CAMPAIGNS AND ELECTIONS

SECOND EDITION

CAMPAIGNS AND ELECTIONS
Rules, Reality, Strategy, Choice

SECOND EDITION

John Sides
GEORGE WASHINGTON UNIVERSITY

Daron Shaw
UNIVERSITY OF TEXAS, AUSTIN

Matt Grossmann
MICHIGAN STATE UNIVERSITY

Keena Lipsitz
QUEENS COLLEGE, CITY UNIVERSITY OF NEW YORK

W. W. Norton and Company
New York • London

W. W. Norton & Company has been independent since its founding in 1923, when William Warder Norton and Mary D. Herter Norton first published lectures delivered at the People's Institute, the adult education division of New York City's Cooper Union. The firm soon expanded its program beyond the Institute, publishing books by celebrated academics from America and abroad. By midcentury, the two major pillars of Norton's publishing program—trade books and college texts—were firmly established. In the 1950s, the Norton family transferred control of the company to its employees, and today—with a staff of four hundred and a comparable number of trade, college, and professional titles published each year—W. W. Norton & Company stands as the largest and oldest publishing house owned wholly by its employees.

Editor: Peter Lesser
Project Editor: Linda Feldman
Editorial Assistant: Samantha Held
Managing Editor, College: Marian Johnson
Managing Editor, College Digital Media: Kim Yi
Production Manager, College: Sean Mintus
Media Editor: Spencer Richardson-Jones
Media Editorial Assistant: Michael Jaoui
Marketing Manager, Political Science: Erin Brown
Design Director: Rubina Yeh
Designer: Lissi Sigillo
Photo Editor: Ted Szczepanski
Assistant Photo Editor: Kathryn Bryan
Permissions Manager: Megan Jackson
Composition: Westchester Book Composition
Manufacturing: Maple Press

Permission to use copyrighted material is included on page C-1.

Library of Congress Cataloging-in-Publication Data

Sides, John.
   Campaigns and elections : rules, reality, strategy, choice / John Sides, Daron Shaw,
Matt Grossmann, Keena Lipsitz. — Second edition.
      pages cm
   Includes bibliographical references and index.
   ISBN 978-0-393-93852-4 (pbk.)
   1. Political campaigns—United States. 2. Elections—United States. I. Shaw, Daron R.,
1966-   II. Grossmann, Matthew. III. Lipsitz, Keena.
   JK1976.C333 2015
   324.70973—dc23

                                                                              2015009309

W. W. Norton & Company, Inc., 500 Fifth Avenue, New York, NY 10110
wwnorton.com
W. W. Norton & Company, Ltd., Castle House, 75/76 Wells Street, London WIT3QT

CONTENTS

7

Interest Groups   178

8

Media   202

9

Presidential Campaigns   236

13
Voter Choice   366

14
Democracy in Action or a Broken System?   396

This book aims to present a comprehensive treatment of political campaigns in the United States. It is structured around four key components that shape American campaigns: the *rules* that govern the electoral process; the *reality* that candidates confront when a campaign begins; the *strategies* employed by important campaign actors, including candidates, parties, interest groups, consultants, and the media; and the *choices* made by voters, which are themselves a response to the rules, reality, and strategies.

The rules that govern the electoral process include institutions such as the Electoral College, as well as the laws that govern campaign finance. The reality that parties and candidates confront consists, in part, of current events, the state of the economy, the presence of an incumbent in the race, and the partisan leaning of their constituents. The importance of rules and reality is augmented by the fact that candidates cannot easily change them. Instead, they structure candidate strategy in important ways. The strategic choices made by candidates comprise the familiar elements of modern campaigns, including message development, television advertising, fund-raising, and voter mobilization. These choices mesh with rules and reality to create the "outputs" of campaigns that are manifest to voters. The response of voters to these outputs goes a long way toward answering the question, "Do campaigns affect voters?" We contend that any good answer to that question is a version of "it depends," and we devote significant attention to what magnifies or diminishes the effects of campaigns.

Throughout the book, we also draw attention to the *democratic functions* of campaigns. We discuss debates about the roles campaigns should play in our democracy and how well contemporary campaigns achieve those goals. We focus on four standards. The first, free choice, means that citizens can participate free of coercion or manipulation. The second, political equality, means that laws cannot disadvantage certain groups of citizens—as, for example, Jim Crow laws disadvantaged southern blacks before the civil rights era. The third, deliberation, refers to the quality of the information that citizens receive from the candidates, the media, and other political actors. Is it sufficient to ensure that citizens can make an informed choice? Of course, deliberation also requires that citizens have the time and motivation to think about electoral choices. The fourth standard, free speech, refers to the constitutional protections that affect whether and how the government might regulate political campaigns. Could, for example, the government require that opposing candidates spend identical amounts of money, so that neither candidate will dominate the airwaves? In discussing such debates, we do not promote any one viewpoint, but instead seek to describe how these values can inform both why campaigns are the way they are, and whether we should attempt to reform them. We emphasize the difficulty of meeting all of these standards simultaneously. It is more likely that making campaigns "better" by one standard will make them "worse" by another. For example, ensuring that citizens receive certain kinds of information may violate the candidates' right to free speech.

This book aims to be comprehensive. We discuss electoral rules and realities not only at the national level but also in the fifty states. We focus on campaigns at all levels of office, including presidential, congressional, state, and local. Doing so illuminates both similarities and differences. For example, although state elections and local elections mimic national elections in key respects—such as by having election dates fixed on the calendar, rather than occurring at the discretion of elected officials themselves—any individual state's elections may differ in the specifics, such as the precise date that elections are held. Similarly, although candidates at all levels of office have the same basic goal—to craft a compelling message and thereby win election—they do so with vastly different levels of resources and thus with different kinds of campaign strategies. A presidential campaign spends more on catering in a week than many local campaigns spend in total.

We also seek to be comprehensive in another respect: by including the perspectives of both campaign professionals and academics. We take into account the views of professionals who work "on the ground" during campaigns and who usually believe that their efforts are consequential. The instructor resources that accompany this book—available at wwnorton.com/nrl—include exercises that simulate some of the decisions that campaign professionals must make.

We also take into account the views of political scientists, who have traditionally been more skeptical about the effects of campaigns, and the views of political theorists, who debate the democratic functions of political campaigns. Ultimately, we hope to provide an insider's perspective on the choices that political actors face in campaigns while simultaneously offering a judicious account of the impact of campaigns on voter attitudes and electoral outcomes.

Perhaps above all, we hope that the book engages readers as citizens. Most Americans experience political campaigns primarily as spectators and profess to dislike what they see. Thus, we want to help readers think critically about two things: what campaigns actually do and what campaigns should do. The former entails identifying when, how, and for whom campaigns matter. With this knowledge, readers will have a more sophisticated view of campaign effects—one that does not attribute great significance to every twist and turn but does not rule out influence entirely. The question of what campaigns should do is meant to engage readers in a broader conversation about the ideals that underpin the electoral process, and whether the process can be reformed to better approximate those ideals.

Revisions to the Second Edition

Highlights of the new edition include:

- The previous edition's chapter on political parties and interest groups has been split into two chapters, with expanded coverage of both topics.
- There is updated coverage of the 2014 campaigns and election results, particularly in Chapters 4 (Financing Campaigns), 10 (Congressional Campaigns), and 12 (Voter Participation).
- Chapter 3 (The Transformation of American Campaigns) features new content on data, analytics, and field experiments.
- Chapter 12 (Voter Participation) now includes a more streamlined discussion of people's individual motivations for voting and social contexts that motivate voters or their voting decisions, as well as an expanded discussion of group differences in electoral participation and whether voters are representative of nonvoters.
- There are several new "In Practice" boxes, including a feature on online fund-raising in Chapter 4 (Financing Campaigns) and a feature on the spillover effects of ballot initiatives in Chapter 11 (State and Local Campaigns).
- Many chapters open with new and timely anecdotes, including former House Majority Leader Eric Cantor's defeat in the Republican primary ahead of the 2014 elections (Chapter 6: Parties), the Koch Brothers' outsized campaign spending efforts in the 2012 election cycle (Chapter 7: Interest Groups), and the media's coverage of Mitt Romney's "47 percent" remarks ahead of the 2012 elections (Chapter 8: Media).

Resources to accompany this book

The following resources, developed specifically to accompany this book, are available to students and instructors:

Norton Coursepacks. Easily add high-quality Norton digital media to your online, hybrid, or lecture course—all at no cost. Norton Coursepacks work with and leverage your existing Learning Management System, so there's no new system to learn, and access is free and easy.

- **Practice quizzes** let students test your knowledge of the chapter.
- **Chapter outlines** provide an overview of the chapter.
- **Flashcards** help students review the key terms from each chapter.

Instructor Resource Website (wwnorton.com/nrl). Accessible to confirmed instructors only, this site includes:

- **PowerPoint slides** of all figures and tables from the text. These are also provided in JPEG format.
- **Test questions** for every chapter.
- **Activity modules**, with detailed instructions for in-class and outside assignments, as well as materials for these activities. These modules allow students to apply what they have learned in the text as they work through hands-on simulations of several aspects of campaigns.

Acknowledgments

We are grateful to those who have assisted us in writing this book. Many scholars read portions of the book at various stages: Scott Adler, Brian Arbour, Suzanne Chod, David Dulio, Philip Habel, Danny Hayes, Valerie Hyman, Phil Jones, Ray LaRaja, Mingus Mapps, Seth Masket, Nate Persily, Andrew Reeves, Travis Ridout, Joe Romance, Wayne Steger, Jessica Trounstine, and Jonathan Winburn.

For their thoughtful feedback on the first edition, we thank:

Jamie L. Carson, University of Georgia
Anthony Corrado, Colby College
Peter L. Francia, East Carolina University
Michael Franz, Bowdoin College
John Gastil, Pennsylvania State University

Matt Guardino, Providence College
Michael G. Hagen, Temple University
Benjamin Highton, University of California, Davis
Eitan Hersh, Yale University
Seth Masket, University of Denver
Hans Noel, Georgetown University
Kathryn Pearson, University of Minnesota
Markus Prior, Princeton University
Michael Tesler, University of California, Irvine
Emily Thorson, George Washington University
Jennifer Wolak, University of Colorado

We thank Jake Haselswerdt for providing research assistance. We also thank W. W. Norton for supporting and nurturing this project—including our editors, Ann Shin and Pete Lesser, for their expert guidance and feedback; associate editor Jake Schindel; editorial assistants Caitlin Cummings and Samantha Held; e-media editors Lorraine Klimowich and Michael Jaoui; project editors Kate Feighery and Linda Feldman; copy editors Jodi Beder and Jennifer Harris; and production managers Ben Reynolds and Sean Mintus.

John Sides
Daron Shaw
Matt Grossmann
Keena Lipsitz

CAMPAIGNS AND ELECTIONS

SECOND EDITION

CHAPTER 1

Introduction

On November 2, 2004, President George W. Bush was elected to a second term and the Republican Party retained control of both the U.S. Senate and House of Representatives. At a press conference two days later, Bush seemed empowered by his victory. He said, "I earned capital in the campaign, political capital, and now I intend to spend it." A week after Bush's election, his chief political strategist, Karl Rove, eagerly described the scope of Bush's victory:

> This was an extraordinary election. [Bush won] 59.7 million votes, and we still have about 250,000 ballots to count. Think about that—*nearly 60 million votes!* The previous largest number was Ronald Reagan in 1984, sweeping the country with 49 states. We won 81 percent of all the counties in America. We gained a percentage of the vote in 87 percent of the counties in America. In Florida, we received nearly a million votes more in this election than in the last one.[1]

Some commentators, even liberal ones, agreed with Rove and believed there had been a fundamental change in American politics, one that would lead to continued Republican dominance.[2] This was, by all accounts, Rove's goal all along.

The post-election euphoria of Bush and Rove proved short-lived. The war in Iraq, which had begun in March 2003, dragged on and on. Following the U.S.-led invasion, protracted sectarian violence engulfed Iraq and U.S. military casualties continued to mount. The American economy also began to weaken, a trend hastened by the financial crisis that shook both Wall Street and Main Street in the fall of 2008. In the months that followed, the United States would experience

---

[1] Joshua Green. 2007. "The Rove Presidency." *The Atlantic*, September. www.theatlantic.com/magazine/archive/2007/09/the-rove-presidency/6132/ (accessed 1/12/15).

[2] One example was Michael Lind, writing at the blog *Talking Points Memo*. See: http://themonkeycage.org/2012/11/12/the-perils-of-democrats-euphoria-or-why-the-2012-election-is-not-a-realignment/ (accessed 1/12/15).

the deepest economic downturn since the Great Depression. In the last month of his presidency, Bush's approval rating dropped to about 30 percent. The capital he thought he'd earned in 2004 was long gone.

In the 2006 midterm election, the Democratic Party struck its first blow, taking back control of the House and Senate. This was the first time since 1994 that the Democrats controlled both chambers. The Democrats elected the first female Speaker of the House, Nancy Pelosi of California, and quickly sought to make good on their campaign promises — specifically, a six-point agenda that they called "A New Direction for America," or, for short, "Six in '06." In her speech after being elected Speaker, Pelosi said, "The election of 2006 was a call to change — not merely to change the control of Congress, but for a new direction for our country."

That new direction got a further boost on November 4, 2008, when the Democratic nominee, Barack Obama, won the presidency — a victory all the more noteworthy because he became the first African American to hold the office. In his victory speech, Obama was no less ambitious than Bush: "This is our time — to put our people back to work and open doors of opportunity for our kids; to restore prosperity and promote the cause of peace; to reclaim the American Dream and reaffirm that fundamental truth — that out of many, we are one." Working with his large congressional majorities, Obama moved swiftly to act on those ambitious goals. He and congressional Democrats succeeded — over

Core of the Analysis

Focusing on four aspects of campaigns — rules, reality, strategy, and citizen choice — helps us understand the outcomes of American elections:

- The *rules* refer to laws and constitutional doctrines that govern the electoral system and affect how campaigns are carried out and ultimately who wins elections.
- Broader economic and political *realities* shape the tenor of public opinion and often place limits on how much campaigns can affect opinion.
- The *strategies* employed by candidates, political parties, interest groups, and the media reflect their unique interests and agendas and can, when circumstances are right, affect public opinion as well.
- The *choices made by citizens* — whether and how to vote — depend on a mix of long-standing habits, current realities, and new information from the campaign itself.
- The democratic values of free choice, political equality, deliberation, and free speech help us evaluate campaigns.

nearly unanimous Republican opposition—in passing a stimulus package intended to help the economy, a climate change bill in the House, and, most notably, health care reform in March 2010.

But once again, the success of the party in power proved short-lived. By the next midterm election in November 2010, the economy was no longer in a tailspin, but it was only limping toward recovery. Obama's approval rating was about 45 percent—20 points lower than when he was inaugurated. All of these facts spelled trouble for the Democrats in Congress. In the 2010 elections, the party lost six seats in the Senate and a whopping 63 seats in the House of Representatives. The number of seats lost in the House was the largest experienced by the president's party since 1938. In a press conference after the election, Obama acknowledged that the Democrats had taken a "shellacking."

In 2012, Obama and Democrats bounced back. Obama beat Republican Mitt Romney by the comfortable margin of nearly 4 points and the Democrats gained seats in both the House and Senate. But Republicans retained control of the House of Representatives, thereby complicating Obama's ability to pursue an ambitious second-term agenda.

In 2014, Republicans once again dominated the midterm election. They expanded their House majority and won a Senate majority as well. For the last two years of his presidency, Obama would confront an even more powerful Republican congressional majority.

These ten years from 2004 to 2014 brought important changes in party power and tempered the ambitions of two presidents. Table 1.1 shows that frequent shifts between the Democratic and Republican parties have been the norm across presidential elections in the past 150 years. These shifts point toward one of the central questions of this book: *What explains the outcomes of American elections—presidential, congressional, and state and local?* Addressing this question entails attention to others. Why do some candidates choose to run and others do not? Why do some candidates win and others lose? There are many interpretations of elections, but far fewer solid answers to these questions.

An obvious answer might be the campaign itself. A political campaign combines elements of two other, nonpolitical types of campaigns. In some ways, it is like a military campaign, with the goal of winning a contest and vanquishing an opponent. It is also like an advertising campaign, with the goal of persuading citizens to buy a product. One might think that political campaigns are always consequential, with millions of dollars being spent, professional strategists scheming, advertisements blanketing the airwaves, and armies of volunteers pounding the pavement. But this is not necessarily so. Elections depend on the overall state of the country, which even brilliant campaigning cannot change.

TABLE 1.1 Percent of Popular Vote Won by Presidential Candidates, 1856–2012*

Year	Democrat	Republican	Independent Candidates or Third Parties	Year	Democrat	Republican	Independent Candidates or Third Parties
1856	**45.3%**	33.1%	21.6%	1936	**60.8%**	36.5%	2.7%
1860	29.5%	**39.7%**	30.8%	1940	**54.7%**	44.8%	0.5%
1864	45.0%	**55.0%**	0.0%	1944	**53.4%**	45.9%	0.7%
1868	47.3%	**52.7%**	0.0%	1948	**49.6%**	45.1%	5.4%
1872	43.8%	**55.6%**	0.6%	1952	44.3%	**55.2%**	0.5%
1876	50.9%	**47.9%**	1.2%	1956	42.0%	**57.4%**	0.7%
1880	48.2%	**48.3%**	3.5%	1960	**49.7%**	49.6%	0.7%
1884	**48.9%**	48.3%	2.9%	1964	**61.1%**	38.5%	0.5%
1888	48.6%	**47.8%**	3.6%	1968	42.7%	**43.4%**	13.9%
1892	**46.0%**	43.0%	11.0%	1972	37.5%	**60.7%**	1.8%
1896	46.7%	**51.0%**	2.3%	1976	**50.1%**	48.0%	1.9%
1900	45.5%	**51.6%**	2.8%	1980	41.0%	**50.8%**	8.2%
1904	37.6%	**56.4%**	6.0%	1984	40.6%	**58.8%**	0.7%
1908	43.0%	**51.6%**	5.4%	1988	45.7%	**53.4%**	1.0%
1912	**41.8%**	23.2%	35.0%	1992	**43.0%**	37.5%	19.6%
1916	**49.2%**	46.1%	4.6%	1996	**49.2%**	40.7%	10.1%
1920	34.2%	**60.3%**	5.5%	2000	48.4%	**47.9%**	3.8%
1924	28.8%	**54.0%**	17.1%	2004	48.3%	**50.7%**	1.0%
1928	40.8%	**58.2%**	1.0%	2008	**52.9%**	45.6%	1.5%
1932	**57.4%**	39.7%	2.9%	2012	**51.0%**	47.1%	1.9%

* Winner's percentage in bold.
Source: Dave Leip's Atlas of U.S. Presidential Elections. www.uselectionatlas.org/ (accessed 1/12/15).

Hence the second central question of this book: *How much does the campaign itself matter?*

It is easy to imagine how campaigns might matter. Campaigns could convince citizens to support one candidate or oppose another, or motivate them to go to the polls on Election Day. Professional campaign operatives frequently argue that campaign strategies accomplish these things. Indeed, it is hard to see how they could believe otherwise: their livelihoods depend on it! Political scientists, however, approach the question differently: rather than relying on personal experience, they use different kinds of evidence to determine how much the campaign actually matters. This entails acknowledging that the campaign's impact, however meaningful, could prove secondary to that of other events. For example, what was more important for Obama's victory in 2008: the $730 million that he spent campaigning or an unpopular George W. Bush and a tanking economy? And what was more important for him in 2012: the $1.1 billion that he and his allies spent or the fact that the tanking economy had actually turned around on his watch?

The fact that Obama spent so much money raises the third central question of this book: *How should we evaluate the American electoral process?* One complaint is that American campaigns are just too expensive, and the incessant fund-raising distracts and possibly corrupts politicians. People wonder whether the system allows the best candidates to emerge. They question whether campaigns are fair, informative, truthful, and engaging. They worry that citizens fail to learn what they need to know in order to make political decisions, or that constant mudslinging alienates citizens and leads them to stay home on Election Day. It is important to think through these complaints analytically — to ask, for example, whether negative campaigning really turns citizens off. But it is also important to think critically about what elections and campaigns *should* be like. Then we will understand not only how much campaigns affect citizens but also how much they help or hurt our democracy.

A Framework for Understanding Campaigns and Elections

In this book, we use a simple framework to understand **campaigns** and **elections** in American politics. This framework emphasizes four aspects of campaigns and elections:

- The *rules* that govern elections.
- The broader *reality*—economic, political, and historical—that parties and candidates confront as they decide whether to run or how to campaign.
- The *strategic choices* that various actors—including candidates, the media, political parties, and interest groups—make.
- The *choices of citizens*, who will ultimately decide the outcome.

The goal of this framework is to identify the major features of the American electoral system that ultimately influence the actual outcomes of elections—who wins and who loses. We will also see how the elements of the framework depend on each other. For example, the strategic choices of candidates depend on both the electoral rules and the broader reality that candidates confront. Similarly, the choices of citizens, especially in the voting booth, may depend on rules and reality, but also on the strategies of candidates, parties, the media, and others, all of whom broadcast information that may influence citizens' feelings about the candidates. In the following sections, we elaborate on each element of this framework.

Rules

Any sports fan can see that the rules of the game matter. When college and professional basketball created a longer-distance shot worth three points, it changed the game, making sharpshooting players more valuable and helping teams who had more such players. Although we cannot replay history, it seems likely that teams have won numerous games that they otherwise would have lost if not for three-point shooting.

Elections are no different. Rules affect their every aspect: who is qualified to run for office, when the election is held and thus when the campaign begins, the size and characteristics of constituencies, how much money can be donated and spent, who is eligible to vote, and, ultimately, who wins the election. All of the actors involved in the election—citizens, candidates, parties, interest groups, the media—find themselves subject to rules. For example, sixteen-year-olds cannot vote. Thirty-year-olds cannot be president. Candidates and parties cannot accept unlimited amounts of money from a wealthy donor. Interest groups cannot coordinate their campaign spending with the candidates it would benefit. Television stations cannot sell advertising time to one candidate but refuse to sell it to the opponent.

The rules of elections are important because, in many cases, they cannot be changed easily. Changing a rule may require legislation or a Supreme Court decision—at the extreme, a constitutional amendment. Even in the simplest cases, rule changes typically do not happen during the campaign itself. Thus, as the campaign gets under way, the rules constitute a hand that all the candidates are dealt and thereby constrain candidate strategy in important ways. Consider some of the basic rules about campaign finance. Existing laws limit the amount of money that any individual can donate but do not limit the amount of money that any candidate can spend. The former means that candidates must devote a lot of time to fund-raising as they try to amass campaign funds from many individual donors. The latter means that some wealthy people will be tempted to run for office and spend their own money to finance their campaigns. The challenges of financing a campaign under the

In 2014, voters elected a new Republican majority in the Senate and expanded the existing Republican majority in the House of Representatives, led by Speaker John Boehner. Why were the Republicans so successful in 2014? Did smart campaigning enable them to take control of Congress? Or were other factors more important than campaign strategy?

existing rules also seem to discourage potential female candidates. In a survey of women and men in professions, such as law and business, that frequently lead to political careers, women were less likely than men to say that they had contemplated running for office, and many women cited the challenges of raising money as a dissuading factor.[3]

Reality

The context in which an election occurs—what we call "reality"—also strongly affects a candidate's success or failure. In 2004, Barack Obama ran for U.S. senator in his home state of Illinois. His opponent was Jack Ryan, a wealthy former businessman who was working as a volunteer at a local Catholic school. Early polls gave Obama a substantial lead, but many respondents described themselves as undecided. Ryan had been divorced from the actress Jeri Ryan in 1999, and in June 2004, after a lawsuit by the *Chicago Tribune* and other media outlets, a judge unsealed the court proceedings from that divorce. In those proceedings, Jeri Ryan alleged that her husband asked her to have sex with him in sex clubs in New Orleans, New York, and Paris. When this information became public, Ryan withdrew from the race. In his place, Alan Keyes stood as the Republican candidate. Keyes was a staunch conservative who had run and lost handily in several other elections, including two ill-fated attempts at the Republican presidential nomination in 2000 and 2004. He established residency in Illinois only days before he began running for this Senate seat. Obama trounced him by 43 points.

To take another example, in early 2008, when Barack Obama ran for the Democratic nomination for president, there was an unpopular war in Iraq, an unpopular Republican president, and the beginnings of a deep recession. After Obama became the nominee, the economic crisis worsened, with several large banks failing or nearly failing—requiring extraordinary government action to save them and prop up both the financial system and the larger economy. Obama again beat his opponent, this time Senator John McCain of Arizona, by a decisive margin.

Both of these stories illustrate the importance of the broader reality candidates face. Here, "reality" refers to several factors in particular: the candidates' biographies, the records of the political parties, and recent and current political and economic events, such as a war or recession. These elements of the broader context are similar in one crucial respect: they are rarely under the control of the candidates themselves. Ryan's divorce, the nomination of

---

[3] Jennifer L. Lawless and Richard L. Fox. 2008. "Why Are Women Still Not Running for Public Office?" *Brookings Institution Issues in Governance Studies*, May.

Keyes, the war in Iraq, the economic recession: Obama made none of these events happen. They happened to him or to his opponents or to the public and arguably increased his chances of winning his Senate seat and then the presidency. Ultimately, the things that candidates can control, such as their campaign strategy, may not overcome the effects of events that conspire against them.

Outside events can be more influential than campaigns

A first important component of reality is the background of the candidates themselves. This may involve their personal lives—for Jack Ryan, his divorce—or their professional lives, including prior service in elected office. Candidates cannot rewrite their biographies from scratch. What they have done or said in the past will follow them, including both the good and the bad. Candidates try to capitalize on the best aspects of their biography, such as a happy family, service to the community or country, and support of popular policies. Opponents bring up the worst aspects, such as lies, unpopular actions, and scandals.

1. Backround
2. Legacies
3. Current events
4. The economy

A second component of reality involves the legacies that political parties bequeath to candidates. The major parties have each developed reputations for giving attention to specific key issues as well as for their positions on those issues.[4] The Democratic Party has traditionally favored using government resources to help people. The Republican Party has favored lowering taxes, partly in an effort to shrink the size of government. An anti-tax Democrat or a pro-welfare Republican is at odds with these legacies and can have difficulty convincing citizens that their positions are sincere. The parties have also developed coalitions of supporters from different groups in society. The Democratic Party's early commitment to civil rights, despite the resistance of Southern Democrats, earned it the lasting loyalty of African Americans. The Republican Party's conservative position on social issues, such as abortion and gay rights, garnered the support of many evangelical Christians. Candidates find it difficult to make inroads with groups that have not traditionally supported their party.

Another component of reality is current or recent events that are directly connected to government policies and the formal powers of political office. For example, foreign policy crises and wars are particularly important for the electoral prospects of presidents and presidential candidates. The terrorist attacks of September 11, 2001, led the public and Congress to rally behind President Bush. The Republican Party even picked up seats in the 2002 midterm elections, despite the fact that the president's party typically loses seats in midterm elections. By 2004, Bush had lost the goodwill of many

---

[4] John Petrocik. 1996. "Issue Ownership in Presidential Elections, with a 1980 Case Study." *American Journal of Political Science* 40, 3: 825–50.

Democrats, but September 11, as well as the Iraq War, still loomed large over the campaign. War and national security issues were central to Bush's message and that of his opponent, Senator John Kerry, in 2004. Ongoing wars can also help or hurt the **incumbent** president (the president currently holding office). Consider Lyndon Johnson, who decided not to run for reelection in 1968 because of the long, costly Vietnam War. Foreign affairs and war may not be completely outside politicians' control, in that presidents help decide how to conduct foreign relations and whether and how to wage war. But presidents cannot control other countries and their armies, and they often confront the unexpected. The same is true for other elected officials and in other policy areas.

A final and especially important component of reality is the economy. Just as the public tends to prefer peace over war, it prefers prosperity to poverty. And the public holds incumbent officeholders, particularly the president, responsible for economic conditions. As we will discuss in more detail in later chapters, incumbents presiding over a robust economy will typically win a larger share of the vote than those presiding over a weak economy. As with foreign affairs and war, elected officials often have some influence on the economy. For example, as happened soon after Barack Obama took office

The state of the economy is an important part of the "reality" campaigns face, and voters often punish incumbents during economic downturns. In 2010, then–Senate Majority Leader Harry Reid faced an unusually tough campaign for reelection in Nevada.

in 2009, the president and Congress can pass bills that attempt to stimulate the economy or that provide government support to unemployed Americans. These types of measures can be important, but they are often less effective than politicians and the public would like. The ups and downs of the economy depend on many factors outside any politician's control.

Taken together, these elements of reality affect candidate strategies, the decisions of citizens, and, ultimately, election outcomes. Their impact on election outcomes makes it difficult to credit campaign strategy for every victory and blame it for every defeat. Incumbent candidates running during a time of peace and prosperity may win easily, even if their campaigns were full of strategic miscalculations. These same candidates running during an unpopular war and a weak economy may lose, no matter the brilliance of their campaign strategy.

[handwritten margin note: already prez]

Strategy

The impact of rules and reality can lead to doubts about the effects of campaign strategy. But campaign strategies do matter. One need look no further than fluctuations in the candidates' poll numbers during a campaign. In 2008, Bush's unpopularity and the weak economy advantaged Obama. However, had the election been held in early September, McCain, basking in the glow of the Republican National Convention, would have won according to the polls. Why did McCain's lead dissipate? Why did Obama's lead continue to grow throughout the rest of September and October? Questions like these draw our attention to the potential impact of campaign strategy.

Campaigns involve a variety of actors. Most visible are the candidates. Their strategic choices involve every facet of a campaign: whether to run in the first place, what issues to emphasize, what specific messages or themes to discuss, which kinds of media to use, and which citizens to target. Candidates' personal campaign organizations, sometimes with paid professionals on board, create much of the visible campaign activity, from yard signs and bumper stickers to television advertising and YouTube videos. Political parties engage in similar strategic debates about the best agenda, message, and targeting strategy. Parties also deploy resources on behalf of their candidates, including ads, voter registration drives, and get-out-the-vote operations on Election Day. The same is true of interest groups, who raise and spend money in support of favored candidates. And, throughout the campaign, the news media are crucial. Although candidates can communicate directly with citizens through advertising, many citizens receive information from news media outlets. Thus, the news media's coverage of the campaign may also matter.

[handwritten margin note: • Parties • Interest groups • Media]

All of these actors are in part following their own strategies and in part responding to others. Candidates routinely try to "stay on message" but often respond to their opponents' claims. Parties and interest groups often structure their campaign activity to complement that of their favored candidates, but at times the strategies of the candidates and those of parties and interest groups diverge. Interest groups, for example, are far more likely than candidates to air negative advertisements. The media depend on political parties, interest groups, and, especially, candidates for news but often impose their own definition of newsworthiness. The media's agenda frequently diverges from those of the candidates—in short, the media are often talking about something different from the candidates.[5] This is one reason candidates frequently criticize the coverage they receive.

Campaign strategy is the element of elections that candidates and other actors can control. They may not be able to end a war or make the economy grow, but they can craft a slogan, produce a television advertisement, give a speech, and kiss a lot of babies at campaign rallies. Much money is spent doing all of these things. The ultimate question is how much difference it makes.

campaign strategies have power

Citizens' Choices

In any democratic political system, an election's outcome depends on the people. Eligible American citizens have two choices to make in an election: *whether* to vote and *how* to vote. Rules and reality affect these choices. Campaign strategists aim to influence these choices as well, by convincing people to support a particular candidate and encouraging supporters to vote on Election Day. The central question is: How susceptible are citizens to campaign influence? Answering this question also means determining how much citizens are affected by broader realities such as the state of the economy, which might matter more than the campaign itself.

Citizens are not blank slates. They have preexisting political habits and opinions. Some vote in every election. Others never vote. Some tend to vote for Democrats, and some for Republicans. Habits put limits on what a campaign can accomplish. No matter how much money candidates spend, or how catchy and engaging their advertisements are, they will not be able to persuade some citizens to support them or to vote. Moreover, at times campaigns struggle simply to command the public's attention. Some people do not follow politics closely and are not interested in watching the news,

---

[5] Danny Hayes. 2009. "The Dynamics of Agenda Convergence and the Paradox of Competitiveness in Presidential Campaigns." *Political Research Quarterly* 63, 3: 594–611.

candidate debates, or political advertisements. Simply put, many votes are not up for grabs, and those that are may not easily be won with the tools of modern campaigns. Indeed, undecided citizens may respond more to "reality" than to campaign messages.

Journalists often describe campaigns as important, as do campaign consultants, naturally enough. Victorious candidates are presumed to have run skillful campaigns. The day after the 2008 election, the front page of the *New York Times* had this headline adjacent to a victorious Obama: "Near-Flawless Run from Start to Finish Is Credited in Victory." After Obama's 2012 victory, a *Slate* article referred to the "talent of the Obama team" and called his campaign "formidable."[6] Losing candidates are presumed to have run flawed, less talented, and less formidable campaigns. Neither presumption is warranted, absent scientific evidence of how much the campaign mattered. Gathering this evidence and demonstrating its persuasiveness are difficult tasks.

Evaluating Campaigns and Elections

Thinking about rules, reality, strategy, and citizen choice helps illuminate what actually happens in campaigns. The next question is: What should happen? Here, "should happen" does not mean "my candidate should win." Rather, we mean: What is good for the democratic political system in which we live?

In democratic systems, campaigns are crucial processes. They are a time during which citizens typically pay the most attention to politics. They also provide a level of interaction between leaders and citizens that is rarely attained at other times. Thus, a lot is at stake in getting this process "right." However, a large majority of the public professes not to like campaigns very much. In a poll conducted immediately after the 2012 election, respondents were asked to grade various people's performance during the campaign: Obama, Romney, the press, pollsters, and campaign consultants. No one made higher than a C+. Indeed, respondents even gave voters a C+.[7] In general, the public routinely complains that campaigns are too long, too costly, and too negative. In the public's eyes, much can and should be done to reform campaigns.

---

[6] John Dickerson. 2012. "How Obama Won Four More Years." *Slate* (7 November). www.slate.com/articles/news_and_politics/politics/2012/11/how_obama_won_he_had_a_better_team_that_ran_a_first_rate_campaign.html (accessed 1/12/15).

[7] See www.people-press.org/2012/11/15/low-marks-for-the-2012-election/ (accessed 1/12/15).

But campaign reform is not a simple matter. There may be good reasons for the status quo, however objectionable it is to some Americans. Moreover, any reform is likely to involve trade-offs, improving things by one measure but worsening them by another. It is helpful, then, to establish a set of standards by which we can evaluate campaigns. Each of these standards represents a potential goal of a democratic political system. Together they may not capture every conceivable goal, but they do represent a starting point. We will refer to them in many subsequent chapters, as we seek to understand not only how campaigns and elections operate but also whether they can or should be improved.

The first standard is *free choice*. For elections to be truly democratic, citizens must be free from coercion or manipulation. To facilitate their choice, they must also have adequate information about the contending candidates and parties. Campaigns that involve violent intimidation of opposition party supporters do not meet this standard, nor do campaigns in which the incumbent regime controls all major news outlets. In the United States, such behavior is rare but is known to occur. For example, during the 2006 election, a letter was sent to approximately 14,000 residents of Orange County, California, all of whom had Latino surnames or foreign birthplaces. Suggesting that immigrants might go to jail for voting, the letter, written in Spanish, had the apparent intent of discouraging Latino citizens from voting and thereby hurting the reelection prospects of the Latina incumbent, Representative Loretta Sanchez. Sanchez's Republican opponent, Tan Nguyen, was convicted in 2010 for lying to federal investigators about whether he played any role in sending the letter.

Even if such dramatic attempts at coercion are rare, we may ask whether the information that citizens receive in American campaigns is sufficient to ensure free choice. What if, for example, a well-funded incumbent is competing against a poorly funded challenger? Chances are, citizens will hear much more from the incumbent than the challenger. Is this a problem? What if the situation is even more lopsided, and there is no challenger for this incumbent? For example, in the 2014 election, only about 40 percent of U.S. House primary elections featured at least two candidates.[8] Does it violate the standard of free choice when there is only one choice?

A second standard is *political equality*. Citizens must, by this standard, be equal in the eyes of the law. Laws that disadvantage certain citizens violate this standard. One example is Jim Crow laws in the South. These laws, which were in effect in many Southern states from 1876 until 1965, effectively

[handwritten margin notes: Campaign standards 1. Free choice 2. Political equality 3. deliberation 4. Free Speech]

---

[8] See http://ballotpedia.org/National_contested_primary_average_during_the_2014_U.S._congressional_elections (accessed 1/12/15).

disenfranchised blacks using a variety of means, such as literacy tests and poll taxes. Blacks, who were often less educated and less affluent than whites, were more likely to fail these tests and be unable to afford the tax. Although Jim Crow laws were eventually abolished, voter eligibility requirements continue to have implications for political equality. For example, requiring potential voters to supply identification, such as a driver's license, will disproportionately affect those without such identification, who tend to be elderly or members of racial minorities. Thirty-four states have passed laws that require identification in order to vote.[9]

The standard of political equality could be applied to candidates as well. The example of the rich incumbent and the poor challenger may violate this standard. But this standard also raises some challenging questions. Must every pair of opposing candidates have identical amounts of money to spend campaigning? What if a challenger has raised little money because he or she seems to lack important qualities or qualifications, leaving potential donors reluctant to give?

A third standard is *deliberation*. Deliberation speaks not just to the quantity but also to the quality of information available to citizens. Interaction between the opposing candidates can be evaluated by this standard. For example, in a truly deliberative interaction, the candidates highlight points of similarity and difference between them. This helps citizens decide whom they prefer. Media coverage of the campaign can be evaluated by this same standard. Does the news give citizens information on the similarities and differences between the candidates? Critics often complain that it does not, because campaign reporting is more focused on the latest polls than on the policy proposals of the candidates. The 2008 election provides but one of many examples. A study by the Project for Excellence in Journalism found that more than half of campaign news stories in 2008 were framed around strategy, tactics, and polling. Only 20 percent were framed around discussions of policy. In 2012, there was less horse-race coverage, but it still exceeded coverage devoted to policy.[10] Is the public learning enough about the real differences between the candidates when their views on issues are so rarely discussed? Before we are too quick to criticize the media, we must also ask: Does this focus on strategy rather than policy merely reflect the

---

[9] See www.ncsl.org/research/elections-and-campaigns/voter-id.aspx (accessed 1/12/15).

[10] Project for Excellence in Journalism. 2008. "Winning the Media Campaign: How the Press Reported the 2008 Presidential General Election." http://www.journalism.org/2008/10/22/winning-media-campaign/ (accessed 1/12/15); Project for Excellence in Journalism, 2012. "Winning the Media Campaign 2012." www.journalism.org/2012/11/02/winning-media-campaign-2012/ (accessed 1/12/15).

desires of news consumers, who are happy to read about polls but not so interested in long articles about the candidates' views on complicated aspects of policy?

A fourth standard is *free speech*. This is a linchpin of the American political system, one enshrined in the Bill of Rights. Upholding free speech may in fact complicate attempts to promote equality or deliberation. Eliminating disparities between incumbents and challengers in the interest of equality entails limiting the amount of "speech" that incumbents have—for instance, by restricting how and how much they campaign. One way to do this is with campaign finance laws, which affect how much candidates can raise and spend. Ensuring deliberation would place restrictions on what the candidates and news media talk about, perhaps by forcing candidates to engage each other on specific issues, even if they would rather not discuss those issues. Either could be said to violate the standard of free speech.

Designing the ideal campaign or election is a difficult task, especially because the four standards discussed here are not always compatible. But these standards are still useful ways by which to evaluate the rules and

One democratic value is equality—but what does this mean in the context of elections? Should rich candidates be prohibited from outspending poorer opponents? In the 2014 Illinois gubernatorial race, incumbent Democrat Pat Quinn (right) was outspent by Republican Bruce Rauner (left), who drew on his personal fortune to give his campaign $38 million of the $89 million it raised. Quinn raised $58 million. Rauner ultimately won 50 percent of the vote to Quinn's 46 percent.

institutions that govern the electoral process—such as the Electoral College and campaign finance laws—as well as the strategies pursued by candidates. Americans commonly complain when candidates attack their opponents. Is this always a bad thing? These standards can help us address that question. They also help us evaluate the behavior of citizens. Does the attention Americans pay to the campaign and their knowledge of the candidates live up to democratic ideals?

Conclusion

To understand and evaluate campaigns, we take into account the perspectives of both political professionals and political scientists—who, as we noted at the beginning of this chapter, often have quite different perspectives on how much campaigns affect elections. Professional campaign operatives and consultants are focused on the nuts and bolts of campaigning—the how-to's—and tend to believe that campaigns have important effects on citizens. Political scientists formulate broader theories of campaigns and elections and then test those theories with empirical research on public opinion, media coverage, and campaign activity. They tend to be more cautious in attributing significance to campaign strategy. However, campaign consultants are increasingly drawing on ideas and tools from political and social science to test the effects of campaign tactics. Our goal is to provide a sense of what happens on the ground in campaigns, and also whether it ultimately matters—to individual voters and to election outcomes.

The next chapter outlines the basic rules of the electoral process in the United States. Chapter 3 describes how American political campaigns have evolved throughout history. Chapter 4 describes how contemporary campaigns are financed—another aspect of the rules that has important consequences for strategy. Chapter 5 discusses the major elements of modern campaign strategy, drawing on political science theories and evidence as well as the thinking of political consultants; much of this chapter focuses on the behavior of candidates. Chapters 6 to 8 consider the specific roles played by other actors: political parties, interest groups, and the media.

Chapters 9 to 11 delve into three specific categories of campaigns: presidential, congressional, and state and local. An important theme throughout the book is that the rules, realities, and strategies inherent to campaigns may differ across levels of office. Thus, it is important to examine how each type of campaign typically unfolds. Chapters 12 and 13 turn the focus to citizens, including their decision whether or not to participate in elections and their decision to support a particular candidate. These two chapters devote particular attention to how much campaigns affect each decision. Finally, Chapter 14 evaluates contemporary American campaigns by the standards presented earlier. Some discussion of these standards also appears in other chapters, but this final chapter provides a broader perspective on whether American campaigns and elections reflect a "broken system" or effective "democracy in action."

KEY TERMS

campaign (p. 7)
election (p. 7)
incumbent (p. 11)

FOR DISCUSSION

1. What are the central differences in how political consultants and political scientists tend to think about the impact of campaigns?
2. Why do the rules constrain candidates when they are campaigning? Why don't candidates simply change the rules to benefit their campaigns?
3. What are several dimensions of "reality" that might affect campaign strategies and election outcomes?
4. Why would the standards of deliberation and equality potentially come into conflict with the standard of free speech?

CHAPTER 2

The American Electoral Process

In the spring of 2001, Barack Obama, a state senator in Illinois, was a year removed from his most stunning political defeat. In the 2000 Democratic primary for a U.S House seat, he had challenged another black Democrat, the incumbent congressman Bobby Rush, and lost by 31 points. Obama struggled to win votes in some parts of Rush's district, particularly black neighborhoods where professors at the University of Chicago — even African American professors like Obama — were viewed with suspicion. Obama had more appeal in South Side neighborhoods around the university, and also North Side neighborhoods closer to downtown, including the so-called Gold Coast along Lake Michigan. The Gold Coast is home to many wealthy (and mostly white) Chicagoans, an ideal group from which to raise money for a political campaign. The problem was that as a state senator, Obama did not represent the North Side and its Gold Coast; his district was on the South Side.

One day that spring, Obama went to a room in a downtown building in Springfield, a room guarded with fingerprint scanners and coded keypads. Inside the room were computers on which a select few employees of the Illinois Democratic Party worked. Their job was to draw legislative districts. The Democrats had won control of the Illinois House and now, the year after the 2000 census, were drawing up a new set of state legislative districts — as was the Republican majority in the Illinois Senate. Obama sat with a Democratic consultant, John Corrigan, and drew himself a new district, one that started in the South Side and then stretched north to the Gold Coast. It was a "radical change," said Corrigan.

After a protracted battle, the Democrats succeeded in implementing their districts. This gave Obama a new district well suited to funding his political ambitions, and it also helped the Democrats win a majority in the Illinois Senate in the 2002 elections. This majority helped Obama by allowing him to more easily establish a record of legislative accomplishments. With this newfound potential for raising money and promoting legislation, Obama was poised to run for the U.S. Senate in 2004.[1]

This chapter is about the rules of campaigns and elections, the first part of the framework introduced in Chapter 1. All democracies depend on rules to govern political life. The anecdote from early in Obama's political career illustrates their importance. Obama was lucky: he had some influence over redistricting, which determined who his constituents would be. Most of the time, political leaders, candidates, and parties do not have this luxury. Rules are often fixed by law, sometimes even by the Constitution itself, and cannot be changed quickly or easily to benefit a party or candidate.

The rules of the American electoral process help us to answer many crucial questions pertaining to campaigns. This chapter explores five of them: who can run for office, when elections are held, where to run, who can vote, and who wins. For each, we first explore what the rules are. The answers are not always straightforward, due in part to a second consideration: who makes the rules. The Constitution, Congress, state legislatures, and political parties all have some say. The rules are not the same for every level of office or in every state. But even general answers are informative.

Knowing what the rules are and who makes them leads to the "why" question: Why these rules and not others? Rules reflect ideals or values — that is, conceptions of what is a good or fair electoral process. For example, a good electoral

Core of the Analysis

- Elections are conducted according to rules that determine who runs, when elections are held, where candidates run, who can vote, and who wins.
- The rules often vary across states and levels of office because they are designed by multiple decision makers, including the framers of the Constitution, Congress, state legislatures, local officials, and political parties.
- The rules reflect values about what constitutes a "good" election, but they often further certain values at the expense of others.
- Many rules are largely outside of the control of candidates, political parties, and voters, especially once the campaign has begun.
- The rules strongly affect the decisions of every relevant actor during a campaign, including candidates, parties, interest groups, the media, and voters.

---

[1] This anecdote comes from Ryan Lizza. 2008. "Making It: How Chicago Shaped Obama." *New Yorker*, July 2.

process might feature a vigorous competition between two candidates — one that provides information to citizens and motivates them to vote. But competitive elections are also more expensive, as candidates have an incentive to raise more money so that they can effectively communicate with citizens. Many people wish that elections were not so expensive and fear that soliciting campaign contributions corrupts candidates. So whether one favors increased competition might depend on what one considers more important: informing voters or mitigating the potential for corruption. Inevitably, electoral rules reflect compromises and almost never fully codify any particular value, reflecting instead trade-offs among competing values. Small wonder, then, that electoral rules are often so controversial.

We turn now to the major rules of American elections. In this chapter, we will see that perhaps the most important aspect of electoral rules, especially from a candidate's or party's point of view, is the consequences of these rules for campaign strategy and for whether candidates are likely to win or lose. Perhaps Barack Obama had philosophical objections to a system in which his party got to redraw the Illinois political map to help both him and his party. But ultimately he did not try to change the rule; he merely tried to make it work in his favor.

When Barack Obama was a member of the Illinois legislature, the rules for redistricting determined who his constituents were. Advantageous district boundaries helped set Obama up for a successful U.S. Senate campaign in 2004.

Who Can Run

Who is eligible to run for office? In the American political system, the qualifications usually involve a minimum age, American citizenship, and a minimum time living in the community one seeks to represent. For federal office, the Constitution spells out these requirements. A candidate for the House of Representatives must be at least 25 years old, a citizen for seven years, and an "inhabitant" of the state the district is in. The qualifications for senator are similar, except that the candidate must be at least 30 years old and a citizen for nine years. These more restrictive qualifications are because the framers of the Constitution believed that the Senate demanded more from its members than did the House. James Madison wrote, "The propriety of these distinctions is explained by the nature of the senatorial trust, which, requiring greater extent of information and stability of character, requires at the same time that the senator should have reached a period of life most likely to supply these advantages."[2]

The requirements for president are even more restrictive. Candidates must be at least 35 years old and U.S. residents for at least 14 years (although the Constitution does not specify when that period of residency must have occurred). Moreover, they must be native-born citizens of the United States. Naturalized citizens may run for the House and Senate.

Candidates for state and local offices typically must meet requirements for minimum age and residency, although different localities have different rules. For example, in Louisiana, candidates for governor need to be at least 25 years old, and citizens of the United States and Louisiana for at least the five years before the election. In Minnesota, candidates for governor must also be at least 25, but need only have lived in the state for the year before the election. Candidates for the Louisiana state legislature must be at least 18 years old, state residents for the preceding two years, and residents of their legislative district for at least the preceding year. Candidates for the Minnesota legislature must be at least 21 years old and must be residents of the state for one year and of the district for at least six months immediately preceding the election. Other states have their own stipulations about age and residency.

Despite these differences, federal, state, and local qualifications for office reflect a common set of values. One is competence. Age requirements help ensure that candidates have the intellectual and emotional maturity to handle the job. To be sure, age is an imperfect measure of competence. There have

---

[2] *Federalist Papers*, no. 62.

been cases where older politicians, due to age or infirmity, lost a significant degree of competence but still held office. In 1919, President Woodrow Wilson suffered a debilitating stroke. His wife, Edith, took over and saw to it that important tasks were delegated to the proper cabinet secretaries—all of whom were kept in the dark about the president's condition.[3] But although any age threshold is somewhat arbitrary, it would be foolish to have no thresholds whatsoever. Whatever the talents of thirteen-year-olds, they are probably not ready to be leaders of the free world.

A second value reflected in these qualifications is loyalty. Requiring candidates to be citizens of the United States helps to ensure that they will work for its interests and not those of another country. Residency requirements for state offices reflect a similar concern—the desire to have representatives who will work for their constituents' interests and not those in some other district or state. Residency requirements also imply a third value: familiarity with those a candidate seeks to represent. Having lived among his or her constituents could help a candidate better understand their needs. Of course, citizenship does not ensure loyalty and residency does not ensure good representation, but both kinds of requirements may foster these ideals.

Outside of age, citizenship, and residency, there are relatively few requirements in widespread use. Two more deserve brief mention, however. First, although it is not codified in the U.S. Constitution or state constitutions, the dominance of political parties in American elections virtually requires candidates to be party members in order to seek office. Party membership does not necessarily imply years of loyal service, and often parties will accept defectors from a competing party with open arms. That said, candidates cannot credibly hopscotch back and forth among parties, and this leads most of them to commit to a single party. This commitment is valuable to parties, who want to ensure that candidates represent the views of party members. **Independent candidates**—those unaffiliated with a party—often face significant challenges in simply getting on the ballot, as do candidates from smaller political parties. States typically require candidates to collect a certain number of signatures from voters to get on the ballot. In some cases, this requirement is not too onerous; for a potential candidate for the U.S. House of Representatives, Tennessee requires only 25 signatures from registered voters who reside in that House district—a tiny fraction of the 700,000 or so residents in a district. But in Texas, a potential candidate for governor must get a number of signatures equal to a larger fraction (1%) of all voters in the previous gubernatorial election. One percent

---

[3] August Heckscher. 1991. *Woodrow Wilson*. New York: Scribner.

may not sound like a lot, but for a candidate in the 2014 gubernatorial election, that entailed about 48,000 signatures.

Second, politicians can sometimes be disqualified from seeking reelection if they have already served in an office for a specified length of time. The shorthand for such a rule is **term limits**: limits on the number of terms politicians can serve in a particular elected office. For example, because of the Twenty-second Amendment (1951), the president can serve only two terms. Members of Congress have no term limits; laws passed by some state legislatures to impose term limits on members of Congress were overturned by the Supreme Court in 1995.[4] However, term limits on governors and state legislators are not prohibited. Thirty-six states limit the number of terms a governor may serve, typically to two.[5] Fifteen states limit the number of terms a state legislator may serve.[6] Term limits imply a certain vision of representation: good representatives are closer to the people, and this can best be achieved with frequent turnover. Otherwise, representatives may go to their respective capitals, spend years in office, and lose perspective on what their constituents want. Critics of term limits tend to emphasize a different ideal: good representatives are more experienced and more knowledgeable about public policy. Under term limits, the argument goes, legislators have little incentive to develop expertise because they will soon be out of a job. Note the tension between the values underlying minimum age and residency requirements on the one hand, and term limits on the other. Minimum age requirements are intended to ensure basic competence, and residency requirements to ensure a better connection with constituents. But to the extent that a longer tenure in office builds representatives' competence and their connection to their constituents, term limits will harm both.

In some respects, the rules regarding age, citizenship, and residency are rarely a constraint on candidates. Most potential candidates are not motivated to run for office until they are older. Nearly all meet the necessary requirement for U.S. citizenship, with the exception of naturalized citizens, such as former California governor Arnold Schwarzenegger, who are not eligible to run for president. Residency is only occasionally an issue, and this is usually not because candidates fail to meet the letter of the law but because opponents claim that although they maintain a home in the state or district,

---

[4] *U.S. Term Limits, Inc. v. Thornton*, 514 U.S. 779 (1995).

[5] For more information, see http://knowledgecenter.csg.org/kc/system/files/4.9_2013.pdf and http://ballotpedia.org/States_with_gubernatorial_term_limits (accessed 1/27/15).

[6] National Council of State Legislatures. "The Term Limited States." www.ncsl.org/default .aspx?tabId=14844 (accessed 1/27/15).

they really live elsewhere (for example, in Washington, DC), or that they arrived too recently in a state to represent it well (as the example of Alan Keyes in Chapter 1 illustrates). In fact, party membership and term limits probably have a larger impact on who can run. The advantages that come with party membership discourage candidates who do not identify with either major party. Term limits regularly force elected leaders to leave office or run for a different office, even when they would prefer to run for reelection to the same office.

The natural criticism of eligibility requirements hinges on the standard of free choice that we discussed in Chapter 1. One might argue that such requirements restrict the choices that citizens have by eliminating candidates who might otherwise be qualified but for one characteristic. Some critics of term limits make precisely this argument: it should not be a law that requires politicians to leave office but the will of the voters as demonstrated by the election of another candidate. The same might be said of other requirements. For example, citizens might also be able to evaluate whether a candidate is mature enough to hold office even without a law that sets a minimum age. The implication is not that eligibility requirements are inherently unnecessary, simply that imposing them tends to prioritize other values (such as competence or loyalty) over free choice.

The standard of deliberation is relevant here as well. Any requirement that restricts the candidates who can run for office might degrade the quality of deliberation by giving voters less information and possibly limiting the variety of information. This is easiest to see when considering the plight of many independent candidates, who face an uphill battle even to be listed on the ballot. Critics argue that ballot access laws deny voters the ability to consider alternative candidates, particularly those not affiliated with the Democratic or Republican parties. With fewer candidates running, there is less information in circulation, especially information that might come from perspectives different from those offered by the two major parties. Of course, some hurdle for ballot access may be necessary to prevent unserious candidates from appearing on the ballot. The question is how high that hurdle should be.

When Elections Are Held

When do candidates start campaigning for office? At the federal level, the timing of elections is set by the Constitution. Elections for the House of Representatives are held every two years; for the Senate, every six years; for president, every four years. These terms in office vary in part because the framers of the Constitution envisioned a different kind of representation from each type of office. House members were meant to be in closer contact with the people, and shorter terms help ensure more frequent interaction. By contrast, senators were expected to be more insulated from public opinion and thus better able to deliberate about public policy. George Washington said that "we pour legislation into the senatorial saucer to cool it."[7] For all federal offices, the date of the general election is, by law, the first Tuesday after the first Monday in November.

States typically follow the same practices, with similar terms in office for legislators (typically two or four years) and governors (typically four years). They use the same November election date that was established by federal law in 1845. States do vary in what year they elect governors—some hold gubernatorial elections during years with a presidential election, others during even-numbered years (without a presidential election), or, in Virginia and New Jersey, in every other odd-numbered year. Many local elections are not held concurrently with federal elections.

General elections are actually the second stage of the process. Most candidates must first secure the support of their party. This is typically determined in a **primary election**, where candidates compete with others from their party for the nomination for a particular office. States have a great deal of leeway in setting the date of their primary, although for the presidential nominations process (discussed further in Chapter 9), the parties pressure states to obey a particular calendar. Candidates in some states thus face an earlier primary than candidates in other states. Only after a primary election victory do candidates then compete in the general election.

Not every country has fixed election dates. In many parliamentary systems, there are only minimum requirements for when elections are held. For example, in Israel, they must be held at least every four years, but a majority of the legislature or the president can call for an election at any point. Once an election has been called, the candidates have roughly four weeks to campaign before Election Day. The incentive this creates is obvious: whenever possible, prime ministers prefer to call elections when their party is likely to win.

The timing of American elections creates different incentives and powerfully affects candidate strategy. Because politicians and potential candidates at every level of office know when the next election is scheduled, they can begin preparing for it well in advance. This creates a campaign that is longer

---

[7] U.S. Senate. "Senate Legislative Process." www.senate.gov/legislative/common/briefing/Senate_legislative_process.htm (accessed 1/27/15).

than in many other countries and that requires extraordinary effort from candidates. Presidential candidates often begin campaigning for the nomination years before the November general election. In preparation for the 2016 election, former Florida governor Jeb Bush announced on December 16, 2014, that he was exploring the possibility of running—more than a year before the first primary election and nearly two years before the November 2016 general election.

Politicians routinely express their dislike for this life. After announcing his retirement from the Senate in 2010, Evan Bayh (D-IL) wrote, "raising in small increments the $10 million to $20 million a competitive race requires takes huge amounts of time that could otherwise be spent talking with constituents, legislating or becoming well-versed on public policy."[8] But most politicians appear unwilling to take chances on letting opponents get a jump on them. They raise money constantly. They travel to their states or districts nearly every week to interact with constituents. They conjure up creative ways to appear in the news media whenever possible.

What is good and bad about this **permanent campaign**? On the one hand, a permanent campaign may help improve the quality of deliberation in the campaign. The longer the candidates campaign, the more information citizens

Jeb Bush announced that he was exploring the possibility of running for president in December 2014—nearly two years before the 2016 election.

[8] Evan Bayh. 2010. "Why I'm Leaving the Senate." *New York Times*, February 20.

receive because news coverage and advertising persists for weeks if not months.[9] A permanent campaign can also improve the quality of representation because such a campaign keeps politicians in constant contact with citizens and perhaps better aware of their needs and interests. Critics respond that much of this effort is for naught: citizens often do not pay much attention until the election is close at hand; all of the early campaigning may be a waste of time and money. Candidates seem to agree, as they intensify their campaigning as the election approaches.

A permanent campaign may also hurt the ideal of free choice by dissuading some good candidates from running. Some talented people, faced with the prospect of endless fund-raising and nights away from home, will simply opt out. And for those who do run, campaigning takes time away from learning about policy or writing legislation. The permanent campaign may therefore detract from good governance. This is all the more true if the permanent campaign keeps politicians focused only on short-term electoral benefits even though the country's problems demand long-term solutions.

Where to Run

Where do candidates run for office? For some offices, such as president, senator, and governor, the boundaries of the constituency are easily determined and do not change. The president represents the country as a whole—although, as discussed in Chapter 9, candidates focus their campaigns on "battleground states." Senators, governors, and any other statewide officeholders represent their states. But for others, notably members of the House of Representatives and state legislatures, the answer to this question is more complicated.

Single-Member Districts

With a few exceptions, federal and state legislators are elected in **single-member districts**. That is, each state is subdivided into districts and each district is represented by one legislator. In a handful of states with small populations, such as Alaska and Wyoming, there are no subdivisions and the state is represented by one member of the U.S. House of Representatives. A system of single-member districts contrasts with a system in which each district is represented by multiple representatives. This is the case in **at-large elections**. For example, for elections to its House of Delegates, Maryland is

---

[9] Randolph T. Stevenson and Lynn Vavreck. 2000. "Does Campaign Length Matter? Testing for Cross-National Effects." *British Journal of Political Science* 30, 2: 217–35.

divided into 47 districts, each of which elects three representatives. Vermont's House of Representatives is composed of some districts represented by one state legislator and some represented by two legislators. Nevertheless, single-member districts are the norm.

Reapportionment

The number of U.S. House districts in each state is proportional to the state's population. The actual number of districts is determined by the process of **reapportionment**. After the decennial census, the number of representatives in each state may be adjusted depending on changes in state populations.[10] For example, after the 2010 census, Georgia, South Carolina, Utah, Arizona, Nevada, and Washington each gained a seat in the House, while Florida gained two seats, and Texas gained four seats. A number of states lost a seat—mainly Midwestern states such as Michigan, Illinois, Iowa, and Missouri—while New York and Ohio each lost two seats. Occasionally, reapportionment generates controversy. After the 1920 census, representatives from rural areas blocked reapportionment because they feared that it would shift power to rapidly expanding urban districts, with potential policy consequences such as the repeal of Prohibition.[11] In 2000, Utah came up 857 residents short of earning an additional seat, which went to North Carolina instead. Utah representatives were upset because the census did not count Utah residents who were traveling abroad as Mormon missionaries—even as the census counted military personnel living overseas, which advantaged states like North Carolina that are home to large military bases. In 2009, two Utah representatives introduced legislation to require the census to count all Americans living overseas; as yet, no such requirement has been passed.

Redistricting

Far more controversial than deciding the number of seats is the process of drawing district boundaries, known as **redistricting**. Redistricting affects both state legislative and U.S. House district boundaries. As a state senator, Obama was involved in redistricting his state legislative seat. The fights over U.S. House district boundaries are usually more visible in the news media. In most states, both state and congressional district boundaries are drawn by the state legislature, often with the governor's approval required.

---

[10] For additional detail on how this is done, see Brian J. Gaines and Jeffery A. Jenkins. 2009. "Apportionment Matters: Fair Representation in the U.S. House and Electoral College." *Perspectives on Politics* 7, 4: 849–57.

[11] Daniel Okrent. 2010. *Last Call: The Rise and Fall of Prohibition*. New York: Scribner.

Less frequently, states use independent commissions, although in some states the legislature picks the members of the commission, making it something less than independent and neutral between the parties.

Malapportionment and "One Person, One Vote"

The major requirements for U.S. House and state legislative districts are two. First, districts must have nearly equal numbers of residents. This prevents **malapportionment** and ensures that representatives each have essentially the same number of constituents. It was not always this way. Prior to a series of Supreme Court decisions in the 1960s, malapportionment was widespread in both congressional and state legislative districts. While urban areas had typically grown in population relative to rural areas, districts had not been redrawn due to the influence of rural legislators, leaving rural districts with far fewer constituents per representative. In the mid-twentieth century, rural areas held the majority of seats in state legislatures even though more than two-thirds of Americans lived in urban areas.[12]

The Court's dismantling of this system began in 1962 with the case *Baker v. Carr*.[13] In this case, the Court established that issues regarding reapportionment and redistricting were justiciable—meaning that the courts could intervene even though these issues had historically been the domain of legislatures. Without *Baker v. Carr*, subsequent decisions on questions of legislative districts would not have been possible.

The next important case was *Gray v. Sanders* (1963).[14] The case involved Georgia's "county unit" system of deciding the winner of primary elections. The candidate who won the majority of votes in each county unit was awarded that unit, and the candidate who won the most units was declared the victor. The problem was that the units were not equal in size, which sometimes led to bizarre outcomes. In 1946, for example, one winning candidate actually received 16,000 fewer votes than the loser, but won the vast majority of county units. In rejecting this system, the Court established the important principle of **"one person, one vote."** Because the Fourteenth Amendment (1868) guarantees equal protection under the law, states must have electoral systems in which each person's vote counts equally. Under the county unit system, the vote of a person in a sparsely populated county unit counted more than the vote of someone in a more populous unit.

---

[12] Stephen Ansolabehere and James M. Snyder, Jr. 2008. *The End of Inequality: One Person, One Vote and the Transformation of American Politics*. New York: W. W. Norton.

[13] 369 U.S. 186 (1962).

[14] 372 U.S. 368 (1963).

The Court noted, however, that the Constitution allows deviations from this principle in two important cases. One is the U.S. Senate, which is famously malapportioned. According to the 2010 census, California had 37.2 million residents, or about 18.6 million for each of its two senators, while Wyoming had about 563,000 residents, or only about 281,500 residents for each senator. The other involves the Electoral College, which is the institution that formally elects the president. Each state is assigned a number of electors equal to its number of representatives and senators combined. The inclusion of senators in this tabulation makes the votes of the residents of less populous states count a bit more.

The establishment of the "one person, one vote" rule had implications for drawing district boundaries. First, these Court decisions made redistricting actually happen. Previously, many state legislatures simply failed to redistrict after the census even when their state constitution required it. As long as redistricting was left entirely up to the state legislatures, there was no means of forcing them to do it, and naturally the parties in power that were advantaged by existing arrangements were reluctant to do so. Second, the Court's decisions mandated that districts had to be roughly equivalent in population. In two 1964 cases, *Wesberry v. Sanders* and *Reynolds v. Sims*, the Court invalidated Georgia's congressional districts and Alabama's state legislative districts, respectively, because both states districts were drawn so that they had dramatically different populations.[15] Subsequent Court decisions have established a strict standard of equivalence: today, even small deviations among U.S. House districts might be held unconstitutional, while greater leeway is given to deviations among state legislative districts. For state legislative districts, deviations of 10 percent or less are typically accepted, although that standard is not set in stone and deviations under 10 percent may be considered suspect in some cases.[16]

The "one person, one vote" rule transformed American elections, legislatures, and public policy. As Stephen Ansolabehere and James Snyder write in their history of this rule, "all states eradicated gross disparities in legislative district populations within five years. The American states began in the 1960s as the most unequal representative bodies in the world, and they finished the decade adhering to one of the strictest standards of equal representation."[17] Although it did not eliminate the ability of self-interested politicians to influence legislative district boundaries—see the discussion of

---

[15] *Wesberry v. Sanders*, 376 U.S. 1 (1964); *Reynolds v. Sims*, 377 U.S. 533 (1964).

[16] See *Cox v. Larios*, 542 U.S. 947 (2004).

[17] Ansolabehere and Snyder, *End of Inequality*, pp. 187–88.

gerrymandering later in this chapter—the application of the rule did produce state legislatures that were much more representative of state populations in their partisan and ideological complexion. It also led to a more equitable distribution of government spending within states. Equal votes really did result in more equal power.

Racial Minorities and Voting Rights

The second requirement for congressional districts involves racial minorities. After Reconstruction, southern states took various steps to dilute the voting power of African Americans. One way was to draw district boundaries so as to split up black communities, placing a small number of blacks into each district and thereby limiting their ability to elect a candidate reflecting their background and preferences. In 1960, the Supreme Court took a step toward prohibiting this practice, arguing that a redrawing of the Tuskegee, Alabama, city boundaries to exclude most black voters violated the Fifteenth Amendment (which gave the right to vote to citizens regardless of race).[18] In 1965, Congress addressed this issue by passing the **Voting Rights Act** (VRA), which forbade states from intentionally diluting the voting power of minorities, including not only blacks but also Native Americans, Asian Americans, and Hispanics. In 1982, amendments to the Voting Rights Act established an even stricter standard: the voting power of minorities could not be diluted even as an unintentional by-product of some other action. The Voting Rights Act also singled out as "covered" jurisdictions specific states and counties with a history of persistent discrimination, including virtually every county in several southern states. Those counties had to submit any change in voting procedures or electoral laws to the Department of Justice for "pre-clearance." Only after the Department of Justice signed off on the change could it be implemented.

How would we know if district boundaries dilute the voting power of minorities? The Supreme Court took up this question in *Thornburg v. Gingles* (1986).[19] A group of African Americans claimed that the redistricting plan passed by the North Carolina General Assembly would have prevented blacks from electing representatives of their choosing. (Lacy Thornburg was the attorney general of North Carolina at that time; the named plaintiff was Ralph Gingles.) The Court ruled in favor of the plaintiffs, and in so doing established three criteria for demonstrating that district boundaries dilute minority voting power. First, the minority must be both sufficiently large and geographically concentrated to comprise a majority in a single district.

---

[18] *Gomillion v. Lightfoot*, 364 U.S. 339 (1960).

[19] 478 U.S. 30 (1986).

Second, the minority must be politically cohesive, meaning that members tend to have similar political preferences. Third, racially polarized voting, wherein the majority typically votes as a bloc for a candidate other than the one the minority prefers, must be present. The decision has been interpreted as a broad endorsement of the Voting Rights Act as amended in 1982.[20]

In 2013, however, the Supreme Court struck down the part of the VRA that defined which states and counties were "covered."[21] A narrow majority of the Court argued that this definition, which was based on data from the 1960s and early 1970s, was no longer valid. The majority argued that the formula was "based on 40-year-old facts having no logical relationship to the present day." Although the Court left intact the provision that states and counties must seek pre-clearance, there is currently no way to enforce pre-clearance if there is no formula to define which states and counties must seek pre-clearance. Congress would have to pass a legislation that establishes a new formula and, to date, it has not done so.

But there are other ways that the federal government can use the VRA to ensure that redistricting does not dilute the voting power of minorities. Another section of the VRA prohibits discriminatory voting laws, and conceivably the Justice Department could bring suit against a state if it believed the state's redistricting plan would hurt minorities. For this reason, it is not clear how much the Court's 2013 ruling will affect the next round of redistricting after the 2020 census.

Besides "one person, one vote" and the constraints on diluting minority voting power, there is little else that formally constrains the drawing of district boundaries. Districts are often drawn to be relatively compact and also contiguous. Contiguity means that a district is not comprised of "islands" of territory within a state, as would be the case for a district that was made up of a couple neighborhoods in San Francisco, a couple in Los Angeles, and nothing in between. Districts are also often drawn to correspond to **communities of interest**, such as existing towns or cities. These guidelines are not codified as formal rules at the federal level; however, some states require that districts respect community boundaries.

Gerrymandering

Without more explicit rules, those drawing the district boundaries can engage in **gerrymandering** (with the resulting set of districts constituting a

---

[20] See T. Alexander Aleinikoff and Samuel Issacharoff. 1993. "Race and Redistricting: Drawing Constitutional Lines after *Shaw v. Reno*." *Michigan Law Review* 92, 3: 588–651.

[21] *Shelby County v. Holder*, 570 U.S. ___ (2013).

"gerrymander"). Gerrymandering is the deliberate manipulation of district boundaries for some political purpose. Its results are most evident in oddly shaped districts. The term was coined in response to a redistricting plan that was implemented under Massachusetts governor Elbridge Gerry in 1812. The plan included a district that some thought resembled a salamander, and "Elbridge Gerry's salamander" begat "gerrymander."

Gerrymandering can serve multiple aims. It can create districts that maximize the number of voters who are racial minorities, thereby helping to ensure the election of representatives who are racial minorities themselves. Districts in which racial minority voters make up the majority of voters are

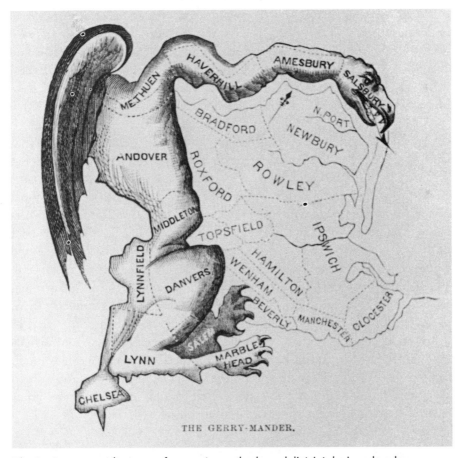

THE GERRY-MANDER.

The term *gerrymander* comes from a strangely shaped district designed under Governor Elbridge Gerry in Massachusetts in 1812. Gerry's goal — and the goal of many gerrymanders since — was to give an electoral advantage to partisan allies. However, gerrymanders may also have other purposes.

sometimes called **majority-minority districts**. Gerrymandering can also protect incumbents by ensuring that their districts are populated with voters likely to support them. Gerrymandering frequently has a partisan motivation. The party in control of the redistricting can try to maximize the number of seats it can win. To do so, it may "pack" voters from the opposite party into as few districts as possible. It may "crack" apart an existing district where the opposite party has been dominant, forcing that district's incumbent into a new district with many constituents who do not know him or her. "Kidnapping" forces two incumbents from the opposite party to compete against each other.

Much about gerrymandering seems objectionable on its face, but the Supreme Court has let many gerrymanders stand. It has raised objections to some redistricting plans geared toward empowering African Americans under the auspices of the Voting Rights Act, however. The most famous case was a North Carolina plan that included a district (the 12th District) some 160 miles long, which was drawn to include black communities in several different cities and was sometimes scarcely any wider than the interstate highway that connected these cities (see Figure 2.1). In *Shaw v. Reno* (1993),[22] the Court's majority described this district as "highly irregular," expressed considerable discomfort with racial gerrymanders in general, and argued that they were subject to the Court's highest standard of review, known as "strict scrutiny," because they could in theory violate the Fourteenth Amendment's equal protection clause. This district was then subject to years of court battles, including three further Supreme Court cases, as well as much tinkering with its boundaries.[23] Ultimately, the Supreme Court upheld the district only after North Carolina successfully argued that its boundaries reflected a political goal—to create a safe Democratic seat—rather than a racial goal. These and other Court decisions have not eliminated race-conscious redistricting, but they have forced states that draw such districts to justify them on different, and more demanding, terms. It is also worth noting that in nearly all of these cases, the Court was narrowly divided, five to four, signaling that there were sharp disagreements on racial gerrymandering—much as there were sharp disagreements on the Court about whether and how to apply the Voting Rights Act to contemporary redistricting plans and other electoral laws that might affect racial minorities.

---

[22] 509 U.S. 630 (1993).

[23] Those decisions were *Shaw v. Hunt*, 517 U.S. 899 (1996), and *Hunt v. Cromartie*, 526 U.S. 541 (1999 and 2001).

FIGURE 2.1 **North Carolina's 12th Congressional District, 1992–98**

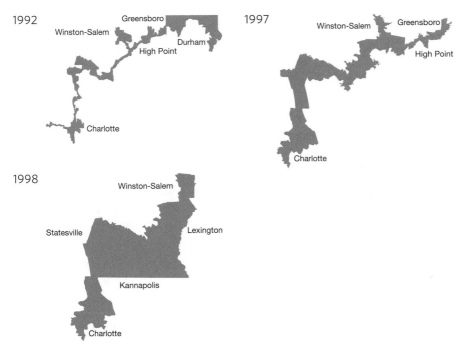

Source: National Conference of State Legislatures. "North Carolina Redistricting Cases: The 1990s." www.senate.leg.state.mn.us/departments/scr/redist/redsum/NCSUM.HTM (accessed 1/27/15).

The Court's concern about racial gerrymandering does not extend to other forms of gerrymandering. In 1973, the Court upheld a Connecticut plan that created separate Democratic and Republican strongholds and thereby provided considerable protection for incumbents.[24] The Court saw benefits in the plan because it provided a legislative body that mirrored the partisan composition of Connecticut voters. Subsequent decisions confirmed that incumbent protection was not necessarily problematic in the view of the Court.[25] The Court has also refused to declare partisan gerrymanders unconstitutional. The Court has confirmed that the questions raised by partisan gerrymanders are justifiably the domain of the courts under the Equal Protection Clause,[26] but in that case and in later cases, it has not sought to define or apply a standard by which partisan gerrymanders could

---

[24] *Gaffney v. Cummings*, 412 U.S. 735 (1973).

[25] See Nathaniel Persily. 2006. "The Place of Competition in American Electoral Law," in *The Marketplace of Democracy: Electoral Competition and American Politics*, eds. Michael P. McDonald and John Samples. Washington, DC: Brookings Institution Press, pp. 171–95.

[26] *Davis v. Bandemer*, 478 U.S. 109 (1986).

be evaluated. This was evident most recently when the Court considered, but did not invalidate, a Pennsylvania partisan gerrymander.[27] However, in that case several justices indicated the need for such a standard, suggesting that the constitutionality of partisan gerrymanders is far from settled. Indeed, one of those justices, the now retired John Paul Stevens, has proposed a Constitutional amendment that would prevent partisan gerrymanders.

Reapportionment and especially redistricting constrain political candidates in an important way: candidates have only limited control over who their constituents are. Their input is limited by the timing of redistricting, which occurs only every 10 years following the census. The 10-year cycle is not set by law. In 2003, the Republicans in the Texas state legislature initiated a new round of redistricting, taking advantage of the fact that Republicans had won control of the legislature in 2002. The resulting plan shifted the Texas congressional delegation from 17 Democrats and 15 Republicans as of 2002 to 11 Democrats and 21 Republicans after the 2004 elections. This example is, however, the exception rather than the rule; most states adhere to the norm of redistricting after the decennial census. Moreover, candidates may be constrained by the process by which district boundaries are drawn. In those states where the state legislature decides on the district boundaries, politicians in the minority party may have little if any input. Constituencies are thus somewhat fixed and constitute part of the reality that candidates must face.

How does limited control over the constituency affect candidate strategy? In some cases it may forestall a candidate's political career: in a district strongly skewed toward one party, a candidate of the opposite party is unlikely to win and, perhaps, to run for office in the first place. At the same time, a particular redistricting cycle may endanger or even end the career of someone already in office, particularly if district boundaries change dramatically and the incumbent must confront large numbers of new constituents who are not supporters. Campaign messages also reflect the realities of district boundaries and constituent demographics. The issues that candidates emphasize, the groups they target, and actions they take if elected to office all reflect the nature of their constituency.

The redistricting process and the prevalence of gerrymandering raise philosophical questions as well. Gerrymandering can limit the competitiveness of legislative elections and instead favor an incumbent legislator or a particular party, leaving opposing candidates or parties on very unequal

---

[27] *Vieth v. Jubelirer*, 541 U.S. 267 (2004).

The Technology behind Redistricting

The process of redistricting involves precise decisions about where to draw district boundaries. No matter whether the goal is to promote competition, protect incumbents, or favor a political party's candidates, the architects of the new map scrutinize neighborhoods down to the city block and street — looking for any potentially favorable adjustment. How do they do this?

Years ago, the process of redistricting could be extraordinarily labor-intensive. It involved teams of people poring over paper maps, often with calculators in hand to tabulate past voting results and figure out the partisan complexion of particular areas. District boundaries would be sketched in different-colored markers. Contemporary redistricting, however, draws heavily on computer technology. Geographic information systems (or GIS) can store data about geographical units, allowing users to draw new boundaries with clicks of the computer mouse. These systems first came to prominence in the 1991 redistricting, when all but four states used GIS in their congressional or state legislative redistricting.[1] Some states also relied on consulting firms who could provide specialized expertise in GIS.

By the next round of redistricting, in 2001, there had been further innovation. Computers were more powerful and redistricting software was widely available. Essentially, anyone with a laptop could purchase this software, download geographical data from the U.S. Census Bureau or a state government agency, and draw their own district boundaries. Some software packages will automatically draw district boundaries based on a particular criterion — making the process even easier. It is more difficult, however, for software to take account of all relevant criteria — such as the need to make districts that have equal populations, are somewhat compact, abide by the Voting Rights Act, and so on. Thus, the participants in the redistricting process — such as state legislators — must do more than simply approve the district boundaries the software has produced.

Computer software remains an imperfect tool, and its increasing prominence has troubled some observers. They fear that because politicians can rely on more precise data and more powerful computing, they can draw even better gerrymanders. For example, in his dissenting opinion in the *Vieth v. Jubelirer* (2004) decision, Supreme Court justice David Souter cited concerns about the use of technology in redistricting and wrote, "[T]he increasing efficiency of partisan redistricting has damaged the democratic process to a degree that our predecessors only began to imagine."

At the same time, there are limitations on what computers can do. Moreover, many controversial gerrymanders — including Elbridge Gerry's original in 1812 — preceded the development of computers. If politicians want to create oddly shaped districts, they probably do not need a computer to do so. In fact, the widespread availability of redistricting software actually allows people besides politicians — including interest groups and citizens — to try their hand at redistricting. If you are interested, see publicmapping.org.

---

[1] Micah Altman, Karin Mac Donald, and Michael McDonald. 2005. "From Crayons to Computers: The Evolution of Computer Use in Redistricting." *Social Science Computer Review* 23, 2: 334–46.

footing. Their underdog status makes it difficult for opposing candidates to raise money and effectively advertise their candidacy. The resulting election may fall short of the ideals of both free choice and deliberation. Although voters are not being coerced into making a choice, their choices may be limited because gerrymandering makes it difficult for certain candidates to run. In such cases, citizens receive less information than they would if the election were competitive, and thus find it harder to deliberate about the candidates' relative merits.

At the same time, gerrymandered districts may actually make elections more representative. Districts drawn to guarantee that a particular party wins usually have a large majority of voters from that party. Most voters in that large majority will typically feel well represented by their representative. Compare that to a district where voters are divided 51–49 percent between the two major parties. If the majority always wins with 51 percent of the vote, a much larger fraction of voters than in the gerrymandered district—possibly even 49 percent—will feel poorly represented. Partisan loyalties are not the only relevant loyalties either. Gerrymandered districts can also give racial minorities a chance to elect the representative of their choice. None of this means that competitiveness is unimportant or undesirable, simply that it must be balanced against alternative considerations.

The debate over redistricting involves other concerns as well. For example, critics argue that in gerrymandered districts, the favored party's candidates will cater only to that party's base, becoming more ideologically extreme and further polarizing the parties in the state legislature or Congress. Concerns about redistricting's effects on competition and polarization have led a number of states to reform their redistricting process—for example, by placing responsibility with a commission rather than the state legislature and by instituting more detailed rules about how districts can be drawn. Washington State, for instance, requires that its commission exercise its powers "to provide fair and effective representation and to encourage electoral competition." There is evidence that redistricting processes that involve courts and commissions produce a larger number of competitive districts than processes involving only the state legislature.[28]

At the same time, even as redistricting often advantages the party that controls the process, political science research suggests that its effects are

---

[28] Jamie L. Carson, Michael H. Crespin, and Ryan D. Williamson. 2014. "Reevaluating the Effects of Redistricting on Electoral Competition, 1972–2012." *State Politics and Policy Quarterly* 14, 2: 165–77.

not always as large as critics suggest. It does not necessarily advantage incumbents, reduce competitiveness, or exacerbate political polarization.[29] Furthermore, there are limits to how much redistricting reforms can increase competition. In some areas of the country, preexisting residential segregation naturally produces politically homogeneous communities. It would be difficult, for example, to carve out a Republican congressional district in Berkeley, California—unless one were willing to draw some pretty contorted salamanders.

Who Can Vote

Electoral rules affect not only candidates but also citizens. The central question concerning citizens is who is eligible to vote. The qualifications for voting have changed a great deal throughout American history. Early restrictions based on race were invalidated by the Fifteenth Amendment (1870) and, perhaps more consequentially, by the Voting Rights Act of 1965. Restrictions based on sex were invalidated by the Nineteenth Amendment (1920). Restrictions based on wealth were invalidated by the Twenty-fourth Amendment (1964), which banned **poll taxes**, fees that one had to pay in order to vote and that were also used to disenfranchise black voters in the South. Restrictions based on level of education were invalidated by the Voting Rights Act, which banned the use of **literacy tests**—another way by which southern blacks were disenfranchised. Restrictions based on age were relaxed by the Twenty-sixth Amendment (1971), which lowered the voting age from 21 to 18. These reforms dramatically expanded the size of the American electorate.

Two remaining restrictions are in place nationwide: the minimum voting age of 18 and the requirement that eligible voters be native or naturalized citizens. Other restrictions vary across states. States differ in how they treat

---

[29] The evidence with regard to the incumbency advantage and polarization is fairly clear. There is more debate about the effects of redistricting on competitiveness. See Alan I. Abramowitz, Brad Alexander, and Matthew Gunning. 2006. "Incumbency, Redistricting, and the Decline of Competition in U.S. House Elections." *Journal of Politics* 68, 1: 75–88; John N. Friedman and Richard T. Holden. 2009. "The Rising Incumbent Reelection Rate: What's Gerrymandering Got to Do with It?" *Journal of Politics* 71: 593–611; Andrew Gelman and Gary King. 2004. "Enhancing Democracy through Legislative Redistricting." *American Political Science Review* 88, 3: 541–59; Michael P. McDonald. 2006. "Drawing the Line on District Competition." *PS: Political Science and Politics* 39, 1: 91–94; Nolan McCarty, Keith Poole, and Howard Rosenthal. 2009. "Does Gerrymandering Cause Polarization?" *American Journal of Political Science* 53, 3: 666–80.

Date of Examination_____

Name of Applicant_____

Address of Applicant_____

QUESTIONS	ANSWER	ANSWER OF APPLICANT
1. Who is President of the United States?	Harry S. Truman	
2. What is the term of office of the President of the United States?	four years	
3. May the President of the United States be legally elected for a second term?	Yes	
4. If the President of the United States dies in office who succeeds him?	Vice-President	
5. How many groups compose the Congress of the United States?	Two-The Senate and House of Representatives	
6. How many United States Senators are there from Georgia?	Two	
7. What is the term of office of a United State Senator?	Six years	

Literacy tests, like this one used in Georgia in 1949, limit who can vote. Laws that require literacy tests were invalidated by the Voting Rights Act of 1965.

criminals and the mentally ill. Although nearly every state bans convicted felons from voting while in prison—only Maine and Vermont permit inmates to vote—states differ in whether they allow convicted felons to vote while on parole or probation. They also differ in whether they deny convicted felons the right to vote after their sentence is served and in the process by which felons can regain the right to vote.[30] These laws have become increasingly consequential, as the number of convicted felons has grown over time. State laws about the mentally ill are similarly wide-ranging, although it is not clear how often any restrictions related to voting by the mentally ill are actually enforced.

States also differ in whether they require citizens to register as a member of a political party in order to participate in primary elections. In a **closed primary**, only citizens registered with the party can vote in that party's primary. In a **semi-closed primary**, both unaffiliated voters and those registered as members of the party can vote in that party's primary. In an **open primary**, all voters can vote in either party's primary, but not both. In a **blanket** (or **jungle**) **primary**, there is a single ballot with the candidates for each party listed, and citizens can mix and match, voting for a Democratic

[30] The Sentencing Project. 2010. "Felon Disenfranchisement Laws in the United States." http://sentencingproject.org/doc/publications/fd_Felony%20Disenfranchisement%20 Laws%20in%20the%20US.pdf (accessed 1/27/15).

nominee for senator, a Republican candidate for governor, and so on. This form of primary was invalidated by the Supreme Court in 2000.[31] The Court argued that it violated the parties' First Amendment right of association because a party's nominee could be chosen in part by people who do not affiliate with that party and who even actively oppose it. The blanket primary survives only in a nonpartisan form. For example, in Louisiana, all candidates are listed on the ballot, and if a candidate wins 50 percent of the vote, he or she is elected to that office after the first round of balloting. If no candidate wins 50 percent of the vote, the top two vote-getters for any office go on to the general election, regardless of their party affiliation. In Washington and California, the same ballot structure is used, but there is no possibility of winning the election outright at the primary stage. The top two vote-getters go on to the general election no matter how much of the vote the front-runner received.

All of these requirements are enforced via a system of voter registration. In every state except for North Dakota, citizens must register to vote and provide evidence that they meet the necessary criteria. Among the states that require registration, there are further differences about when citizens must register in order to be eligible to vote—ranging from 30 days prior to the election to the day of the election itself. Ten states as well as the District of Columbia have implemented **same-day** (or **election-day**) **registration** (Colorado, Connecticut, Idaho, Iowa, Maine, Minnesota, Montana, New Hampshire, Wisconsin, and Wyoming).[32] States are also currently debating the identification that voters must show to prove their identity: 31 states have voter identification laws in force, and 9 of those require photo identification.[33]

All of these requirements affect campaign strategy by affecting the number of citizens who actually vote. The more onerous the requirements, the more likely it is that some eligible citizens cannot or will not register to vote or turn out on Election Day.[34] For example, in 2012, voter turnout in states that did not have Election Day registration was, on average, 10 points lower

---

[31] *California Democratic Party v. Jones*, 530 U.S. 567 (2000).

[32] National Conference of State Legislatures. 2015. "Same Day Registration." www.ncsl.org/research/elections-and-campaigns/same-day-registration.aspx (accessed 1/27/15).

[33] National Conference of State Legislatures. 2014. "Voter Identification Requirements." www.ncsl.org/research/elections-and-campaigns/voter-id.aspx (accessed 1/27/15). North Carolina has also passed a law requiring photo identification that is meant to take effect in 2016. A Wisconsin voter identification law is currently blocked pending the resolution of a court case.

[34] See Raymond E. Wolfinger and Steven J. Rosenstone. 1980. *Who Votes?* New Haven, CT: Yale University Press.

than in states with Election Day registration, although there is some debate about how much of that gap was actually caused by other factors.[35]

Some countries, such as Brazil and Australia, make voting compulsory. Unlike in countries with compulsory voting, the American system leaves the responsibility up to citizens, and many eligible citizens choose not to vote. This leads to a second consequence for campaign strategy, one that reflects both an opportunity for and a burden on candidates and parties. They have the opportunity to mobilize citizens to vote, including perhaps some who otherwise would not have participated. Successful mobilization can help a candidate win. The burden arises because mobilization efforts demand time, energy, and money.

Rules about voter registration affect campaign strategy in a third way: by affecting the types of citizens who are eligible or likely to vote. For example, some research suggests that making it easier for felons to vote helps Democratic candidates—in part, because felons and ex-felons are disproportionately African American, they are more likely to vote Democratic than the population as a whole.[36] Election Day registration seems to encourage the participation of two groups, young people and nonwhites, who are both more likely to vote Democratic than Republican.[37]

For these reasons, candidates and parties naturally tend to resist reforms that they fear will increase voter turnout among members of the opposite party. That said, most such reforms would not necessarily lead to a vastly different political landscape. The predicted changes in turnout among particular demographic groups are not always large; moreover, many elections are won by such large margins that changes in turnout would probably not affect

---

[35] Demos. "What Is Same Day Registration?" www.demos.org/publication/what-same-day-registration-where-it-available (accessed 1/27/15). See also Craig Leonard Brians and Bernard Grofman. 2001. "Election Day Registration's Effect on U.S. Voter Turnout." *Social Science Quarterly* 82, 1: 170–83; Michael Hanmer. 2009. *Discount Voting.* Cambridge: Cambridge University Press.

[36] Jeff Manza and Christopher Uggen. 2004. "Punishment and Democracy: Disenfranchisement of Nonincarcerated Felons in the United States." *Perspectives on Politics* 2, 3: 491–505.

[37] R. Michael Alvarez, Stephen Ansolabehere, and Catherine H. Wilson. 2002. "Election Day Registration in the United States: How One-Step Voting Can Change the Composition of the American Electorate." Caltech/MIT Voting Technology Project Working Paper. www.vote.caltech.edu/drupal/files/working_paper/vtp_wp5.pdf (accessed 1/27/15); Stephen Knack and James White. 2000. "Election-Day Registration and Turnout Inequality." *Political Behavior* 22, 1: 29–44. However, the introduction of election-day registration in Wisconsin appeared to help Republicans more than Democrats. Jacob Neiheisel and Barry C. Burden. 2012. "The Impact of Election Day Registration on Voter Turnout and Election Outcomes." *American Politics Research* 40, 4: 636–64.

the outcome.[38] Predicting the effects of election reforms is fraught with uncertainty, and this uncertainty, along with concerns about adverse effects on their own and their party's electoral prospects, makes politicians wary of reform.

Perhaps the primary value considered throughout the history of voting rights is political equality. Much of the battle for voting rights, such as those for women and African Americans, was about changing laws that denied voting rights to a particular group even as other groups had that right. As noted in Chapter 1, ongoing debates about voting rights still concern political equality. If members of some groups are less likely to possess a particular form of identification, such as a driver's license, and voter identification laws require would-be voters to show a poll worker this identification, does this violate the standard of political equality?

A second relevant value is the level of participation. For many people, "good" elections are ones in which large percentages of eligible citizens vote—and, in their view, turnout in the United States is too low. If so, then rules about voter qualifications should be structured to ensure that as many people as possible can and will participate. Compulsory voting would even be a reasonable step, from this perspective.

But maximizing equality and participation may not be the only relevant goals. It may be justifiable to limit participation, even if those limits fall disproportionately on certain groups. Restrictions with regard to age and mental illness imply a concern about competence; very young people or people who are mentally ill are assumed, correctly or incorrectly, unable or unready to vote. Requiring citizenship implies a concern about loyalty; the people choosing a country's leaders should be "members" of that country themselves. Disenfranchising felons reflects the belief that the right to vote depends on a willingness to obey the law. Requiring party registration for a primary election reflects a belief that a party's candidates should be chosen by voters loyal to that party. Requiring voters to register ahead of the election, or provide identification on Election Day, is intended to prevent such fraud as impersonating another voter or attempting to vote more than once. All of these rationales can be critiqued. For example, cases of voter fraud are rare.[39] The broader point is that electoral rules are geared not simply

---

[38] Jack Citrin, Eric Schickler, and John Sides. 2003. "What If Everyone Voted? Simulating the Impact of Increased Turnout in Senate Elections." *American Journal of Political Science* 47, 1: 75–90.

[39] Justin Levitt. 2007. "The Truth about Voter Fraud." Brennan Center for Justice at New York University School of Law. http://brennan.3cdn.net/c176576c0065a7eb84_gxm6ib0hl .pdf (accessed 4/8/11).

toward promoting strict equality before the law or encouraging citizens to participate; they are intended to further other goals as well.

Who Wins

Once candidates have campaigned and citizens have voted, a crucial question arises: How are votes counted to determine a winner (or winners)? In the United States, most elections adhere to a simple winner-take-all principle. That is, the person with the most votes (a plurality of votes) wins the election. For example, in order for a presidential candidate to win a state and therefore receive all of that state's Electoral College votes, the candidate need only win more votes than any other candidate in that state. A plurality is not necessarily a majority, or more than half of the votes. **Plurality rule** is more common than majority rule in American elections, although some states do have rules in place to ensure that for certain offices the winning candidate does get a majority. This often entails a runoff election between the top two vote-getters, as in the Louisiana system discussed earlier.

The American system of plurality rule in single-member districts differs from that of many other democracies. A helpful contrast involves those countries whose legislatures are chosen by **proportional representation**, such as Israel (see Box 2.1). In these systems, seats are allocated to parties in proportion to the percentage of the vote they received. A party that wins 20 percent of the vote can expect to receive 20 percent of the seats, although many countries have a threshold such that a party must win at least some minimum percentage of the vote to gain any seats. To achieve proportionality, these systems often do not have single-member districts but either nationwide elections or districts with multiple winners. Voters vote for a slate of candidates chosen by the party, rather than for an individual candidate nominated via a primary election. To be sure, proportional systems differ from each other in their specific rules, and some countries combine features of both kinds of systems. But this general description highlights the major points of contrast between these systems and the American system.

A candidate competing in a plurality election must get the most votes; second place, even by a margin of only one vote, gives the loser nothing. One implication of this was spelled out by the French political scientist Maurice Duverger, in what became known as **Duverger's Law**: In a system with single-member districts and plurality voting, there is a strong tendency for only two parties to emerge, and candidates not affiliated with either of those parties face serious obstacles. This is because in an election with more than two candidates, voters in a plurality system often engage in **strategic voting**—voting for a candidate who is not their first choice but has a better chance of winning. Some supporters of independent candidates or candidates from minor parties do not want to "waste" their vote on a candidate who has little chance of winning a seat. And so they end up defecting to whichever of two major-party candidates they like better (or dislike less). Third-party or independent candidates typically fare poorly. Duverger's Law helps explain why the American party system is characterized by long periods of two-party dominance. By contrast, in a system that uses proportional representation, candidates from smaller parties may still win some seats, even if they have no chance of winning the most votes, so their supporters are less likely to defect.

The use of plurality rather than proportional rules in the United States gives candidates a strong incentive to affiliate with a major party. It also gives parties and candidates the incentive to invest significant effort only in

BOX 2.1

Proportional Representation in Israel

Unlike election to the U.S. Congress, election to the federal legislature in Israel, called the Knesset, relies on a system of proportional representation. A brief overview of this system provides some useful contrasts with the American system.

First, the Israeli system does not have districts. Representatives to the Knesset are elected in nationwide elections and do not represent any specific districts.

Second, voters in Israel are voting for party lists, not for individual candidates. Party leaders compose these lists, as opposed to having voters nominate candidates via primary elections. The order of candidates on the party list determines who ultimately gets a seat. If a party wins only one seat, then the first person on that party's list joins the Knesset.

Third, parties are given seats in the Knesset in proportion to the number of votes they receive, with one stipulation: to be given any seats, the party must receive at least two percent of the vote. This relatively low threshold is quite favorable to small parties. In the Israeli election in 2013, 12 different parties won seats in the legislature. As an example of how proportional the allocations of seats are, consider the top vote-getter, the Likud Party: it received 23.3 percent of the votes and 25.8 percent of the seats (31 out of 120). In the 2014 House elections, Republican candidates received 52.9 percent of the major-party vote nationwide, but controlled 56.8 percent of seats (247 out of 435).

competitive races. For example, political parties raise money that they can then spend on behalf of any of their candidates. Where is that money best spent? In an uncompetitive district where it might help the party's candidate win, say, 30 percent of the vote instead of 15 percent? Probably not. In a winner-take-all election, 30 percent of the vote earns nothing more than 15 percent. Instead, parties will target more competitive districts where this money might make the difference between winning and losing. The same logic applies to presidential candidates, given the winner-take-all nature of the Electoral College. It makes little sense for candidates to campaign in states where they are virtually guaranteed to win or to lose. They go instead to the "battleground" states where the outcome is in doubt and additional campaign dollars may make the difference.

The dominance of the two major parties is one criticism of the American system and is frequently cited as a reason for favoring a system of proportional representation instead. Proportional representation, the argument goes, enhances free choice by providing more options for voters. These increased options may also enhance the deliberative potential of elections, as a wider range of issues and policy proposals are likely to be discussed. Fewer votes are "wasted" because more citizens are encouraged to select their first choice. In particular, minorities—whether political, racial, or otherwise—may find it easier to elect representatives of their choice under a proportional system. Some supporters also argue that citizens are more likely to vote because they have an option that truly represents their preferences, although there is not much evidence that turnout is higher in proportional systems.[40]

On the other hand, proportional representation is sometimes criticized for promoting a multiparty system that often results in elections lacking a clear winner. In a proportional system, it is common for no one party to win a majority of seats in the legislature. Then two or more parties must form a coalition to achieve a majority and govern the country. Critics argue that negotiations among parties may produce coalitions that voters did not anticipate or intend. To take a hypothetical example, imagine that a country had three parties, Left, Right, and Center, and none got the majority of the vote. It turns out that most voters of the Center Party prefer the Left Party to the Right Party. But after the election, Center and Right form a coalition. Is this

---

[40] André Blais. 2007. "Turnout in Elections," in *Oxford Handbook of Political Behavior*, eds. Russell J. Dalton and Hans-Dieter Klingemann. Oxford: Oxford University Press, pp. 621–35.

what Center Party voters want? If they had known that this coalition would result, might they have voted for the Left Party instead?

A second criticism is that proportional representation produces less stable government. Coalitions can be fragile. If one party leaves the coalition, the coalition may fall apart, necessitating a new election. Finally, proportional systems often lack the personal form of representation that can be provided in single-member districts, where representatives have a long history in the community and know their constituents well.

Supporters of proportional representation have answers for all of these criticisms, noting that instability is far from inevitable and that personal representation may provide little consolation to constituents who sharply disagree with their homegrown representative. The larger point remains: any set of rules will promote certain values over other values.

Conclusion

This chapter has discussed the basic rules of the American electoral system — rules that govern nearly every aspect of the electoral process. Even in this brief overview, it is clear that the American system reflects no grand logic. It is the result of many compromises that are guided by multiple decision makers, including the framers of the Constitution, the Supreme Court, and federal, state, and local lawmakers. As such, the rules can change over time and vary across states and localities. The rules are also products of contending values about what a "good" election looks like. Whether rules strike observers as fair or unfair will depend in part on which values they hold dear. Moreover, it is challenging to construct electoral rules that uphold all these values simultaneously. Trade-offs are inevitable.

The rules that govern elections affect all of the actors whose roles we describe in later chapters. The rules provide the framework for the decisions of candidates, parties, and citizens alike. They are rarely as newsworthy as a candidate's gaffe or a hard-hitting campaign advertisement, but they are important nonetheless. Electoral rules are all the more important because they are not easy to change and remain largely outside of the control of candidates, parties, and citizens. Passing new laws and amending the Constitution are difficult. Candidates instead adapt. The rules then become part of the hand that candidates are dealt, at least once the campaign is under way.

Even seemingly arcane rules can be consequential. The adoption of the new district that Obama helped draw as a state senator literally came down to a piece of paper that was picked out of a hat. The Democrats, who controlled the Illinois House, had drawn up one set of districts. The Republicans, who controlled the Illinois Senate, had drawn up another. The two parties could not agree, and a redistricting commission composed of four Democrats and four Republicans was convened to select the new map. When it, too, failed to reach agreement, the Illinois Supreme Court submitted the names of one Democrat and one Republican to break the deadlock. One of those names was to be drawn from a hat—a hat made to resemble Abraham Lincoln's stovepipe hat, no less—and that person would then be the tie-breaking vote on the commission. The Democrat's name was drawn and his vote enacted the Democrats' map and thus Obama's new district. The rest, as they say, is history.

KEY TERMS

independent candidates (p. 24)

term limits (p. 25)

primary election (p. 27)

permanent campaign (p. 28)

single-member districts (p. 29)

at-large elections (p. 29)

reapportionment (p. 30)

redistricting (p. 30)

malapportionment (p. 31)

one person, one vote (p. 31)

Voting Rights Act of 1965 (p. 33)

communities of interest (p. 34)

gerrymandering (p. 34)

majority-minority districts (p. 36)

poll taxes (p. 41)

literacy tests (p. 41)

closed primary (p. 42)

semi-closed primary (p. 42)

open primary (p. 42)

blanket/jungle primary (p. 42)

same-day/election-day registration (p. 43)

plurality rule (p. 46)

proportional representation (p. 46)

Duverger's Law (p. 46)

strategic voting (p. 47)

FOR DISCUSSION

1. What are arguments for and against term limits?
2. What formal rules and informal norms govern the drawing of U.S. House districts during redistricting?
3. How might different rules about who can vote affect how candidates campaign?
4. How does the American system's combination of single-member districts and plurality rule disadvantage minor political parties and independent candidates?

CHAPTER 3

The Transformation of American Campaigns

On November 4, 2012, Politico published an article titled "R.I.P. Positive Ads in 2012."[1] Relying on an analysis of television advertisements in 2012 by the Wesleyan Media Project, the article painted a bleak picture of presidential campaign discourse in the race between Barack Obama and Mitt Romney:

> Many predicted this would be the most negative presidential campaign in history, with outside groups blanketing swing-state airwaves with attack ads. But few thought the hostility would erupt quite so intensely from the candidates themselves. Barack Obama and Mitt Romney are tearing each other up on the television airwaves in the final days of Election 2012, setting a record for the most negative campaign ads in presidential election history . . . the slew of negative ads also shows just how close this race is in the seven or eight battleground states that will decide the election. The campaigns "recognize anything that moves 1 percent of the voters may make the difference between winning and losing," said Darrell West, author of "Air Wars," a book on TV advertising in campaigns. "In that situation, they'll use anything they've got." Even as Hurricane Sandy pummeled the East Coast last week, the negative barrage continued. "They will stay negative. Too much on the line. Too close," GOP ad man Fred Davis said.

There is some truth to Politico's characterization of 2012, and even a cursory glance at that election provides reasons why it turned ugly. The 2012 presidential election featured a Democratic incumbent who had presided over a difficult and uneven economic recovery and had championed a controversial overhaul of the nation's health care system. Opposing him was a wealthy Republican heir to a famous American political family, who had run a venture capital company and

---

[1] Donovan Slack. 2012. "R.I.P. Positive Ads in 2012." Politico, November 4. CNN Politics, September 15. www.politico.com/news/stories/1112/83262.html (accessed 6/6/14).

governed a liberal state. Furthermore, the fascinating mix of race and religion at the top of the parties' tickets created an unusual dynamic, one that produced some explosive charges and story lines.

But was 2012 "the most negative presidential campaign in history"? Negativity has always been a central feature of American political campaigns. In fact, the negativity that occurred in 2012 pales in comparison to that seen in some previous campaigns. For example, in the election of 1828, a local newspaper printed this attack against Democratic candidate Andrew Jackson: "Gen. Jackson's mother was a common prostitute brought to this country by the British soldiers. She afterwards married a mulatto man, with whom she had several children, of whom Gen. Jackson was one." In 1860, Abraham Lincoln was attacked as "a fourth-rate lecturer, who cannot speak good grammar and who, to raise the wind, delivers his hackneyed, illiterate compositions at $200 a piece." As if that were not enough, Lincoln was also characterized as "a horrid wretch . . . Sooty and scoundrelly in aspect, a cross between the nutmeg dealer, the horse swapper, and the night man, a creature fit evidently for petty treason, small stratagems, and all sorts of sports."[2]

This chapter focuses on the lessons past campaigns teach us about contemporary American campaigns. Are there certain patterns and characteristics that appear time and time again? Or have the American electorate and its candidates evolved so that the essential nature of campaigns is dynamic and shifting? In this chapter, we argue that the rules and the reality that drive election campaigns change infrequently, producing continuity in most aspects of American

---

Core of the Analysis

- Many aspects of modern campaigns can be seen in campaigns throughout American history.
- Changes in the conduct and content of campaigns have been produced by changes in rules, reality, strategy, and the electorate.
- Campaigns can be sorted into roughly four eras, each of which is distinguished by distinct forms of campaigning.
- There are also commonalities across these eras, particularly in the length, expense, and content of American campaigns.
- The increasingly competitive and polarized party system and the penetration of the Internet may or may not signify a new era for campaigns.

---

[2] These examples come from Paul Boller. 1984. *Presidential Campaigns*. New York: Oxford University Press.

campaigns. But when these factors do change, they tend to do so abruptly, producing periods in which campaigns innovate and campaign strategies evolve. There have been at least four major eras of American political campaigns: 1788–1824 ("Pre-Democratic Campaigns"), 1828–92 ("Mass Mobilization Campaigns"), 1896–1948 ("Progressive Era Campaigns"), and 1952 to the present ("Candidate Campaigns"). Each is distinct enough from the others to warrant its own category, but each also contains elements common to the other eras.

We will also see that the American campaign as we know it today has roots in the 1950s but really took on its current characteristics around 1972. This was due to four central factors: (1) changes in campaign finance and party nomination rules, (2) a new political reality driven by social upheaval and the Vietnam War, (3) changes in strategy driven by the rise of the survey and marketing industries and the expansion of television, and (4) the expansion of the electorate to include previously disenfranchised blacks and 18- to 20-year-olds. Some observers have argued that in more recent years, the increased competitiveness of elections, the polarization of the parties, and new technological advances — most notably, the development of the Internet — have ushered in a new era. As we will see, it is unclear whether we are currently in a new period of campaigning that differs significantly from previous eras. We will explore this question toward the end of the chapter.

The First Campaign Era: Pre-Democratic Campaigns, 1788–1824

In some ways, the earliest era of campaigning is unique. The first two presidential contests, which resulted in unanimous elections of George Washington, were like no others in American history. Washington was considered the logical choice for the job—indeed, there are some who believe the Constitution would not have been ratified had lawmakers not assumed Washington would serve as the first president—and there was no serious campaign against him. Unsurprisingly, the sum total of Washington's campaign expenditures in 1788 was to provide two casks of Virginia spirits for electors.[3] Similarly, the election of John Adams as Washington's successor in 1796, though contested, involved only trace elements of the partisan effort, conflict, and machinations that emerged a scant four years later.

---

[3] Boller, *Presidential Campaigns.*

The 1800 election marked a turning point within the first era in American election campaigns (Figure 3.1), which we refer to as the **era of pre-democratic campaigns**. Adams's first term as president was distinguished by the unraveling of the uneasy truce that had held during Washington's tenure. In its place, two camps emerged. On one side was the **Federalist Party**. The Federalists believed in a strong federal government, preferred to ally with Great Britain, and were suspicious of the radicalization of the French Revolution. The Federalists, who were especially numerous in New England and the mid-Atlantic states, were led by many of the architects of the Constitution, including John Adams and Alexander Hamilton. On the other side was the **Democratic-Republican Party**. The Democratic-Republicans distrusted the expanding federal government and suspected that it only served the commercial interests of the northeastern states. They preferred an alliance with France, even in the face of the French Revolution, to an alliance with Great Britain and its monarchy. Democratic-Republicans, who were numerous in the southern states, were led by Thomas Jefferson and his trusted ally James Madison.

The actions of these two camps as the presidential election of 1800 approached illustrate one of our major themes: the importance of the rules that govern campaigns and elections. At that point in time, presidential electors were chosen by state legislators and not by ordinary citizens. In fact, citizens did not come to dominate the presidential election process until the 1820s, which is why we characterize this era as one of "pre-democratic campaigns." Because state legislators were so consequential, presidential candidates sought their support and attempted to influence the composition of state legislatures. They also tried to get legislatures to adopt rules that would give them more votes in the Electoral College. Jefferson's Democratic-Republicans, for example, worked hard to win a majority of districts in Pennsylvania's lower house in early 1800 and then attempted to change Pennsylvania's rules so that all of the state's electors would go to the candidate whose party commanded a legislative majority. The Pennsylvania Senate, where Adams's Federalists had a majority, blocked the move. This state-by-state effort to craft favorable electoral rules offers the earliest glimpse of the emphasis on "battleground states" that dominates contemporary presidential campaigns.

The importance of state legislators also led to another innovation in strategy: the first organized attempts to get eligible citizens to the polls. In New York, Aaron Burr built a political network that helped the Democratic-Republicans win crucial seats in the state legislative elections of 1798—seats that would prove important in 1800, when Burr became Jefferson's running

FIGURE 3.1 Four Major Eras of Political Campaigns

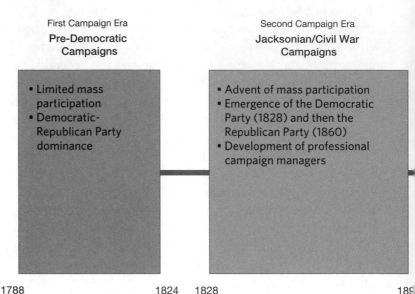

mate. In building this network, Burr employed several strategies that later became staples of political campaigns, including identifying sympathetic citizens and turning them out to vote on Election Day.

The 1800 election also featured the kind of negative campaigning that pundits today sometimes bemoan. There were attack ads, many of which centered on Jefferson's sympathies with the French Revolution as well as his religious faith (or lack thereof). Here is one passage from a Federalist newspaper, attacking Jefferson and other members of the "anti-federal junto":

> Citizens choose your sides. You who are for French notions of government; for the tempestuous seas of anarchy and misrule; for arming the poor against the rich; for fraternizing with the foes of God and man; go to the left and support the leaders, or the dupes, of the anti-federal junto. But you that are sober, industrious, thriving, and happy, give your votes for those men who mean to *preserve the union* of the states, the purity and vigor of our excellent Constitution, the sacred majesty of the laws, and the holy ordinances of religion.[4]

[4] Edward J. Larson. 2007. *A Magnificent Catastrophe*. New York: Free Press, p. 93.

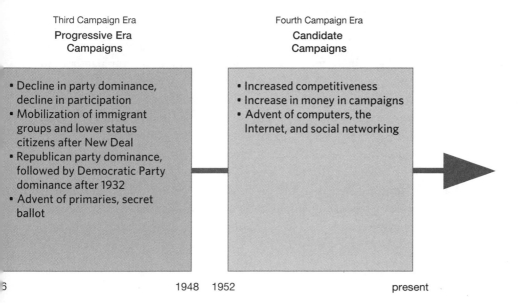

The central difference between the 1800 election and contemporary presidential elections is how little campaigning the candidates themselves actually did in the earliest presidential campaigns. For the most part, the organizational activity and the negative campaigning were carried out by surrogates. Adams did some campaigning during a trip from Massachusetts to Washington, D.C., in the spring of 1800. But it was mainly Hamilton and other Federalists who worked to influence legislative elections and wrote letters and articles excoriating Jefferson and his Democratic-Republican allies on every issue of the day. Jefferson stayed mainly in his Virginia home, Monticello, communicating by letter with Madison, Burr, and other Democratic-Republican leaders.

The election of 1800 culminated in Jefferson's victory. Discontent over the prospect of higher taxes and more intrusive government worked against Federalist arguments. Moreover, the Federalists made several key mistakes, such as supporting the Alien and Sedition Acts, which had been passed in 1798 under the Adams administration and which made it illegal for the press to publish "false, scandalous, and malicious writing" about the government or its officials.

The next 25 years brought relative stasis to American political parties and campaigns. Federalist presidential candidates attempted to hold electors in their New England base while winning over electors in the mid-Atlantic and southern states by emphasizing the need for greater national government support of commercial development and infrastructure. Meanwhile, Madison and James Monroe maintained—and in ways expanded on—the coalition established by Jefferson. Candidates continued to campaign behind the scenes, writing letters, encouraging supporters, dictating strategy, and suggesting lines of argument and attack. The brutality of 1800 abated somewhat, but campaigns were marked by substantive differences as well as personal attacks.

However, conditions were changing even as Jefferson assumed the presidency in the spring of 1801. Most notably, states began changing their rules so that presidential electors would be chosen by a statewide popular vote. Moreover, they also began changing their standards for citizenship in ways that significantly expanded the eligible electorate. This set the stage for a more democratic mode of campaigning.

The Second Campaign Era: Mass Mobilization Campaigns, 1828–92

The two decades between 1820 and 1840 saw the development of the first mass democratic electorate. Politicians began to campaign to this electorate, thus changing the nature and meaning of campaigning. The 1828 presidential campaign was particularly important in setting the tone for all subsequent American campaigns. Although the level and sophistication of campaigning varied over time and from place to place after the 1828 election, its innovations became increasingly widespread.

The 1828 campaign arguably began four years earlier, when a political slight against Andrew Jackson produced a personal vendetta. In the presidential election of 1824, Jackson was the most popular candidate running. He received 41 percent of the national vote, winning 7 states worth 99 electoral votes. Unfortunately for Jackson, there were 261 total electoral votes, and 131 votes were needed to win the presidency. His competitors, John Quincy Adams (84 electoral votes), William Harris Crawford (41 electoral votes), and Henry Clay (37 electoral votes), had more than enough electoral votes among them to prevent the race from being decided in the Electoral College. Because no candidate won an Electoral College majority, the election was decided in the U.S. House of Representatives, where, as stipulated in the Constitution, each statewide congressional delegation was to cast a single vote. In this case, a reputed deal between the Speaker of the House,

Henry Clay, and supporters of John Quincy Adams resulted in the election of Adams. Jackson was outraged. Perhaps more significant, so were his supporters.

Jackson and a handful of confidants, stung by the "stolen" election of 1824, began to lay plans to avoid what they felt would be another "theft" in 1828. As in modern presidential campaigns, all of this began well in advance of the election itself. Jackson's message centered in part on his status as a war hero. (Jackson had won fame by defeating the British army at the Battle of New Orleans in 1815.) It also centered on his promise to "clean house" and fight northeastern commercial interests that had become entrenched in Washington and who, Jackson argued, enriched themselves at the expense of the country's "common folk."

Jackson's campaign operation provided the template for all subsequent American campaigns, and especially presidential campaigns. The first element of that template was its structure. The campaign was led by a small group of friends and supporters who were motivated by their personal loyalty to Jackson. These individuals recruited political operatives in important

In the nineteenth century, candidates were more likely to engage personally in campaigning when the election was expected to be close. When Stephen Douglas ran for the U.S. Senate in 1858, he campaigned vigorously against Abraham Lincoln in a closely fought race, as this cartoon depicts.

counties. The operatives were not paid, but Jackson's promise to "clean house" led them to (reasonably) expect that they would receive jobs in a Jackson administration. This expectation—that working on the campaign could lead to a government job—remains to this day.

The second element of the template was the emphasis on organizing voters. This may seem like an obvious strategy, but in fact it was an important innovation. It was made possible by changes in state voting laws—such as abolishing the requirement that citizens own property in order to vote—which enfranchised a larger segment of the electorate and thus created more eligible citizens to target. Jackson's operatives were in charge of mobilizing eligible voters in their counties.

The third element of the template concerns how these voters were organized. As in previous campaigns, Jackson's followers promoted his candidacy with a sustained public relations campaign in local newspapers, writing letters and enlisting the aid of sympathetic editors. But the need to appeal to a mass electorate necessitated a new tactic: entertainment. This and subsequent campaigns featured rallies, public speeches, picnics, torchlit parades, songs, slogans, and bombastic rhetoric. Policy issues took a backseat to partisan allegiances and personalities. Thus, even though many criticize modern campaigns for their superficiality, the 1828 election shows that American campaigns have long emphasized style over substance.

This emphasis on mass politics gave rise to a further innovation: candidates themselves increasingly campaigned for office. To be sure, many candidates were still reticent about campaigning, but as early as the 1840s it was no longer an entirely unheard-of concept. For example, when Stephen Douglas ran for the U.S Senate in 1858, he campaigned tirelessly on his own behalf, making dozens of speeches across the state of Illinois. During the course of this campaign, Douglas participated in seven public debates with his opponent, a state legislator named Abraham Lincoln. As was often the case for candidates in this era, Douglas's actions were influenced by his expectation that the election would be close. Candidates appeared more likely to embrace electioneering when facing tough competition.

All of these elements pioneered in 1828 were visible in many subsequent campaigns during this era. The 1840 election is a good example. After Jackson's victory in 1828, his supporters formed the core of what was to become the **Democratic Party**. Beginning in 1832, the Democrats faced stiff competition from the newly formed **Whig Party**, which favored congressional authority over presidential authority and supported a program of modernization and economic protectionism. This competition came to a head in 1840, when Whig candidate William Henry Harrison attempted to

When the Democrats claimed that William Henry Harrison was the type of man who would live off his pension, sitting on his porch drinking hard cider, Harrison's supporters turned the charge around to portray Harrison as a man of the people. In this 1840 engraving, Harrison is depicted welcoming a veteran with his "hard cider hospitality."

unseat Jackson's successor, incumbent Democratic president Martin Van Buren.

Just as Jackson's campaign did in 1828, Harrison's campaign emphasized his war record, particularly his role in the battle of Tippecanoe, a famous victory for U.S. forces against an American Indian Confederation in the Indiana Territory in 1811. The Democrats charged that Harrison was the sort of fellow who would just as soon live off his pension, sipping hard cider on the porch of his log cabin. Harrison's campaign countered by turning this into a virtue, presenting Harrison as a man of the people—just as Jackson had done 12 years earlier. Meanwhile, the emphasis on mobilizing eligible voters continued apace. More citizens—80 percent of those eligible—voted in 1840 than in any previous presidential contest, thanks in part to campaign rallies, parades, and other hoopla. Harrison won relatively easily.

Even the growing disagreements over slavery and the Civil War itself did not create striking changes in political campaigns. As the Whig Party split up over the issue of slavery, a series of anti-slavery parties emerged: the Free

Soil Party, the Liberty Party, and (finally) the **Republican Party**. Although the Republicans were a party dedicated to the preservation of the Union and hostile to slavery, they adopted the campaign tactics and copied the campaign strategies of the Whigs. In the 1860 election, fought on the eve of the Civil War, the Republicans chose not to emphasize the policies of their nominee, Abraham Lincoln. Instead, in almost every broadside and campaign missive they spoke of Lincoln's honesty and his connection with the common man. After the end of the Civil War, campaigns continued to focus on pageantry, personality, and symbolic (rather than substantive) issues. In the presidential elections of 1868 and 1872, for example, the newly dominant Republicans nominated General Ulysses S. Grant, and focused their campaigns on reminding Americans who had been on the winning side in the war.

The 1876 presidential election provides a striking example of campaigning from this period. By 1876, the Republicans were faltering after the scandal-plagued second term of President Grant. In the election for his successor, Rutherford Hayes, a Republican, faced off against Samuel Tilden, a Democrat. Hayes and Tilden agreed on almost all of the major issues of the day, but, once again, the campaign was rancorous. Republicans continued to link the Democrats with the South's secession during the Civil War. One supporter of Hayes said this: "Every man that endeavored to tear the old flag from the heavens that it enriches was a Democrat. Every man that tried to destroy this nation was a Democrat. . . . The man that assassinated Abraham Lincoln was a Democrat. . . . Soldiers, every scar you have on your heroic bodies was given you by a Democrat!"[5] For their part, Democrats thought up some bold lies, too. Hayes was said to have stolen the pay of dead Civil War soldiers in his regiment, cheated Ohio out of vast sums of money as governor, and shot his own mother.

Perhaps more important, the resolution to the 1876 presidential election brought about one of the major changes that would contribute to a new era of political campaigns. Four states—Oregon, South Carolina, Louisiana, and Florida—had disputed election results, and Hayes needed all four of them to win, while Tilden needed only one. An election commission was appointed, with five senators, five representatives, and five Supreme Court justices. Seven of the members were Republicans, seven were Democrats, and one was independent. But the independent—Justice David Davis—was elected to the Senate by the Illinois legislature before the commission completed its work and had to be replaced by Justice Joseph Bradley, a Republican.

---

[5] Boller, *Presidential Campaigns*, p. 134.

Bradley voted with the Republicans on all disputes, and Hayes ended up winning the election. As part of their efforts to appease outraged Democrats, Hayes and the Republicans agreed to pull federal troops out of Louisiana and South Carolina, hastening the end of the **Reconstruction** era efforts to enfranchise African Americans in the South. The end of Reconstruction meant an end to widespread black participation in southern politics and essentially delivered the South to the Democrats for the next 100 years.

In a second change that affected campaigning, the latter half of the 1800s saw the gradual weakening of the partisan press. Candidates and parties had helped create and fund supportive newspapers for nearly a century, but that was changing. During the American Revolution and in the days after the ratification of the U.S. Constitution, most newspapers were essentially party organs, writing stories that promoted a particular political agenda. By the 1830s, some East Coast cities—with their burgeoning middle- and working-class populations—began to see the development of the "penny press": for one cent (more traditional newspapers cost six cents) people could get information on crime, gossip, and adventure. By the late 1800s, many newspapers

A TRUCE—NOT A COMPROMISE, BUT A CHANCE FOR HIGH-TONED GENTLEMEN TO RETIRE GRACEFULLY FROM THEIR VERY CIVIL DECLARATIONS OF WAR.

The 1876 presidential race, between Republican Rutherford Hayes and Democrat Samuel Tilden, brought up bitter rivalries from the Civil War. The election was so close that it was decided (controversially) by an election commission. This 1877 cartoon calls for an end to the rancor surrounding the election.

had become more financially independent, thanks in part to sensationalized coverage of people and events, such as that evident in the newspapers of publishing moguls William Randolph Hearst and Joseph Pulitzer. News-papers did not need the funds provided by political parties, and so their connections to those parties began to weaken. At the same time, journalism was becoming increasingly professionalized, with an emphasis on objec-tivity and impartiality. This was, for example, the approach emphasized in elite metropolitan newspapers such as the *New York Times*. The norm of impartiality began to crowd out the openly partisan journalism of earlier periods.

A third and final change was that political party organizations, which had been growing stronger during the nineteenth century, were about to face challenges. Their growth was particularly notable in such cities as New York and Boston, where waves of immigrants became the loyal foot soldiers of local party organizations and were often rewarded with government jobs and services. The parties functioned as **political machines**—a uniquely American combination of mass politics and government programs, with more than a whiff of money and corruption. In the urban campaigns of the 1800s, issues were almost incidental, particularly when compared to party performance and loyalty. Similarly, candidates were often irrelevant; their personal background and qualifications were less important than their party membership. Political power was wielded by party bosses, who never stood for election.

Although machine politics were never as pervasive as is sometimes assumed, they were still controversial. The crushing economic depression of the 1890s helped usher in a new era, one that would hamstring the parties, elevate the importance of individual candidates, and demobilize segments of the American electorate.

The Third Campaign Era: Progressive Era Campaigns, 1896–1948

The third era of campaigns, which began with the 1896 presidential elec-tion, had two important features: the continued trend toward more per-sonal campaigning, with candidates increasingly involved in day-to-day electioneering, and reforms that weakened political parties and their abil-ity to mobilize potential voters, resulting in a dramatic decline in voter participation.

Candidates for the House of Representatives and Senate had routinely campaigned on their own behalf throughout the 1800s, giving speeches, writing letters, and frequently meeting their opponents in debates. Even a few presidential candidates took their turns on the campaign trail, openly seeking the support of American voters.

But the 1896 election was different. The Democratic nominee for president, William Jennings Bryan, ran a campaign that was especially aggressive in its appeal to Americans. He traveled over 18,000 miles by train, made more than 600 speeches (sometimes 10 or 20 in a day), and addressed 5 million people over the course of the campaign (Figure 3.2). His campaign speeches were filled with religious imagery, and his entire effort took on the aura of an evangelical crusade.

Bryan's Republican opponent, William McKinley, ran a much quieter but no less energetic campaign. After the Democratic National Convention, in which Bryan delivered his famous "Cross of Gold" speech, appealing to farmers and factory workers by proclaiming support for easing the money supply and rejecting close adherence to the gold standard, Republican strategists were worried. But McKinley refused to mimic Bryan's efforts.

FIGURE 3.2 Contemporary Map of Bryan's Campaign Travels, 1896

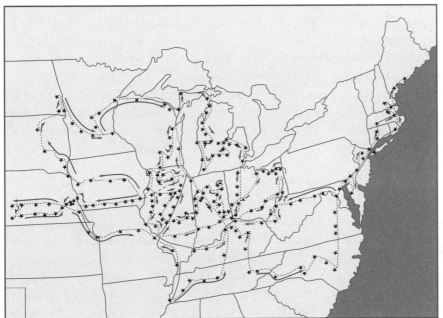

I cannot take the stump against that man. . . . If I took a whole train, Bryan would take a sleeper; if I took a chair car, he would ride a freight train. I can't outdo him and I am not going to try. . . . If I should go now, it would be an acknowledgement of weakness. Moreover, I might just as well put up a trapeze on my front lawn and compete with some professional athlete as go out and speak against Bryan.[6]

Instead, McKinley emulated Benjamin Harrison's 1888 **front-porch campaign**, conducting business from his home in Canton, Ohio. His manager, Mark Hanna, arranged for hundreds of delegations representing different interest groups and demographic groups to visit McKinley, whereupon the candidate would deliver a short speech that was often reprinted in the newspapers. McKinley also raised and spent $7 million (the equivalent of about $194 million today) and enlisted 18,000 speakers across the country on his behalf. Bryan spent only $300,000 (the equivalent of about $8 million today) and, lacking the support of many influential Democrats, largely spoke on his own behalf. These differences between McKinley and Bryan illustrate how reality—in this case, the backgrounds, connections, and abilities of the candidates—influenced their campaign strategies. Despite Bryan's efforts, McKinley beat him by five points.

While the 1896 presidential election was distinct from those that came before and immediately after, it reshuffled the parties' coalitions (with the Republicans gaining the upper hand) and proved to be a harbinger of modern campaigns.

In the 1912 presidential election, the candidates were also quite involved in their campaigns. This election featured an unusual three-way race. The candidates included not only the incumbent president, Republican William Howard Taft, and his Democratic opponent, Woodrow Wilson, but also Theodore Roosevelt, who ran for president as the nominee of the **Progressive (or "Bull Moose") Party** after being denied the Republican nomination by Taft's forces.

Taft mostly sat on the sidelines, giving few speeches and almost no interviews. But for the first time, two major presidential candidates—Wilson and Roosevelt—campaigned vigorously and personally. Roosevelt toured the country by rail, made hundreds of speeches, and worked the press with intensity and candor. Wilson also spent extensive time on the campaign trail. The passion of the campaign was embodied in the events of October 14, when Roosevelt was shot at close range before a speech in Milwaukee. Refusing to be driven to the hospital, Roosevelt insisted on giving his

---

[6] Boller, *Presidential Campaigns*, p. 173.

speech, which lasted for well over an hour. Later, doctors found that the bullet had fractured his fourth rib and lodged near his lung. He took two weeks off from the campaign, while Wilson and Taft halted their own activities out of a sense of fairness and respect. But Roosevelt was soon back on the trail, and by Election Day he had utterly exhausted his voice. With increasingly few exceptions, this was to be the new style of presidential campaigns: personal, aggressive, and relentless.

The second major development of this era was the reforms that weakened political parties. Up until the turn of the century, the Republican and Democratic parties had been extremely effective at mobilizing citizens to vote. But the Progressive movement—a loose association of activists dedicated to reforming government—believed that strong party organizations were often corrupt and empowered party bosses at the expense of ordinary citizens. The Progressives helped institute or advance three significant strands of reform.

One important reform built on the creation of the federal **civil service** in 1872.[7] The civil service gave federal government jobs to individuals on the basis of their professional qualifications and not party loyalty, which was naturally the most important criterion when party organizations controlled government jobs. At the turn of the century, the number of civil service positions in the federal government expanded considerably. This undermined the parties' abilities to incentivize and compensate campaign workers.

Two other strands of reform concerned elections. One was ballot reform, in particular, the adoption of the **Australian ballot**, which protects the secrecy of voter preferences and prevents parties from monitoring voters and rewarding or punishing them accordingly. Second was the use of primary elections to determine nominees. Primaries, which were adopted in a small number of states during this era, took power out of the hands of party leaders, who typically selected candidates for office, and gave it to voters.

These reforms once again provide examples of how rules affect campaign strategy and the subsequent behavior of voters themselves. In this case, the reforms reduced the control parties had over candidates and voters. Individual candidates could then tailor messages to fit specific constituencies rather than simply adopting the positions of their party. Voters, now more anonymous because of the secret ballot, were freer to defect from the party line.

Perhaps most important, these reforms had an unintended chilling effect on voter participation and turnout. In major cities such as New York, Boston,

---

[7] The term *civil service* has two distinct meanings: (1) A branch of governmental service in which individuals are employed on the basis of professional merit as proven by competitive examinations, or (2) the body of employees in any government agency other than the military. We are referring to the first of these definitions.

and Philadelphia, reforms that limited the benefits that parties could offer to encourage campaign workers crippled the mobilization and outreach efforts of parties. At the same time, in the South, selective enforcement of ballot reforms was used as a means to disenfranchise eligible black voters. For example, the secret ballot served as a de facto literacy test: many blacks could not read, and because their vote was now to be secret, no person could assist them in the voting booth (these rules were not so rigorously enforced for Southern white voters). As a consequence, turnout plummeted. Even in the wild and woolly election of 1912, turnout was 20 points lower than in the 1896 election. Subsequent national events like the Great Depression and World War II also failed to increase turnout to its previous levels. Turnout in the presidential elections between 1932 and 1948 averaged 58 percent— compared to 74 percent in the second era of campaigns (1828–92).

This third era of campaigning came to a close amid more important transformations in the nature of news media. The continued movement away from the partisan press toward a more professional style of reportage created the need for candidates and parties not only to counter the negative stories in the outlets of the partisan opposition but also to shape how journalists reported on the campaign.

At the close of this era, important technological innovations also began to change campaign strategy. The days of torchlit parades and four-hour speeches were passing into history. A more complete continental rail system, soon to be followed by air travel and a national network of interstate highways, gave candidates greater ability to travel. Campaigns could adjust strategies more quickly as the telephone replaced telegrams and letters. Even something as simple as the microphone allowed candidates and their surrogates to address larger crowds. Finally, the radio emerged as a revolutionary way for people to reach mass audiences, although its campaign potential would not be realized until the 1940s and '50s. But all these changes taken together were not as transformational as the technology that would inaugurate the fourth era of campaigns: television.

The Fourth Campaign Era: Candidate Campaigns, 1952–?

Since the 1950s, American political campaigns have been defined by television. The development of broadcasting technology and the proliferation of television sets across the United States in the 1950s ushered in a new age of political communication. Although campaigns continued to revolve around

retail politics—door-to-door canvassing, speeches to crowds by the candidates and their supporters, and other in-person interactions—well into the 1960s, presidential and Senate candidates of the 1950s began to develop detailed strategies for producing and placing television and radio advertisements. Dwight Eisenhower's 1952 and 1956 presidential election campaigns purchased advertising in specific time slots in selected media markets in battleground states. The New York advertising agency Doyle Dane Bernbach devised similar strategies for both John F. Kennedy in 1960 and Lyndon Johnson in 1964.

The rise of television had four important consequences for campaign strategy: it elevated the role of fund-raising, shifted power from parties to individual candidates, altered the content of political messaging, and changed the geographic unit for targeting and measuring the effects of the campaign. First, the allure of reaching millions of potential voters through television ads was something few campaigns could resist. But the cost of television advertising dwarfed the expenses of candidate travel, campaign literature, and wages for staff and workers. As a result, parties and candidates had to spend more time and effort on fund-raising. Indeed, the need to raise money in order to produce and air television ads has become one of the most prominent features of American politics today. As we note in Chapter 4, many House candidates report spending as much as half of their day raising money during election years. These fund-raising demands increased the pressure on office-holders (and candidates) to recruit and train more staffers, and to do so early in the campaign cycle. The demands also meant that accountants and lawyers became commonplace in campaigns.

Second, the rise of television shifted the focus away from political parties and onto individual candidates. We have noted that American campaigns have always tended to focus on personalities rather than policies. But this tendency was magnified with the advent of a medium that put candidates into the living rooms of American voters. Television made politicians stars in a more personal and immediate way than ever before.

Third, television changed the content of political communication, further emphasizing the sloganeering that had dominated American campaigns since the 1830s. The restricted length of television commercials—political ads usually last no more than 30 seconds—makes it imperative to communicate a message quickly and memorably. Moreover, political ads compete not only against other campaign ads but also against expensively produced, and often very entertaining, commercial product ads.

Finally, the rise of television has shifted the strategic focus of consultants away from precincts, cities, and counties and onto media markets. The fundamental unit of analysis in campaigns had long been the county. But television advertisements are bounded by signal reach and are measured at the level of the media market. These media markets have become the fundamental units of political and campaign analysis. Consultants are constantly evaluating media market demographics—the characteristics and loyalties of the voters—calibrating and recalibrating the cost per persuadable voter (see Chapter 5) of advertising in certain markets based on TV ad rates and how many swing voters there are in a specific locale.[8]

More generally, the logic and sequencing of a television advertising campaign has come to dominate the strategy of most high-level political campaigns. The itinerary and the talking points of any candidate on a given day often reflect the television advertising strategy, as candidates visit the markets in which their advertisements are running and repeat the messages contained in those advertisements. Campaigns thus look to reinforce their TV advertisements with other sorts of campaign activity.

A separate development of the fourth campaign era rivals the rise of television in its effect on campaigns: the rise of primary elections as the dominant means for selecting candidates. The nominating conventions that marked the 1800s and the first half of the 1900s were still the method of choice for choosing candidates well into the 1960s. But the exclusion of black voters from selection processes throughout the South and the dramatic protests at the Democratic National Convention in 1968 by voters who felt excluded from the nomination system resulted in reforms that led states to opt for primary elections. By the mid-1970s, over 40 states were using primary elections of some sort to select candidates.

The move to primary elections reinforced some of the effects of television's rise. Candidates often needed to raise and spend money to compete in both the primary and the general election. This necessitated raising money earlier, which in turn necessitated building an effective campaign organization as much as eighteen months before Election Day. Primary elections also changed how candidates thought about their campaign message, as they needed to develop a message that distinguished themselves from other candidates in the same party. Some observers argue that this meant taking more ideologically extreme positions in order to appeal to presumably more

---

[8] The rise of television has affected campaigning in other countries, as well. But in many of these other countries, political advertising is restricted. In some countries, laws limit or even prohibit commercial advertising. Elsewhere, television stations are owned by the government and there is little or no advertising on the public airwaves.

partisan and ideological primary voters.[9] Others argue that primary elections make campaigns more focused on biography and personality because candidates have no other way to distinguish themselves from competitors within their party, most of whom share their views on issues. For example, in the 2008 Democratic presidential primary, Hillary Clinton and Barack Obama differentiated themselves from each other mainly in terms of who had the most experience (Clinton's argument) or who would best bring about change (Obama's argument).

While not as significant as television or primary elections, the proliferation of polling is another noteworthy development of the fourth campaign era. Campaigns have always attempted to craft popular messages and present the most appealing side of their candidate. But the application of a branch of mathematics called probability and statistics to the mass public turned guesswork into a science. George Gallup, among others, pioneered the field of **survey research** in the 1930s and '40s, in which representative samples were drawn from the broader population in order to produce more accurate estimates of public opinion. The commercial applications of survey research were obvious, but political practitioners soon discovered its utility for candidates for office.

Widespread polling by campaigns did not occur until the 1960s and especially the 1970s, when telephones became sufficiently widespread to ensure both the representativeness of survey samples and cost-effectiveness. Since that time, polling has become a staple of campaigns, and top pollsters have become famous and sought-after individuals. Polls have also increased our understanding of what citizens think and how they will react to issue positions and messages. Some claim that polls and pollsters have effectively trivialized and cheapened political discourse as candidates simply advocate whatever message appears popular with citizens. Regardless of whether that is true, polling has particular relevance in an era where television advertising is central. Polls help candidates formulate and test messages before spending millions of dollars to broadcast them.

A final change in this fourth era speaks to an important reality that candidates confront: the balance of partisanship in the electorate as a whole. This era began with the Democratic Party somewhat dominant in national politics. Despite Republican success in presidential elections—the GOP won 9 out of 16 presidential elections between 1952 and 2012—the Democrats

---

[9] This, in turn, could create difficulties for candidates who take more ideologically extreme positions to win primary elections, but then have to reposition themselves as more centrist for the general election (see Chapter 13).

largely controlled the U.S. Congress until the 1994 election. Their advantage stemmed in part from the simple fact that since President Franklin Delano Roosevelt's New Deal, more people have identified themselves as Democrats than as Republicans. The allegiance of many to the Democratic Party was an apparent result of the perceived success of the Roosevelt administration.

But by the 1990s, the Democrats' advantage began to diminish. The Democratic Party's support of civil rights reform, a woman's right to an abortion, and gay rights cost them support among several groups, such as white southerners and Catholics, that had been linked with the Democratic Party. Their gains among other groups, especially blacks, were not enough to make up the difference (Figure 3.3). For example, in 1952, much more of

FIGURE 3.3 **Average Percent Democratic Margin in Presidential Elections among Key Social Groups**

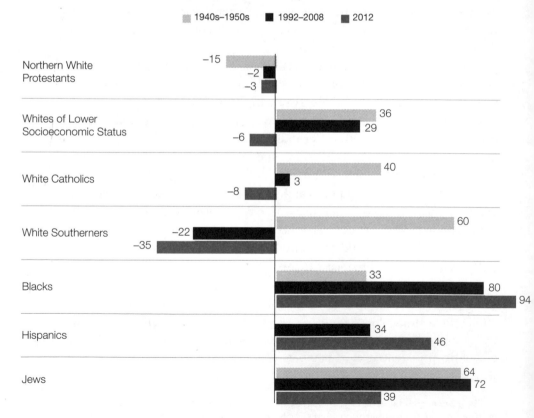

Source: Gallup Poll, 1940–48 Gallup Year Books; American National Election Studies, 1952–2012.

the public identified with or leaned toward the Democratic Party (59 percent) than the Republican Party (36 percent). But by the 1990s, the Democrats' 23-point edge had shrunk by half—to an average of 12 points over the period between 1990 and 2008.[10] This slimmer margin, combined with the wholesale transformation of the South from solidly Democratic to largely Republican, produced a series of very competitive elections and ultimately allowed the Republicans to take control of the House of Representatives in 1994 for the first time in 40 years. (See Chapter 13 for the demography of the 2012 presidential vote.) It is not surprising that a more competitive electoral environment creates even greater incentives for candidates to raise and spend money. Moreover, with the presidency or control of the Congress much more in play, candidates and parties focus even more on a handful of competitive districts and battleground states.

The innovations of technology and polling, combined with the shift to primary elections and increasingly competitive national elections, have made modern campaigns qualitatively different from their forebears. At the same time, there is continuity between the past and modern campaigns. The need to raise money to run a campaign is nothing new; this fourth era simply made it a much more significant task. Similarly, the personalized campaigns of the modern era—where candidates take to the airwaves to present themselves to potential voters—merely magnify a tendency that has always been present in American campaigns. Indeed, despite the many dim opinions of modern campaigns, it is not clear that they are less substantive or any more negative than campaigns were in the past. Table 3.1 provides a review of the main characteristics of campaigns in the four major eras.

What About Today?

The new technologies that have been crucial to this fourth era are beginning to sound anachronistic today. After all, campaigns no longer rely exclusively on television. What about the Internet, including YouTube, Facebook, and Twitter? Have we moved into a new era of electioneering—one dominated by electronic communication and social networking? Have these new technologies, and other recent developments, transformed campaigns? Let us consider the ways in which campaigns today both differ from and resemble previous campaigns. Ultimately, it would appear that new developments,

---

[10] These data are from the American National Election Study, www.electionstudies.org /nesguide/toptable/tab2a_2.htm (accessed 5/13/11).

TABLE 3.1 Characteristics of the Four Major Eras of Campaigns

Campaign Era	Focus of Campaigns	Campaign Method/Style
First (1788–1824)	Limited electorates for most races; state legislatures choose presidential electors.	Candidates do not campaign themselves, but encourage, cajole, and direct from behind the scenes. Use of friends, surrogates, and a partisan press.
Second (1828–92)	Mass electorates for all races. Campaigns seek to expand the participation of supportive groups, and reach out in attempts to persuade unaffiliated groups.	Some candidates campaign personally and directly, but many still emphasize indirect campaigning that relies on party organizations and personal relations. Campaigns are taken to the people. Many characteristics of contemporary campaigns emerge—for example, slogans, songs, parades, conventions.
Third (1896–1948)	Campaigns tend to be fought over peripheral issues, while personalities and broad appeals dominate. Parties continue to use labor-intensive methods to mobilize eligible voters, but they no longer control the jobs or the ballot. Mass communication technologies begin to change the style and nature of campaigns by the end of the era.	Personal campaigning becomes the norm by the time of FDR. The general election campaign lasts from early October until Election Day.
Fourth (1952–?)	Campaigns focus on raising money in order to pay for television advertisements. They also attempt to position candidates to win the support of their party base (to protect against a primary-election challenge) as well as the general electorate.	Candidates campaign personally for both money and votes. Mass communication efforts dominate and one-on-one outreach fades, at least until the 2000s. Campaign supporters work to "spin" media to present their interpretation of news and events.

however important they may be, do not outweigh the ways in which contemporary campaigns resemble their ancestors.

New Developments

Clearly, technological innovations have influenced campaign strategy. For example, innovations in the measurement of public opinion, such as **focus groups** (in which small groups of people are asked their detailed impressions of candidates, advertisements, and so on) and dial groups (in which people are asked to use a 0–100 dial to rate their reactions to what they are seeing on a screen) have allowed campaigns to estimate more precisely who they should be talking to and what they should be saying.

Moreover, campaigns no longer have to rely on the information they can collect via polls or other indirect means. Both parties have constructed enormous databases with information on the vast majority of Americans.[11] These databases build on the information in state voter files, which record addresses, whether people actually vote, and, sometimes, party registration. The data are then merged with data from census reports as well as from private marketing firms. A typical profile for any individual might include name, age, address, phone, voting history, political donations, estimated income, race, family structure, mortgage data, magazine subscriptions, and other indicators. This enables campaigns to engage in more sophisticated targeting strategies, using this information to estimate people's political views and the likelihood that they will turn out to vote. Campaigns can even target special interest groups—say, subscribers to *Guns & Ammo* magazine.

In 2012, practitioners and pundits noted the emergence of **"big data"** and campaign **"analytics"** and pondered their impact on the conduct and quality of campaigns. In the context of American elections, *big data* refers to the development noted earlier—large data sets containing extensive information on individual voters. *Analytics* refers to the use of sophisticated statistical models to identify politically meaningful patterns in these voter data. How do big data and analytics impact campaigns? They allow campaigns to identify with great precision specific groups of voters for particular forms of outreach. For example, campaigns might use big data and analytics to identify voters who are particularly open to persuasion if contacted and presented with information about a candidate's views on gun-owner rights.

---

[11] Jon Gertner. 2004. "The Very, Very Personal Is the Political." *New York Times Magazine*, February 15. www.nytimes.com/2004/02/15/magazine/15VOTERS.html (accessed 8/12/10).

In addition to the proliferation of data and statistical modeling, 2012 also saw the rise of **field experiments** as an important new way for campaigns to test outreach and persuasion. Field experiments randomize subjects (in this case, voters) into treatment and control groups and then compare outcomes. For example, a campaign might test the effectiveness of different subject headings on a fund-raising e-mail to potential contributors by conducting the following field experiment: identify a group of 1,000 potential donors; randomly assign 333 of them an e-mail with the subject heading "Give now"; randomly assign another 333 an e-mail with the subject heading "We need you"; randomly assign another 333 to a control group that received no mail. Then see whether the number of click-throughs is different across the three groups. Both the Obama and Romney campaigns conducted field experiments, although the systematic and rigorous commitment of the Obama team to scientific testing was unprecedented.

New developments in the media have multiplied the ways candidates can disseminate their message and target viewers. The rise of cable television and talk radio is one such development. Both have increased opportunities to target advertisements at relatively small but demographically distinct audiences. For example, conservative candidates can reach a large and like-minded audience through the talk-radio shows of hosts like Rush Limbaugh and Sean Hannity. The development of cable news networks such as CNN, Fox News, MSNBC, and HLN (formerly Headline News) also presents new opportunities (or possibly burdens) for candidates. Because these networks broadcast news virtually 24 hours a day, it means that candidates can put out a new message and see it picked up and rebroadcast almost instantly. At the same time, continuous news can create distractions for candidates, who may also feel compelled to respond to stories that quickly circulate on these networks even though they would prefer to talk about other issues entirely.

Then there is the computer revolution, accompanied by the development and popularization of the Internet, the attendant emergence of political, candidate, and social networking websites, and the rise of e-mail and text-messaging technologies, all of which facilitate the widespread and instantaneous transmission of information. Although larger proportions of people still consume traditional media like television and newspapers, consumption of information online is growing quickly—a trend we discuss in Chapter 8.

So rather than simply air television advertisements and send out generic mail pieces, campaigns today engage in a variety of more targeted, personal campaign activities. They post videos for the subscribers to their YouTube pages. They send out blast e-mails to raise funds from small groups with similar issue interests. They direct volunteers from a community to visit

How Technology Has Changed Campaigns

I n the 1990 election for Texas governor, Republican Clayton Williams ran against Democrat Ann Richards. Williams, seeking to become only the second Republican governor of the Lone Star state since Reconstruction, spent freely from his personal fortune on television advertisements. In October and early November, Williams's campaign called potential supporters at their homes, and sent literature through the mail. He did not, however, have a website. Neither he nor his staff used e-mail. Needless to say, the campaign did not have Facebook or Twitter accounts. They did not post videos to YouTube. Even in the context of 1990, there was little innovation or excitement associated with the Williams campaign.

Twenty years later, in the 2010 election for Texas governor, Republican Rick Perry was running for an unprecedented third term. Perry did not have a personal fortune to spend. He did not have lawn signs or billboards. He chose not to debate his Democratic opponent, the former Houston mayor Bill White. Instead, Perry deliberately relied on a small set of campaign techniques that he and his staff — most notably, chief consultant David Carney — believed to be effective based on research they had conducted from 2006 to 2008. Computers and technology were critical to both the research and their preferred campaign techniques.

The Perry campaign set up Facebook and Twitter accounts for the governor early in 2009, and posted frequently thereafter. Sometimes Perry highlighted articles or speeches of note, sometimes he offered commentary. The campaign assiduously monitored "likes" and negative comments on Perry's Facebook postings, as well as his "friends" on Facebook and his "followers" on Twitter. They also used Facebook and Twitter to drive traffic to Perry's website and to collect e-mail addresses for additional outreach.

The governor's website became the focal point of his campaign effort. Perry's Web page guru, Jordan Root, constantly tinkered with the site based on feedback he received from visitors and from quantitative analyses. For example, Root found that links on Perry's site to interviews with newspapers like the *Wall Street Journal* were counterproductive because people would not return to Perry's site once they had linked to the original article. He also decided that every page on the Perry site needed a prominent "CONTRIBUTE/VOLUNTEER" icon so that visitors wouldn't forget about rendering such support.

In addition, the website emphasized Perry "home headquarters." Visitors could establish a Perry home headquarters by doing three things: (1) publicly identifying oneself as a Home Headquarters, (2) identifying 12 pro-Perry voters from among their friends, family, and coworkers, and (3) turning those 12 voters out to vote during early voting. Perry was not the first candidate to do this, but the particular emphasis placed on this effort shows how the Internet has become critical in the recruitment, organization, and direction of volunteer activity.

specific households, where they will talk to potential voters and make specific appeals driven by polling information, and send their responses back to the campaign using smartphones.

The narrowing gap between numbers of self-identified Democratic and Republican voters has been accompanied by another trend: the ideological sorting and polarization of the parties. **Sorting** means that people's partisan preferences have become more closely aligned with their political views. Liberals have moved to the Democratic Party, while conservatives have moved to the Republican Party. In the past, parties were not so ideologically homogeneous. This trend has the potential to reshape campaign strategy. It may become harder for candidates to find ways to persuade voters who identify with the opposing party to support them; after all, it is unlikely that they will have enough common political ground. Instead, candidates may focus even more on mobilizing their own party's faithful, "the base." The expansive databases of information about individual citizens helps make this possible, as candidates can more accurately locate those people who are already likely to support them. Once candidates have identified likely supporters, they can then take advantage of such media as cable television, the Internet, and text-messaging to communicate with those supporters.

Other demographic changes are afoot in the American electorate. As noted earlier, the electorate has expanded in key ways as a result of the enfranchising of 18- to 20-year-olds and the removal of impediments that had made it difficult for some blacks to vote. But an even more important transformation may be at work. More specifically, there is the nation's growing ethnic diversity. Immigration and high fertility rates have greatly increased the share of the American population that identifies as Asian or Latino. For example, the Census Bureau projects that by 2050, whites will make up less than 50 percent of the population; Latinos will make up 30 percent, compared to 16 percent in 2010.[12] Campaign strategists are already seeking ways to reach these populations. Spanish-language political advertisements have become commonplace. In 2010, the California gubernatorial candidate Meg Whitman produced an advertisement in Chinese. It will be even more interesting to see whether the agendas and opinions of these populations lead candidates to develop different messages. For example, a candidate who seeks to appeal to Latinos may need to talk about immigration differently than a candidate who seeks to appeal to whites. The fact that Latinos and Asian Americans have tended to vote Democratic has raised concerns

---

[12] The projections are available at www.census.gov/population/www/projections/files/nation/summary/np2008-t6.xls (accessed 5/13/11).

among some Republicans, who believe that their party needs to broaden its appeal in this diversifying electorate.

The Case for Continuity

These changes in technology, the media, and demography are no doubt important, but they do not necessarily make campaigns today significantly different from the campaigns of the fourth era. In fact, some apparent innovations are modern-day versions of campaign strategies from centuries past. For example, the rebirth of partisan or ideological media on talk radio and cable news harks back to the partisan press of the 1800s. Similarly, sending volunteers door to door to mobilize potential voters, even if they are carrying smart phones or iPads, is fundamentally similar to the campaigning of old-school party organizations. Indeed, these recent trends in campaigns make them look like updated versions of nineteenth-century campaigns rather than the slick, mass-media-obsessed campaigns of the 1980s.

In other respects as well, contemporary campaigns have not changed that much. For example, the proliferation of primary elections in the 1960s and '70s was most responsible for lengthening campaigns—today's campaigns are not significantly longer than campaigns were in the 1980s. Presidential campaigns in 1988 and 1992 began in earnest during the late summer of the year before the election; in 2011, none of the presumably major Republican challengers to Barack Obama declared their candidacy before May 1 (Tim Pawlenty and Mitt Romney announced exploratory committees on March 22 and April 11, respectively).

If campaigns have not gotten significantly longer of late, have they gotten more expensive? As we will show in Chapter 4, the presidential elections of 2008 and 2012 set all-time records for candidate fund-raising and expenditures. In fact, federal election campaigns in the United States in 2012 cost over six billion dollars. But it is unclear whether this spike in 2008–12 will be sustained. The overall trend in American campaign spending over the past 150 years is uneven, with ebbs and flows. It is still too early to declare that fund-raising and spending have been transformed.

Other frequent complaints about recent campaigns concern their content: they don't focus enough on policy, they lack substance, they are too negative, and so on. As we have suggested throughout this chapter, American political campaigns have always focused on personality more than policy. Even now, with the political parties taking increasingly distinct positions on the issues, this polarization is not always reflected in how candidates campaign. Candidates are often reluctant to sacrifice their broader electoral appeal in favor of party loyalty or ideological purity. This behavior derives in part from American electoral institutions and rules. Officeholders represent single districts and are elected through plurality elections. When the "winner takes all," there is less incentive to do anything that might reduce your risk of winning. Candidates do care about policies, of course, but you cannot implement a policy if you do not win the election.

Thus, in American campaigns issue positions are often ambiguous (see Chapter 13). Candidates say they are for "middle-class tax cuts," or "saving Social Security," or "strengthening American defense." The logic here is straightforward: candidates know that specific issue positions involve costs and trade-offs, that may alienate some voters, so they tend to endorse broadly popular goals rather than any specific means of achieving those goals. Of course, present and past campaigns have involved clear and specific policy differences. Nevertheless, there is a venerable tradition of policy ambiguity in American campaigns.

Similarly, negative campaigning is hardly a recent invention. American political campaigns have been negative ever since Federalists were calling Thomas Jefferson an infidel. This does not mean that negative campaigning is necessarily more common or more important to vote choice than positive campaigning, now or then. It means that American campaigns have always involved contrasting the relative merits of the candidates, which typically necessitates providing unflattering information about one's opponent. But are contemporary campaigns any more negative than those of earlier campaign eras? It is difficult to say. No one has conducted a study comparing the information received by typical Americans in 1840 and in 2012, for example. If such a study were done, it seems likely it would reveal that today's voter would get substantially more information and a similar ratio of positive to negative information.

Conclusion

In this chapter, we have made the case that the United States has seen substantively different campaign eras. These differences have arisen for a variety of reasons, but chief among them is the transformation in information and communications technology, particularly the development of broadcast media such as television. At the same time, campaigns throughout U.S. history have shared common qualities, including a focus on the candidates' biographies and personalities and a willingness to attack opponents. Thus, although most Americans believe that campaigns have gotten "worse," it is difficult to prove that this is true. As we noted in Chapter 1, the quantity and quality of information provided to citizens is an important criterion by which to judge campaigns. We are quite certain that more information is available to Americans today than 200 years ago, and it is far from clear whether that information is less useful or more superficial. This does not make contemporary campaigns "good" in any absolute sense, and there are reasonable arguments about how they might become better. Still, a historical perspective can be important in making such assessments.

KEY TERMS

era of pre-democratic campaigns (p. 55)

Federalist Party (1796–1828) (p. 55)

Democratic-Republican Party (1796–1824) (p. 55)

Democratic Party (1828–present) (p. 60)

Whig Party (1832–1852) (p. 60)

Republican Party (1860–present) (p. 62)

Reconstruction (p. 63)

political machines (p. 64)

front-porch campaign (p. 66)

Progressive/"Bull Moose" Party (1912–14) (p. 66)

civil service (p. 67)

Australian ballot (p. 67)

retail politics (p. 69)

survey research (p. 71)

focus groups (p. 75)

big data (p. 75)

analytics (p. 75)

field experiments (p. 76)

sorting (p. 78)

FOR DISCUSSION

1. In what ways are today's campaigns similar to those of the second campaign era (1828–92)?

2. Thinking back to the second and third campaign eras, under what circumstances were candidates more likely to campaign personally for elected office? Why would this have been the case?

3. How did the rise of television and primary elections influence campaigns?

4. Some have argued that the Internet and the computer revolution have reinvigorated the more personal approach to campaigning that characterized earlier campaign eras. Do you agree or disagree with this argument?

CHAPTER 4

Financing Campaigns

Every election year, commentators and citizens bemoan the amount of money spent in American elections. The 2012 presidential election was no different. Together President Obama and Mitt Romney spent more money than any other presidential candidates since 1976, when the Federal Election Commission (FEC) instituted a comprehensive system for documenting fund-raising. Obama spent $684 million and Romney spent $433 million.[1] Whereas the combined spending of all presidential candidates in the primary and general elections was $66.9 million in 1976 — the equivalent of $272 million in 2012 dollars (Figure 4.1) — the presidential candidates spent a stunning $1.4 billion in 2008 and 2012. Small wonder, then, that 75 percent of respondents in a May 2012 poll said that there is too much money in politics.[2]

To be sure, 2008 and 2012 were somewhat unusual elections. In 2008, both parties had contested primaries. The Democratic primary was especially long and expensive thanks to the tight battle between Obama and Hillary Clinton. Several primary candidates in 2008 and all of the serious ones in 2012 shunned **public funding**, funds provided to candidates by the federal government in exchange for their agreeing to restrictions on fund-raising from private donors. In 2008, Obama was the first general election candidate to refuse such funding, which is why he was able to spend more than double what McCain spent. In 2012, both Obama and Romney declined public funds. The main reason spending did not increase between 2008 and 2012 is because Obama had no serious primary challengers.

---

[1] Open Secrets. 2012. "2012 Presidential Race." www.opensecrets.org/pres12/ (accessed 2/4/15).

[2] Patricia Zengerle. 2012. "Most Americans Think Campaign Money Aids Rich." Reuters, May 24. www.reuters.com/article/2012/05/24/us-usa-campaign-spending -idUSBRE84N1RB20120524 (accessed 2/4/15).

FIGURE 4.1 Presidential Candidate Spending, 1976–2012

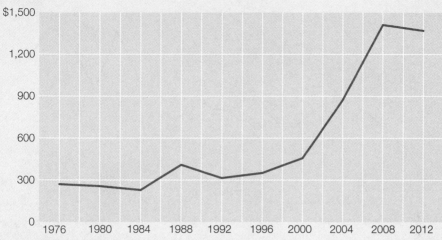

Spending in millions (2012 dollars)

Source: Center for Responsive Politics.

Core of the Analysis

- The rules governing campaign finance place caps on donations but not on spending, which has allowed the cost of American campaigns to increase.

- These rules have an important implication for strategy: candidates and parties must raise the money necessary to fund their campaigns. Private donations are more important than public funding provided by the government.

- Campaign finance rules also allow independent groups, corporations, and labor unions to raise and spend money to try to elect or defeat candidates of their choice.

- These rules reflect a fundamental philosophical trade-off between two competing values: the right of donors and candidates to free speech and the need to guard against the potentially corrupting influence of money.

FIGURE 4.2 Congressional Candidate Spending, 1980–2014

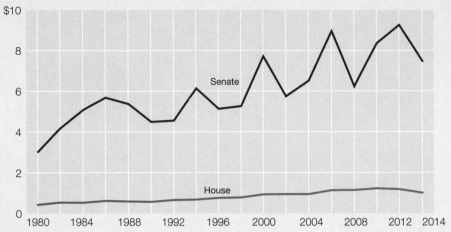

Average spending in millions (2012 dollars)

Source: Campaign Finance Institute. House: www.cfinst.org/pdf/vital/VitalStats_t2.pdf; www.cfinst.org/pdf/vital/VitalStats_t5.pdf (both accessed 3/21/13); and Michael Malbin.

Spending in congressional elections has increased as well, albeit less steeply than in presidential elections. The average candidate in a general election for the House of Representatives spent about $427,000 in 1980 and just over $1 million in 2014.[3] The trend in Senate races is more variable, in part because it depends on which states have Senate races in any given year, but spending has still increased over time. The average general election candidate for Senate in 1980 spent about $3 million; the average Senate candidate in 2014 spent $7.6 million (Figure 4.2).

Candidates are not the only ones raising and spending more money. The political parties are also raising much more money in congressional elections, which they donate to candidates, spend on behalf of candidates, and use to mobilize voters—among other things. In the 1992 electoral cycle, the Republican and Democratic parties raised roughly a combined $630 million. In the 2012 cycle, they raised $1.3 billion (Figure 4.3).[4]

What does all this money buy? More than half of the average campaign's expenditures go to efforts to persuade and mobilize voters. One study of a typical House campaign found that candidates spent about 22 percent of their

---

[3] These figures are in 2012 dollars.

[4] These figures are in 2012 dollars and include all fund-raising by the Democratic and Republican national committees, as well as by their respective campaign committees for the House of Representatives and the Senate.

FIGURE 4.3 Political Party Spending in All Federal Races, 1992–2014

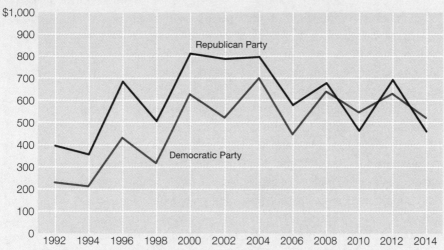

Total spending in millions (2012 dollars)

Source: www.cfinst.org/pdf/vital/VitalStats_t13.pdf (accessed 5/4/15) and Michael Malbin.

budget on television ads, 16 percent on mail sent to voters and other campaign literature, 13 percent on radio and newspaper ads, and 1 percent on voter registration and get-out-the-vote drives. The bulk of the rest went to staff salaries (18 percent), office supplies and rent (11 percent), and fund-raising (9 percent).[5]

Despite their cost, it is not obvious whether American political campaigns are "too" expensive. By some metrics, they are cheap. For example, Americans spent more on almonds in 2014 than was spent in that year's midterm election.[6] Some even wonder why American campaigns are not more expensive; given the value of government policies to interest groups and corporations, they contribute remarkably little money to political candidates and parties.[7] Ultimately, it may not be necessary to determine whether American political campaigns are too costly. The important question for political scientists is *why* American elections cost what they do. Much of the answer lies in the rules of American campaign finance.

---

[5] Paul Herrnson. 2008. *Congressional Elections*, 5th ed. Washington, DC: Congressional Quarterly Press, p. 84.

[6] Binyamin Appelbaum. 2014. "Who Wants to Buy a Politician?" *New York Times Magazine*, December 9. www.nytimes.com/2014/12/07/magazine/who-wants-to-buy-a-politician.html (accessed 1/4/15).

[7] Stephen Ansolabehere, John M. de Figueiredo, and James M. Snyder, Jr. 2003. "Why Is There So Little Money in U.S. Politics?" *Journal of Economic Perspectives* 17, 1: 105–30.

As we discussed in Chapter 2, electoral rules govern crucial aspects of political campaigns. Campaign finance rules affect both sides of campaign finance: donors, including individuals and interest groups, and spenders, including political candidates, parties, and interest groups. With regard to donors, the rules determine who can give, to whom they can give, and how much they can give. With regard to recipients, the rules determine whether, how much, and when they can spend. As with the electoral rules discussed previously, there is no single set of campaign finance laws. Federal law governs federal elections, but state and local laws govern state and local elections. Any state's campaign finance laws may differ from federal law and from the laws of other states.

Campaign finance rules affect candidate strategies, most notably by allowing (or, perhaps, forcing) candidates to raise money for their campaigns. Although systems of public financing exist, American campaigns largely depend on private donations. Campaign finance rules also empower parties and interest groups, each of whom can raise and spend money on behalf of the candidates they favor or against candidates they oppose. As we discuss later, recent Supreme Court decisions have allowed a greater role for interest groups, including corporations and labor unions, which has in turn raised some fears that they will have too powerful an impact on elections.

Campaign finance rules are controversial. Like all rules, they reflect particular values. The challenge is that more than one value is relevant in political campaigns. One is the right of citizens and candidates to express themselves: without money, certain modes of expression are impossible. Another is the need to insulate candidates from the potentially corrupting influence of money: we want leaders to make decisions based on what is good for the country, or at least their constituents, not simply what is good for donors to their campaign. The trade-offs are evident: limiting the money raised and spent on campaigns might mitigate the potential for corruption, but it might also infringe on the right to free expression. In this chapter, we begin by explaining the rules central to financing federal campaigns. In the process, we describe the important legislation and Supreme Court decisions that have shaped these rules. We also describe how state campaign finance laws differ from federal law. We will once again see that the central consequence of these laws, from the perspective of candidates, parties, and interest groups, concerns campaign strategy and each candidate's chances of winning. It is usually not possible for candidates to change the rules, only to make them work to their advantage.

Rules for Donors

The rules for donors involve two basic questions: who is allowed to give and how much they can give. The central feature of this aspect of campaign finance law is the limits placed on donors and particularly on the amount of money that they can give to candidates and parties.

Who Can Give?

There are two main types of donors in American political campaigns: individuals and organized interest groups. Individual Americans are free to donate to a candidate, political party, or interest group, provided that they are either citizens or permanent residents. And while Americans have to be 18 to vote, there are no restrictions as to the age of political donors. Minors can give, as long as it is their money and they do so voluntarily.

Organized interest groups can also donate, as long as they are not themselves tax-exempt groups. (Otherwise, the federal government would be indirectly subsidizing political campaigns by allowing groups to keep money they would have paid in taxes and then give it to particular candidates.) Potential donors therefore include corporations and labor unions but not charities and churches. Neither corporations nor unions, however, can donate simply by giving some of their revenue directly to candidates or parties. Corporate donations were banned in 1907 with the passage of the **Tillman Act**. Labor union donations were banned in 1947 with the passage of the Taft-Hartley Act. Instead, corporations and labor unions must establish separate **political action committees (PACs)**, which are groups that directly work toward the election of candidates, to pass or defeat a piece of legislation, or to advance a political agenda. Some small amount of corporate revenue can be spent to set up the PAC, but thereafter the PAC must raise money on its own. The PACs that give the largest amounts to political campaigns typically represent labor unions or industry associations (for example, the National Association of Realtors or the National Beer Wholesalers Association).

Membership organizations (groups with members who pay dues) must also establish PACs in order to give to candidates. Thus, there are PACs that represent groups with issue-oriented or ideological agendas, such as the National Rifle Association and Planned Parenthood. Political parties and political leaders can establish their own PACs as well. Political party organizations with PACs include the Democratic Senatorial Campaign Committee and the Republican Congressional Campaign Committee. The PACs of political leaders, sometimes called "leadership PACs," raise money and donate to candidates whom those politicians favor. For example, Representative Nancy Pelosi

(D-CA), showing affection for terrible puns, has her "PAC to the Future." The Republican leader, John Boehner, calls his "Freedom Project."

Campaign donations by PACs have increased sharply over time. PAC donations to congressional candidates grew from $120 million in 1978 to $423 million in 2014 (Figure 4.4). But this increase conceals an important fact: individuals donate more money to campaigns than do PACs. This is somewhat counter to the impression fostered by media coverage, which exaggerates PAC contributions.[8] In 2013, individuals contributed 53 percent of the funds raised by House candidates, while PACs contributed 37 percent.[9] The remainder came from donations from parties, the candidates themselves, and a few other sources.

FIGURE 4.4 PAC Contributions to Congressional Candidates, 1978–2014

Total PAC contributions in millions (2012 dollars)

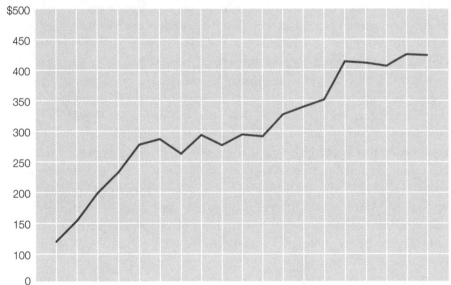

Source: Campaign Finance Institute. www.cfinst.org/pdf/vital/VitalStats_t10.pdf (accessed 5/4/15) and Michael Malbin.

[8] Stephen Ansolabehere, Erik C. Snowberg, and James M. Snyder, Jr. 2005. "Unrepresentative Information: The Case of Newspaper Reporting on Campaign Finance." *Public Opinion Quarterly* 69, 2: 213–31.

[9] The Campaign Finance Institute. 2013. *Campaign Funding Sources for House and Senate General Election Candidates, 1984–2014.* www.cfinst.org/pdf/vital/VitalStats_t8.pdf (accessed 4/29/15).

Campaign finance law also provides for the disclosure of donors. New rules about disclosure were established in 1971 by the **Federal Election Campaign Act (FECA)** and then revised by amendments to this act in 1974. Candidates, parties, and PACs must each maintain a central committee where all donations are received. They are then required to file regular reports with the **Federal Election Commission (FEC)** identifying anyone who has given them at least $200, with additional reports filed immediately before and after the election. In the final days of the campaign, any donation of $1,000 or more must be reported within 48 hours. In turn, the FEC maintains a searchable database of campaign donors. One can see that, for example, Ben Affleck, identified in the database as an actor living in Santa Monica, California, has given money to various Democratic candidates, including Barack Obama, Massachusetts Senator Elizabeth Warren, and New York Senator Kirsten Gillibrand. Another actor, Chuck Norris of Dallas, Texas, has given money to a wide array of Republican candidates, including Senator John Cornyn of Texas, George W. Bush, and Mike Huckabee (with whom Norris campaigned extensively in 2008).

How Much Can They Give, and to Whom?

Under federal campaign finance law, there are limits on campaign donations. These limits were established by the amendments to FECA in 1974 and remained unchanged until 2002, when new legislation, the **Bipartisan Campaign Reform Act (BCRA)**, adjusted the limits upward and indexed them to inflation, meaning that the limits will continue to increase in the future.[10] The limits are imposed on individuals, political party committees, and PACs, and affect what they can give to candidates, parties, and PACs, and, in some cases, their total giving to all candidates and parties. Table 4.1 summarizes the limits in effect for the 2013–14 election cycle. As of 2014, individuals can donate $2,700 to any candidate per election, for a maximum of $5,400 for the primary and general elections combined. There was previously an overall limit on how much individuals could give to all federal candidates combined, but this limit was struck down by the Supreme Court in 2014.[11] PACs can give no more than $5,000 per election to any candidate. (See Table 4.2a on p. 93 for more on these contribution limits.)

---

[10] This, and all of the major provisions of BCRA, were upheld by the Supreme Court in *McConnell v. Federal Election Commission*, 540 U.S. 93 (2003). However, as we discuss later, a 2010 decision, *Citizens United v. FEC*, overturned some provisions.

[11] *McCutcheon v. Federal Election Commission*, 572 U.S. ___ (2014).

TABLE 4.1 Contribution Limits in the 2013–14 Election Cycle

	To Candidate	To National Party Committee	To State, District, and Local Party Committee	To Other Committee (e.g., PAC)	Overall Limits
Individual	$2,700 per election	$33,400 per year	$10,000 combined per year	$5,000	No limit
National party committee	$5,000	No limit	No limit	$5,000	$46,800 to Senate candidates per campaign
State, district, and local party committee	$5,000	No limit	No limit	$5,000	No limit
PAC	$5,000	$15,000	$5,000 combined per year	$5,000	No limit

Source: Federal Election Commission. "How Much Can I Contribute?" www.fec.gov/ans/answers_general
.shtml#How_much_can_I_contribute (accessed 9/19/14).

Most states follow federal law in imposing limits on individual and PAC contributions for gubernatorial and other state-level races. Twelve states—Alabama, Indiana, Iowa, Mississippi, Missouri, Nebraska, North Dakota, Oregon, Pennsylvania, Texas, Utah, and Virginia—have no such limits.[12] The actual limits of the other states, however, vary widely. As of the 2015–2016 election cycle, individual donors could give a candidate for the Massachusetts state legislature no more than $2,000 over these two years, while in Ohio, donors could give state legislature candidates up to $12,532.34.[13] State restrictions on donations by PACs and parties are similarly diverse.

---

[12] National Conference on State Legislatures. 2013. "State Limits on Contributions to Candidates." www.ncsl.org/Portals/1/documents/legismgt/Limits_to_Candidates_2012 -2014.pdf (accessed 1/4/15).

[13] For the Massachusetts limits, see: www.ocpf.us/Legal/ContributionLimits. For the Ohio limits, see: www.sos.state.oh.us/sos/upload/candidates/2015limitchart.pdf (accessed 3/25/15).

The limits on how much individual donors can contribute mean that candidates have to spend much time and effort amassing enough contributions to fund their campaigns by attending fund-raisers, wooing potential donors, and soliciting contributions. Here, Wendy Davis, the Democratic candidate for governor of Texas in 2014, shakes hands at the Lady Bird Johnson fund-raiser in Dallas. Davis lost badly to Republican Greg Abbott.

Political Parties and Soft Money

Current federal restrictions on contributions are now more far-reaching than they were before BCRA passed in 2002. Before 2002, political parties, such as the Democratic National Committee and Republican National Committee, could raise **soft money**. These were donations that were not subject to contribution limits or disclosure provisions. Donations subject to these rules are **hard money**. During the 1990s, the parties became increasingly successful at raising soft money: in 2000, the Democratic and Republican parties raised a combined $457 million.[14]

Soft money contributions could be spent on registering and mobilizing voters and on some kinds of political advertisements, but not on **express advocacy**—that is, directly advocating for a particular candidate. Spending on ads that stopped short of express advocacy was permitted; the key was whether an ad used words like "vote for" or similar **magic words**. Parties

---

[14] OpenSecrets. "Soft Money Backgrounder." www.opensecrets.org/parties/softsource.php (accessed 4/9/11).

found ways to craft ads that conveyed a clear partisan message anyway, often by merging criticisms of a candidate from the opposite party with **issue advocacy**, or arguments for positions on a particular issue. Consider this ad from a 1998 Wisconsin congressional race, in which a party organization, the Democratic Congressional Campaign Committee, targeted Mark Green, the Republican candidate:

> Mark Green has taken over $22,000 from the healthcare industry's lobbyists. It's no wonder that he voted against keeping our medical records private, allowing HMOs and insurance companies to make our records public. It's no wonder he wanted to let negligent healthcare providers off the hook, even when they operated under the influence of drugs or alcohol. Tell Mark Green our healthcare isn't for sale. Support HMO reform.

The ad avoids the magic words and is ostensibly about an issue—namely, reform of health maintenance organizations (HMOs) and insurance companies. Nevertheless, the partisan intent is clear. Citizens are not fooled, either. In a 2000 study, participants watched several party-sponsored ads that were intended as issue advocacy but which included critical statements about the opposing presidential candidates. The vast majority of participants, about 80 percent, said that the primary objective of the ad was to "persuade you to vote against a candidate," not to "present an issue."[15]

The ability of parties to raise soft money was a big loophole in the rules. A labor union or corporation could not give a million dollars directly to a candidate but could give it to party committees. Critics argued that this created the appearance of, and perhaps the reality of, corruption. And so BCRA banned soft money. The only money that national parties can raise is hard money that is subject to contribution limits. Although critics of BCRA feared that it would impoverish the parties, this has not come to pass. In fact, the Democratic and Republican National Committees raised $726 million in 2012, significantly more than they raised before BCRA.[16]

Independent Groups

BCRA did not close a second loophole, however. Independent groups, who are unaffiliated with political parties or candidates, are able to raise soft money without contribution limits (see Table 4.2b on p. 97). As we discuss

---

[15] David Magleby. 2000. *Dictum without Data: The Myth of Issue Advocacy and Party Building.* Provo, UT: Center for the Study of Elections and Democracy.

[16] OpenSecrets. "Political Parties Overview." www.opensecrets.org/parties/index.php (accessed 3/21/13).

TABLE 4.2a A Donor Taxonomy

	Candidate Committee	Political Party Political Action Committee (PAC)	Federal PAC
Example	McCaskill for Missouri	Democratic Congressional Campaign Committee	American Meat Institute PAC
Description	Committee formed by the candidate to raise and spend money during the campaign	PACs formed by the parties that donate money to the candidates or spend it for other purposes, such as get-out-the vote efforts	PACs organized by interest groups that collect contributions from members or employees and then donate to candidates, parties, or other PACs
Limits on contributions to the group	Individuals: $2,700 per election PACs: $5,000 per election Corporations: cannot give except via a PAC	Individuals: $30,400 per year to a national party committee PACs: $15,000 Corporations: cannot give except via a PAC	Individuals: $5,000 per year PACs: $5,000 per year Corporations: cannot give except to their own PAC
Limits on how the group can use its money	A candidate committee cannot contribute more than $2,000 to another candidate committee or $5,000 to a PAC.	A political party PAC can give no more than $5,000 a year to a candidate committee or another PAC. (A party PAC can also give no more than $46,800 to all Senate candidates combined.)	A federal PAC can give $5,000 per election to a candidate, $5,000 per year to another PAC, and $15,000 per year to a party PAC.
Are donors disclosed?	Yes, to the Federal Election Commission	Yes, to the FEC	Yes, to the FEC

later, this money may not be given to candidates, as traditional PACs do. Rather, it is spent independently of candidates on things such as political advertising, although the goal is still to help elect or defeat candidates. Spending by these groups increased dramatically after BCRA's passage and then again after the 2010 *Citizens United* decision. Thus, their spending in presidential elections increased from $13 million in 1992 to $321 million in 2008, then climbed dramatically to $1.1 billion in 2012 (Figure 4.5). Independent group spending in midterm elections has increased sharply as well.

There are three main legal categories of independent groups, some identified by a confusing array of numbers and letters that correspond to designations under the federal tax code, as administered by the Internal Revenue Service. The crucial differences among them involve federal laws about whether they must disclose their donors and whether and how they can be involved in campaign activity.

The first category of groups is **independent expenditure committees**—a type of actor that came into existence only during the 2010 campaign. These are PACs that pool donations from various sources and then use the funds to advocate explicitly for or against candidates. Because these PACs are not associated with a specific political party, corporation, or interest group, but gather contributions from multiple sources—individual donors, corporations, unions, and so on—they have been termed **super PACs**. Unlike traditional

FIGURE 4.5 Spending by Independent Groups, 1990–2014

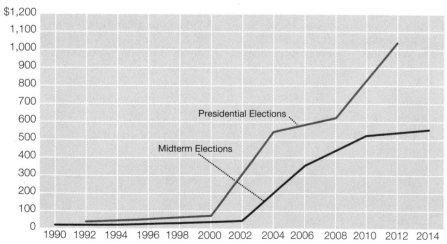

Spending in millions (2012 dollars)

Note: These data are the totals spent by independent groups (not including party committees), in 2012 dollars.
Source: Center for Responsive Politics.

PACs, they can collect donations of unlimited amounts as a consequence of *Citizens United*. They are required to disclose their donors. Super PACs were initially created by people seeking to influence national elections, but over time they have become increasingly involved in state elections as well.[17] For example, super PACs may raise money from wealthy donors but then give that money to other organizations working to influence elections for governor or state legislator.

The second category of independent groups are **527 organizations**. (The number 527 refers to a specific section of the tax code.) 527s are officially designated as political organizations under the tax code and are also required to disclose their contributors to the Internal Revenue Service. These organizations came to the fore in 2004, the first election after BCRA's ban on soft money for parties. 527s like America Coming Together (ACT), MoveOn .org, and the Swift Boat Veterans for Truth raised and spent a substantial amount of money—over $600 million.[18] ACT, perhaps most famous for sponsoring an ad featuring the actor and comedian Will Ferrell lampooning George W. Bush, spent over $78 million. As we will discuss in Chapter 5, the Swift Boat Veterans for Truth aired perhaps the most controversial ads of the 2004 campaign. Because donations to 527s are not subject to contribution limits, wealthy Americans can give them large amounts of money; the financier George Soros gave $24 million to nine different left-leaning 527s in 2004.[19] After 2004, 527s played less of a role. MoveOn.org shut down its 527, partly because the Obama campaign asked it not to use its 527 to support Obama. Nevertheless, 527s still spent about $490 million in the 2008 election. In the wake of the *Citizens United* decision, many interests turned to super PACs as their preferred vehicles for raising campaign funds because they can openly support or oppose a candidate by name. As a result, 527s spent less in the 2012 election ($535 million) than in 2004.

The third category of independent groups is known as **501(c) organizations**. These groups are designated as nonprofit organizations, are not required to pay taxes, and are not required to disclose their donors. There are various kinds of 501(c) organizations that are further designated with an additional number. For example, 501(c)3 organizations include charities, churches, and

---

[17] Derek Willis. 2014. "The Special Powers of Super PACs, and Not Just for Federal Elections." *The New York Times*, December 8. www.nytimes.com/2014/12/09/upshot/the -special-powers-of-super-pacs-and-not-just-for-federal-elections.html (accessed 1/4/15).

[18] OpenSecrets. "527s: Advocacy Group Spending in the 2010 Elections." www.opensecrets .org/527s/index.php (accessed 1/4/15).

[19] OpenSecrets. "Top Individual Contributors to Federally Focused 527 Organizations, 2004 Election Cycle." www.opensecrets.org/527s/527indivs.php?cycle=2004 (accessed 1/4/15).

educational institutions. An example would be the March of Dimes. 501(c)4 organizations, such as the League of Women Voters, are designated as "social welfare" organizations under the tax code, meaning that their goal is to "operate primarily to further the common good and general welfare of the people of the community (such as by bringing about civic betterment and social improvements)."[20] 501(c)5 organizations include agricultural, horticultural, and labor organizations. For the purpose of U.S. campaigns, the most important 501(c)5 organizations are labor unions. 501(c)6 organizations include business leagues and chambers of commerce—most important among them the U.S. Chamber of Commerce.

Tax laws place restrictions on the campaign activities of 501(c)3 and 501(c)4 organizations. Organizations with 501(c)3 status are prohibited from participating in political campaigns, although some occasionally attempt to bend or skirt the law. For example, a 501(c)3 organization might post a sign on its property endorsing a candidate. By contrast, 501(c)4 organizations are allowed to participate in campaign activity as long as that activity is not their "primary purpose." During the 2010 election, 501(c)4 organizations became prominent, particularly those working to support Republican candidates. These organizations, which like many 527s used nondescript names like Crossroads Grassroots Policy Strategies, attracted some donors, particularly corporations, who did not want their identities revealed. Some questioned whether groups like Crossroads were flouting the law by making campaign activity their primary purpose, although it appears unlikely that these groups will be investigated. For one, there is limited staffing and funding at the Internal Revenue Service.[21] Moreover, when the IRS attempted to determine whether groups applying to become 501(c)4 organizations were likely to be primarily political organizations, a scandal arose over whether the IRS was targeting conservative groups in particular. The scandal could make it less likely that the IRS will begin to regulate these groups more stringently. And even if the IRS did, this would not address another concern of critics, which is that these groups can legally raise and spend money without disclosing their donors.

[20] Internal Revenue Service. 2014. "Social Welfare Organizations." http://www.irs.gov/Charities-&-Non-Profits/Other-Non-Profits/Social-Welfare-Organizations (accessed 1/4/15).

[21] Michael Luo and Stephanie Strom. 2010. "Donor Names Remain Secret as Rules Shift." *New York Times*, September 20. www.nytimes.com/2010/09/21/us/politics/21money.html (accessed 1/4/15).

TABLE 4.2b A Donor Taxonomy: Independent Groups

	Independent Expenditure-Only Committee	527	Nonprofits 501(c)4, (c)5, (c)6
Example	American Crossroads	American Solutions Winning the Future	Crossroads Grassroots Policy Strategies, U.S. Chamber of Commerce
Description	A PAC that pays for communications that can support or oppose a candidate by name.	A tax-exempt group that raises money for political activities, including voter mobilization and issue advocacy. These groups haven't typically supported or opposed a candidate by name, but are beginning to.	Tax-exempt groups that can engage in political activity, but it cannot be their primary purpose. These groups haven't typically supported or opposed a candidate by name, but are beginning to.
Limits on contributions to the group	Unlimited	Unlimited	Unlimited
Limits on how the group can use its money	These groups cannot donate to a candidate or PAC or coordinate their spending with parties or candidates.	These groups cannot donate to a candidate or PAC or coordinate their spending with parties or candidates.	These groups cannot donate to a candidate or PAC or coordinate their spending with parties or candidates.
Are donors disclosed?	Yes, to the FEC	Yes, to the Internal Revenue Service	No, unless the contributor gives money for a specific political advertisement

Source: Adapted from "A Donor Taxonomy." 2010. *New York Times.* September 21. www.nytimes.com /imagepages/2010/09/21/us/politics/21money-graphic.html?ref=politics (accessed 3/16/15).

Rules for Spenders

The spenders in American political campaigns include candidates, parties, PACs, and independent groups. The rules for spenders involve three basic questions: how much they can spend, and when and how they can campaign. These rules, particularly with regard to independent groups, are among the most controversial aspects of campaign finance law.

How Much Can They Spend?

Central to American campaign finance law is this principle: contributions are limited, but spending is not. The federal government cannot limit how much candidate campaign committees, party committees, PACs, or independent groups such as 527s spend on campaign activity. And candidates can spend an unlimited amount of their own money on their campaign—that is, they can "self-finance."

Originally, FECA contained both spending and contribution limits. But when the FECA provisions were challenged in the Supreme Court in the 1976 case **Buckley v. Valeo**,[22] the Supreme Court upheld only the contribution limits. The Court reasoned that although donating to candidates was an act of speech subject to First Amendment protections, the federal government had a compelling interest in preventing the possibility of corruption, which might arise if a candidate could raise large amounts of money from a few donors. Thus, contribution limits were declared constitutional. However, the Court ruled that there was no compelling interest in limiting spending, and thus the spending limits violated the free speech clause of the First Amendment.

At the federal level, spending can be limited only in presidential races, and then only with the agreement of the candidates. FECA set up a system of public financing for presidential elections, which was upheld by the Court in *Buckley* and remains in place today. Public financing comes from tax dollars; there is, in fact, a box on federal tax forms that taxpayers can check if they want to give a small amount of money to help finance federal campaigns. In the nomination phase, public financing comes in the form of matching funds. If candidates have raised a certain amount in a certain number of states, the federal government will give them funds equal to the contributions from individuals, up to $250 for any single contribution. Thus, if an eligible candidate received 1,000 donations of $250, or $250,000, she would receive an additional $250,000 in matching funds. The requirement

---

[22] 424 U.S. 1 (1976).

to raise at least some money helps to ensure that only viable, serious candidates qualify for matching funds. If candidates accept matching funds, however, they must then agree to a spending limit. In 2012, the limit was approximately $46 million overall, with specific limits by state depending on population size.[23] Again, the public-funding system is voluntary and some candidates refuse matching funds in the primaries because they want to raise and spend more than this limit. In 1980, Republican John Connally was the first primary candidate to take this step. In 1996, Steve Forbes became the next candidate to do so. By 2012, it had become accepted practice, with every Republican candidate as well as Barack Obama refusing matching funds.

Presidential general elections also have a public financing option. After each party holds its nominating convention, the nominee for that party can receive a fixed amount of money from the federal government. This amount is indexed for inflation and varies from election to election. In 2012, it was $91.2 million. The candidate must then agree to spend only that amount—although, of course, party committees and independent groups may also be spending money in ways that help the candidate. Until 2008, every major-party presidential candidate accepted public funds for the general election.[24] That year, Obama refused public funding, allowing him to spend more than McCain. In 2012, both Obama and Romney spurned public funds.

Public financing systems also exist in about half of the states. As in the presidential system, all are optional and come with strings attached, such as minimum fund-raising requirements, pledges to limit or refuse private donations, and spending limits. For example, in New Jersey, gubernatorial candidates must, as of 2014, raise $380,000 to be eligible for public financing. The state will then match every $3,800 in private contributions with $7,600 in public money—up to $3.5 million for the primary election campaign and $8.2 million for the general election campaign. However, participating candidates may not spend more than $5.6 million in the primary campaign and $12.2 million in the general campaign.[25]

---

[23] Federal Election Commission. "Presidential Spending Limits for 2012." www.fec.gov /pages/brochures/pubfund_limits_2012.shtml (accessed 1/4/15).

[24] Minor-party and independent candidates are not eligible for federal funds unless they met the vote threshold from the previous election. If they adhere to FECA regulations, they can retroactively apply for public money.

[25] New Jersey Election Law Enforcement Commission. 2014. "Gubernatorial Public Financing: Overview." www.elec.state.nj.us/download/gubernatorial/GubPublicFinPP _122012.ppt (accessed 1/4/15).

Seven states have gone further and established full public funding, also known as **clean elections systems**, for statewide or legislative elections, or both.[26] Maine's system will illustrate. To be eligible, candidates for state offices must gather a certain number of contributions of $5 or more: 60, 175, and 3,250 for state house, state senate, and gubernatorial candidates, respectively. Once candidates decide to accept public financing, they receive a grant from the state and may not receive any further private donations. For example, state senate candidates in Maine in 2014 each received $7,359 for the primary election and $21,749 for the general election. These amounts were set below the average expenditure in previous elections, and thus reflect the further goal of reducing the amount of money spent on campaigns.[27]

When and How Independent Groups May Campaign

A final set of rules applies to when and how campaigning can take place. In line with the lack of limits on campaign spending, the American system also imposes few restrictions on when and how candidates may campaign. In contrast, some other democratic countries restrict televised political advertising. For example, in Belgium, France, Great Britain, and Spain, candidates and parties cannot buy broadcasting time on either commercial or public television. In lieu of purchased time, these countries provide free air time either on commercial or public television, albeit with substantial restrictions on when and how much advertising can be aired.[28] The lack of such restrictions in the American system is one reason why campaigns are so expensive: the largest category of candidate spending is for television advertising, and that advertising can be aired at any point and in whatever amount. It is not surprising that in competitive races, this makes for long campaigns with seemingly endless advertisements.

The American system places more restrictions on independent groups than on the candidates or parties. A first rule is that if these groups want to spend their resources to support a candidate or the candidates of a party, they cannot consult with, coordinate with, or receive help from the candidates or the party. If a labor union PAC wants to help a Democratic candidate, neither that candidate nor her staff can assist with PAC fund-raising, the production

---

[26] National Conference of State Legislatures. 2013. "Public Financing of Campaigns: An Overview." www.ncsl.org/research/elections-and-campaigns/public-financing-of-campaigns-overview.aspx (accessed 1/4/15).

[27] For more information, see www.maine.gov/ethics/mcea/index.htm (accessed 1/4/15).

[28] Christina Holtz-Bacha and Lynda Lee Kaid. 2006. "Political Advertising in International Comparison," in *The Sage Handbook of Political Advertising*, eds. Christina Holtz-Bacha and Lynda Lee Kaid. Thousand Oaks, CA: Sage, pp. 3-13.

of a television advertisement sponsored by the PAC, or the PAC's decision on when and where to air the ad.

Second, there are restrictions on the content of advertising by independent groups. When BCRA was passed in 2002, its proponents were not only concerned with soft money donations to political parties. They also worried that, with a soft money ban for political parties, even more soft money would flow to independent groups, who would use these contributions to engage in issue advocacy, including ads that lacked the "magic words" but were essentially endorsements of (or attacks on) a candidate. BRCA established new rules. First, it defined a new and expanded category of *electioneering communications*: ads that referred to a clearly identified candidate for federal office (regardless of whether the magic words were mentioned), that occurred up to 60 days before a general election or 30 days before a primary election, that were publicly distributed on radio or television, and that were broadcast to an electorate of at least 50,000 people. BCRA then stated that electioneering communication could not be funded with corporate or union treasury funds—that is, the revenue that corporations or unions raise as part of their regular operations. In order to engage in electioneering communication, these groups would have to establish PACs and raise hard money subject to contribution limits and disclosure provisions. Of course, BCRA's rules on electioneering communication contained exceptions. They did not regulate ads that occur outside the 30- or 60-day windows, or other forms of campaigning such as direct mail, online ads, or telephone calls.

Subsequent Supreme Court decisions have weakened these BCRA provisions substantially. The most important decision, **Citizens United v. Federal Election Commission**, was handed down in 2010.[29] Citizens United is a nonprofit organization that received corporate funding to produce a documentary film, *Hillary: The Movie*, which was critical of Hillary Clinton. The group wanted to run commercials advertising the film and to air it on cable television during the 2008 presidential primaries. The FEC considered this to be an electioneering communication—essentially, an argument that Clinton should not be elected—that could not be aired 30 days before a presidential primary. Citizens United asserted that the documentary was factual and politically neutral.

The more conservative justices on the Court took the unusual step of going beyond the narrow questions surrounding the documentary to consider a more fundamental issue: whether corporations and unions could be banned from spending their general treasury funds for electioneering communication.

---

[29] *Citizens United v. Federal Election Commission*, 558 U.S. 08-205 (2010).

Commentators assumed that this signaled the conservatives' willingness to overturn the ban, and, indeed, that was correct. In a 5–4 decision, the Court ruled that the ban was unconstitutional. While corporations and unions are not literally people, the majority argued that "associations of persons" also have a right to free speech. The Court's decision opened the door to advertising by corporations and labor unions—not simply their PACs—that both targeted specific candidates (express advocacy) and was aired within the 30- and 60-day windows. The decision called into question the laws in 24 states that had imposed similar restrictions or bans on independent expenditures by corporations or unions. It also provoked criticism by President Obama in his 2010 State of the Union address, a speech made in front of members of both houses of Congress and the Supreme Court. We discuss this debate in more detail later in the chapter.

Some commentators feared that the *Citizens United* decision would lead to a flood of spending and advertising by independent groups. Analyses in the wake of 2010 suggested that these concerns might have been overblown. In the 2010 election, there was a substantial increase in the amount of money spent by independent groups relative to the previous midterm election in 2006 (see Figure 4.5). However, the spending of other actors, including the candidates and parties, also increased, particularly in Senate races, where the fraction of advertisements that were sponsored by independent groups, as opposed to candidates or political parties, was no greater in 2010 than in 2008. In U.S. House races, this fraction doubled, from 6 percent in 2008 to 12 percent in 2010, but even the 12 percent figure was a much smaller fraction than in 2000, when interest group advertisements constituted 17 percent of all advertisements in House races.[30]

In many ways, it was the election of 2012 that confirmed the worst fears of those who believed the *Citizens United* decision would open the floodgates of spending in campaigns. Outside groups spent $1.1 billion on independent expenditures and electioneering communication for all federal candidates in the primary and general elections of 2012. This was nearly as much as the combined total of what they had spent in every federal election between 1990 and 2010 ($1.2 billion, adjusted for inflation). Thus, the 2012 election featured nearly as much outside group spending as the previous 20 years of elections.[31]

---

[30] Michael M. Franz. 2010. "The *Citizens United* Election: Same as It Ever Was?" *Forum* 8, 4: article 7.

[31] Center for Responsive Politics. 2012. "Total Outside Spending by Election Cycle, Excluding Party Committees." www.opensecrets.org/outsidespending/cycle_tots.php (accessed 3/27/13).

If party and candidate spending in 2012 had also increased dramatically then there would be less cause for concern, but as Figures 4.1, 4.2, and 4.3 demonstrate, that was not the case. As a result, the percentage of all Senate ads sponsored by independent groups doubled from 15 to 30 percent between 2010 and 2012. The percentage of presidential ads sponsored by such groups increased from 19 percent in 2004 to 31 percent in 2012. In House races, there was no notable increase in the proportion of ads sponsored by these groups.[32]

Commentators have also speculated about whether independent spending decides elections, especially because it favored Republican candidates more than Democratic candidates in 2010 and 2012. Outside groups typically target the most competitive races, where candidates and parties are also campaigning heavily. This means advertisements sponsored by independent groups may be drowned out in the general din of the more numerous advertisements from candidates and parties. Indeed, in 2010, Democratic candidates' disadvantage in terms of independent group spending was largely compensated for by their advantage in spending by candidates and party organizations. Similarly, in 2012, Obama compensated for Romney's 3–1 advantage in outside group spending by raising significantly more than his opponent in individual contributions.

Does this mean outside group spending does not matter? Absolutely not. In 2012, if one excludes ads sponsored by interest groups, for every 53 ads that Romney aired in a media market, Obama aired 100 ads in the same media market. When one includes ads by independent groups, for every 82 ads favoring Romney in a media market, there were 100 Obama ads.[33] In other words, it can be argued that outside group spending kept Romney in the game and enabled him to mount a strong challenge against an incumbent president. Thus, an advantage in independent spending does not guarantee that a candidate will win an election, but it certainly improves their chances.

Campaign Finance Rules and Political Strategy

As we discussed in Chapter 2, understanding electoral rules is important because they profoundly influence the actions of citizens, candidates, parties, and interest groups. This is true with regard to campaign finance law as

---

[32] Michael M. Franz. 2013. "Interest Groups in Electoral Politics: 2012 in Context." *Forum* 10, 4: 62–79.

[33] Franz, "Interest Groups."

well. Here, we identify some of the implications of the campaign finance system for each category of actors.

Citizens

Consider first the strategies pursued by individual citizens. By making private donations central to campaign fund-raising, the American system allows private citizens another avenue by which to express their political voice, one distinct from voting and writing to a member of Congress, for example. As with other forms of political participation, donating provides citizens another means by which they can establish a tie with candidates and hold elected leaders accountable for their performance in office. Donations are a particularly powerful way to encourage accountability: the central goal of any candidate is to be elected, and it is virtually impossible to do so without the resources provided by donations.

How do citizens decide what candidates to support with donations? In some cases, the decision is straightforward: a donor may give to a candidate who shares her values and goals. But the decision is often strategic as well. Consider, for example, primary elections, in which there are often few differences between the candidates. How might donors decide then? One important factor is whether donors expect a candidate to win. If two candidates have similar platforms, donors often prefer to support the likely winner rather than "waste" their money on a likely loser. Potential donors will thus look to various indicators of candidates' viability, including polls, news coverage, and donations by other individuals and interest groups.[34]

Candidates

Campaign finance rules profoundly affect political candidates. By not limiting spending, the American system gives candidates the incentive to raise and spend as much as possible. By limiting the amount of each donation, the system makes it particularly onerous to raise money because candidates must raise it from a larger number of donors. If there were no limits on the size of donations, a candidate could conceivably fund his campaign with money from a single rich donor. Instead, candidates ask for contributions from thousands of donors, with phone calls, at receptions and dinners, and so on. One study of House candidates in the 1996 and 1998 elections found that a substantial fraction (42 percent) reported spending at least a quarter of their time engaged in fund-raising. Almost a quarter of these candidates

---

[34] Diana Mutz. 1995. "Effects of Horse-Race Coverage on Campaign Coffers: Strategic Contributing in Presidential Primaries." *Journal of Politics* 57: 1015–42.

(24 percent) reported spending at least half their time fund-raising.[35] More recently, an orientation given to newly elected Democratic members of Congress by the Democratic Congressional Campaign Committee recommended that they spend four hours each day making phone calls to raise funds.[36] Given this reality, candidates must seek out efficient ways to raise money. The Internet is helpful, as fund-raising online does not require receptions or dinners. Another strategy is to recruit "bundlers," relatively wealthy donors who can also enlist a set of friends and acquaintances to donate. Bundlers are so valuable that campaigns use catchy names to recognize them. For the 2000 and 2004 Bush presidential campaigns, bundlers were called "Pioneers," "Rangers," and "Super-Rangers" if they supplied $100,000, $200,000, and $300,000, respectively, in donations.

Candidates will likely face even greater incentives to raise money in the wake of the *Citizens United* decision. The increase in independent spending in 2010 may heighten candidates' fear of an advertising blitz sponsored by independent groups, much of which is likely to attack them.

Fund-raising takes considerable time and energy and will continue to do so. But not every candidate faces the same burden. The American system of campaign finance advantages incumbents to a significant degree. As we discuss further in Chapter 10, incumbent members of Congress are typically much more successful than challengers in raising money. They are better known. They already have the status and power that makes them valuable to donors and interest groups. They are usually perceived as the likely victor. All of this stacks the deck against challengers.

The campaign finance system may also benefit wealthy candidates. The lack of spending limits means that candidates can fund their own campaigns, potentially giving wealthy individuals a significant advantage over the less wealthy. Thus, American elections often feature candidates who spend large amounts of their personal wealth to get elected. For example, in the 1992 presidential campaign, Ross Perot spent $63 million of his own money running as an independent candidate. Self-financing can discourage some potential opponents from running against a wealthy, self-financed candidate.

However, the experiences of self-financed candidates also suggest that personal wealth does not guarantee victory. First, it is important to remember

---

[35] Paul S. Herrnson and Ronald A. Faucheux. 2000. "Candidates Devote Substantial Time and Effort to Fundraising." http://www.gvpt.umd.edu/herrnson/reporttime.html (accessed 1/4/15).

[36] Ryan Grim and Sabrina Siddiqui. 2013. "Call Time for Congress Shows How Fundraising Dominates Bleak Work Life." *Huffington Post*, January 8. www.huffingtonpost.com/2013/01/08/call-time-congressional-fundraising_n_2427291.html?1357648217 (accessed 1/4/15).

Experiments in Online Fund-raising

Candidates frequently send dozens if not hundreds of e-mails to their supporters, asking them to contribute money, or more money, to the campaign. For Barack Obama's 2012 campaign, these e-mails were a crucial part of its fund-raising strategy. More so than Mitt Romney, Obama relied on donations in small amounts to fund his campaign, although he also took in plenty of large donations too.[1] How did the Obama campaign motivate supporters to give and give again? They invested in a little science.

In particular, the Obama fund-raising team conducted experiments with their fund-raising e-mails. Before they sent a blast e-mail to their list of supporters, they selected small groups of supporters at random and sent each group a different version of the e-mail. These groups would see different subject lines, different text, different colors, and so on. Then the Obama team would see which e-mail elicited the most donations. The "winning" e-mail would then be sent to all supporters.

For example, in one experiment, the Obama team determined that the subject line "I will be outspent" raised far more money than "If you believe in what we're doing" or "Do this for Michelle." More generally, the Obama team determined that a casual tone and even occasional profanity ("Hell yeah, I like Obamacare") also increased donations. Most of these findings were not anticipated in advance. The Obama team would routinely bet on which e-mails would be most successful in each experiment. For the most part, they were wrong. Amelia Showalter, Obama's director of digital analytics, said, "We were so bad at predicting." This is why the science was so valuable.[2]

But science goes only so far. The Obama team discovered that new e-mail tactics tended to work for a while, but then they would wear off and new tactics were required. Moreover, what worked best in the Obama campaign did not necessarily work as well in other campaigns. Showalter described how the Obama campaign's e-mails tended to raise more money when they were shorter, but Senator Elizabeth Warren's campaign found that longer e-mails written by Warren herself tended to be most effective for them.[3]

Nevertheless, these experiments have spawned many more by other candidates, party committees, and interest groups. All of this science is likely to increase the efficacy of online fund-raising.

---

[1] See www.cfinst.org/pdf/federal/president/2012/Pres12_30G_Table4.pdf (accessed 1/4/15).
[2] Joshua Green. 2012. "The Science behind Those Obama Emails." *Bloomberg Businessweek*, November 29. www.businessweek.com/articles/2012-11-29/the-science-behind-those-obama-campaign-e-mails (accessed 1/4/15).
[3] John Sides and Lynn Vavreck. 2014. "Obama's Not-So-Big Data." *Pacific Standard*, January 21. www.psmag.com/navigation/politics-and-law/obamas-big-data-inconclusive-results-political-campaigns-72687/ (accessed 1/4/15).

that many candidates are essentially forced to spend their own money because they are facing strong opposition and could easily be defeated if they only use what they raise from other donors, or because they are languishing in the polls and desperately need to give their campaign a jolt. In the 2004 presidential primaries, Senator John Kerry mortgaged his house so that he could loan $6.4 million to his campaign, which was struggling at that time. Second, dollars raised from other donors appear to produce more votes than dollars provided by the candidate. This may reflect the additional benefits of cultivating a network of supportive donors. Private donations signal the strength of the candidate to the media and political elites. It will surprise no one that a candidate would give his or her own campaign $3 million—after all, it is the candidate's money, and the candidate wants to win. But if 3,000 people give the candidate $1,000 each, it may convince others that the candidate is a serious contender. Moreover, the act of fund-raising may generate local media coverage of fund-raising events and may strengthen a candidate's ties to crucial interest groups and blocs of voters. Thus the possibility of self-financing entails a complex series of strategic calculations.[37]

As we discussed earlier, in presidential elections, candidates may accept public funding. But this necessitates another strategic calculation, because the public funding comes with a spending limit. For a lesser-known candidate in the presidential primaries, accepting the money may be an easy decision. Unfamiliar candidates struggle to raise private donations and may be able to spend far more if they accept matching funds, despite the accompanying spending limit. Better-known candidates will be tempted to rely on private donations because they believe that there are many individuals and interest groups who will donate to them, and thus more money to be raised from private rather than public funds. Many believe that the fact that no major-party candidates in the 2012 primary or general elections accepted public funds signaled the death knell of the public financing system for presidential elections. This is very likely true unless the level of public funding is raised high enough to make it attractive to candidates once again.

By accepting private donations, candidates face another strategic imperative: keeping donors happy. Donors can withhold their money to ensure accountability, and it is up to the candidate to make sure they are not disappointed. Here is the problem, however. As we describe in more detail later, donors are not at all representative of voters as a whole. What donors want may not match up with what voters want. Thus, candidates may find

---

[37] See Jennifer Steen. 2006. *Self-Financed Candidates in Congressional Elections.* Ann Arbor: University of Michigan Press.

themselves forced to take one position to please donors but another position to please voters—a difficult balancing act and one that often attracts criticism if contradictory positions become public knowledge.

Political Parties and Interest Groups

Under the current rules, political parties and interest groups, including corporations and unions, can raise and spend their own money on campaign activities. BCRA's ban on soft money has not hindered the parties in this regard. The Supreme Court's decision in *Citizens United* gave interest groups even freer rein to spend independently. This poses both an opportunity and a challenge for candidates. On the one hand, they may benefit from the campaign activity of their party and of interest groups who support them. On the other hand, they may find that their party and ostensibly supportive interest groups are not interested in helping them. They may also be attacked by the opposing party and its aligned groups. Thus, the presence of parties and interest groups can both facilitate and complicate the efforts of candidates.

A dispute within the Democratic Party during the 2006 election illustrates the complex ways in which the strategies of candidates and parties interact. The chair of the Democratic National Committee (DNC), the former Vermont governor and 2004 presidential candidate Howard Dean, advocated a "50-state strategy"—one that would invest the DNC's money in building up the Democratic party organization in every state, even in states where the party rarely won elections. This was a boon to many Democrats in such states, who typically did not attract much support from the party. At the same time, the chair of the Democratic Congressional Campaign Committee (DCCC), Rahm Emanuel, had a very different strategy: he sought to use DCCC money to bolster Democratic House candidates in competitive races, and thought it was wasteful to spend party money in states where the party had little chance of winning. This was a boon to Democrats in hard-fought campaigns, but not to Democrats in Republican-dominated states. No matter which strategy the party pursued, some Democratic candidates would benefit more than others.

Like political parties, interest groups must make strategic decisions about which candidate to support, through either donations or independent expenditures. This will depend on their agenda. Groups that find their interests well served by current officeholders will pursue an "access" strategy, working to support incumbents of both parties and, via their contributions, guarantee access to these incumbents so that they can press their agenda. This creates an incentive for incumbent candidates to be responsive to groups to ensure their support during the campaign. Groups that tend to have a more ideological agenda, one further from the average officeholder, will pursue a "replacement" strategy, seeking to replace incumbents with new representatives who share this agenda. These new representatives will typically come from one party or even one ideological faction within the party.[38] The Club for Growth, a group that promotes conservative economic policies, is famous for targeting incumbent "RINOs"—Republicans in Name Only—that it considers too moderate. Of course, incumbent candidates will not sit idly by if they are threatened with such a challenge. They may take new steps to placate the interest groups and convince them not to support the challenger. If that is unsuccessful, they may adjust their own positions on issues to be more in line with their challenger's, thereby negating some of the rationale for replacing them. In the 2010 Arizona Senate race, John McCain, the incumbent, faced a conservative challenger, J. D. Hayworth, in the Republican primary. Hayworth's presence led McCain to take more conservative positions on several issues. McCain soft-pedaled his earlier advocacy for campaign finance reform and BCRA, even though he had been one of its staunchest advocates.

The agendas of candidates and their interest group supporters may not be well aligned—a very plausible scenario, given that under current campaign finance law, candidates and interest groups are not permitted to coordinate their campaign activities. A supportive interest group may emphasize different issues or themes or adopt a different set of tactics than the candidate it supports. For example, parties and interest groups tend to air far more negative campaign ads than do candidates. At times, this may not bother candidates, who can take the high road and let others do the dirty work. But at other times, candidates may have to disavow a particularly aggressive ad aired by a supporter. In the 1988 presidential election, the National Security Political Action Committee (NSPAC) aired an ad attacking the Democratic candidate, Michael Dukakis, for a Massachusetts program that allowed prisoners to leave jail temporarily for furloughs as part of a rehabilitation effort. The ad focused on one prisoner, William Horton (the ad called him "Willie"), who, while on furlough, raped a woman and assaulted her fiancé. The ad featured a photograph of Horton, who was black, and became controversial after critics argued that it played on racial fears. The campaign of Dukakis's opponent, George H. W. Bush, ultimately requested NSPAC to withdraw it, although some have argued that the Bush campaign knew

---

[38] See Michael M. Franz. 2008. *Choices and Changes: Interest Groups in the Electoral Process.* Philadelphia: Temple University Press.

about the ad in advance and delayed their request for its withdrawal to give the ad time to have an impact.[39]

Ultimately, candidates may find that much of the campaigning that takes place, even on their behalf, is out of their control. As such, it may both help and hurt their campaign, at least as they see it. By expanding the number of actors eligible to raise and spend money, the American system of campaign finance creates loose alliances among candidates, parties, and interest groups that contain significant tensions even as these players seek a common goal.

The Debate over Campaign Finance Reform

The American system of campaign finance is perennially controversial, as the debate over the *Citizens United* decision illustrates. To understand this controversy, it is worth considering the values that underlie the campaign finance system, discussing the tensions among these values, and evaluating proposed reforms to the system. As noted earlier, two important values underlying campaign finance law are freedom of speech, as discussed in Chapter 1 and as enumerated in the First Amendment; and guarding against corruption, and in particular the corrupting influence of money. Debate about campaign finance also engages other values discussed in Chapter 1, especially free choice and political equality.

The Supreme Court has weighed those values in different ways when considering the rules imposed on donors and spenders. In *Buckley v. Valeo*, the Court argued that donations to a candidate pose a significant threat of corruption, but that spending on behalf of a candidate (for example by an interest group) does not. It also argued that donations are not as meaningful as spending in terms of their communicative content. Donations serve only to convey general support but not the reasons for that support. Spending, on the other hand, is central to communicating one's ideas during a campaign. Both of these arguments buttressed the Court's decisions to limit donations but not spending. Concerns about free speech also led to the Court's decisions in *Citizens United*, which struck down laws that restricted the spending of independent groups.

---

[39] The Federal Election Commission conducted an investigation into whether there was illicit cooperation between the Bush campaign and the independent group that produced the ad. The commission was deadlocked 3–3 on the question (not surprising given the presence of three Republicans and three Democrats on the Commission) and thus did not produce a conclusive ruling. www.insidepolitics.org/ps111/independentads.html (accessed 1/4/15).

The Case against the Status Quo

The chief objection to these legal decisions (and to the American system in general) is that they allow money to have too much influence on politics. This has at least four possible negative consequences. First, it is hard on candidates, who must raise money incessantly, even to the detriment of other, possibly more beneficial activities, such as policy making. It may also discourage some talented individuals from running in the first place, especially ones who have no ability to self-finance as an alternative to raising private donations. In a 2008 survey of potential political candidates, 29 percent of women and 21 percent of men said that the prospect of soliciting campaign contributions would "deter them from running for office."[40]

Second, critics fear that money simply buys elections, meaning that whoever can spend the most wins. They point to the fund-raising disparities between incumbents and challengers and to the extraordinarily high rate at which incumbents win. This criticism is based on the values of free choice and political equality. Voters do not really have a choice, the argument goes, when a well-funded incumbent can scare off many potential challengers and then easily defeat the poorly funded challenger who decides to run. Is it fair that campaign finance rules create such inequality, whereby some candidates have vastly more resources to spend than others?

Third, critics argue, the campaign finance system favors those wealthy enough to donate, giving them a greater voice in politics than those who cannot donate and violating the value of political equality. Wealthy individuals are far more likely than the poor to donate to candidates. Indeed, campaign contributions have become increasingly concentrated among the wealthiest individuals, as their wealth has grown and as they have become more interested in politics.[41] Moreover, critics claim, interest groups that represent wealthy Americans and business or corporate interests are more powerful than groups representing, for example, the poor or working class. In the 2011–12 election cycle, business PACs contributed about $2.7 billion to congressional and presidential candidates, while labor PACs contributed just $177 million.[42]

---

[40] Jennifer Lawless and Richard Fox. 2008. "Why Are Women Still Not Running for Office?" *Issues in Government Studies* 16. Washington, DC: Brookings Institution Press.

[41] Adam Bonica, Nolan McCarty, Keith T. Poole, and Howard Rosenthal. 2013. "Why Hasn't Democracy Slowed Rising Inequality?" *Journal of Economic Perspectives* 27(3): 103–24.

[42] OpenSecrets. "Business-Labor-Ideology Split in PAC & Individual Donations to Candidates, Parties, Super PACs and Outside Spending Groups." www.opensecrets.org/bigpicture/blio.php (accessed 1/4/15).

Fourth, critics point to the fact that some outside groups can raise and spend money without disclosing their donors. This prevents observers and voters from knowing the identities or agendas of the people trying to influence election outcomes. This is all-the-more problematic, critics argue, since these outside groups are raising donations in unlimited amounts. For example, of the $180 million raised by the 501(c)4 organization Crossroads GPS during the 2012 election cycle, $22.5 million came from a single donor, whose identity is unknown.[43]

Fifth, and perhaps most important, critics argue that the current system does not do enough to combat corruption, or at least the appearance of corruption. Critics note that candidates and political parties still find ways to raise large amounts of money that violate the spirit of campaign finance law. For example, candidates and their parties sometimes establish "joint fundraising committees," as did both McCain and Obama in 2008. A donor can write a single check to this committee; this donation is then distributed to the candidate, national party committees, and perhaps state parties. Such donations cannot exceed contribution limits, but nevertheless, critics argue, the overall impact of a single large check gives wealthy donors added clout. Furthermore, committees are established to fund the presidential nominating conventions, which can raise unlimited sums from corporate and union general treasuries and PACs. This is because of an FEC loophole defining convention funds as "motivated by a desire to promote the convention city and not by political considerations"—a proposition critics find highly dubious.[44]

Fundamentally, critics are concerned that the money that donors and organized interests give and spend can influence elected leaders. Stories about the possible influence of money are common. During the debate over health care reform in 2009, a *Washington Post* story noted that Max Baucus (D-MT), then-chair of the Senate Finance Committee, who was a key figure in drawing up health care legislation, was also a "leading recipient of Senate campaign contributions from the hospitals, insurers, and other medical interest groups hoping to shape the legislation to their advantage."[45] Another story implicated Christopher Dodd (D-CT), who had received numerous contributions from hedge funds even as the Senate Banking

---

[43] Matea Gold. 2013. "One single donation to Crossroads GPS in 2012: $22,500,000." *Washington Post*, November 15. www.washingtonpost.com/blogs/the-fix/wp/2013/11/15/one-single-donation-to-crossroads-gps-in-2012-22500000 (accessed 1/4/15).

[44] *Federal Register* 68, 153 (8/8/2003): 47401–2.

[45] Dan Eggen. 2009. "Industry Cash Flowed to Drafters of Reform." *Washington Post*, July 21.

Committee, which Dodd then chaired, was considering legislation that would regulate those funds.[46] A 2002 survey of state legislators also found that many believed that campaign contributions had at least some influence on the content and passage of bills in their state's legislature.[47] In the minds of critics, campaign contributions may lead to policies favored by donors, rather than policies that would serve other important goals and perhaps even the general good of the country.

A proposed solution to many of these potential problems with campaign finance rules is public financing, and especially a clean elections system like that in Maine. Clean elections systems can help equalize resources among candidates by providing equal amounts of public funding to all candidates and by forbidding any other fund-raising by the recipients of public funding. With equal amounts of funding, the campaign might then be more competitive, improving the quality of information provided to voters and giving them a more meaningful choice. In addition, with almost all campaign financing coming from the government, there is little to no chance that wealthy donors or interest groups will have a disproportionate or corrupting influence. Advocates of clean elections have proposed a similar system for federal elections, the Fair Elections Now Act, which could, in the words of one of its proponents, make "elected officials beholden to the people they're supposed to represent instead of the wealthy special interests."[48]

Complicating the Case for Reform

How well do the arguments for campaign finance reform withstand empirical scrutiny? And are there good arguments in support of the system as it stands? Answers to these questions suggest that the American system of campaign finance, however imperfect, may have its merits.

Arguments for reform include two primary claims about the current system: simply stated, money buys elections and money buys legislators' votes. But can we verify that these statements are true? The first claim is difficult to assess. Consider that incumbents tend to raise much more than challengers. Is this disparity in fund-raising the actual reason that incumbents win? Or do incumbents raise so much because they are already anticipated to

---

[46] Manu Raju. 2010. "Hedge Fund Managers Invest on Hill." *Politico*, April 13. www.politico.com/news/stories/0410/35704.html (accessed 1/4/15).

[47] Lynda Powell. 2012. *The Influence of Campaign Contributions in State Legislatures*. Ann Arbor: University of Michigan Press.

[48] Public Campaign. "Bipartisan Fair Elections Now Act Reaches Majority of Majority in U.S. House." www.publicampaign.org/pressroom/2010/02/04/bipartisan-fair-elections-now-act-reaches-majority-of-majority-in-us-house (accessed 1/4/15).

win, and donors often prefer to give to the likely winner? And how do we separate the effects of incumbents' fund-raising advantage from the other advantages they have as incumbents, including their work on behalf of constituents and consequent visibility? These sorts of advantages may help explain why incumbents were re-elected at such high rates even *before* they were so dominant in fund-raising. For example, in the early 1980s, House incumbents were typically spending about 1.5 times as much as challengers; in the 2000s, they typically spent about 2.5 or 3 times as much. But incumbents' reelection rates in the early 1980s were above 90 percent, slightly higher than in the 2000s, even though their fund-raising advantage increased in the 2000s. Thus, the high reelection rate of incumbents is not necessarily due *only* to their fund-raising advantage.

This may explain why more stringent campaign finance rules do not necessarily transform elections, making them more competitive and incumbents more vulnerable. For example, neither bans on spending by corporations nor different levels of limits on individual donations are associated with incumbent defeats.[49] The evidence on the effects of clean elections is also somewhat equivocal. Public financing programs appear to reduce the amount of time that candidates spend fund-raising for themselves and thereby to increase the time spent interacting with voters, but it may also increase the time candidates spend fund-raising for their party. Public financing programs do appear to reduce the advantages of incumbents and make elections more competitive, but they may also make legislatures more polarized by reducing the influence of interest groups that tend to support moderate candidates.[50]

The claim that money buys legislators' votes also needs examination. There is relatively little evidence that it actually occurs. First, because of contribution limits, the amount that any donor or interest group can give is small, relative to the large amount of money that many candidates routinely

---

[49] Raymond J. LaRaja and Brian F. Schaffner. "The Effects of Campaign Finance Spending Bans on Electoral Outcomes: Evidence from the States about the Potential Impact of *Citizens United v. FEC.*" *Electoral Studies* 33: 103–14; Thomas Stratmann and Francisco J. Aparicio-Castillo. 2006. "Competition Policy for Elections: Do Campaign Contribution Limits Matter?" *Public Choice* 127, 1: 177–206.

[50] Peter L. Francia and Paul S. Herrnson. 2003. "The Impact of Public Finance Laws on Fundraising in State Legislative Elections." *American Politics Research* 31, 5: 520–39; Andrew Hall. 2014. "How the Public Funding of Elections Increases Candidate Polarization." Working paper available at https://dl.dropboxusercontent.com/u/11481940/Hall _publicfunding.pdf (accessed 1/4/15); Michael Miller. 2014. *Subsidizing Democracy: How Public Funding Changes Elections and How It Can Work in the Future.* Ithaca, NY: Cornell University Press; Powell, *The Influence of Campaign Contributions in State Legislatures.*

raise and spend. Candidates who raise millions of dollars are not likely to "sell" their votes to a PAC for a measly $5,000.

Second, many donations to campaigns are strategic: the donors do not want to waste their money on someone who will never support their agenda. Instead, they give to members who are already supportive, perhaps because these members simply have beliefs about policies that are similar to the donors' or because members are responding to their constituents, who also agree with donors. Consider this hypothetical example. The National Farmers Union PAC gives an incumbent congressman $5,000 for his reelection campaign. The congressman represents a rural district in Iowa whose economy revolves around growing corn. After the election, he votes to give additional government subsidies to corn farmers. Did he vote this way because he simply believes that government subsidies are necessary, because many of his constituents are farmers and others who benefit from subsidies, or because he got that PAC contribution?

None of this is to say that campaign donations are ineffectual. Some research suggests that donations are more likely to buy the involvement of an elected official on an issue, if not his vote. Donations appear to motivate representatives to be more active in promoting the issue on congressional committees, for example. However, this is true only for representatives who already share the donors' positions.[51] Donors may also get more "access" to an elected official—that is, a greater opportunity to advocate for their views in front of a representative or her staff.[52] Of course, this does not imply that the representative will always agree with these views. Ultimately, campaign donations may not be quite as powerful an influence as reformers claim and media coverage often suggests.

The American system of campaign finance can also be defended on philosophical grounds. Two of the features that reformers routinely target—private donations and unlimited spending by candidates—could in fact be considered valuable. By allowing private donations to candidates, the American system creates an opportunity for citizens and interest groups to have a voice and help to elect candidates who they believe can best represent them. By allowing unlimited spending, the American system allows for more campaign activity, including advertising that communicates information about

[51] Richard L. Hall and Frank W. Wayman. 1990. "Buying Time: Moneyed Interests and the Mobilization of Bias in Congressional Committees." *American Political Science Review* 84, 3: 797–820.

[52] Kalla, Joshua L., and David E. Broockman. Forthcoming. "Congressional Officials Grant Access to Individuals Because They Have Contributed to Campaigns: A Randomized Field Experiment." *American Journal of Political Science*.

the candidates, activities that mobilize citizens to vote, and so on. This point was made in the *Buckley v. Valeo* decision: "A restriction on the amount of money a person or group can spend on political communication during a campaign necessarily reduces the quantity of expression by restricting the number of issues discussed, the depth of their exploration, and the size of the audience reached." And, indeed, there is evidence that campaign spending helps voters learn about political candidates.[53] Given that Americans still do not always know much about the candidates or vote in large numbers, it could be counterproductive to limit campaign spending.

Leaving aside arguments about the merits of the current campaign finance system, there is one further challenge that critics of the system face: there is often little incentive for incumbent leaders to reform the system. Despite the public's complaints about money in elections, polls reveal that opinions about dramatic reforms, such as public financing, depend on how the poll question is worded. For example, a 2010 poll conducted by Common Cause, a group advocating for public funding found that 63 percent of respondents supported public financing when described this way:

> Under this plan, candidates for Congress could run for office without raising large campaign contributions. Instead they would collect a large number of small contributions from their home state in order to qualify for a limited amount of public funding for their campaign. They would be prohibited from taking any contributions over 100 dollars or any contributions from lobbyists. Contributions of 100 dollars or less would be matched with public funds on a four to one basis, up to a strict limit.[54]

However, a 2007 Gallup poll found that the public actually preferred that presidential candidates *not* accept public financing.[55] Over half of respondents (56 percent) believed that candidates should "opt not to take public financing and spend whatever money they can raise on their own" rather than to "agree to take public financing and accept spending limits." Similarly, in 2013 Gallup found that only 50 percent would vote for a "law that would establish a new campaign finance system where federal campaigns

---

[53] For example, see John J. Coleman and Paul F. Manna. 2003. "Congressional Campaign Spending and the Quality of Democracy." *Journal of Politics* 62(3): 757–89.

[54] See www.lakeresearch.com/news/MoneyPolitics.publicpresentation.pdf (accessed 1/4/15).

[55] Lydia Saad. 2007. "Americans Prefer Presidential Candidates to Forgo Public Funding." *Gallup*, April 27. www.gallup.com/poll/27394/Americans-Prefer-Presidential-Candidates-Forgo-Public-Funding.aspx (accessed 1/4/15).

are funded by the government and all contributions from individual and private groups are banned." The public's reluctance to embrace public financing wholeheartedly reflects their ambivalence about using government money—in other words, their taxes—to fund campaigns.

It is actually not clear that the public pays much attention to how candidates finance their campaigns. In an October 2008 Gallup poll, about 70 percent of voters either did not know whether Barack Obama and John McCain had accepted public financing or were mistaken in their view.[56] Little had changed four years later. Despite record spending by outside groups in 2012, only 25 percent of Americans said that they had heard "a lot" about "increased spending in this year's presidential election by outside groups."[57] More generally, the public typically considers campaign finance reform far less important than the economy, foreign affairs and war, health care, education, and a host of other issues. Indeed, the legislation that became BCRA languished for years until a major scandal involving the energy company Enron—which had developed a close relationship with many elected politicians even as it was covering up financial problems that would eventually lead to bankruptcy—prompted action.

Without a significant push from the public, incumbent leaders are often reluctant to embrace reform. This is entirely rational: they were elected under the status quo. Changing the rules introduces uncertainty into their bids for reelection. Incumbent leaders are especially nervous about public financing because they often believe it will help their opponents to be more competitive—and, of course, this is precisely the outcome desired by some proponents of public financing. The point is not who is wrong or right. The point is that the implications of campaign finance rules for elected leaders often mean that their best strategy is not to change the rules.

Conclusion

Debates about the efficacy of the current system of campaign finance laws in the United States reinforce the important connections among rules, reality, strategy, and citizens. The American system is unusual among democracies

---

[56] Jeffry M. Jones. 2008. "Campaign Financing Appears to Be Non-issue for Voters." *Gallup*, October 30. www.gallup.com/poll/111652/Campaign-Financing-Appears-NonIssue -Voters.aspx (accessed 1/4/15).

[57] The source is a July 2012 *Washington Post* poll: www.washingtonpost.com/politics /polling/americans-unfamiliar-outside-campaign-spending/2012/08/02/gJQA9lWLRX _page.html (accessed 1/4/15).

in that candidates and other actors have been given a wide degree of latitude with respect to what they can say, when they can say it, and how they pay for it. Recent changes in campaign finance law have increased the amount of money in federal election campaigns, mostly by allowing interest groups to solicit and spend funds more freely. Some observers have gone so far as to suggest that trying to keep money out of politics is like trying to keep ants out of a kitchen: plugging one hole will only lead the ants to find another as long as there is any sugar around. Nevertheless, proponents of campaign finance reform seek to plug as many holes as possible, even as others defend the current system and do not mourn the failures of regulation. This again highlights the fact that campaign finance rules reflect a fundamental philosophical trade-off between free speech, on the one hand, and the potentially corrupting influence of money, on the other.

KEY TERMS

public funding (p. 82)

Tillman Act (p. 87)

political action committee (PAC) (p. 87)

Federal Election Campaign Act (FECA) (p. 89)

Federal Election Commission (FEC) (p. 89)

Bipartisan Campaign Reform Act (BCRA) (p. 89)

soft money (p. 91)

hard money (p. 91)

express advocacy (p. 91)

magic words (p. 91)

issue advocacy (p. 92)

independent expenditure committees (p. 94)

super PACs (p. 94)

527 organization (p. 95)

501(c) organizations (p. 95)

Buckley v. Valeo (p. 98)

clean elections systems (p. 100)

Citizens United v. Federal Election Commission (p. 101)

FOR DISCUSSION

1. According to Supreme Court decisions about campaign finance, why are contributions to candidates limited while spending by candidate is unlimited?

2. What are the costs and benefits to a candidate of funding their campaign via: (a) money raised from private donors; (b) public funding; and (c) their own money?

3. How did BCRA and the *Citizens United* decision affect the ways in which political parties and interest groups can raise and spend money in elections?

4. What are reasons for and against the argument that money corrupts politicians?

CHAPTER 5

Modern Campaign Strategies

In the summer of 1988, Vice President George H. W. Bush trailed the Democratic nominee, Michael Dukakis, by 16 points in the polls. Prior to the Republican Party's August convention, Bush's campaign team convened to discuss the latest polling results. Bob Teeter, Bush's pollster, gave a lengthy description of the mood of the country, including the public's issue priorities and positions, but stalled and stammered when he came to public perceptions of Bush's personal characteristics. He tried, as best he could, to suggest that the vice president was not perceived as being "very forceful." Bush blanched at this, pointing out his service in World War II, his stint as director of the CIA, and his time as ambassador to China. Teeter tried to explain that the public had a more general impression, one rooted in a "gut reaction." This reaction had to be corrected if Bush were to escape from the shadow of President Reagan and win the White House. Bush pushed Teeter on the specifics behind the numbers; Teeter hemmed and hawed, unsure how to explain the problem without offending the vice president. Finally, James A. Baker III, a Bush confidant, intervened: "What Bob is telling you, George, is that the people think you're a pussy, and we need to turn you into a prick."[1]

This example demonstrates in coarse but effective terms that the basis of a good campaign strategy is, first, to recognize the reality of the campaign, or the broader context in which the campaign is being run. The next step is to set an appropriate goal that, if achieved, will win the election. The beauty of the Baker quote is its simplicity: George H. W. Bush's main problem in 1988, the reason he was lagging behind Democratic challenger Michael Dukakis, was that Americans did not think Bush was strong enough to lead the country. The campaign (and its candidate) needed to recognize this and take bold steps to change perceptions of Bush. They did this by having Bush aggressively contrast his positions on crime and defense with Dukakis's. Both the style and substance of Bush's speeches and advertisements sought to portray him as tough — tough on criminals, tough

---

[1] Story related to Daron Shaw by someone present at the August 1988 meeting.

on enemies of the United States, and tough on his Democratic opponent. In the end, Bush swayed a sufficient number of independents — 64 percent of whom supported him — to win the White House.[2] His "tough guy" strategy may not have won him the race, but it is difficult to see how he would have won had his campaign not dealt with what many analysts called "the wimp factor."

The goal of this chapter is to describe and consider the role of strategy (and strategists) in American political campaigns. We begin by defining strategy and discussing how a modern campaign develops a strategy. Next, we outline the important strategic decisions of a campaign, examining both professional practice and academic research. Among other things, we argue that campaigns are selective with respect to what they say and who they say it to. Some voters are critical to victory and they receive most of the campaign's attention. The skill with which a campaign identifies and convinces these voters can be important for the outcome of the election. We then examine what a campaign looks like, how it is organized, and the role of political consultants. Finally, we discuss the normative implications of the rise of more professionalized, strategic campaigns.

Core of the Analysis

- A campaign must develop a strategy in order to compete effectively in a competitive district or state.
- Campaigns try to mobilize supporters and persuade undecided voters.
- Campaign strategy involves decisions about whether to run, which issues to emphasize, what positions to take on issues, whether to attack the opposition, and how to allocate resources to different constituencies and media.
- These strategic decisions depend strongly on the broader rules and realities that candidates confront.
- Campaign organizations have general features in common but vary considerably depending on the size and scope of the campaign.
- Modern political campaigns rely on professionals to devise and execute their strategies, and to organize their campaigns.

---

[2] This figure is based on results from the 1988 American National Election Study, www.electionstudies.org/nesguide/2ndtable/t9a_1_2.htm (accessed 12/10/10).

How Are Campaign Strategies Constructed?

Assuming a candidate has decided to run—a decision we will consider in greater detail later in this chapter—there are many tasks the campaign must address immediately. The campaign needs a physical space for a headquarters, so that people have a place to work. The candidate has to announce his or her candidacy. There are people who must be contacted, including past candidates and party leaders, whose expertise, advice, and endorsement are all potentially valuable. The campaign needs to identify the main issues the candidate intends to run on and prepare position papers. Finally, the campaign must purchase some of the staples of the modern campaign: computers, computer servers, Wi-Fi and Internet connections, smart phones, and materials for brochures, bumper stickers, buttons, and pamphlets.

But perhaps more than anything else, a campaign needs to quickly develop a **campaign strategy**. Put simply, a strategy is a proposed pathway to victory. It is a plan for how to win, and it is driven by an understanding of who will vote for the candidate and why they will do so. The political scientist Joel Bradshaw posits four key propositions for developing a successful campaign strategy.[3] First, in any election the electorate can be divided into three groups: the candidate's base, the opponent's base, and the undecided. Second, past election results and survey research make it possible to determine which people fall into each of these three groups. Third, it is neither possible nor necessary to get the support of all people everywhere to win the election. Research should allow a campaign to determine how best to mobilize the candidate's base and persuade the undecideds. Both mobilization and persuasion are central to a campaign's efforts. Fourth, and last, once a campaign has identified how to win, it can act to create the circumstances to bring about this victory. In order to succeed, campaigns should direct campaign resources—money, time, and message—to key groups of potential voters and nowhere else. Resource allocation is therefore defined by strategy.

Vote Targets

Implicit in these propositions is the need to develop specific **vote targets** (or vote goals). These targets are based on estimates of what the upcoming election will look like: how many total votes the campaign believes will be cast

---

[3] Joel Bradshaw. 2004. "Campaign Strategy," in *Campaigns and Elections American Style*, 2nd ed., eds. James A. Thurber and Candice J. Nelson. Boulder, CO: Westview Press: 38–40.

in the election, how many it will need to win, how many votes its candidate can expect no matter what, and how many **persuadable** (or **swing**) **votes** are out there.

Campaigns typically derive vote targets by examining data from recent comparable elections. For example, let us say that our candidate is running for governor in a general election in Ohio. The simplest way to develop an estimate for the total votes to be cast in the upcoming election is to look across the most recent gubernatorial elections (see Table 5.1).

Notice that we are not looking at turnout in presidential years, which is invariably higher than in midterm elections; we only want to look at data from comparable elections. Notice also that the Ohio turnout rate varies a bit from year to year, from a low of about 47 percent in 2002 to a high of about 53 percent in 2006. The number of registered voters, however, appears to increase every year. It increased by 746,226 from 2002 to 2006, and by 177,754 from 2006 to 2010. For the 2014 election, it is reasonable to assume that (1) turnout will be about 50 percent of registered voters, and (2) the number of registered voters will be greater than 8,037,806. In a real election campaign, we would be able to access updated registration numbers from the Ohio secretary of state. For illustrative purposes, though, let us assume that registration will increase by approximately 200,000 for our election. That gives us 8,237,806 registered voters. If we assume that 50 percent of those who are registered vote in the governor's race, the total number of votes cast will be about 4,118,903.

So how many votes do we need to win? This depends, of course, on the number of candidates in the race. If it is simply a contest between major party

TABLE 5.1	**Turnout in Ohio Gubernatorial Elections, 2002–10**		
Year	Registered Voters	Total Votes	Turnout Rate
2002	7,113,826	3,356,285	47%
2006	7,860,052	4,185,597	53%
2010	8,037,806	3,956,045	49%
Average	**7,670,561**	**3,832,642**	**50%**

Source: Ohio Secretary of State, Elections and Ballot Issues.

candidates—Republican versus Democrat—our candidate will need slightly more than 50 percent of the vote. If there are minor party or independent candidates, a candidate could conceivably win with less than 50 percent (a plurality, but not a majority). But let us assume that we have a two-party election on our hands. A bare majority (50.1 percent) of our expected electorate would be 2,063,570. Most campaigns round up when estimating a vote target because they want to avoid a situation where they meet their vote target but lose the election because of unexpectedly high turnout. So let us be very cautious and say our target is 2.2 million votes.

Next, our campaign should have an expectation about what our candidate's base vote is. In other words, how many votes would a "bad" candidate from the party get in an election in which conditions favored the other side? Again, most campaign strategists turn to past results to estimate this (Table 5.2).

Consider things from the perspective of the Republican candidate. The election results vary a great deal—from a Republican high of almost 58 percent in 2002 to a low of just under 37 percent in 2006. In many ways, 2006 was a low-water mark for the Republican Party, both in Ohio and across the nation. Republican president George W. Bush was deeply unpopular, a controversial war was dragging on in Iraq, and the economy was beginning to show signs of recession. Moreover, in Ohio, the Republican gubernatorial candidate, Ken Blackwell, was widely regarded as having run an especially inept campaign. Thus, we can take the 2006 result as an estimate of the Republican base vote, the minimum that a Republican candidate can expect to win. If we use the figure of 37 percent of the expected turnout, our estimate of the Republican base vote is 1,523,994.

TABLE 5.2 Votes Won in Ohio Governor Elections, 2002–10			
Year	Republican Candidate	Democratic Candidate	Other Candidates	Republican Candidate's Percentage
2002	1,865,007	1,236,924	126,977	58%
2006	1,474,331	2,435,505	113,019	37%
2010	1,889,186	1,812,059	156,224	49%

Source: Ohio Secretary of State, Elections and Ballot Issues

To generate an estimate of the persuadable vote, we need an upper estimate of what a candidate from our party can achieve. In other words, how many votes would a "good" Republican candidate get in an election in which conditions favored the Republican Party? The 2002 election provides just such an example. The public rallied behind President Bush and the Republicans after the terrorist attacks of 9/11 and when the economy seemed to be slowly emerging from the recession of 2000–2001. Furthermore, the Republican gubernatorial candidate Robert Taft was a popular figure from a legendary Ohio political family. Let us therefore take his 58 percent result as an estimate of the high end for a Republican candidate. The difference between these extremes is 58 minus 37 percent, or 21 percent. So our estimate of the persuadable vote for our upcoming Ohio governor's race is 21 percent of the total expected vote of 4.1 million, or approximately 865,000 voters.

This last estimate is critical. To recap, we assume that approximately 4.1 million voters will cast ballots in the Ohio governor's election in 2014. We have a vote target of 2.2 million, and we estimate that our base vote is slightly over 1.5 million voters. The swing vote in the state is 865,000. To get from our base (1.5 million) to our target (2.2 million), we need to win 700,000 of the 865,000 swing votes (81 percent). It is important to observe that while this is how many campaigns estimate the number of swing voters, it does not translate into individual "targets"—that is, we have an idea about how many voters can be swayed, but we do not know which individuals are most likely to be persuaded to vote for our candidate (more on this later).

We can also generate vote targets for each county in the state based on previous election results—for example, we might use the three most recent elections to calculate the average contribution of each county to the total statewide party vote (Table 5.3). For example, take Cuyahoga County, where the city of Cleveland is located. It contributed, on average, 7.6 percent of the total Republican vote in Ohio in the past three elections. For the 2014 election, we would multiply this number by the total statewide vote target (2.2 million) to generate a target for Cuyahoga of 167,204 Republican votes. This can be done for every county and even the precincts within a county.

Profiling Vote Targets

How can the campaign hope to win over the swing voters it needs to meet its target? First and foremost, the campaign must identify who these voters are. Campaigns typically use surveys and, to a lesser degree, focus groups to do this. Initially, the campaign will conduct surveys to ascertain what sorts

TABLE 5.3 **Election Results and Vote Targets for Selected Ohio Counties (Republican Candidates)**

County	2010 Kasich Votes	2006 Blackwell Votes	2002 Taft Votes	Average Contribution to Republican Vote Total	Vote Target for 2014 Election (based on a statewide target of 2.2 million)
Cuyahoga	148,611	107,258	142,874	7.6%	167,204
Franklin	169,487	122,601	156,712	8.6%	188,395
Hamilton	143,222	141,374	160,223	8.6%	188,918
Montgomery	89,218	76,189	95,891	5.0%	110,235
Statewide	1,889,186	1,474,331	1,865,007	—	2,200,000

Source: Ohio Secretary of State, Elections and Ballot Issues.

of people are persuadable. Almost all campaign surveys are **probability samples**, in which some number of individuals from a certain population are randomly selected and asked a set of questions. The key to a probability sample is that every individual in the population of interest has a known probability of being selected. Because selection is random, a small number of completed interviews (usually between 400 and 1,000) reveal the general opinions held throughout the population, with a known and relatively small (or at least acceptable) margin of error. In much the same way a doctor can make inferences about your health based on a small sample of your blood, we can make inferences about public opinion based on a small sample of randomly chosen citizens.

Thinking back to our governor's race, a survey (or poll) can thus be used to ask registered voters in Ohio whom they intend to vote for in the upcoming election. For those people with a preference, we can also ask how strongly they prefer their candidate. A survey allows us not only to identify how many people are currently undecided or might be moved from their current preference but also to see if persuadable voters are more common among certain groups, such as women, young people, or Latinos. In addition, we can examine the issue preferences of persuadable voters to develop a plan for winning them over.

Once surveys have been analyzed, many campaigns conduct in-depth interviews with small groups of persuadable voters to gather additional data and test specific issue positions. These are called **focus groups**. They have been a part of political campaigns since the mid-1980s, when campaign consultants noticed that businesses were using them to enhance their understanding of client preferences. They range in size between 8 and 20 participants, and are led by a "facilitator" whose job is to pose questions and encourage full participation from all members. Focus groups differ from polls in that participants are not selected randomly. In fact, they are intentionally recruited based on certain characteristics that the campaign associates with persuadable voters (for example, gender, age, or ethnicity). Because of this, focus group participants do not necessarily represent what the larger population thinks; they are simply suggestive of how certain subgroups think about politics and the election. And while focus groups do not provide statistically generalizable information, they provide a depth of information that campaigns often find valuable.

Together, polls and focus groups give a campaign a strong sense of what sorts of voters they need to win over and the kinds of appeals that will most effectively accomplish this. This knowledge can be used to craft stump speeches, position papers and press releases, and television and radio advertisements.

The second step to identifying swing voters involves rating the persuadability of all registered voters in the district. This step involves two major tasks. Both tasks represent large and expensive undertakings, and thus they are typically done only in presidential, gubernatorial, U.S. Senate, and hotly contested U.S. House races. Smaller state and local campaigns, as we discuss in Chapter 11, may rely on cheaper and less sophisticated strategies.

The first task is to acquire a list of registered voters and augment it with demographic information on each voter. As we discussed in Chapter 3, the major political parties have compiled extensive databases on voters, including names, addresses, phone numbers, previous voting history, demographic attributes such as gender or race, and financial and consumer data such as home values.

Then, the campaign uses information from the poll about who is persuadable to determine how open each voter on the list is to appeals from its candidate. In other words, the campaign builds a statistical model of persuadability based on the results of the poll, and then uses this to predict the persuadability of every individual in the voter file. The campaign can then isolate specific voters for mailings, phone calls, or in-person visits, all based on a combination of data from the poll and the voter list. This process, called

microtargeting, was developed in the 2000 and 2002 elections to allow individual-level targeting. Microtargeting avoids the need to make **voter identification (or voter ID) calls**, in which every voter on the voter list is called and asked her preferences for the upcoming race.

It is difficult to microtarget based on a standard campaign poll. A poll of 500 people, for example, will not have a sufficient number of people in certain groups—such as college students—to make reliable inferences about what these groups think. Nor will a standard poll ask enough questions about a respondent's background to take advantage of the information available in voter databases. Thus, microtargeting typically requires a very large poll—say, of 6,000 or more respondents—with additional questions about the respondents' backgrounds and habits. Microtargeting is expensive, but it's much less expensive than a round of statewide voter ID calls.

The Context of Voter Targeting

Targeting voters effectively requires not only polling data and an accurate voter list but also an understanding of the reality associated with the particular election. Perhaps the most important aspect of the reality is whether the candidate is an incumbent. For the incumbent, the election is to some degree a referendum on how things have gone on her watch. Citizens will associate prevailing conditions—the state of the economy, crime rates, traffic flow, and so on—with the incumbent candidate and will reward or punish her accordingly. In this context, it is more difficult to persuade voters; people have seen the incumbent in action and have formed opinions. Conversely, if the candidate is a challenger running against an incumbent, he will try to convince people that the incumbent has done a poor job and that it is time for a change. In addition, the challenger will be less familiar to constituents in the district. People prefer someone they know, and they are more likely to recognize the name of the incumbent than that of the challenger. In sum, when an incumbent is running for reelection, most of the campaign is about defining her record. Targeting is thus constrained by real-life conditions.

If there is no incumbent, the central question remains who will do a better job, but people do not have recent and relevant experience to guide their assessments. Perhaps more to the point, in an **open-seat** race it is much easier to craft a strategy to persuade people to support your candidate. Other factors can come to the fore.

Another important reality is the partisan makeup of the district. As we discussed in Chapter 2, the characteristics of a candidate's constituency affect nearly every dimension of campaign strategy. If 60 percent of voters in the district are Democratic, 20 percent are Republican, and 20 percent describe themselves as independent, the Democratic candidate will likely emphasize traditionally partisan appeals (and will usually win). The Republican candidate will need to win over some independents and Democrats, and is therefore likely to emphasize candidate-related appeals. This was the case in the 2010 U.S. Senate race in Massachusetts between Martha Coakley, a Democrat, and Scott Brown, a Republican, in which Brown pulled off a 52–47 percent upset victory in a heavily Democratic state. He focused on voter anger with the status quo and convinced some Democrats that the race was about something besides traditional party labels.

But consider another district in which 30 percent of voters are Republican, 30 percent are Democratic, and 40 percent describe themselves as independent. Here the campaign will likely target the broad swath of independents. This was the case in the Nevada U.S. Senate race in 2010, where the incumbent Democrat, Harry Reid, defeated the Republican challenger, Sharron Angle. Angle's ties to the Tea Party movement and her unorthodox views on several issues helped Reid paint her as an extremist. He won 57 percent of independents en route to a surprisingly easy win.

In a special election for the U.S. Senate in January 2010, Republican Scott Brown defeated Democrat Martha Coakley in heavily Democratic Massachusetts. In addition to turning out Republicans, Brown targeted independents and moderate Democrats by focusing on his personal traits and pragmatic approach.

Although both state and national factors matter, they are not all-powerful. For example, Brown (a Republican) won in arguably the most Democratic of states. Reid (a Democrat) won in a year when Republicans swept the House and almost took the Senate. The dominance of the Democratic Party in Massachusetts and the sour national mood in 2010 (both of which contribute to what we refer to as the political "reality" of a given election) shaped their respective campaign strategies, but both campaigns were able to target and mobilize electoral majorities.

Strategic Campaign Decisions

Thus far, we have emphasized the nature of strategy but have said little about how it influences the specific decisions that face every political campaign. We now examine a range of strategic decisions that face most campaigns, paying particular mind to the similarities and differences between campaign professionals and political scientists in how they think about these decisions.

The Decision to Run

We are so used to thinking about who wins and loses elections that sometimes we forget an important prior question: who decides to run for office in the first place? Elections are significantly shaped by who chooses to run and who sits things out. For example, in 1992, New York governor Mario Cuomo's decision not to run for president opened the door to Arkansas governor Bill Clinton. In 1996, General Colin Powell's decision not to run all but assured Kansas senator Bob Dole of the nomination. In 2004, former vice president Al Gore decided not to run, enhancing the prospects for Massachusetts senator John Kerry. In 2008, Vice President Dick Cheney and former Virginia governor George Allen never considered running for president, helping to make Arizona senator John McCain a front-runner. In 2016, Hillary Clinton's decision to run for president will have a major effect on who chooses to run on the Democratic side as well as on the substance of both the primary and general election campaigns. The effect of these decisions—while most obvious at the presidential level—is felt in races at all levels.

Political consultants and political scientists have similar views about what drives the decision to run. When thinking about whether to run for office, there are several important factors for a candidate and her advisers to consider. One is *motivation*. Does the candidate want to run for office, or is she being dragged reluctantly into the fray? While we tend to think of politicians as uniformly ambitious, many are ambivalent about moving up the political ladder. For example, an incumbent might prefer his current position to running for higher office and potentially losing. If local and statewide offices are prestigious and attractive, fewer talented politicians will want to seek higher office.[4] A concrete example of ambivalence comes from the 2008 presidential campaign. After the election was over, the campaign manager for Representative Ron Paul, a candidate for the Republican nomination, said of Paul, "We couldn't get him for six months to say that he wanted to be president."[5] For candidates who do want to run, it is also important to understand the reasons that they want to run. Their motivations—duty to country, particular policy goals, and so on—will help inform strategic campaign decisions.

In gauging motivation, it is also important to know how the candidate's family feels about her candidacy. For example, does she have a spouse who is willing to assist and endure the campaign? Does she have children? Is she willing to move the family around and use them in the campaign? Maybe more to the point, is the candidate willing to endure the potentially embarrassing scrutiny of her immediate and extended family? And does she have secrets that she would like to keep from her family? A concern about separation from his children was one thing that made Barack Obama hesitate before declaring his candidacy in 2008. One of his advisers, David Plouffe, told an audience after the campaign, "He's got young kids and he's very close to them. That was really the biggest hurdle—could he reconcile his desire to see his family a lot?"[6]

A second factor to consider is *resources*. Perhaps the most important question here is whether the candidate can raise money. As we discussed in Chapter 4, the American system of campaign finance puts the onus of fund-raising on the candidate, and little can be accomplished without money on hand. Besides money, other resources that affect a candidate's decision to run include credentials (has the potential candidate held an office that gives her relevant experience?) and time (can she take time off work and away from her family to campaign effectively?).

A third factor is whether the candidate can assemble a campaign organization. Does she have an experienced, enthusiastic staff? Is there adequate outside help available, or have the best pollsters, consultants, media people, and field organizers already committed to other campaigns? Modern-day

---

[4] Cherie Maestas, Sarah A. Fulton, L. Sandy Maisel, and Walter J. Stone. 2006. "When to Risk It? Institutions, Ambitions, and the Decision to Run for the U.S. House." *American Political Science Review* 100: 195–208.

[5] Institute of Politics. 2009. *Campaign for President: The Managers Look at 2008.* New York: Rowman & Littlefield, p. 22.

[6] Institute of Politics, 2009, p. 29.

campaign organizations often look like small armies. It is ideal to put an organization in place at the beginning of the campaign.

A final factor for a candidate and advisers to consider in deciding whether to run is the *opportunity* (or lack thereof) presented in the election. Opportunities derive from the realities that candidates face at a particular time and place. Opportunities are crucial because they often determine *when* a candidate will run, as opposed to whether she has a general inclination to run. Smart candidates will wait until the odds are in their favor. The probability of winning is especially affected by the realities of the election. What is the makeup of the electorate? For example, would the candidate be willing to run when the electorate is primarily composed of members of the opposite party? And what is the nature of the competition? Will the candidate face a competitive primary challenger? Will she face a competitive general election opponent? What are the resources that the opponents have? What about conditions in the country? How is the economy doing? How popular is the incumbent president? All of these things may influence whether the candidate feels she can win.

The role of opportunity suggests that candidates can be thought of as "strategic politicians."[7] In some ways, potential candidates are rational actors looking to maximize the chances that they will win. Given the costs of running, and the potential damage to their reputation if they run and lose, they are unlikely to run unless they believe there is a significant chance they will win. Thus, strategic politicians rarely challenge dominant incumbents, rarely run in a district where they are outnumbered by partisans from the other side, and rarely run if the prevailing national mood is against their party.[8] Conversely, they look for races where the incumbent is retiring or weak. They tend to run in districts where most voters share their party affiliation. They tend to run if there is a national tide favoring their party. This mentality creates something of a self-fulfilling prophecy: strategic politicians rarely run unless they calculate favorable odds, so incumbents almost never face tough competition unless other factors are decidedly against them. To

---

[7] Gary C. Jacobson and Samuel Kernell. 1983. *Strategy and Choice in Congressional Elections*. New Haven, CT: Yale University Press.

[8] Candidates will occasionally run for office even though their prospects are not good. Sometimes they run because the upside of victory is enough to offset the downside of a loss. Long-shot presidential candidates fall into this category. At other times, candidates run in order to lay the groundwork for a later run for office. For example, up-and-coming Texas Republican Ted Cruz (the former solicitor general) challenged the much-better-known and well-financed Lieutenant Governor David Dewhurst for the 2012 GOP Senate nomination, possibly calculating that even a losing effort could enhance his status with the public and fund-raisers. (Cruz won the primary and general elections.)

be sure, not every candidate will appear rational. There are plenty of quixotic campaigns being waged every election year. But there are still strong incentives for politicians to think strategically about the decision to run.

Political science research on the decision to run suggests that three of these factors—motivation, resources, and opportunity—matter simultaneously. A good example comes from the research of Jennifer Lawless and Richard Fox on why so few women hold elective office, relative to their share of the population. This research has shown that, although women candidates are as likely as male candidates to win elections, they are less likely than men to run in the first place. In part, this is a question of motivation. Women report less enthusiasm for the rigors of campaigning, such as fund-raising. They also seem to perceive themselves as lacking in resources. One such resource is their credentials: women are less likely than men to see themselves as qualified. Another resource is time: even women who are employed full time in high-status professions, such as law or business, report spending more time on household tasks and child care than do men in similar professions. Finally, they see fewer opportunities. Relative to men, they are more likely to believe that elections in their community are competitive, that raising money will be difficult, and that female candidates are less likely to win.[9]

Issue Priorities

Perhaps the most obvious strategic question of a campaign involves issues. Which issues should a candidate emphasize? Candidates select issues for their campaign agenda with care and then seek to emphasize only those issues—"staying on message," as the saying goes. Choosing issue priorities is a critical strategic decision because candidates want to control the campaign agenda wherever possible. Some issues will work to a candidate's advantage, and some will not. A candidate who keeps the focus on issues where the public favors her policy positions may win over persuadable voters and perhaps win the election. For example, in the 2008 presidential election Barack Obama wanted to focus attention on the economy, health care, and the Bush administration's handling of Iraq, while John McCain wanted to focus on national security, taxes, and limiting government. In some ways, the main fight in the campaign was more about the agenda than specific proposals. Once most Americans decided the election was a referendum on the state of the economy, Obama (arguably) had won.

---

[9] Jennifer Lawless and Richard Fox. 2005. *It Takes a Candidate: Why Women Don't Run for Office.* New York: Cambridge University Press.

Campaign consultants also believe strongly in the importance of agenda control. Many of them assume that citizens do not care much about politics and only pay attention to the "loudest" moments of the campaign. Thus, while citizens' perceptions are malleable, candidates only have a couple of shots at telling them what the election is about. The result is that campaigns focus on one or two issues, **framing** (or presenting) them in simple, easy-to-understand terms. Each side attempts to define what matters.

Why might candidates choose some issues and not others? Here, the reality that candidates confront is crucial. Events outside of their control put certain issues on the agenda, leading the public to prioritize those issues and leaving candidates little choice but to address them. In the 2004 presidential election, John Kerry and George W. Bush both felt compelled to talk about terrorism because of the terrorist attacks of September 11, 2001, and the ongoing war in Iraq. In the 2012 presidential election, both Obama and Mitt Romney talked a great deal about the economy. The issue was nettlesome for both sides, as Obama had been unable to turn the economy around in his first term, while many still blamed Romney's Republican Party for the collapse of 2008. Still, when certain issues become national priorities, as the economy did in 2012, it is common to see opposing candidates with similar agendas.

Candidates also base their agendas on the traditional strengths of their parties. In Chapter 1, we noted that the reputation a political party has developed for attention to a particular issue gives that party greater credibility on the issue. This example of a reality of campaigns and elections is known as **issue ownership**, a term that suggests that parties come to "own" issues because of their reputations.[10] Observers would typically say that the Republican Party owns the issues of national security, taxes, and crime, while the Democratic Party owns health care, education, and entitlement programs like Social Security and Medicare.

If candidates emphasized only the issues their party owns, then we would expect to see them talking past each other, rather than engaging one another on the issues. In reality, although candidates sometimes put greater emphasis on their party's "owned" issues, they often talk about all sorts of other issues, even those "belonging to" the other party.[11] In part, this is because national events demand it. Also, strategic candidates may be able to frame

---

[10] John R. Petrocik. 1996. "Issue Ownership in Presidential Elections, with a 1980 Case Study." *American Journal of Political Science* 40: 825–50.

[11] John Sides. 2006. "The Origins of Campaign Agendas." *British Journal of Political Science* 36, 3: 407–36.

any issue in a way that is favorable to them. In the 1996 presidential election, Democrat Bill Clinton discussed the issue of crime, which had been traditionally seen as an area where the Republican Party had an advantage, by emphasizing prevention strategies, such as community policing, rather than punishment strategies, such as longer prison sentences.[12]

Campaign agendas are also influenced by the candidate's own personal experiences and reputation. Regardless of the reputation of their party, candidates often develop areas of policy interest, expertise, and accomplishments. They can talk credibly about these issues by highlighting their own achievements. For example, in the 2000 presidential election, George W. Bush emphasized education a great deal, even though this was supposedly an issue owned by the Democratic Party. As governor of Texas, he had worked to improve primary and secondary education, and he believed that the state's progress gave him the credibility he needed to "trespass" on the Democrats' territory. Although personal experience can matter, candidates do discuss many issues with which they have limited expertise or experience. This again suggests that candidates are confident that they can frame issues in favorable ways, no matter what the reality is.

Issue Positions

While formulating their agendas, candidates also have to determine what positions they should take on these issues. In doing so, they face a choice: Should they simply take a position that is popular with citizens, or should they seek to persuade citizens to adopt their own point of view?

The logic of taking popular positions can be explained using the **median voter theorem**.[13] This theorem assumes that voters can be arrayed on a spectrum that captures the range of positions on a particular issue — from, say, liberal to conservative. Candidates seek to position themselves on that spectrum nearest to the hypothetical voter who would provide the winning vote for them: the median voter. The median voter is the person who falls in the exact middle of the spectrum. That is, half of all voters are more liberal than this hypothetical person and half are more conservative. The candidate who wins the median voter, as well as all of those voters who are on the same side as the candidate, wins the election.

---

[12] David B. Holian. 2004. "He's Stealing My Issues! Clinton's Crime Rhetoric and the Dynamics of Issue Ownership." *Journal of Politics* 26: 95–124.

[13] Anthony Downs. 1957. *An Economic Theory of Democracy.* New York: Harper & Row; Harold Hotelling. 1929. "Stability in Competition." *Economic Journal* 39, 153: 41–57.

A diagram may help to illustrate. The bell-shaped curve in Figure 5.1 represents how many voters are positioned at each point along this spectrum, arrayed from left ("L") to right ("R"). The median voter is labeled "M." The two candidates are labeled "A" and "B." Currently, Candidate A appeals to more voters than Candidate B because he is closer to the median voter M. Both candidates could improve their support by adopting policy positions that move them closer to M.

The median voter theorem may seem too abstract to guide campaign strategy. After all, campaigns want to appeal to real voters, not some hypothetical median voter. However, the basic logic of the median voter theorem is quite evident in how campaign professionals and political commentators think about campaigns. For example, we often hear about candidates who are "moving to the center," with the presumption that this enables them to appeal to more "moderate" or "independent" or "swing" voters whose support would allow them to win the election.

There are several reasons that the prediction of the median voter theorem might not hold true. For one, candidates are constrained in the positions they take. If moving toward the median voter means contradicting some previous position, then the candidate may damage his credibility and risk earning a label like "flip-flopper"—as with John Kerry in 2004 and Mitt Romney in 2012.

Candidates also have different constituencies to appeal to, with views that often differ from those of the hypothetical median voter. Candidates must raise money by appealing to donors, recruit volunteers by appealing to activists, and earn endorsements by appealing to interest groups. Donors, activists, and interest groups tend to have very strong opinions about

FIGURE 5.1 The Median Voter Theorem

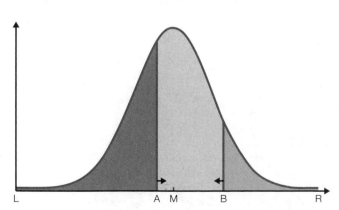

political issues—opinions that are often more ideologically extreme than those of the average citizen. Taking moderate positions on issues may have more costs than benefits if it alienates ideologically driven supporters.

The challenge of appealing to multiple constituencies with different opinions may lead candidates to avoid specific positions on issues. In Chapter 3, we noted that American campaigns have often centered on biography and personality, offering only vague platitudes about political issues. There may be advantages for candidates in this, even though it seems counter to the conventional wisdom that candidates must take clear stands on the issues. Keeping their positions vague allows candidates to say things that are unobjectionable and popular—"I want to save Social Security" or "Our children need a good education." Various constituencies may interpret such statements as endorsing their particular positions, even when candidates have not done so explicitly. Candidates who take vague positions also provide less for the media and opposing candidates to pick apart. Studies of campaigns find that ambiguity is common and that, consequently, citizens often do not know candidates' positions on specific issues.[14]

This lack of knowledge among citizens points to one final problem with the median voter theorem: it assumes that citizens know where they stand on issues, know where the candidates stand, and vote accordingly. But as we noted earlier, there is reason to suppose that the average citizen is not that attentive to the campaign or to politics generally. Certainly many campaign professionals believe this, and much political science research supports this view. In Chapter 13, we discuss the assumption of the median voter theorem, as well as the strategies by which voters choose candidates, in more detail.

If the average citizen does not assess the candidates based on their issue positions, then candidates may be empowered to pursue another strategy: attempting to persuade voters to support their positions on issues. Whether candidates can do so speaks to a more general question: the ability of campaigns to affect what citizens think. Just as candidates attempt to frame the election around particular issues, they would like to persuade citizens to adopt their positions on those issues. In Chapter 13, we discuss at greater length how successfully candidates can do this. As we will see, campaign consultants and political scientists come to somewhat different conclusions on this question, with political scientists more skeptical than campaign consultants about how much candidates can change public opinion.

---

[14] Benjamin Page. 1978. *Choices and Echoes in Presidential Campaigns.* Chicago: University of Chicago Press.

Whether to Attack

Few things attract more attention during campaigns than attacks, which may come from candidates, parties, interest groups, and others. Despite the apparent proliferation of attacks, whether to campaign negatively—or "go negative"—is a complex decision that is largely contingent upon the reality of the race.

Negative campaigning can be defined simply as any criticism leveled by supporters of one candidate against the opposing candidate.[15] By contrast, **positive campaigning** (sometimes called *advocacy*) focuses only on the background, record, and views of the sponsoring candidate. Of course, campaigns are not limited to one or the other. A campaign message or advertisement may mix positive and negative information. Such advertisements, sometimes called **contrast advertisements**, focus on the differences—in qualifications, record, or issue positions—of the main candidates in the race.

Campaigns make decisions about other specific aspects of a negative message. One aspect is a campaign's content: Should the negative ads criticize a candidate for her stand on issues that concern voters, or for her personal qualities? Another aspect is civility: Should a negative campaign be critical but respectful, or is it useful to be ugly or mean-spirited? However, in this discussion, we simply focus on the general question of whether to campaign negatively, and not on specific questions about how to do so.

According to some political scientists and many campaign practitioners, the main factor affecting whether to attack is the political reality surrounding the race—in particular, which candidate is the front-runner and which the underdog. The candidate who is ahead in the polls is less likely to attack than the candidate who is behind. This finding emerges in both academic research and in a survey of campaign consultants.[16] For this reason, incumbents are less likely to attack than their opposition. Only if support for the opposing candidate appears to be increasing would an incumbent seek to define him via negative campaigning. For example, an incumbent with a lot of political baggage who is facing a well-financed, impressive challenger may wish to go negative before the challenger begins campaigning in earnest. This happened in the 2010 Senate race in Nevada, when the incumbent, Harry Reid, aired early **attack ads** against the challenger, Sharron Angle. Little-known

---

[15] John G. Geer. 2006. *In Defense of Negativity: Attack Ads in Presidential Campaigns.* Chicago: University of Chicago Press, p. 23.

[16] Stergios Skaperdas and Bernard Grofman. 1995. "Modeling Negative Campaigning." *American Political Science Review* 89: 49–61; John Theilman and Allen Wilhite. 1998. "Campaign Tactics and the Decision to Attack." *Journal of Politics* 60, 4: 1050–62.

challengers, or any candidates lagging in the race, may feel they need to attack. Many challengers are not well known in their districts. Yet challengers run little risk of further increasing the incumbent's name recognition advantage by airing negative ads because incumbents are already well known in their districts. Moreover, attacking the incumbent raises doubts about his fitness for office and can open the door for a challenger. Attacks on the incumbent are also more likely than positive campaign messages to draw news media coverage.[17]

Although it seems like common sense to advise front-runners to stay positive and underdogs to go negative, large-scale studies of campaign messages and advertisements in American presidential elections suggest that front-runners and underdogs do not always follow this advice.[18] Sometimes incumbents run campaigns that are more negative than the challengers'. Indeed, it is not uncommon for candidates well ahead in the polls to pound away on the underdog. In the 1964 election, Democrat Lyndon Johnson had a commanding lead throughout the campaign, but still relentlessly attacked the Republican candidate, Barry Goldwater.

There's another potential issue with negative campaigning: it may not actually win votes. As we will see in Chapters 12 and 13, it is far from certain that negative advertising affects whether citizens vote or for whom they vote. Ultimately, there is enough uncertainty with regard to who should go negative and to what extent negative campaigning affects voters to produce a wide range of professional opinion on the matter.

Where to Campaign

Whether a candidate is running for president or for city council, the decision about where to deploy precious campaign resources is always hotly debated. Should the presidential candidate go to Florida or to Ohio for that last-minute campaign stop? Should the city council candidate have greeted voters entering the polls in Precinct 1 or in Precinct 4? The assumption shared by consultants and scholars is that a campaign's resources must be allocated strategically to achieve maximum effect.

After George W. Bush's reelection in 2004, campaign consultants began to refer to his model of campaigning as the **Bush model**, in contrast to the

---

[17] Travis N. Ridout and Glen R. Smith. 2008. "Free Advertising: How the Media Amplify Campaign Messages." *Political Research Quarterly* 61, 4: 598–608.

[18] Geer, *In Defense of Negativity*; Emmett H. Buell, Jr., and Lee Sigelman. 2009. *Attack Politics: Negativity in Presidential Campaigns since 1960*, 2nd ed. Lawrence: University of Kansas Press.

Clinton model of former president Bill Clinton.[19] The Bush model focuses on mobilizing partisans. In the 2004 presidential election, Bush's campaign worked exceptionally hard to identify and reach out to Bush supporters in places like the Florida panhandle and southern Ohio. These people, the Bush team assumed, would probably vote for Bush if they could be persuaded to turn out. Much of the campaign was therefore targeted at supportive areas where turnout and enthusiasm lagged.

By contrast, the Clinton model focuses on persuading independent and weakly partisan voters. Prior to the 1996 presidential election, Clinton's team developed a series of issue positions that were tailored to the sensibilities of these voters. These were not necessarily the "big" issues of the day, but rather a series of minor but symbolically important concerns, such as school uniforms to combat gang activities and additional federal funding for municipal police. These issues and positions were then communicated in an extensive television advertising campaign during the summer of 1995 that targeted top media markets with large numbers of independent voters.

The relative efficacy of the Bush and Clinton models may depend on context. A political newcomer, like Barack Obama in 2008, has a chance to reach out to independents and weakly partisan voters and convince them to support his candidacy. A more established candidate, conversely, may have a record that limits her "flexibility" when it comes to winning over independent voters, but could target and mobilize core supporters. Incumbent candidates, especially those in the more polarized context of today's politics, are therefore more likely to embrace the Bush model.

There are, of course, combinations of the Bush and Clinton models. Most campaigns seek to mobilize partisans *and* persuade independents. To do so, they rely on detailed plans for allocating resources. As discussed earlier, most major campaigns use polling and voter identification data to estimate the number of persuadable voters in their state or county. They can then price out the cost of a visit or television ad in that state or county, and calculate the price per persuadable voter. A campaign is thus able to rank-order all states or counties (or precincts) by cost-effectiveness, and can allocate dollars based on this ranking. Other factors may induce a campaign to visit a certain county or advertise in a certain market, but professional campaigns tend to adhere closely to their analytical rankings. Political science research confirms this.[20] For example, research on presidential campaigns from 1992 through 2008 shows that television advertising expenditures were mostly

---

[19] Mark Halperin and John F. Harris. 2008. *The Way to Win*. New York: Random House.

[20] Daron R. Shaw. 2006. *The Race to 270*. Chicago: University of Chicago Press.

based on price-per-persuadable-voter estimates.[21] Campaigns below the presidential level are not as exacting in their deployment of resources. This is partly because the consulting talent, available data, and allocation options decrease with more localized elections, making it more difficult to develop and execute a rigorous plan for resource allocation.

How to Campaign

Should the campaign use its funds to run television advertisements on the broadcast networks? Or should it purchase cable television advertisements instead? Would radio advertisements be better? Or maybe Internet advertisements? What about billboards, lawn signs, bumper stickers, and buttons? And how much time and effort should be spent on the ground game—face-to-face campaigning by the candidate, staff, and volunteers? These are nuts-and-bolts decisions that a campaign strategist must make. In some respects, they are questions of tactics as opposed to strategy. Tactics are the means by which strategic goals are accomplished and thus they are often driven by strategic calculations.

Tactics are most affected by available resources. Candidates would prefer to draw on as many tactics as possible—saturating every form of mass media with advertisements, for example—but often they cannot afford to do so. If candidates have enough money to run advertisements on broadcast television, which is the most expensive medium and also likely to reach the largest audience, then they will. If they do not, then the question becomes whether other mass media, such as cable television or radio, are affordable. Campaigns with even fewer resources often rely more on the ground game, which consists of personal campaigning by the candidate and outreach by volunteers, both door-to-door and over the phone. Well-funded campaigns will combine a ground game with the "air war" of advertising on radio and television.

In the past decade, there has been something of a renaissance of interest in the ground game. Both political consultants and political scientists believe that personal contact with potential voters is effective, especially if the contact is from familiar and credible sources of information, such as friends and neighbors—that old-fashioned door knocks and other forms of personal outreach are often more effective than direct mail or phone banks. Political science studies have confirmed this: personalized contact is much more effective than mail or telephone calls in mobilizing citizens to vote, although

---

[21] Taofang Huang and Daron Shaw. 2009. "Beyond the Battlegrounds: Electoral College Strategies in the 2008 Election." *Journal of Political Marketing* 8, 4: 272–91.

How Candidates (Try to) Use New Media

In Chapter 3, we saw how changes in technology affected fund-raising and volunteer-recruitment efforts. New forms of media, including those aimed at audiences on the Internet, are becoming increasingly prominent in other aspects of campaigns as well. Candidates, political parties, and interest groups create websites, blog about the campaign, and communicate with supporters via Facebook and Twitter.

Campaigns also often try to produce or push content that "goes viral," meaning it is redistributed continuously online and becomes fodder for the news. In the second presidential debate in 2012, for example, President Barack Obama countered Mitt Romney's comment that the U.S. "Navy is smaller now than at any time since 1917" with a zinger that won the night. "You mentioned the Navy, for example, and that we have fewer ships than we did in 1916," Obama told Romney. "Well, Governor, we also have fewer horses and bayonets, because the nature of our military's changed." The "horses and bayonets" comment delighted the Twittersphere: The hashtag #horsesandbayonets became the number one trend on Twitter in the United States and third in the world. At one point, the phrase was mentioned on Twitter nearly 60,000 times in one minute, according to data from Topsy, a social Web analytics tool. The Obama campaign capitalized on the traffic, buying the search term "Bayonets" on Twitter. Within minutes of Obama's comment, a "Horses and Bayonets" Tumblr featuring GIFs and images went live, and a Horses and Bayonets Facebook page already had more than 3,000 likes.

New media are valuable to candidates because these media empower citizens to produce their own content, giving them a sense of ownership in the campaign. In 2008, the recording artist will.i.am produced an online song and video called "Yes We Can," using footage from Obama's New Hampshire primary-night speech. The video was played millions of times on YouTube, won an Emmy award, and was eventually used by the campaign.

At the same time, this empowerment of citizens to produce their own content limits the control candidates have over their campaign message. In 2008, an employee of a website development firm working for the Obama campaign produced a Web video attacking Hillary Clinton that was uploaded to YouTube. The video borrowed from a 1984 Apple Computer ad that portrayed Microsoft as an authoritarian menace. The Obama campaign denied involvement and the employee was forced to resign. In another incident, Barack Obama offered free websites and blogs to his supporters at my.barackobama.com. Some users who objected to Obama's positions on civil liberties issues used these websites to blast Obama. Because the criticisms were coming from Obama supporters, the traditional media gave them more credence.

Candidates also must understand other limits of new media. They are unlikely to reach many undecided voters, as visitors to candidate websites are overwhelmingly committed supporters. Moreover, using new media to mobilize supporters is not always successful. Research has shown that sending e-mails to supporters does not necessarily make them more likely to register or vote.[1] In sum, new media give candidates a new array of tools but certainly no magic bullets. (We take a closer look at new media in campaigns and elections in Chapter 8.)

[1] David W. Nickerson. 2007. "Does Email Boost Turnout?" *Quarterly Journal of Political Science* 2, 4: 369–79.

phone calls made by professional telemarketers can be effective, especially compared to phone calls with a prerecorded voice.[22]

In recent elections, both parties have invested significant resources in developing a field organization that can carry out personalized mobilizations. Union organizations arguably started this move in the 1998 and 2000 campaigns. Republican Party organizations, spooked by the Democrats' get-out-the-vote machine that built on the efforts of the unions, countered with their own volunteer efforts in 2002 and 2004. In 2008 and 2012, the Obama campaign created an extensive field organization of trained volunteers. In fact, the more modern, online forms of social networking—candidate websites, Facebook, and Twitter—are being used to drive the sorts of in-person outreach that, after the advent of television, had seemed like a thing of the past. For example, Steve Hildebrand, the deputy national campaign director for Obama's 2008 campaign, said, "We didn't make the assumption that people signing up on our website meant that they were going to help the candidate or even vote for him. From the beginning, we had an initiative to take our online force offline."[23]

Thus, offline forms of personal contact will likely continue to be significant, alongside online organizing and, in the case of advertising, on-air messages. For the moment, however, television advertising continues to be the linchpin of contemporary campaigns, especially in statewide and federal races.

Organizing for Strategic Success

The various strategic decisions we have discussed do not get made by themselves. When a candidate decides to run for office, she needs to identify knowledgeable people to help her design a strategy and then set up an organization so that important questions are decided and plans are implemented. But the fact that campaigns face common dilemmas in determining and implementing a strategy does not mean than there is one common solution—in fact, there is no such thing as a "typical" campaign. Campaigns vary in their resources: some have huge budgets and target millions of citizens, and some have tiny budgets and target hundreds or only dozens. Naturally, they will have diverse organizations as well. Moreover, although many

---

[22] Donald P. Green and Alan S. Gerber. 2004. *Get Out the Vote!* Washington, DC: Brookings Institution Press.

[23] Quoted in Tim Dickinson. 2008. "The Machinery of Hope." *Rolling Stone*, March 20. www.rollingstone.com/news/coverstory/19106326 (accessed 12/10/2010).

campaign organizations include similar positions of authority—with strategists who (no surprise) are in charge of developing strategy and a campaign manager who is in charge of organizing the campaign and implementing the strategic plan—these positions do not always have the same job description or the same place in the organization's hierarchy. Campaign managers are not necessarily at the top of the organization. A chief strategist is usually, but not always, a centrally important position. Political directors are typically in charge of organizing the field staff, but some engage in overall messaging strategy as well. Personal relationships can drive the structure of the organization, with positions created to accommodate specific people that the candidate wants for specific purposes.

It is instructive to examine briefly the campaign organizations of Mitt Romney and Barack Obama in the 2012 presidential race. Although presidential campaigns offer a "deluxe" example of what a campaign can be, smaller campaigns try to do many of the same things, if on a much smaller scale in terms of people and resources. The presidential campaign of the Republican nominee Mitt Romney evolved throughout the year. Initially, Romney's campaign team (Figure 5.2) moved from state to state as the GOP's primary season unfolded. After clinching the nomination, the organization in Boston was solidified and fleshed out below the top positions; additional senior advisers were added, with fund-raising, paid media, and polling becoming focal points. The team included a finance chair (in charge of overseeing raising campaign money), a political director (in charge of operations, grassroots, outreach, and education), a communications director (in charge of press relations, advertising, and promoting message and image), and a pollster (in charge of identifying target voters and developing appropriate issue and message points). Intent on avoiding the "who's in charge?" problems that plagued the McCain campaign throughout much of 2008, lines of authority for the Romney team were clearly established, with Stuart Stevens serving as the point person for strategic decisions and Matt Rhoades serving as the final word on organization and staffing.

Barack Obama's 2012 presidential campaign, like his 2008 campaign, is best represented as a sort of loop (or circle), in which information flowed in a particular pattern but which also allowed different players to be involved in the decision-making process. Obama had numerous people serving in key positions, and it was not always clear who outranked whom (Figure 5.3). Nevertheless, David Axelrod, senior strategist, had the final say on most important decisions, while Jim Messina, the campaign manager, and David Plouffe, who was able to act as something of an overlord for the organizational apparatus, were usually deferred to on matters involving voter

FIGURE 5.2 **Mitt Romney's Presidential Campaign**

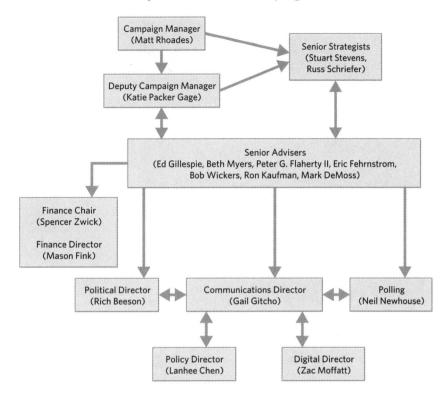

outreach, volunteers, and targeting. The Obama campaign thus maintained the traditional distinction between a campaign strategist and a campaign manager noted earlier: campaign strategists are usually in charge of developing a plan and honing the candidate's message, while campaign managers are usually in charge of running the day-to-day operations of the campaign. The Obama team also featured more specific, task-oriented departments and personnel—most notably, messaging (tasked with ensuring that all elements of the campaign were focused on the same issues and themes), innovation (tasked with Internet, e-campaigning, social media, and the development and integration of big data), and field (tasked with coordinating local, regional, and state volunteer and paid staffing work).

FIGURE 5.3 Barack Obama's Presidential Campaign

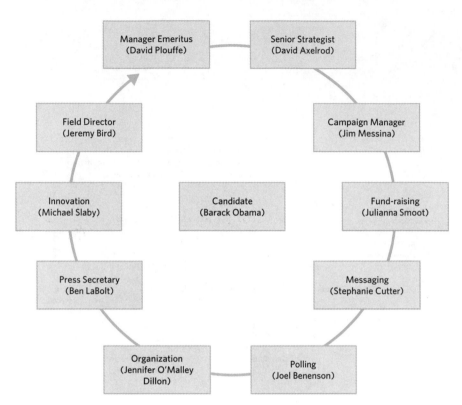

Who Are Campaign Strategists?

As described in Chapter 3, the modern American campaign is candidate-centered and dominated by television. This means that candidates recruit and develop their own advisers. The importance of television for communicating messages made people with expertise in public opinion and television advertising exceptionally valuable for candidates. As a consequence, a class of professional campaign consultants emerged in the 1950s; these professionals have become the main purveyors of strategic advice in American elections.

The Backgrounds of Campaign Strategists

Although the development of professional campaign consultants is relatively new, there have always been strategists in American campaigns. Alexander

Hamilton may have been the most famous political consultant of the early days of the new Republic, as he constantly schemed and plotted how to win elections for those who shared his Federalist views. James Madison was only slightly less aggressive as Thomas Jefferson's top political strategist, although Jefferson himself was also an active strategist. Indeed, we could put together quite a catalog of campaign strategists from before the modern campaign era.

In today's campaigns, how does someone become a campaign consultant or strategist? First, there are those who become proficient at a specific campaign endeavor, and parlay this into a broader role crafting and overseeing strategy. For example, in the 1960s and 1970s, people with a background in public relations or consumer advertising were much sought after by campaigns, as candidates attempted to develop personal loyalty among constituents through persuasive self-promotion. Public relations and advertising professionals naturally favored using market research to drive messaging, and using mass media (especially television) to deliver these messages. Roger Ailes, who worked for Richard Nixon, Ronald Reagan, and George H. W. Bush, and is now president of Fox News, is a good example.

People with a background in journalism or speechwriting have also become successful strategists. Some have moved up by serving as the liaison between the candidates and the news media, while others have served as speechwriters before taking on the broader role of strategist. Democrats Bill Moyers (who served Lyndon Johnson) and Bob Shrum (who worked for eight Democratic presidential candidates, including Edward Kennedy and John Kerry) are prime examples.

Pollsters, who are trained in the art and science of ascertaining what the public is thinking, have also become campaign strategists. Doug Schoen, Bill Clinton's pollster, later served as Hillary Clinton's presidential campaign strategist. Bob Teeter, a legendary Republican pollster, served as George H. W. Bush's presidential campaign strategist and manager in 1992.

More recently, people who are good at direct mail or telemarketing campaigns have used this success as a way of becoming general strategists. Both of these activities require a strong sense of which voters the candidate should address and what messages move them. Republican strategist Karl Rove dominated direct mail campaigning in Texas before taking up much broader responsibilities for George W. Bush.

Finally, the emergence of campaign management schools has provided another route by which aspiring strategists can hone their craft. As yet, there are few examples of campaign school graduates becoming superstars, but the ranks of congressional and even presidential campaigns are now populated with people who cut their teeth at these academies.

A different path to becoming a campaign strategist consists of developing relationships with particular candidates and marshaling them through their political careers. These individuals may have only a few clients throughout their careers, but they play a major role for those clients. James A. Baker III built his career in law but entered politics at the urging of his friend George H. W. Bush. He served in the Ford, Reagan, and Bush administrations, but only in a handful of campaigns, the most prominent of which involved Bush. Baker's particular value to Bush was as someone who had his best interests at heart, someone who could tell him the unvarnished truth, and someone who knew his strengths and weaknesses inside out. Only Baker could have given Bush the salty advice described at the beginning of this chapter.

Regardless of their path into the business, professional campaign strategists have attained much greater visibility in recent decades and are even referred to as gurus. Their lionization can be traced to a classic work of campaign journalism, Theodore White's *The Making of the President*.[24] White's narrative of the 1960 campaign details the machinations of Robert Kennedy and other advisers to John F. Kennedy, noting their disciplined targeting of states and voting groups and aggressive voter registration strategy, among other things. White also discusses the opposing side, in particular Richard Nixon's disastrous pledge to campaign in all 50 states, and the challenge of attacking the elusive and charismatic Kennedy. The implication was clear—JFK's victory was, at least in part, due to the cool, methodical, professional campaign strategy developed by his team. The elevation of the strategist had begun, and soon many would become well known: Hamilton Jordan (for Jimmy Carter), Ed Rollins (for Ronald Reagan), James Baker and Lee Atwater (for George H. W. Bush), James Carville and Dick Morris (for Bill Clinton in 1992 and 1996, respectively), Karl Rove (for George W. Bush), and David Axelrod (for Barack Obama in 2008 and 2012).

Despite the visibility of superstar strategists, we know very little about their actual impact on contemporary elections. Commentaries like *The Selling of the President* have criticized the mass marketing techniques so often employed in contemporary campaigns, on the advice of consultants.[25] But little has been written on how much campaign consultants actually help candidates win. What evidence exists suggests that hiring consultants is no panacea.[26] In part, this may reflect how much both campaign strategy and

---

[24] Theodore S. White. 1964. *The Making of the President, 1960*. New York: Atheneum.

[25] Joe McGinniss. 1969. *The Selling of the President*. New York: Simon & Schuster.

[26] Stephen Medvic. 2001. *Political Consultants in U.S. Congressional Elections*. Columbus: Ohio State University Press.

The "superstar" strategists of recent years have included David Axelrod, left, and Karl Rove, right. Axelrod is credited with helping Obama win in 2008 and 2012 and served in the Obama administration, while Rove is known for devising George W. Bush's strategies in 2000 and 2004 and also went on to work in the White House.

election outcomes are constrained by the rules governing elections and the reality that candidates face. Political scientists are therefore less likely than campaign professionals to attribute the success of candidates to the strategic genius of their advisers. This skepticism is at the heart of the more general disagreement between campaign consultants and political scientists with respect to whether campaigns "matter."

Conclusion

In this chapter, we have delineated what a campaign strategy is, discussed several key strategic decisions that campaigns make, and considered the perspectives of both campaign consultants and political scientists. We have also discussed how campaigns organize to make strategic decisions, and examined who campaign strategists are. The central notion is straightforward: campaign strategists want to win elections, and everything they do can be understood as a rational, if sometimes imperfect, effort to achieve this goal. Practitioners and academics tend to agree on many of the factors that candidates can and should consider when deciding if they should seek higher office, emphasize a particular issue, run an attack ad, or focus resources on a particular constituency. The central question, however, is how much these strategic decisions matter—a topic we will return to in subsequent chapters.

How should we view campaign strategy in light of the philosophical ideals spelled out in Chapter 1? We will explore this topic at greater length in Chapter 14, but we can highlight one issue here. Intrinsic to campaign

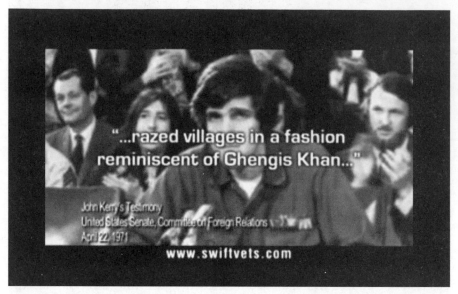

In 2004, a group called Swift Boat Veterans for Truth ran ads questioning presidential candidate John Kerry's record as a war hero in Vietnam. Was Kerry's hesitation in responding to these ads during his campaign a fatal strategic mistake?

strategy is this notion: some citizens are more valuable than others. That is, campaigns routinely identify subsets of citizens to target—such as swing voters or voters in a certain geographic area—and ignore many others. This approach may run counter to several ideals. The laserlike focus of campaigns on partisan supporters or swing voters or any other groups may violate the ideal of political equality. Of course, we are most concerned that citizens are equal in the eyes of the law, not in the eyes of campaign consultants. Nevertheless, this decision involves a trade-off of values. Similarly, targeted voters inevitably receive much more information about the campaign than do other voters, challenging the ideal of deliberation. The information that voters receive clearly differs depending on whether they are the targets of a campaign's strategy. That campaign strategy may fail to live up to these ideals reflects this simple fact: campaign strategy is fundamentally about winning elections, not about upholding civic standards.

KEY TERMS

campaign strategy (p. 122)

vote targets (p. 122)

persuadable/swing votes (p. 123)

probability sample (p. 126)

focus groups (p. 127)

microtargeting (p. 128)

voter identification/voter ID calls
 (p. 128)

open seat (p. 128)

framing (p. 134)

issue ownership (p. 134)

median voter theorem (p. 135)

negative campaigning (p. 138)

positive campaigning (p. 138)

contrast advertisements (p. 138)

attack ads (p. 138)

Bush model (p. 139)

Clinton model (p. 140)

FOR DISCUSSION

1. Do campaigns attempt to convince all voters to support their candidate? Why or why not?

2. What factors influence whether or not a candidate chooses to run for an office?

3. Why are challengers more likely than incumbents to run negative advertisements?

4. How has the rise of public opinion polling influenced campaigns?

CHAPTER 6

Political Parties

On the morning of June 10, 2014, House Majority Leader Eric Cantor attended a monthly meeting with Republican donors and lobbyists at a Starbucks on Capitol Hill. The group was looking ahead, raising money for the general election campaigns of threatened Republican incumbents. Cantor showed no signs of fear about his own campaign in Virginia. Later that evening, college professor and political newcomer David Brat defeated Cantor in the Republican primary by a margin of 11 percent. Cantor's loss, the first ever by a House Majority Leader in a primary, shocked political professionals and reporters.

Cantor was hardly the first incumbent to face primary opposition or to lose. Primary challenges and losses were consistently higher in the 1970s and peaked in 1992 — though most incumbents face no intra-party challenger and most of those that do still win by large margins.[1] Cantor's status as an incumbent and Republican Party leader helped him raise $5.5 million, compared to just over $200,000 for Brat. National Tea Party organizations stayed out of the campaign; Brat could not convince even organizations that wanted to oust Cantor that he was a viable candidate. Brat did benefit from the support of talk radio hosts Mark Levin and Laura Ingraham as well as favorable coverage from local media. Brat portrayed Cantor as out of touch with the district, citing Cantor's support of Wall Street and openness to immigration — but many other Tea Party challengers made similar arguments and had less success. Cantor recognized the threat late in the campaign, driven in part by misleadingly positive poll numbers provided by his own pollster (who claimed Cantor was up by a 34 percent margin).

Cantor's loss was surprising because it was so atypical. A party's primary is supposed to be its own chance to select a nominee; the choice of party leaders usually wins the support of party voters. Yet American parties are not top-down and unified hierarchies; the support among fellow House members that made Cantor a congressional leader did not translate into automatic nomination in his

---

[1] Robert Boatright. 2013. *Getting Primaried: The Changing Politics of Congressional Primary Challenges.* Ann Arbor: University of Michigan Press.

own district. Even those who share the party's goals, like local activists and conservative talk show hosts, may not support its legislative leaders. The decisions made by the party's legislative branch, like Cantor's support for the bank loan program under President Bush (derided as a "bailout"), may not play well with a party's base. Cantor's limited efforts to achieve compromise on immigration, designed to help the national party appeal to an increasingly Hispanic electorate, did not help much in a district with few Hispanics — especially in a largely white Republican primary electorate.

Political parties provide the structure for American elections, but voters ultimately determine election results. Party organizations have diverse roles in campaigns — recruiting candidates, running advertisements, and mobilizing voters — but citizens have to support a party's decisions to enforce their will. Yet parties are not like other outside groups. They have a permanent place in American politics, helping to order the competition between candidates. For most candidates and many voters, decisions about whom to support in any one election follow from a more basic political decision: selecting a party, one of the two major sides of American political competition. Despite occasional losses by party leaders, America's two major parties are remarkably stable and resilient: Cantor was quickly replaced by another party stalwart for his leadership position in the House. Even in Virginia, Republicans who supported Cantor voted for Brat in the general election and the party replaced one reliable supporter in Congress with another.

In this chapter, we will address several questions about the role of political parties in campaigns. What are political parties and why do we have them? Why do we have only the Democrats and the Republicans? How do parties behave in campaigns and how is their role evolving? Of course, no discussion of parties is complete without consideration of interest groups, which usually take one party's side

Core of the Analysis

- Political parties strategically intervene in elections by recruiting candidates, airing advertisements, and mobilizing voters.
- Political parties have not lost much influence, despite attempts by some reformers to weaken them.
- The two major political parties have adapted to changing issues and slowly changed their voting coalitions, in the process becoming more ideologically polarized.
- Political parties fall short of achieving some democratic values, but it is unlikely that democracy could function without them.

in a campaign; parties and interest groups are often intertwined, but we post-pone discussion of interest groups to Chapter 7. This chapter also considers broader questions about how parties fit into American politics. How do parties strategize about campaigns? How do electoral rules and political and economic realities influence their strategies? Are parties contributing to polarization or adapting to a changing society and new policy issues? Each of these questions raises key philosophical concerns: Do parties serve or undermine democratic values in campaigns? Even if Americans are dissatisfied with parties, do viable alternatives exist? To address these questions about parties, we first have to understand their behavior.

What Are Political Parties and How Are They Organized?

Political parties are groups of people with the shared interest of electing pub-lic officials under a common label. The two major political parties in the United States, the Democrats and the Republicans, share the goal of win-ning elections. Each party has policy goals, of course, but it is their electoral goals that unite parties and distinguish them from other kinds of groups.

American political parties are nevertheless amorphous groups, including everyone from elected officials to fund-raisers to individual voters. It can be difficult to answer seemingly straightforward questions about political par-ties. For example, who is in charge of the Democratic and Republican par-ties? The president is usually the most prominent spokesperson for his party; during presidential campaigns, the presidential nominees generally have this role. Barack Obama became the leader of the Democratic Party in 2008 as the party's nominee for president, although he held no formal position within the party organization. When a party loses a presidential election, it often creates a leadership vacuum that is not filled until four years later. Outside of the presidency, who is in charge of the Republican Party? The closest to an official head, Republican National Committee (RNC) chairman Reince Priebus, was elected in 2011 as a largely unknown candidate running on the promise that he would be different from Michael Steele, the previous chair-man, who was dogged by controversy. (In the most notorious episode, Steele had to explain a $2,000 RNC expenditure at a bondage-themed West Holly-wood topless nightclub in 2010.) Yet Priebus does not run any government departments, vote in Congress, or appear on voter ballots. Senate Majority Leader Mitch McConnell and House Speaker John Boehner are the governing heads of the Republican Party. In 2010, former RNC chairman Ed Gillespie and political operative Karl Rove created new organizations, known as Crossroads and Crossroads GPS, to compete with the RNC by raising money and coordinating support for Republican Party candidates. The Republican Party also has separate chairs for its House and Senate campaign committees and state parties. Yet reporters have often looked to former presidential candidate Mitt Romney or even talk show host Rush Limbaugh to represent the views of the Republican Party.

Party membership is equally unclear. If your friend says that she is a Republican, this does not necessarily mean that she is officially registered with the party. In many states, individuals do not need to register with a

Who speaks for the Republican Party? a. Senate Majority Leader Mitch McConnell and House Speaker John Boehner; b. Republican National Committee Chairman Reince Priebus; c. Conservative radio talk show host Rush Limbaugh; d. 2016 candidate Jeb Bush; 2012 Republican presidential nominee Mitt Romney; or someone else?

TABLE 6.1 Three Aspects of the Major American Parties

Aspect of Party	Democrats	Republicans
Party-in-the-electorate	• Democratic registrants • People who identify themselves as Democrats • Democratic primary voters • Democratic general election voters • Democratic campaign volunteers and activists	• Republican registrants • People who identify themselves as Republicans • Republican primary voters • Republican general election voters • Republican campaign volunteers and activists
Party-as-organization	• Democratic National Committee • Democratic Senate Campaign Committee • Democratic Congressional Campaign Committee • State and local party committees • Leadership PACs	• Republican National Committee • Republican National Senate Committee • Republican National Campaign Committee • State and local party committees • Leadership PACs
Party-in-government	• President (Barack Obama) • Senate Minority Leader (Harry Reid) • House Minority Leader (Nancy Pelosi) • Democratic State and Local Elected Officials	• Senate Majority Leader (Mitch McConnell) • Speaker of the House (John Boehner) • Republican State and Local Elected Officials

political party in order to vote in that party's primary; in some states, there is no official party registration at all. Perhaps we should consider anyone who thinks of herself as a Democrat or Republican to be a member of the party. Yet political scientists have found that even people who view themselves as independents—meaning they are unaffiliated with either party—often vote consistently for one party's candidates. The same is true of elected officials who call themselves independent. As of 2014, two U.S. senators, Bernie Sanders of Vermont and Angus King of Maine, were listed as Independents, but both work with the Democratic leadership.

To make sense of political parties, the political scientist V. O. Key suggested three manifestations of political parties: the **party-in-the-electorate**, the **party-as-organization**, and the **party-in-government** (see Table 6.1).[2] The

[2] V. O. Key, Jr. 1952. *Politics, Parties, and Pressure Groups*. 3rd ed. New York: Crowell.

party-in-the-electorate includes all citizens who identify with the party. This is where your friend who claims to be a Republican would fit. The party-as-organization comprises the institutions that administer party affairs, including the official bodies that raise funds and create the rules for the party. This is where Priebus and the RNC fit. The party-in-government consists of the elected leaders and appointed government officials who shape party policy goals. This is where Obama, McConnell, and Boehner fit. Each of these manifestations of the party is somewhat independent of the others. Partisans in the electorate do not decide how party leaders operate. Reince Priebus speaks for the party organization, but he cannot tell Republican senators how to vote. In studying campaigns and elections, we pay most attention to the party-as-organization, which assists the candidates, and the party-in-the-electorate, which votes for them. Some scholars have expanded the definition of the party-as-organization to include Leadership PACs (committees attached to party leaders that donate to other candidates) and interest groups that usually support one party, calling the parties "multi-layered coalitions" of diverse actors that share mutual goals and collaborate regularly.[3] Indeed, the parties appear to share mailing lists across an "extended party network" with individual candidates, allied interest groups, and ideological news outlets.[4]

Why Do We Have Parties?

Parties have the potential to help make democratic government work in several ways. First, they aggregate and articulate interests. Every citizen and politician has his or her own interests and ideas, but democracy requires that they work with others in order to achieve these goals. Parties help individuals to decide which of their principles and goals are most important and to find people that agree with them. Second, parties organize coalitions. If every ethnic, religious, and economic group nominated its own candidates, it would be difficult for any group to obtain a majority of the vote. Parties enable groups to unite under broader umbrellas. Third, parties coordinate elections and mobilize voters. Without them, candidates would have to convince voters individually that they share their views; and they would have to

---

[3] Paul Herrnson. 1999. "The Roles of Party Organizations, Party-Connected Committees, and Party Allies in Elections." *Journal of Politics* 71, 4: 1207–24.

[4] Gregory Koger, Seth Masket, and Hans Noel. 2009. "Partisan Webs: Information Exchange and Party Networks." *British Journal of Political Science* 39: 633–53.

mobilize their own constituencies. Party labels make it easier for voters to form opinions about the candidates. Fourth, parties coordinate the legislative process. While this role is not as important for elections, it does allow voters to learn how their vote will likely translate into public policy. Finally, parties facilitate collective political action. Both electing candidates and governing require individuals to work together, and parties provide a crucial means by which people join together in pursuit of shared goals.

Just because parties have the potential to serve the interests of democracy, however, does not mean this is the reason they were created. Most of the Founders feared parties, even as they later participated in them. As he left office, George Washington warned of "the baneful effects of the spirit of party." Nevertheless, political parties quickly developed and took on increasingly important roles in American government. Political parties serve the needs of politicians who want durable legislative majorities in order to pass legislation.[5] They also want a reputation or "brand" that voters recognize and can use when voting. They need an infrastructure that helps persuade and mobilize voters during elections. Parties serve all of these functions. Political parties may also have developed to promote the policy goals of various interest groups, who often affiliate with parties in order to advance their policy goals.[6] By working through a party, interest groups seek to influence policy by choosing which candidates the party nominates and which candidate ultimately wins each election. The alternative to a political party—negotiating with individual candidates and legislators to support a group's agenda—is far more costly.

The Democratic and Republican Parties

Two major political parties have dominated the U.S. political system. The Democratic Party traces its history to the 1828 election of Andrew Jackson. The Republicans emerged as their major challenger with the 1860 election of Abraham Lincoln. Since the 1920s, the two major parties combined have always controlled at least 95 perent of House and Senate seats and won at least 90 percent of Electoral College votes for the presidency.

Ideologically, the Republican Party is more conservative and the Democratic Party is more liberal (see Figure 6.1). The Democratic Party favors

---

[5] John Aldrich. 1995. *Why Parties?* Chicago: University of Chicago Press.

[6] Marty Cohen, David Karol, Hans Noel, and John Zaller. 2008. *The Party Decides: Presidential Nominations Before and After Reform*. Chicago: University of Chicago Press.

FIGURE 6.1 Ideological Distribution of Party Members, Activists, and Donors

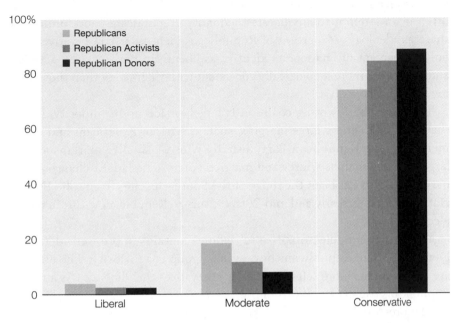

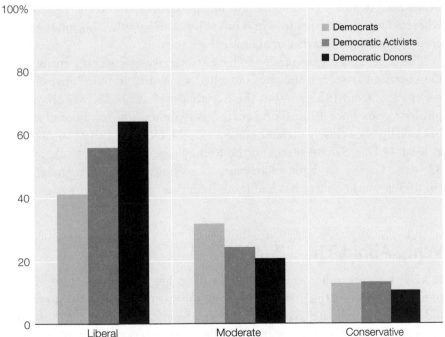

The figure shows the percent of members of the Democratic and Republican parties who identify as liberal, moderate, or conservative as well as the same distributions for partisans who reported two or more campaign activities (activists) and those that reported donating money to political causes (donors).

Source: Data from the 2012 American National Election Studies.

more government intervention in the economy than the Republican Party, often in an attempt to ameliorate inequality. Republicans more uniformly share an ideology; 74 percent of Republicans identify as conservatives, but only 41 percent of Democrats identify as liberal. In both parties, activists and donors are more ideologically consistent with their party than those who merely identify with it.

The Democratic voting coalition is largely made up of minority groups that vote for them by large margins, such as African Americans and union members. The Republican Party usually wins by smaller margins among larger groups, such as whites and married voters. The largest change in the party coalitions has been the move of the Southern states from solid Democratic voting in the early and mid-20th century to Republican voting in recent elections.

The American electorate as a whole contains more self-identified Democrats than Republicans but neither group is a majority. The electorate also contains more self-identified conservatives than liberals. As a result, Republicans usually benefit from framing their opponents as liberals but face regular pressure from their ideological base (see Box 6.1). Nationally, Republicans need to win a greater share of independents than do the Democrats, whereas Democrats have to win more votes than Republicans among moderates because they have a smaller ideological base.

The United States has tended to have strong two-party competition. The Democratic Party continuously controlled a majority in the House of Representatives from 1955–94, but the Republicans have had a majority for all but four years since 1995. The Senate has switched control more often but has usually been closely divided; since 1955, the Democrats have always held at least 44 U.S. Senate seats and the Republicans have always held at least 32 seats. There have been more party transitions in the presidency; since the 1930s, neither party has had more than two consecutive presidents.

What About Third Parties?

It is rare for any candidate not affiliated with either major party to get elected to federal office. At the presidential level, the most successful third-party or independent candidates have won at best a handful of states and thus come up woefully short in the Electoral College. This was true for such candidates as Theodore Roosevelt, who ran as the Progressive Party nominee in 1912; Strom Thurmond, who ran as the States' Rights Democratic Party (or Dixiecrat) nominee in 1948; and George Wallace, who ran as the

American Independent Party's nominee in 1968. Roosevelt won only seven states. Thurmond and Wallace did not win any states outside the Deep South. In 1992, an independent candidate, Ross Perot, won 19 percent of the popular vote but no electoral votes. Consumer advocate Ralph Nader received only 2.7 percent of the popular vote as the Green Party candidate in 2000 and less than 1 percent as an independent candidate in 2004.

The most important difficulties third parties have in U.S. elections are posed by the rules of the electoral system. As discussed in Chapter 2, the use of single-member districts and plurality elections favors congressional candidates from the two major parties. Plurality voting within the Electoral College—whereby the candidate who wins the most votes in each state wins all of that state's electoral votes—hurts the chances of national third parties or independent candidates at the presidential level. There are other legal hurdles for third parties, including requirements for getting on the ballot (see Chapter 2). With the playing field tilted so strongly against them, third parties routinely find it difficult to attract media coverage, raise money, recruit experienced candidates, or earn a place in candidate debates. At the state and local levels, the Democratic and Republican parties often conform to the local political terrain. This makes it hard for a third party to develop a regional base of support. Despite these difficulties, third parties and independent candidates are sometimes successful. For example, the Green Party and the Libertarian Party have elected more than 200 officeholders between them, mostly in local elections. Third parties and independent candidates can also influence the issues discussed in campaigns. Both the Democrats and the Republicans felt compelled to respond to Ross Perot's concerns about the federal budget deficit in 1992. But this small amount of policy influence also makes third parties short-lived. One or both of the two major parties can adopt their issue positions and lure their supporters away.

What Roles Do Parties Play in Campaigns?

Political parties play central roles in contemporary campaigns, with the party-in-the-electorate, the party-as-organization, and the party-in-government all having some impact on the electoral process.

The Role of the Party-in-the-Electorate

The vast majority of Americans identify with or lean toward either the Democratic or the Republican Party and vote loyally for candidates from their preferred party. This makes the partisan complexion of a district or

BOX 6.1

What Is the Tea Party?

In 2009, thousands of activists organized protests and attended congressional town hall meetings to oppose Obama's policy agenda, including health care reform legislation. In the 2010, 2012, and 2014 elections, they supported several candidates and were credited with changing election outcomes. They called themselves the "Tea Party movement," emphasizing their link to the values of the American founders by evoking the Boston Tea Party.

Is the Tea Party a viable alternative to the two major parties? Some Tea Party activists were previously active in third parties like the Libertarian Party, the Constitution Party, and the American Independent Party. They also frequently oppose the Republican Party's preferred candidate in primary elections—occasionally to disastrous effect for the Republican Party. For example, in the 2012 Indiana Senate primary, Tea Party favorite Richard Mourdock (pictured here) defeated incumbent Senator Richard Lugar. Following Mourdock's comments that "if life begins in that horrible situation of rape, that is something that God intended to happen," he went on to lose the seat—one that had been held by a Republican for 36 years—to Democrat Joe Donnelly.[1] In 2014, self-identified Tea Party candidates were successful less often in Senate races.

But in other respects, the Tea Party movement substantially overlaps with the Republican Party. Attendees at Tea Party events are far more likely to consider themselves Republicans than Democrats and Republican respondents to public opinion polls are consistently more supportive of their activities.[2] Former and current Republican Party activists and consultants helped organize their protests and campaigns. Republican officeholders and candidates spoke at their events. Most Tea Party activists want to support Republican candidates rather

Richard Mourdock, Indiana state treasurer, defeated incumbent senator Richard Lugar in the 2012 Republican primary but lost the general election to Democrat Joe Donnelly after his controversial comments about pregnancies resulting from rape.

than organize a third party.[3] Their overall goal is not to replace the Republican Party but to move it in a conservative direction.

If not a separate party, is the Tea Party movement an interest group? On the one hand, Washington interest groups like Freedom-Works and Americans for Tax Reform provided logistical support for their initial protests and their town hall meeting attendance strategy. Tea Party activists have also created several nonprofit organizations and PACs to fund candidates and intervene in elections. They also engage in lobbying. On the other hand,

[1] The comments can be viewed here: www.politico.com/blogs/on-congress/2012/10/richard-mourdock-under-fire-for-rape-remarks-139411.html?hp=l1 (accessed 6/26/14).
[2] Vanessa Williamson, Theda Skocpol, and John Coggin. 2011. "The Tea Party and the Remaking of Republican Conservatism." *Perspectives on Politics* 9, 1: 25–43.
[3] Kate Zernike and Megan Thee-Brenan. 2010. "Poll Finds Tea Party Backers Wealthier and More Educated." *New York Times*, April 15, p. A1.

the Tea Party does not have an organized leadership. And they employ tactics that are more typical of social movements than of organized interest groups. The first Tea Party events were protests, and Tea Party activists describe themselves as learning tactics from the liberal activists of the 1960s. In sum, the Tea Party movement remains something of a hybrid, featuring attributes of a political party, an interest group, and a social movement, but remaining largely aligned with the broader Republican Party.

state a central feature of the reality that candidates confront. In Chapter 5, we discussed how candidates and campaign consultants carefully count partisans of both camps as well as independent or undecided voters when planning their campaign strategy. The party-in-the-electorate is important in another way: it forms the volunteer base of each party. Party volunteers knock on doors, make phone calls, and talk to others in support of their party's candidates. In local elections for city council, school board, or county commission, volunteer networks and party activists are often the only visible party involvement.

The Role of the Party-as-Organization

The party-as-organization plays a central role in political campaigns. Party organizations such as the national committees, state committees, and legislative campaign committees recruit candidates and raise money for them. Recruiting candidates is harder than it might seem: in 2012, 33 percent of state legislative candidates faced no opposition candidate from the other party.[7] Parties try to recruit quality candidates who are well known to the electorate and have relevant experience for the office they seek. Candidates who have previously held elected office are much more likely to win future elections, so they are often the first people party organizations try to draft. For instance, the Republican-affiliated organization GOPAC recruits and trains candidates to run for state and local offices. Under the leadership of Newt Gingrich, it was credited with helping to build the farm team of candidates that enabled the 1994 Republican takeover of Congress. In addition to recruiting candidates, parties also work to minimize retirements within their ranks because incumbents are more likely to win elections than newcomers.

---

[7] A full list of unopposed candidates is available at http://ballotpedia.org/Candidates_with
_no_general_election_opposition_in_2012_state_legislative_elections (accessed 1/15/15).

Traditionally, the party organization also selected the party's nominees for general elections. Before 1972, unpledged party delegates selected presidential nominees at the national conventions (as discussed in Chapter 3). That changed with reforms to the presidential nomination system that emphasized primaries and caucuses. Primary elections became more important in nominations for lower-level offices as well, although party nominees for some statewide or local offices are still selected at party conventions or by party leaders. In many states, party organizations can also replace candidates who are no longer able to run or select nominees for special elections. For example, after incumbent senator Paul Wellstone was killed in a plane crash in October 2002, the Minnesota state party quickly put former vice president Walter Mondale on the ballot as a replacement. And even where party organizations no longer officially nominate their own candidates, party officials can influence primary results with their money or endorsements. They often discourage primary challengers, leaving only one candidate. When party leaders unite behind one front-runner, their preferred candidate usually wins the primary election.

The other main task of party organizations is to raise money for their candidates. As discussed in Chapter 4, parties are quite successful at raising money, despite the ban on soft money contributions. They contribute some of this money directly to individual campaigns. They sometimes pay campaign consultants, pollsters, and other vendors of campaign goods and services. Parties also spend money to produce and broadcast television advertisements, build local party organizations and pay for get-out-the-vote drives.

Parties are now spending considerable sums on candidates' behalf, much of it on television advertisements. During the 2004 election cycle, party expenditures increased dramatically and shifted away from **coordinated expenditures** (Figure 6.2). As discussed in Chapter 4, campaign finance rulings in the courts opened the way for unlimited party independent expenditures. Parties' initial use of this option was circumscribed; today, both parties spend predominantly on independent expenditures. Democratic committees had the overall spending advantage in 2004 and 2008 but Republican committees spent more in 2012.

Party organizations also play an important role in mobilizing voters to participate in elections. People who are contacted by a political party during a campaign are more likely to vote, more likely to persuade others how to vote, more likely to work on behalf of a candidate, and more likely to contribute money.[8]

---

[8] Steven J. Rosenstone and John Mark Hansen. 1993. *Mobilization, Participation, and Democracy in America*. New York: Macmillan Publishing Company.

FIGURE 6.2 Party Committee Coordinated and Independent Expenditures

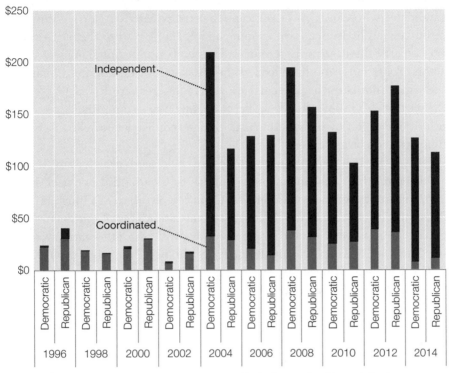

Source: Data from Federal Election Committee, summarized by the Congressional Research Service

Yet the parties consistently fail to contact most citizens. According to the American National Election Studies, the percent of citizens who report contact from either of the political parties went from a high of 31 percent in 1982 to a low of 19 percent in 1990. The current trend is toward more mobilization. In all elections since 2002, at least 40 percent of citizens were contacted by one of the parties. Political science experiments consistently show that knocking on voters' doors or calling them on the phone increases their likelihood of participation; these experiments have led political consultants to recommend more mobilization activities and seem to have had some effect on the parties' resource allocation decisions.[9]

---

[9] Donald Green and Alan Gerber. 2008. *Get Out the Vote: How to Increase Voter Turnout.* 2nd ed. Washington, DC: Brookings Institution Press.

One reason not all citizens are contacted is that party organizations tend to concentrate their resources on races that are closely contested and most likely to tip the balance of power in legislatures. They want their resources to maximize the number of their representatives who get elected by helping candidates who can win. This means that many candidates with minimal resources and little chance of winning do not get help from the parties. The way a party distributes its resources also sends important signals to other actors. Politicians who have leadership PACs will often donate to many of the same candidates that the parties invest in. Interest groups affiliated with the parties also follow their lead. Party organizations sometimes make their priorities explicit by distributing lists of targeted districts or winnable elections to guide other actors.

Parties can also direct resources to where their needs are greatest. Due to a substantial fund-raising advantage in 2008, Obama did not need party expenditures to compete with John McCain; as a result, the Democrats could direct more resources to their congressional candidates. Republican Party organizations were critical to helping McCain but their intervention was less important in 2012, when Mitt Romney was helped by a substantial Super-PAC spending advantage.

Of course, parties are not necessarily unified when developing a campaign strategy. Former party leaders Howard Dean and Rahm Emanuel regularly battled over whether the Democratic Party should devote resources to all of the states or only to competitive races. Another traditional conflict within party organizations is the trade-off between ideological purity and electability. Parties want elected officials who support their party's agenda. Yet sometimes candidates who are more ideologically moderate and less consistently partisan are more likely to win elections, especially in swing districts where voters are evenly divided along partisan lines.

In 2006, Congressman Joe Schwarz of Michigan's 7th District was challenged in the Republican primary by Tim Walberg, a former state representative. Republican politicians and party organizations supported the moderate Schwarz but many interest groups supported the more conservative Walberg. Walberg beat Schwarz in the primary and prevailed in the general election. But two years later, he lost the congressional seat to Mark Schauer, a Democratic state senator. In 2010, Walberg sought to challenge Schauer in the congressional race, but the NRCC recruited Brian Rooney, the brother of a Florida congressman, to run against Walberg in the Republican primary. Most observers saw the primary as pitting ideological consistency against electability: Walberg was conservative but, given his 2008 loss, perhaps not electable. In a better year for conservatives and Republicans, however,

Choosing a Gubernatorial Nominee

Entering the 2010 Michigan gubernatorial campaign, the Republican Party was confident. State public opinion had moved against the Democrats, including Governor Jennifer Granholm, who was retiring. The most popular potential Democratic candidate, the lieutenant governor, decided not to run. The expected Republican victory brought several quality candidates into the primary field. Early primary polls showed the race divided between Mike Cox, the popular attorney general from the Detroit area, and Congressman Pete Hoekstra, from the more conservative western part of the state.

Republican leaders and interest groups tried to unify behind a candidate. Cox received endorsements from Right to Life of Michigan PAC and the Michigan Chamber of Commerce along with the previous Republican candidate for governor. Yet western Michigan voters still supported Hoekstra.

Rick Snyder, a businessman with no ties to state party or interest group leaders, began with almost no public support but took advantage of the dissension. At the state's largest party gathering, the Mackinac Republican Leadership Conference, Snyder unexpectedly won the straw poll. Newspapers explained the victory by reporting that Snyder had paid for many college Republicans to enjoy the splendid conference weekend on Mackinac Island, which they used for partying of the traditional variety.

By using his own wealth, Snyder was also able to advertise directly to voters rather than court the state's interest groups. His folksy advertising campaign, begun with a television ad during the Super Bowl, christened him as "one tough nerd," a successful outsider and accountant who would shake up the state's politics.

The state's party establishment and interest groups, meanwhile, did not take him seriously. Republican leaders continued to decide between Hoekstra and Cox because they were seen as more ideologically conservative and loyal to the party than Snyder. Shadowy groups designed to avoid recognition also waged a two-way battle on the airwaves. A group calling itself the Michigan Taxpayers Alert ran ads in support of Cox, attacking Hoekstra for supposed support of tax increases. Another group calling itself the Foundation for a Secure and Prosperous America ran misleading ads on behalf of Hoekstra, attacking Cox for alleged ties to the disgraced Detroit mayor Kwame Kilpatrick. While Cox and Hoekstra responded to attacks from one another, Snyder ran only positive ads and remained largely unscathed.

Snyder benefited not only from lack of consensus among Republican leaders but also from state election law. Because Michigan does not ask voters to register by party, independents and Democrats can decide to vote in the Republican primary. In 2010, nearly twice as many people voted in the Republican primary as the Democratic primary, including many who do not identify as Republicans. Snyder, seen as the most moderate candidate, received many of their crossover votes and won the primary.

Republican leaders ended up with a nominee with few ties to the party. Pro-life interest groups helped bring about a victory by the candidate who supported their cause the least. Snyder took advantage of the opening as conservatives failed to rally behind one alternative. In November, Snyder was elected governor in a landslide. As the incumbent in 2014, he won again—this time with no primary opposition and the support of Republican leaders.

Walberg won the Republican primary and the general election and returned to Congress. It is rare that intra-party feuding reaches this level, but such cases show how decentralized parties sometimes fail to reach consensus.

The Role of Party-in-Government

The party-in-government also influences campaigns and election outcomes. For better or worse, candidates with a party label are tied to the party's elected leaders. With Barack Obama as president, other Democratic politicians are seen as favoring his agenda, and Republican politicians are seen as opposing it. If Obama's approval rating is low, it may hurt all Democratic candidates. If the party leadership in Congress advances a legislative program, it will also reflect on that party's candidates. Many Democratic candidates in 2012, for example, had to defend health care reform, the economic stimulus package, and other controversial legislation associated with their party's actions in government. The same dynamics play out in state races, where candidates are seen as favoring or opposing their current governor's agenda. In legislative races, candidates are also affected by the current balance of power between the parties. The party with a majority in the legislature gets to set the agenda, typically earns more donations from access-oriented contributors, and can time legislation to maximize its impact on elections.

Candidates associated with the political party in power, especially incumbents, are judged on the basis of almost anything that occurs during their party's reign. Even adverse weather conditions like the dust storms of the 1930s, or events that have nothing to do with public policy, such as the 1916 shark attacks that inspired the movie *Jaws*, have been shown to move the mood of the electorate against the incumbent party.[10]

Legislators also must work through their party to pass bills that benefit their districts, such as legislation to support local road projects. Bringing federal money or other benefits to their districts can help increase an incumbent's popularity and prospects for reelection. Legislative party leaders know of this power; they often decide which of their incumbents to favor with local goods or legislative achievements based on the importance of their district in the next election.

---

[10] Christopher H. Achen and Larry M. Bartels. 2012. "Blind Retrospection: Why Shark Attacks Are Bad for Democracy." Working Paper. Vanderbilt University Center for the Study of Democratic Institutions. www.vanderbilt.edu/csdi/research/CSDI_WP_05-2013 .pdf (accessed 6/25/14).

Rules, Reality, and Party Strategies

Like candidates, political parties are strategic actors that have to make decisions within the context of both the reality on the ground and the rules set by government. The major rules that affect the parties are the election laws (Chapter 2) and the campaign finance laws (Chapter 4). The most relevant election laws for parties involve primary elections. There are long-running legal disputes about the extent to which parties can control their own nomination processes, which typically means control over primary elections. Some states mandate open primaries, where independents can vote in either party's election, but many party organizations prefer closed primaries, where only party members can vote. Parties have also attempted to set their own dates for primary elections and administer the voting, but most states demand that party rules conform to state laws and procedures. This often means that the two parties have to hold their elections on the same day. Parties still set many of their own rules and sometimes alter nomination rules to influence the winner of primary elections.

The State of California has implemented a series of reforms intended to weaken the influence of party organizations in primary elections. In 1996 voters enacted a "blanket primary": all of the candidates from both parties were listed on the ballot, allowing voters to vote in the Democratic primary for one office and in the Republican primary for another (see Chapter 2). The Supreme Court struck down this law in 2000, finding that it violated a political party's First Amendment freedom of association. In 2010, California voters passed another initiative that created a new system: candidates from all parties run together in the first round of voting, and the two candidates with the most votes advance to the general election. This means that two Democrats (or two Republicans) might be the only candidates on the final ballot. Under this system, party organizations that convince fewer of their candidates to run for each office have an advantage.

Campaign finance rules affect how parties can raise and spend money. As discussed in Chapter 4, before the Bipartisan Campaign Reform Act of 2002 political parties could accept unlimited contributions—or "soft money"—to spend on party-building activities and issue advertising. BCRA made soft money contributions illegal. Donors reacted by creating the so-called 527 organizations to channel the money that they previously directed to parties. BCRA's ban on soft money has not yet been overturned, despite several rulings weakening its restrictions on independent groups and corporations.

Federal campaign finance law does benefit political parties in one sense: unlike other organizations, such as Super PACs, parties are allowed to coordinate their campaign expenditures with the candidates they support. These coordinated expenditures allow parties to cooperate with candidates in developing messages and communicating them to voters. Party organizations also make independent expenditures that are not coordinated with candidates (see Figure 6.2 on p. 165). A party can thus intervene in a federal election by donating money to the candidate, donating money to state party organizations, coordinating expenditures with the candidate, and running its own advertisements.

Parties are not only affected by rules but are also constrained by the same reality that candidates face. For example, the **party identification** of voters is relatively stable (see Chapter 13); parties cannot easily convince citizens to change their identification and "join" another party. Similarly, parties cannot easily change how the public perceives them and their leaders. "Issue ownership," discussed in Chapter 5, means that the public trusts one party more than another to deal with certain problems. For example, voters have traditionally trusted Democrats more than Republicans to handle education, while Republicans have typically been trusted to handle national security issues.

Parties are also constrained by the prevailing economy. Many citizens come to disapprove of the party that presides over an economic recession and support the party that presides over an economic boom. Parties will often find it harder to recruit quality candidates and prevent incumbents from retiring when economic conditions are unfavorable.

A party's ability to win seats in an election can depend on the current partisan balance in legislatures. The party that controls the majority of seats may find that there are few remaining seats that they can win because they've already won so many of the competitive seats. Meanwhile, the minority can sometimes win back lots of marginal seats with a small swing in the national electorate. In 2010, one of the reasons the Republicans were able to win 63 more seats in the House of Representatives than they previously held was that they had lost so many seats in competitive districts in the 2006 and 2008 elections.

Parties find themselves constrained in part by the decisions of other actors, including candidates and interest groups. At times, these actors may work at cross-purposes with the party they support. Candidates who are fearful of losing independent voters may renounce aspects of their party's accomplishments and agenda. Interest groups that are otherwise allied with the party may even work against that party's incumbents. But parties and their allies among interest groups, consultants, and candidates typically strive to develop similar agendas and to target a similar set of competitive races.

Are Political Parties in Decline?

Although some observers have claimed that political parties are in decline, political scientists are skeptical of these claims. Political parties are certainly not in decline in government. Research shows that political parties in government have become more, not less, unified in the last 40 years and are able to exert better control of the legislative process.

Most arguments for party decline emphasize the apparent disregard for parties within the electorate—substantial percentages of the public identify as "independent," profess to dislike the major parties and their leaders, and favor a system with competitive third parties or independent candidacies. But reading too much into these sentiments is a mistake. As we noted earlier, most citizens who claim to be "independent" still lean toward one of the major parties and tend to vote for that party. These voters are really "closet partisans." Moreover, party identification is actually becoming *more* important in congressional, presidential, and state elections. This does not mean that the majority of citizens are familiar with the platforms of the political parties or have political opinions that are always closely aligned with their preferred party. These things are true of only the most well-informed citizens. Party identification, however, is a useful shortcut for reaching candidate judgments with or without detailed information.

Perhaps the best evidence for party decline comes from the decreasing role of party organizations in elections. In Chapter 3, we discussed how a certain kind of strong party organization known as a "party machine" gradually declined after the nineteenth century because of reforms such as the secret ballot. The rise of candidate-centered elections in the latter half of the twentieth century created a relationship whereby parties service candidates rather than having control over them.[11] There is indeed some evidence that candidates position themselves independent of parties and create their own constituencies, fund-raising operations, and volunteer networks—although parties still provide important resources that help with fund-raising, polling, get-out-the-vote operations, and other aspects of a campaign.

As we have seen, today's party organizations also have less control over selecting nominees to run in the general election than they did several decades ago. In presidential elections, the national party conventions used to select the presidential nominees largely independent of the voters. State parties once performed similar roles. With the rise of direct primaries for presiden-

---

[11] Aldrich, *Why Parties?*

tial and legislative elections, party organization leaders no longer have complete control over who becomes a party nominee.

However, parties may have regained significant influence over presidential nominations. Party leaders can coordinate their support for a candidate during the "invisible primary"—the period of time before the actual presidential primaries begin, when party leaders can observe and interact with potential candidates and each other. The goal of this process is to develop a consensus around one candidate so as to avoid a protracted and divisive primary process. One way in which party leaders signal their support for a candidate is via an endorsement. These endorsements strongly correlate with which candidate wins the nomination, even after taking into account the candidates' support in polls, the amount of money they raise, and the amount of media coverage they receive.[12]

This attempt by decentralized parties to reach consensus is not always successful, as the 2008 primaries suggest: neither Barack Obama nor John McCain won the support of enough party leaders to make the primary election results a foregone conclusion. Instead, both parties, and particularly the Democratic Party, experienced a lengthy and intensely competitive primary season. But in many other presidential election years, the nominee with the most support from party leaders quickly emerges as the winner. In 2012, Mitt Romney led the endorsement race and Obama faced no primary challenger.

Debates over the rise and decline of parties often return to the definitional controversies that began this chapter. Who constitutes the party? If it is anyone who endorses candidates, then the party includes elected officials, party officials, affiliated interest groups, celebrities, and others with access to money or organization. If it is anyone who gives money, it includes PACs, business leaders, professionals, activists, and constituents that want something from government. The more narrowly the party organization is defined, the more it becomes clear that this organization does not resemble a centralized machine, and the more evidence there is for its decline. By contrast, the more broadly parties are defined, the more influence they appear to have.

Party Evolution and Polarization

Although there is little evidence of partisan decline, there have been some changes in the issue positions and social coalitions of the Democrats and the Republicans. The most important geographic change, the move of the South

---

[12] Cohen et al., *The Party Decides.*

from a solid Democratic region to one that leans Republican, coincided with a sorting of voters into partisan camps based on their ideologies. Conservative Democrats, concentrated in but not exclusively from the South, slowly left the party. Liberal Republicans, largely from the northern states, changed parties or became more conservative. Ideological sorting was also helped by religious coalition change. Catholic voters, once a part of the Democratic coalition, became more evenly divided; white evangelicals gravitated toward Republicans.[13]

Some political scientists have argued that these changes were brought about by the rising salience of racial issues in American politics.[14] The civil rights movement split the parties' electoral coalitions, especially the uneasy alliance of white segregationists and African Americans in the Democratic Party. As a result, voters' feelings on civil rights policies like school integration and affirmative action became more important in their overall partisan identification—leading some to switch parties and others to align their racial and economic policy views with their party. This has led to concerns that Republican politicians' campaign messages include "coded racial appeals," discussing immigration, crime, and welfare to tap underlying white racial resentment.[15]

Other scholars argue that the parties have extended their initial conflicts on economic issues to an array of new issues, including race and gender as well as moral issues like abortion.[16] When the Supreme Court struck down anti-abortion laws in the 1973 *Roe v. Wade* decision, Republicans and Democrats (in both Congress and the electorate) were almost evenly divided between pro-choice and pro-life positions on abortion. Today, pro-choice Republicans and pro-life Democrats are rare. The same is true of other issues that formerly divided each party. As a result, citizens now learn a lot more about candidates based on their party affiliation alone and partisans of each stripe find it harder to admire any candidates in the other party.

Increasing party-line voting in Congress (with most Democrats on one side and most Republicans on the other) has led to concerns about

---

[13] Jeff Manza and Clem Brooks. 1999. *Social Cleavages and Political Change: Voter Alignments in U.S. Party Coalitions.* New York: Oxford University Press.

[14] Edward Carmines and James Stimson. 1989. *Issue Evolution: Race and the Transformation of American Politics.* Princeton, NJ: Princeton University Press.

[15] Ian Haney Lopez. 2013. *Dog Whistle Politics: How Coded Racial Appeals Have Reinvented Racism and Wrecked the Middle Class.* New York: Oxford University Press.

[16] Geoffrey Layman, Thomas Carsey, and Juliana Menasce Horowitz. 2006. "Party Polarization in American Politics: Characteristics, Causes, and Consequences." *Annual Review of Political Science* 9: 83–110.

polarization: the idea that the two parties are moving further apart from one another on an underlying ideological spectrum. As legislators have sorted into two parties with diametrically opposed views on most issues, the average opinion of Democrats and Republicans in the American public also seems to be diverging. Partisans are divided on more issues; in each issue area, fewer members of each party agree with the other party. This hardly means that we are a nation of extremists: many voters still express moderation and relatively few have consistently conservative or liberal views on every topic. Increasing division, however, has made it more difficult for politicians to campaign on issue positions likely to draw in voters from the other camp. Since Republicans and Democrats are now more segregated geographically, many legislative districts are also now less competitive.

Evaluating Political Parties

Political parties play important roles in elections but they are also frequently scrutinized and criticized. The major parties tend to have low approval ratings. To evaluate whether parties are helpful or harmful for democracy, we can ask several key questions.

First, do parties help voters make informed choices, or do they manipulate voters? On the one hand, parties and the platforms they create provide voters with clear choices and information about those choices, which helps voters select the candidate with whom they agree on most issues. In fact, simply voting based on party affiliation can be an effective way for some people to identify the candidate whose views accord more with their own.[17] Yet some voters may have different priorities than parties, so they will find the information provided by parties less helpful. As for manipulation, there is evidence that when citizens hold a policy preference different from a trusted party leader, they change their own preferences rather than oppose their party.[18] In addition to manipulation, this may simply reflect citizens blindly following elites.

Second, do parties contribute to free choice? Here too the picture is mixed. The two major political parties provide for competitive elections in many

---

[17] Richard Lau and David Redlawsk. 2001. "Advantages and Disadvantages of Cognitive Heuristics in Political Decision Making." *American Journal of Political Science* 45(4): 951–71.

[18] Gabriel Lenz. 2009. "Learning and Opinion Change, Not Priming: Reconsidering the Priming Hypothesis." *American Journal of Political Science* 53, 4: 821–37.

places, especially at the national level. They are roughly equal in their resources, the quality of their candidates (as judged by experience), and the support they command from voters. Clearly this is better than the one-party systems in some authoritarian regimes. At the same time, the Democratic and Republican parties certainly do nothing to alter the American system's bias against third parties and independent candidates who might represent other preferences among the public; indeed, the major parties often collude to exclude third-party competition.

Third, do parties contribute to deliberation? In one sense, they do. Competition between the major parties helps to clarify similarities and differences in what candidates and parties believe. But in other ways, parties do not contribute to healthy deliberation, especially in a two-party system. Much like candidates, parties try to persuade voters, not promote conversation. They also tend to focus on the narrow range of issues that will appeal to swing voters. In contrast, a multiparty system encourages a much broader range of issue discussion, as different parties emphasize different issues.[19]

Even if we are dissatisfied with the current role of parties, we should ask whether there is a viable alternative to them. Because most major democracies feature parties, it is hard to know what elections would look like without them. It is true that many local elections are nonpartisan (see Chapter 11), but this does not necessarily stop parties from forming, if only informally. Even without official parties, candidates tend to develop stable alliances. One could argue that this is good, in that identifiable "teams" of candidates are easier for voters to evaluate than a mass of Lone Rangers. Some reformers say that there actually should be more parties rather than fewer. They believe that a multiparty system would provide voters more diverse options and better represent the range of views in the public. However, as we noted in Chapter 2, multiparty systems may also make it more difficult for elected leaders to coordinate after elections.

Conclusion

Political parties are key features of American campaigns. Candidates and voters usually have preexisting ties to the Democrats or Republicans and campaigns usually replicate partisan divisions on public policy issues. Party organizations often recruit the candidates and determine their viability,

---

[19] Keena Lipsitz. 2004. "Democratic Theory and Political Campaigns." *Journal of Political Philosophy* 12, 2: 163–89.

directing resources to those most likely to win. Primary elections are largely internal party battles, with partisan leaders and activists helping to determine the nominees. General elections are largely fought along partisan lines, with each party's candidate presenting the party's issue positions and philosophy to voters already predisposed to choose one side in the battle.

But parties are also decentralized and amorphous organizations. A powerful party leader in Congress like Eric Cantor, selected by fellow elected Republicans, might still face a primary challenge in his home district and lose. Partisan activists and individual voters also shape the party's image and help decide its representatives; unfortunately for Cantor, they preferred a less experienced local professor. Nonetheless, we should not mistake the exception for the rule. Most incumbents cruise to victory in their primaries. Even in this case, Republican victory was assured by the makeup of the district: most Republican voters, and most districts where they reside, reliably elect Republicans. The same is true for the Democrats.

In the abstract, most citizens disdain parties. But despite persistent claims of decline, America's two major political parties are here to stay. As groups of citizens, officeholders, and organizations, parties guide voters, they train and organize candidates, and they govern. Attempts to regulate their influence typically succeed only in redirecting it. Whatever burdens parties create for democracies, it is difficult to imagine that democracy could work without them.

KEY TERMS

political parties (p. 154)

party-in-the-electorate (p. 156)

party-as-organization (p. 156)

party-in-government (p. 156)

coordinated expenditures (p. 164)

party identification (p. 170)

FOR DISCUSSION

1. Would American elections improve if party organizations were more involved in selecting party nominees and informing voters about the differences between candidates, or would it be better to leave campaigning to the candidates? How would elections change with more or less party involvement?

2. Democratic and Republican candidates (and voters) now take distinct positions on most issues. Is this a positive trend, because voters can now more easily tell the parties apart and elect candidates who

share their views, or a negative trend, because the two parties are too extreme to compete for moderate voters?

3. Should political parties seek to maximize the seats that they control in Congress, running less loyal and less ideologically consistent candidates in the districts where they have fewer identifiers, or only support those candidates that adhere to the party's platform? Why?

4. What are the most significant changes in the role of political parties in American elections since the 1960s? Have they gained or lost influence? How have their coalitions and issue positions evolved?

CHAPTER 7

Interest Groups

Charles and David Koch, the primary owners of a manufacturing, energy, and mining firm called Koch Industries, have a long history of promoting conservative and libertarian political causes. Through their family foundations, they helped build the main think tanks of the American right: the Heritage Foundation, the American Enterprise Institute, and the Cato Institute. They helped found organizations that became key promoters of the Tea Party movement, including Americans for Prosperity and FreedomWorks. As individuals and through their company, they have long been major donors to political candidates.

In the 2012 election cycle, they substantially increased their political spending in the hopes of defeating President Obama. A large network of interest groups they helped create and facilitate spent $170 million on federal campaigns, more than half of which was directly provided by Koch-linked grants.[1] Charles, David, and Koch Industries also provided more than $5 million in campaign contributions, more than 90 percent on the Republican side.

Democrats resented their efforts. Majority Leader Harry Reid repeatedly complained about their outsized influence, blaming them for the 2013 government shutdown and accusing them of "trying to buy the country" on the Senate floor. A Democratic Super PAC ran television ads directly attacking them as "out-of-state billionaires" fighting to "rig the system," "end Medicare as we know it," and even "cut off Hurricane relief."[2] Even though neither Koch brother is a candidate or a party official, they have become the subject of attack ads. Their donation patterns and elaborate network of organizations, sometimes difficult to trace back to them, influence the financial advantages of candidates and the content of their advertising campaigns.

---

[1] Robert Macguire, "At Least 1 in 4 Dark Money Dollars in 2012 Had Koch Links." Center for Responsive Politics. www.opensecrets.org/news/2013/12/1-in-4-dark-money-dollars-in-2012-c/ (accessed 7/23/14).

[2] FactCheck.org profile of Senate Majority PAC. www.factcheck.org/2014/02/senate-majority-pac/ (accessed 7/23/14).

Although the money they spend on campaigns is far beyond the norm, several aspects of their political activities are emblematic of interest group participation in campaigns. First, the Kochs are the most common type of large donors to interest groups: well-off business officials with clear ties to one party. Second, some of their organizations are traditional interest groups that lobby Congress and produce research, but others are part of a new breed of entities that are developed to take advantage of some feature of tax or campaign finance law. Americans for Prosperity mobilizes voters and lobbies state legislatures, but the American Future Fund and Americans for Responsible Leadership may simply be accounts for collecting money and paying for television ads. Third, the Koch brothers are motivated by a combination of financial interest and ideology. Their companies can gain from federal contracts and low regulation, but their political spending is far beyond their direct foreseeable gain. They also provide considerable charitable contributions for art and education (with no obvious company benefit); politics is another outlet for using their money to advance their ideas.

Interest groups play important roles in American campaigns, but the most involved are often adjuncts of political parties or creations of rich patrons. This chapter explores their roles, focusing both on the traditional role of interest groups in mobilizing segments of the electorate and their contemporary role as vehicles for campaign spending independent of candidates and parties. We first discuss the different types of interest groups and why they have proliferated. The chapter then looks at their involvement in campaigns and how it has co-evolved with changes in campaign finance law. We also focus on their unique roles in initiative campaigns and note that the majority of interest groups still

Core of the Analysis

- Interest groups are varied actors, only some of which get involved in campaigns; they have proliferated, while changing form in response to changes in law.

- Interest groups donate money, run advertisements, and help mobilize voters but have distinct motives from those of the candidates and parties that they support.

- Interest group spending can affect voters' choices, but there is only limited evidence that they redirect campaign agendas or deliver specific constituency votes.

- Interest group activity may seem at odds with many of our hopes for campaigns, but it can increase the diversity of voices in campaigns beyond the candidates.

avoid campaigns in favor of lobbying. The chapter then addresses interest group campaign strategy, in the context of the rules and realities they face, and assesses whether interest groups succeed in changing campaign debate or delivering constituency votes. Finally, we evaluate their role: Are interest groups meddling liars that divert candidates from their messages and mislead voters, or do they add important voices to American campaigns? Are the Koch brothers best seen, as their spokesman suggests, as "patriotic Americans that have devoted their lives to advancing tolerance and freedom in America" or, as Harry Reid argues, as "two power-drunk billionaires" running the Republican Party?[3] Their true role may be more pedestrian, motivated by conservative ideas (and aligned business interests); the Koch brothers have created a network of interest groups to help Republicans win elections — just as other rich individuals fund groups supporting Democrats.

Types of Interest Groups

An **interest group** is a collection of people acting on the shared goal of influencing public policy. Although parties also have policy goals, interest groups differ from parties in key respects. Most important, interest groups do not run their own candidates for office. Often, interest groups seek more particular policy goals than do parties. Interest groups are not always aligned with any one party. Many groups assist or attempt to influence members of both parties. This is true even in campaigns, where some groups will support members of both parties. Finally, some interest groups do not participate in elections at all, focusing instead on lobbying policy makers after they are elected. But because election results influence policy outcomes, many interest groups do participate in campaigns and can be important actors in elections.

There are several major types of interest groups. The largest sector of groups represents businesses. More than 3,000 individual corporations or trade associations have a political office in or near Washington, D.C. These include large groups such as the National Association of Manufacturers and the American Farm Bureau Federation that, through affiliates, regularly give money to campaigns and participate directly in them. Yet most corporations do not have political action committees (PACs), make campaign contributions, or air their own campaign advertisements. Another large sector of interest groups,

---

[3] Kenneth P. Vogel. 2014. "Behind Harry Reid's War against the Koch Brothers." *Politico.* www.politico.com/story/2014/07/harry-reid-koch-brothers-108632.html (accessed 7/24/14).

professional associations, represent occupations; examples include the American Medical Association and the American Bar Association. The largest of these groups participate in elections, but most are small and do not participate in campaigns. A third sector of interest groups, labor unions, regularly participates in campaigns. Most labor unions—for example, the American Federation of State, County, and Municipal Employees (AFSCME) and the Service Employees International Union (SEIU)—usually support Democratic candidates. A smaller number of unions, such as the Teamsters Union, sometimes endorse candidates from both parties. Rather than the direct economic concerns of corporations, unions, and professionals, some interest groups seek to represent broader social groups or ideological perspectives. Groups that represent a social group include the National Association for the Advancement of Colored People (NAACP), which works on behalf of African Americans. Some groups represent a general ideological orientation, such as the American Conservative Union. These groups usually refer to themselves as public interest groups. Other groups advocate for a single issue—in the case of the National Rifle Association (NRA), the rights of gun owners (see Box 7.1). Public interest and single-issue groups are more likely to participate in elections than economic groups, but they are less numerous and have fewer resources.[4] The 2012 campaign also witnessed a large increase in ideological groups created only to advertise in one campaign, rather than for ongoing lobbying.

Interest groups also differ in the extent of their ties to political parties. Unions like the National Education Association have endorsed the Democratic Party candidate in every presidential election of the past few decades; others like the Fraternal Order of Police lean toward the Republicans. Many interest groups share close ties to a party, exchanging mailing lists and voter targets, even if they officially claim to be nonpartisan. Groups may have some incentive to maintain allies in the opposing party: the NRA still gives money to some Democrats, even though the Republican National Committee was a top recipient of its largesse.

Why Does the United States Have So Many Interest Groups?

The United States has a large and growing number of interest groups. The increase has been particularly dramatic since the 1960s. What has caused

---

[4] Jack Walker. 1991. *Mobilizing Interest Groups in America: Patrons, Professions, and Social Movements.* Ann Arbor: University of Michigan Press.

BOX 7.1

How the National Rifle Association Enforces Support for Gun Rights

The National Rifle Association's political influence is legendary. Its reputation was sealed in 1994, when many incumbents that the group opposed, including House Speaker Tom Foley, lost, thereby shifting control of Congress to the Republicans. Several of these members, including Foley, had defected from supporting gun rights on only one significant occasion — by supporting the assault weapons ban in a crime bill — but that was enough to earn the NRA's retaliation. According to many observers, including former president Bill Clinton, the NRA's intervention cost these members their seats in Congress. "The gun lobby claimed to have defeated nineteen of the twenty-four members on its hit list," Clinton reported in his autobiography, "They did at least that much damage and could rightly claim to have made [Newt] Gingrich the House Speaker."[1]

Political scientists are more cautious about attributing influence to interest groups. Many other factors contributed to the Republican Party's victories in 1994, and there is little evidence that the NRA's television ads or the votes of gun rights supporters were the deciding factors. For the NRA's purposes, however, it may not matter. Their reputation benefited regardless, enabling them to exert more influence on members of both parties. Interest groups that intervene in elections can gain in two ways: actual influence on election outcomes, and an enhanced reputation for influence — the NRA has proven adept at both. In 2013, two Democratic state senators in Colorado were recalled after a campaign backed by the NRA. The NRA does not win every battle it enters, but it wins enough to make an impression on politicians wavering in their support of gun rights.

The NRA's CEO, Wayne LaPierre, regularly presides over large showcase rallies that highlight its goals in influencing government.

Can the NRA's influence be neutralized? In 2014, former New York Mayor Michael Bloomberg said he would donate $50 million to build interest groups in favor of gun control. The new groups would run ads against candidates opposed to gun control and organize public supporters. The goal, according to Bloomberg was to "make them afraid of us."[2] Bloomberg is satisfied that he is doing the right thing: "I have earned my place in heaven. It's not even close," he said. Nevertheless, Bloomberg's initial efforts to counteract the NRA did not result in much success: Federal gun control is no closer to enactment, and few, if any, candidates have changed their views or gone down to defeat as a result of Bloomberg's campaigns. The NRA's reputation as an influential political force with a solid constituency behind it has stayed intact.

---

[1] Bill Clinton. 2005. *My Life: The Presidential Years*. New York: Vintage Books, p. 215.
[2] Tim O'Connor and Leslie Larson. 2014. "Former Mayor Michael Bloomberg Pledges $50 Million to Build Network to Fight NRA and Seek Stricter Gun Control Laws." *New York Daily News*. www.nydailynews.com/new-york /bloomberg-pledges-50m-fight-nra-article-1.1757801 (accessed 7/24/14).

this trend? A basic reason is the expansion of government. As governments at all levels in the United States, but particularly the federal government, have taken on more responsibilities, they now regulate more entities and provide resources to more people. This creates an incentive to organize so as to receive more favorable regulations and additional resources.

A second reason for interest group expansion is improved strategies for organizational maintenance. A key innovation was direct mail fund-raising, by which an organization could regularly solicit contributions from an expanding list of like-minded Americans. Today, organizations maintain e-mail lists and websites to further facilitate fund-raising appeals.

A third reason is that prominent social movements have served as models for other groups to mobilize. After the success of the African American civil rights movement, for example, other minority groups mobilized—a trend furthered by the increasing ethnic and religious diversity of the United States. Successful mobilization by one side can also stimulate mobilization by the other. A conservative group called the American Action Network was recently founded to respond to the liberal Center for American Progress, which was originally founded to counter conservative think tanks like the Heritage Foundation. The Heritage Foundation was itself founded to counter the liberal Brookings Institution. This pattern of response and counter-response is common.

A fourth factor in the proliferation of interest groups is the nature of the rules concerning these groups—specifically, the federal tax and campaign finance laws that encourage organizations to create separate affiliated groups for distinct purposes. As noted in Chapter 4, many interest groups are registered with the Internal Revenue Service (IRS) as 501(c) nonprofit corporations or as 527 groups. Interest groups also create political action committees (PACs) to accept contributions and donate them directly to political candidates. Some organizations have a combination of affiliates of different types. For example, EMILY's List, a supporter of female Democratic candidates, is a PAC with affiliated 527s. Progress for America is a conservative 501(c)4 organization with a 527 affiliate. The Center for American Progress is a 501(c)3 with a 501(c)4 affiliate. The NRA is a 501(c)4 with a PAC. State and local laws differ in how these organizations are treated and whether they can participate in state and local elections. As a result, organizations with state or local affiliates can have even more complicated structures.

Campaign finance rules drive the formation of new groups in another way as well. Because the laws require that the sponsors of advertisements be disclosed in the advertisements themselves, some groups create new organizations with names designed to appeal to the electorate. In a 2010 California ballot initiative campaign dealing with auto insurance, the side funded by insurance companies called itself "Californians for Fair Auto Insurance

This advertisement, run by the True Republican PAC in Alabama's 2010 gubernatorial election, attacked a candidate for his belief in evolution. However, reports later surfaced that tied the PAC to the state teachers' association.

Rates" and created the "California Senior Advocates League" to promote its cause. In 2010, the Alabama Education Association, a liberal teachers association, even funded the "True Republican PAC." This PAC disingenuously ran advertisements critical of the teaching of evolution to weaken conservative support for the incumbent GOP candidate in the Republican primary. Campaign finance laws, in other words, encourage the same groups of people to create multiple organizations for legal and public relations purposes.

An increase in campaign activity by interest groups has accompanied the general increase in the number of groups. More interest groups have meant more interest group campaigning. Yet, as Figure 7.1 illustrates, not all upward trends followed the same trajectory. The numbers of lobbyists and PACs have risen only slightly in the past eight election cycles but they have become accompanied by new types of groups: 527s and Super PACs. The largest increase in PACs occurred in the late 1970s and early 1980s. Expenditures by 527s were concentrated in the 2004 election cycle. Independent spending has increased most dramatically since 2006, especially by Super PACs in 2012. 501(c) organizations also began spending considerable sums on election-related activities, but their use is still in its infancy.

FIGURE 7.1 Number of Lobbyists, Contributing Political Action Committees, Super PACs, and 527s, 1998–2014

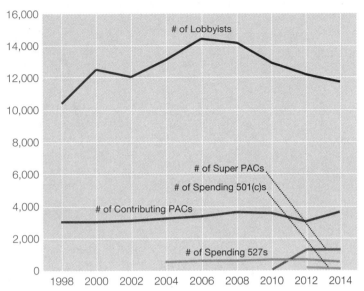

Source: Lobbyist data are from the Center for Responsive Politics, based on data from the Senate Office of Public Records. PAC data are from the Federal Election Commission. SuperPAC and 527 data are from the Center for Responsive Politics, based on Federal Election Committee and Internal Revenue Service data.

Figure 7.2 illustrates trends in the total amounts of money that interest groups donate in federal campaign contributions and how much they directly spend in campaigns (including several types of spending). Since PAC contributions go disproportionately to incumbents who often lack competition, direct spending can be more influential in close elections. It also has some disadvantages for interest groups, since independent spenders cannot coordinate with candidates and often have to pay higher rates for television advertising. In 2012, independent expenditures in federal elections eclipsed total PAC contributions for the first time, tripling the totals from the previous campaign. These trends were caused more by changes in campaign finance laws than by changes in the number of groups trying to influence campaigns (as Figure 7.1 shows). Supreme Court rulings and Federal Election Commission (FEC) interpretations enabled new Super PACs to accept unlimited contributions and spend unlimited amounts to influence elections. In 2012, a small number of them, disproportionately favoring Republicans, directed the large increase in direct group spending. The Republican Super PAC advantage in 2012 allowed Romney to remain competitive in total advertising volume, even though the Obama campaign substantially

FIGURE 7.2 Total Interest Group Campaign Contributions and Direct Campaign Spending 1998–2014

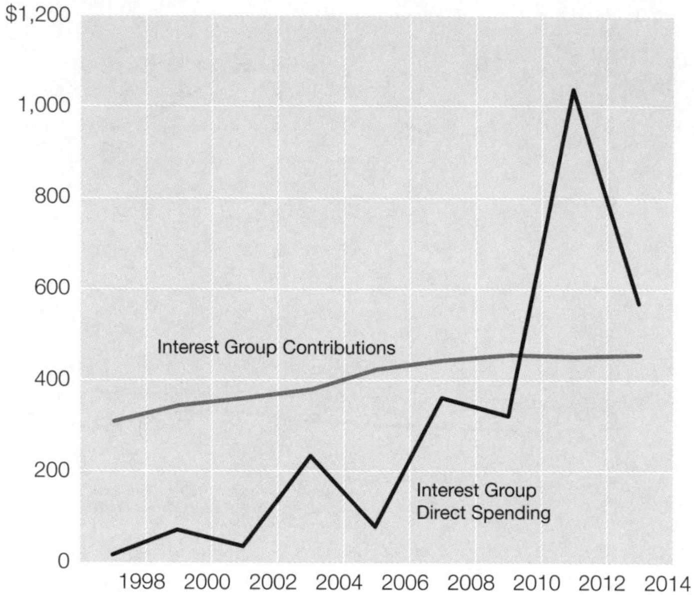

Note: In millions, 2012 dollars.
Source: Data are from the Center for Responsive Politics, based on data from the Federal Election Commission. Campaign contributions include only PAC contributions. Direct spending includes independent expenditures, electioneering communications, and communication costs.

outraised the Romney campaign. In 2014, Democrats were more effective at mobilizing Super PAC dollars than in previous elections.

How Are Interest Groups Involved in Campaigns?

Although the majority of interest groups do not get involved in campaigns, many groups contribute money and endorse candidates. Organizations with members commonly communicate with and attempt to mobilize their members to volunteer and turn out to vote. A small number of interest groups engage in their own advertising, including an increasing number that are founded exclusively for this purpose.

Because of donor disclosure requirements, campaign contributions are the type of interest group electioneering that is easiest to track. Interest groups often donate money to candidates and parties through their affiliated PACs. Total PAC contributions have been increasing since the 1990s, even as the number of PACs has held relatively steady. Most PACs are associated with professional associations, unions, or corporations. Corporate, union, and association executives also make individual contributions to candidates. The Center for Responsive Politics combines PAC giving with donations from individuals associated with an organization in its tracking of total giving by industries over time. In 2012, according to their data, total giving by entities affiliated with business accounted for more than 60 percent of large federal campaign contributions, labor unions contributed 5.4 percent, and ideological interest groups contributed 10.5 percent. Ideological and single-issue PACs are becoming more numerous, but their contributions still account for a small portion of total PAC giving. Within the corporate sector, the financial industry donates more money than any other corporate sector, with companies in law, energy, health, and communications also accounting for a large portion of contributions (see Figure 7.3). Corporate sectors differ not only in how much they donate but in who receives their donations. The building materials and oil and gas industries consistently favor Republicans, while the entertainment and publishing industries consistently favor Democrats. Unions are bigger supporters of Democratic candidates than any industry sector. Although PACs are clearly important donors, their contributions must be put in context: as we discussed in Chapter 4, PACs donate less money to American political campaigns than individuals, although many of these individuals are employees of corporations with political interests.

Interest groups can also participate in elections by running their own advertising campaigns. According to the Center for Responsive Politics, the interest groups most involved in independent expenditure campaigns in 2008 were the SEIU, the NRA, and AFSCME. In 2012, Super PACs dominated outside campaign intervention, spending more than $631 million. Table 7.1 reports the top interest group spenders in the 2012 federal elections. The top Super PACs were American Crossroads, Restore Our Future, and Priorities USA Action. New 501(c) organizations officially claiming to advance social welfare, rather than focus on politics, were nonetheless also funneling money toward campaign advertising. Traditional interest groups like the U.S. Chamber of Commerce, the SEIU, and the NRA also continued to spend at high levels. In total, conservative non-party committees spent well over twice as much as their liberal adversaries (though this may have been a product of the 2012 race, where the Obama campaign raised more money than the Romney campaign and Republicans relied on interest groups to make total spending on each partisan side more even). Together, 2012 interest groups allocated over four times as much as political parties to independent spending.

Campaign advertisements aired by interest groups are much more likely to be negative than those aired by candidates. In 2014, 45 percent of federal

FIGURE 7.3 Total Political Contributions by Industry Sector

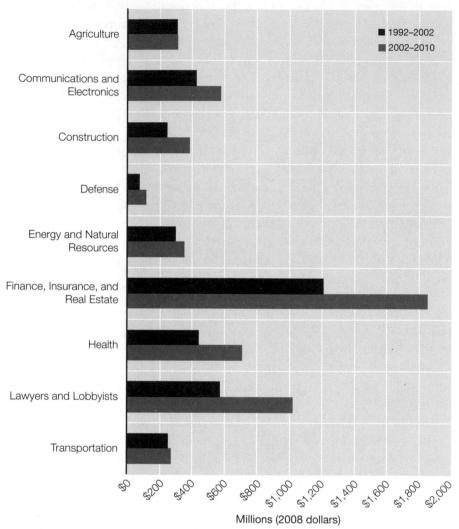

Source: Data from opensecrets.org. Includes individual contributions, PAC contributions, and soft money.

candidate ads were positive and only 24 percent were negative. Among ads aired by interest groups in the same races, only 13 percent were positive and 77 percent were negative.[5] Interest groups are less concerned than candidates or parties with protecting their reputation and are willing to risk any backlash from negative advertising. Interest group ads are less obviously

---

[5] Erika Franklin, Fowler Michael Franz, and Travis Ridout. 2016. *Political Advertising in the United States*. Boulder, CO: Westview Press.

tied to the candidate that they are supporting, although voters may not necessarily distinguish interest group ads from candidate ads. Interest group advertisements are also more likely to focus on policy issues than candidate advertisements. Candidates are more concerned with sharing their biographies, whereas interest groups often want to make the issues that concern them more central to the campaign.

Contributions and independent expenditures may be the easiest way to measure interest group involvement in campaigns, but they are not the only ways in which interest groups try to influence elections. Interest groups also use newer forms of media to get their campaign messages out and support specific candidates. Many groups have large e-mail lists and groups of online supporters on social networking sites like Facebook and Twitter. Many groups mobilize their members to support causes or candidates via donations or other forms of activism. At times, online activists and blogs, such as the liberal Daily Kos, become interest groups in themselves, raising money and endorsing candidates.

Interest groups also sometimes pursue independent efforts to mobilize and persuade voters. Unions have long engaged in grassroots mobilization of their members. In 2004, 527s on the Democratic side, such as America Coming Together, also worked to mobilize voters. Many interest groups produce voter guides or endorse slates of candidates. The Christian Coalition handed out millions of voter guides outside churches in 1994, making it clear that they believed Republican candidates were pro-life and pro-family whereas Democratic candidates were not. In local races, groups often place door-hangers throughout a district, listing all of the candidates that they are supporting.

Interest groups that undertake these campaign activities often claim to speak for broader **constituencies**, such as all voters from a particular ethnic or religious group. Organizations and leaders that represent a particular group can help to reinforce the allegiance of group members in the voting public to a party or set of candidates. Arguably, the loyalty of African American voters to the Democratic Party arises in part because most black leaders are allied with the party.[6] Republican candidates also sometimes attend NAACP conventions, if only to avoid appearing to ignore African Americans. Candidates may also sign on to a group's policy agenda, such as Americans for Tax Reform's "Taxpayer Protection Pledge," which entails a promise not to raise taxes. Candidates signing the pledge expect not only to gain the

---

[6] Paul Frymer. 1999. *Uneasy Alliances: Race and Party Competition in America.* Princeton, NJ: Princeton University Press.

TABLE 7.1 Top Interest Group Spenders in 2012 Elections

Group Name	Amount Spent	Partisan Tilt	Type of Group
American Crossroads/ Crossroads GPS	$176,429,025	Republican	SuperPAC, 501c
Restore Our Future	$142,097,336	Republican	SuperPAC
Priorities USA/ Priorities USA Action	$65,166,859	Democratic	SuperPAC
Americans for Prosperity	$36,352,928	Republican	501c
U.S. Chamber of Commerce	$35,657,029	Republican	501c
American Future Fund	$25,415,969	Republican	501c
Service Employees International Union	$23,011,004	Democratic	SuperPAC, 501c
National Rifle Association	$19,767,043	Republican	501c
FreedomWorks	$19,638,968	Republican	SuperPAC
AFSCME	$18,012,198	Democratic	501c
Club for Growth	$17,960,737	Republican	SuperPAC, 501c
Winning Our Future	$17,007,762	Republican	SuperPAC
Americans for Job Security	$15,872,864	Republican	501c
Americans for Tax Reform	$15,794,552	Republican	501c
League of Conservation Voters	$14,181,521	Democratic	SuperPAC, 501c

Source: Data from Center for Responsive Politics.

support of individuals affiliated with the interest group, but also to signal to all voters opposed to taxes that they share their views.

Interest Groups in Initiative Campaigns

In **ballot initiative campaigns**, where voters decide to support or oppose specific policy changes, interest groups replace the candidates as the main actors. In states and localities where initiatives and referenda are allowed, coalitions of individuals and interest groups often form to pay signature gathering firms to sign up enough registered voters to meet requirements to get an initiative on the ballot. In California, proponents routinely pay $1 or $2 million just for the signature gathering effort before the real campaign begins. Legislatures can also directly put questions on the ballot, and local governing authorities are sometimes required to put measures like tax increases to the voters. No matter how they make their way onto the ballot, committees often form to support or oppose them. Statewide initiatives, especially those that will impact the bottom line of businesses, are more likely to generate active campaigns.

Interest group endorsements and advertising can provide clues to initiative voters, who might not otherwise understand the complex legislative language of initiatives. A study of California voters deciding on five complicated insurance initiatives found that knowing whether the insurance industry, trial lawyers, and consumer activists supported the measures was enough to help voters who could not understand the initiatives emulate the votes of those who did have full information.[7] Voters just had to know whether you favored the position of the insurance industry or the trial lawyers, not which particular law you preferred.

With enough money, even obscure interest groups can put their issues to the voters. In 2014, a wealthy technology businessman tried to qualify an initiative to divide California into six separate states including one named "Silicon Valley," even though polls showed little support and legal experts said voters lacked the authority to break up the state. Because too many signatures were invalid, the initiative was kept off the ballot. Interest group spending can also help defeat initiatives, especially if opponents outspend proponents by a 2–1 margin, but there is little evidence that outsized spending on the positive side can move voters to support a proposition.[8] Money might eventually buy this businessman a place on the ballot, but California is in little danger of splitting up anytime soon.

Why Do Some Interest Groups Avoid Campaigns?

Many traditional interest groups avoid spending money on political campaigns. Most businesses that hire a lobbyist fail to start a PAC. Even some huge firms like Apple and Berkshire Hathaway lack PACs. All of the major

---

[7] Arthur Lupia. 1994. "Shortcuts versus Encyclopedias: Information and Voting Behavior in California Insurance Reform Elections." *American Political Science Review* 88, 1: 63–76.

[8] Liz Gerber. 1999. *The Populist Paradox: Interest Group Influence and the Promise of Direct Legislation*. Princeton, NJ: Princeton University Press.

industries that do donate to candidates still spend considerably more on lobbying and charitable contributions than on campaigns.[9] Few interest groups give the maximum amounts allowed by law to candidates and even fewer spend their own money directly in campaigns.

This points to a difference in the goals of interest groups, compared to political parties and candidates. Interest groups' primary concerns are policy outcomes, rather than who holds power. They care about elections because which party controls government influences whether legislatures pass the laws they favor or oppose and how administrations implement those laws. Groups may also be able to identify particular candidates most likely to support their policy goals. But elections are not interest groups' only opportunities to influence policy: they can also lobby whoever is elected or appointed. If you plan to talk to members of both parties, it may be disadvantageous to have a firm tie to the Democrats or the Republicans.

As judged by their spending habits, most interest groups view spending money on lobbying as a better strategy than spending on campaigns. The issues of interest to many corporations, such as a specific tax exemption or a small appropriation, never come up in campaigns. Interest groups also like to present an apolitical image of expertise and a willingness to work with anyone to achieve shared goals. Appearing to stay above the fray, rather than intervening in elections, may better serve that image.

The combination of some interest groups averse to campaigns and some interest groups invented for the sole purpose of running ads in campaigns means that the most involved groups in elections are not representative of all the groups trying to influence policy. The campaigning groups are much more likely to take a clear partisan side and be motivated by ideology than those who sit on the sidelines.

Rules, Reality, and Interest Group Strategies

Interest groups decide their campaign role in the context of the rules set by government. As we have seen, campaign finance affiliates laws set limits on how much any group can donate, and encourage groups to establish multiple subsidiaries—501(c) organizations, 527 organizations, PACs—in order to stay within the law. Groups are also prohibited from coordinating their advertising or mobilization efforts with candidates. Candidates cannot use

[9] Jeffrey Milyo, David Primo, and Timothy Groseclose. 2000. "Corporate PAC Campaign Contributions in Perspective." *Business and Politics* 2, 1: 75–88.

the resources of interest groups, even office space or printed materials, without counting those resources as in-kind contributions, subject to disclosure and contribution limits. Furthermore, tax law limits the activities of many interest groups if they are organized as tax-exempt nonprofit organizations. Depending on their tax status, interest groups may be prohibited from publicly endorsing candidates or engaging in campaign activity.

Interest group strategies are also constrained by certain realities that they may not be able to change during any particular campaign. Some interest groups represent more popular issue positions than others. Some represent issues that are already of great concern to voters, but others need to stimulate interest in their issue areas. Some groups find it easier to raise money and thus have more resources to use in elections than others. Candidates may inevitably cater to the wealthiest groups and those most able to deliver large numbers of votes.

Interest group strategies also depend on how their agenda and issue positions correspond to those of incumbent politicians.[10] Groups whose agendas are well served by incumbent politicians will typically support them, regardless of party, and will seek to maintain their access to these politicians and thus ensure that government policy continues to match their preferences. Evidence of this strategy can be seen among interest groups that give to members of both parties. For example, the defense and aerospace industry—which has earned many billions of dollars in government contracts—routinely gives considerable sums to both parties. In 2012, the top donor within the industry, Northrop Grumman, gave 42 percent of its donations to Democrats and 57 percent to Republicans. By contrast, interest groups whose views are not well represented among incumbents—typically, ideological and single-issue groups—will seek to replace these incumbents, often with representatives who are more liberal or conservative than the average legislator. The actions of the Club for Growth exemplify this strategy, as the group often seeks to replace Republican incumbents with more conservative alternatives.

Substantial interest group resources—particularly in the form of independent expenditures—are often targeted at a few competitive races. This can complicate life for the candidates in these races. Interest groups often emphasize a message different from that of the candidate they support—a message that may center on their narrow agendas rather than the concerns of the average voter. Their message may also be more controversial: the Willie Horton advertisement discussed in Chapter 4 was broadcast by an interest

---

[10] Michael M. Franz. 2008. *Choices and Changes: Interest Groups in the Electoral Process.* Philadelphia: Temple University Press.

group and ultimately disavowed by the candidate, George H. W. Bush, it was meant to support.

Interest Group Campaign Influence

Interest groups largely engage in the same activities as candidates and parties, meaning that their influence is tied to similar factors. If voters know little about the candidates, one side spends considerably more than the other, and a close race is projected based on fundamental factors, interest group activities can help tip the balance. In races with well-known contenders or even spending, interest group activities—just like candidate and party campaigns—will have a hard time affecting election outcomes. If ads or GOTV efforts are successful in the hands of parties or candidates, interest groups can use the same strategies to achieve similar effects. But interest groups face the same environment as their allies: most favored Romney over Obama in 2012, but had no more luck than the Republican Party or Romney in convincing voters to reject Obama. Similarly, the mobilization of liberal groups in 2014 met the same fate as their Democratic allies. In a banner year for Republicans, most of their preferred candidates lost.

The large increase in interest group campaign activity has stimulated some research on its impact. In the 2012 Republican presidential primary, where Super PACs outspent candidates in many states, Super PACs extended the viability of Rick Santorum, who had limited money, and reduced the influence of candidate wins in the early states on the contests that followed them.[11] A lab experiment where researchers showed these 2012 Super PAC ads to voters found that they reduced voters' evaluations of Romney, indirectly helping Obama even though they were meant to support Romney's primary opponents.[12]

Many reformers are concerned that interest group influence will grow with unlimited spending by Super PACs. Some have even fought back by forming their own. In 2011, comedian Steven Colbert started a Super PAC to dramatize the potential for unlimited and hidden political spending. He raised $1 million, increasing awareness of campaign finance laws among his television viewers but failing to influence many voters with his advertising. In 2014, Harvard professor Lawrence Lessig started the Mayday PAC with

---

[11] Dino Christenson and Corwin Smidt. 2014. "Following the Money: Super PACs and the 2012 Presidential Nomination." *Presidential Studies Quarterly* 44, 3: 410–30.

[12] David Lynn Painter. 2014. "Collateral Damage: Involvement and the Effects of Negative Super PAC Advertising." *American Behavioral Scientist* 58: 510–23.

an odd purpose: to support candidates who want to eliminate Super PACs. He recommends that citizens "embrace the irony" of using Super PACs to fight against Super PACs, but the effort faces an uphill battle: making the issue matter to electable candidates without stimulating overwhelming opposition spending.[13] Thus far, the effort has spent considerable sums (often on long-shot candidacies) to little effect.

Interest groups may be especially likely to influence outcomes where other campaigning is limited, such as in ballot initiative campaigns. In one field experiment, researchers worked with an advocacy group supporting and opposing statewide initiatives in Oregon to send persuasive mailers to randomly selected households, finding that precincts that received the materials were more likely to support initiatives favored by the group and oppose those that the group sought to defeat.[14]

Can Interest Groups Deliver Constituency Votes?

Interest groups often claim to represent constituencies like gun owners, union members, and African Americans. They offer candidates a deal: support our groups' goals and you will win the votes of our members and sympathetic fans in the electorate. But can interest groups actually deliver? Gaining the support of interest groups is likely to translate into votes only if group members perceive a common fate, believe that an organization best represents their interests, and tend to vote together consistently. Gaining a Farm Bureau organizational endorsement, for example, matters more if farmers see themselves as a group that will rise and fall with support for particular agricultural policies. The efforts of interest groups and their leaders may be especially important in local elections, where voters know more about their neighborhood association, union, or business association than they know about many of the candidates. In local elections, there will often be a direct negotiation between candidates and local group leaders over which candidates will receive the votes of group members. All of the local African American neighborhood leaders may endorse one of the mayoral candidates, sending a message that the candidate supports African American interests and promising to mobilize local African Americans through churches and community associations.

---

[13] Nicholas Confessore. 2014. "Big Money to Fight Big Donors." *New York Times*, September 7: A1.

[14] Todd Rogers and Joel Middleton. 2014. "Are Ballot Initiative Outcomes Influenced by the Campaigns of Independent Groups? A Precinct-Randomized Field Experiment Showing That They Are." *Political Behavior.* Published online July 11, 2014 at http://link.springer.com /article/10.1007/s11109-014-9282-4.

Yet candidates cannot be certain that earning the endorsement of groups or their leaders will lead group members to vote for them. Early in the 2008 campaign for the Democratic presidential nomination, Hillary Clinton scooped up endorsements from African American legislators and interest groups, but ultimately this did not translate into enough support from black voters. One of Clinton's strategists, Mark Penn, expected only 70 percent of African Americans to support Obama in the 2008 primaries, but in some states, 90 percent did. This miscalculation was enough to cost Clinton her chance of winning a majority of the delegates to the Democratic convention. More generally, interest groups sometimes exaggerate their ability to "deliver" votes for a candidate. The views of group leaders are often more consistently ideological or strongly partisan than views of group members. Members may also be more divided than leaders in their loyalties to parties or candidates. Ultimately, although candidates typically seek the support of sympathetic interest groups, the number of voters any group can deliver is uncertain.

Unions have traditionally been a major force in Democratic Party politics. Much of the campaigning in Democratic primaries consists of traveling from union hall to union hall gathering endorsements by talking at open meetings or negotiating with leadership. National labor groups like the AFL-CIO and the SEIU are still among the top Democratic Party donors and spend considerably on their own advertising and get-out-the-vote strategies. They also serve as national volunteer networks for Democratic campaigns. But Republican politicians regularly complain that union leadership fails to represent the views of their significant, but minority, Republican membership. Unions also face a declining membership and they increasingly represent government employees rather than private sector workers, making it harder to reach out to the broader working class that they hope to mobilize on behalf of Democrats.

When a constituency is easily identifiable, motivated, and ascendant, interest groups can help channel their energies toward candidates that share their view. Since 2010, the Tea Party Express, FreedomWorks, and Americans for Prosperity have helped to build the infrastructure of Tea Party rallies and campaign activities. They often support the same candidates in Republican Party primaries, stamping them with the moniker of "consistent conservative" and helping to direct conservative voters to the candidates they support. Although not many Americans are official members of these interest groups, many more are sympathetic to the aims of the Tea Party. Interest group endorsements help codify one candidate as the Tea Party candidate, a fact often amplified by talk radio hosts and reported in local media coverage.

Can Interest Groups Change the Campaign Agenda?

Some interest groups have goals beyond electing a particular candidate; they hope to change the **campaign agenda**: the issues at the heart of a campaign. Environmental organizations usually support Democratic candidates, but they also want issues like pollution and climate change to play a more prominent role in campaigns. They may advertise directly on the issues that most concern them, hoping to stimulate candidate and voter discussion on the same issues. The League of Conservation Voters targets 12 candidates it calls the "dirty dozen" who it says oppose clean energy. It funds television ads, voter contact operations, and online videos focused on these candidates' environmental records.

As interest group activity in campaigns has come to be dominated less by single-issue groups and more by ideological and partisan organizations established to funnel money toward advertising, group advertising has become less distinctive. In 2012, interest group and candidate advertising both focused mostly on jobs and taxes, though candidates were slightly more likely to focus on education and interest groups were more focused on health care.[15] If interest groups use the same political consulting firms, run similar focus groups, and use similar survey data to design their advertising, the output is likely to look the same as that of candidates. There is also little evidence that candidates follow the lead of interest groups when they choose to advertise on different issues. Candidates choose their own issue focus and often respond to the issues that their opponents raise, but do not necessarily shift their advertising based on issues raised only by interest groups.

Even with limited resources for advertising, interest groups may help focus the attention of their supporters on the candidates' records on the issues that concern them. Many groups issue scorecards for elected officials, outlining their votes for and against the interest groups' positions. Abortion rights groups regularly declare that Republicans have waged a "war on women" and serve to highlight candidate statements that oppose legal abortion even in cases of rape or incest. Candidates are sometimes forced to respond to these interest group efforts, with reporters asking why they have a poor voting record according to a particular group or asking them to clarify a statement highlighted by a group.

---

[15] Wesleyan Media Project. As reported in Michael Franz. 2014. "Attack of the SuperPACs," in *New Directions in Interest Group Politics*, ed. Matt Grossmann. New York: Routledge: 144–52.

Evaluating Interest Groups

Interest groups are often labeled "special interests" by politicians and even citizens—suggesting that they are opposed to the broader public interest. Some interest group advertising is notoriously misleading, and interest groups cannot be held as accountable as candidates for their deceptions. Interest groups do represent a diversity of perspectives, which helps to ensure that Americans from a variety of backgrounds have a voice. But they are likely to represent constituencies that are wealthier and have more to gain from government policy, which tends to heighten inequalities in political influence.

The independent role of interest groups can be especially important. The normative goal that interest groups most strongly advance is free speech. They empower individuals and organizations other than the candidates. They highlight the concerns of voters and may advocate views other than those that the candidates themselves articulate. Interest groups help serve the standards of free choice, but do not always contribute to equality. They add voices to campaign deliberation, but intend to persuade rather than inform voters.

Would we be better off without interest groups? There have been numerous attempts to limit interest group involvement in American campaigns, most prominently via campaign finance law. However, courts have invalidated some of these laws, arguing that interest groups deserve free speech protection because they advocate for the concerns of their supporters. Even if the courts had not ruled in this way, it seems unlikely that interest groups could be significantly weakened. There will always be incentives for advocates of a cause to band together and seek to influence parties and candidates. In fact, this may benefit democracy, inasmuch as citizens have political views that they want to share with politicians. Interest groups help citizens get politicians' attention. Hillary Clinton was roundly booed in 2007 when she told an audience of liberal bloggers that "lobbyists, whether you like it or not, represent real Americans," citing associations of nurses and teachers.[16] But sometimes, that is true.

Interest group involvement in campaigns also raises some unique concerns. Candidates may feel beholden to interest groups that donate to them or advertise on their behalf. Regardless of whether they change election outcomes, politicians may exchange favors or moderate their positions to stay on their good side. If candidates believe that casino magnate Sheldon Adelson

---

[16] Kim Chipman. 2007. "Clinton Draws Fire from Obama, Edwards over Lobbyists." Bloomberg, August 5. www.bloomberg.com/apps/news?pid=newsarchive&sid =aNCxpEpsbL9g (accessed 6/25/14).

Education Politics

A 2013 election for the Los Angeles School Board was hardly a local affair, attracting the money and attention of New York Mayor Michael Bloomberg, former Washington, D.C., schools chancellor Michelle Rhee, and Netflix CEO Reed Hastings. It became a national proxy fight between education interest groups, with supporters of district-level reform and charter schools (including Bloomberg, Rhee, and Hastings) supporting one set of candidates and their opponents (especially teachers' unions) supporting an alternative slate. Similar interest groups fought in Denver's school board elections in 2011, with neither side winning their full slate.

The battle over education reform has largely been playing out within the Democratic Party, the primary home to both teachers' unions and many charter school enthusiasts, but the combatants have not limited themselves to (largely nonpartisan) school board elections. In the 2013 Boston mayoral runoff between two Democrats, charter supporters sided with former teacher John Connolly while labor unions supported Martin Walsh (the eventual victor). Mayors like Bloomberg have taken control of education policy from their school boards, meaning that mayoral elections can sometimes determine the fate of school reform efforts.

Neither side limits its fight to the local level either. In 2011, Rhee's organization, Students First, lobbied on behalf of a Michigan state legislative effort to raise the cap on charter schools and followed up by supporting the mostly Republican candidates who sided with the effort. Interest groups in Washington State helped legalize charter schools via a 2012 statewide ballot initiative campaign that gathered bipartisan support.

Two national-level interest groups exemplify the divide within the Democratic Party: Democrats for Education Reform, which often supports pro-charter candidates; and the Network for Public Education, which was founded by Diane Ravitch, an education historian who has become the leader of charter school opponents. The partisan politics of education have become even stranger with the fight over the Common Core, a set of national education standards promoted by business groups, unions, and the Obama administration and adopted by nearly all states before becoming a lightning rod, attracting opposition from Tea Party Republicans as well as criticism from Ravitch and those on the ideological left.

Education interest groups have different motives from parties or candidates. They seek to change policies through whatever venues are available. That sometimes means lobbying a school board or state legislature, but it also can mean running an initiative campaign, endorsing candidates in a local or state race, or backing a national effort to influence Congress or the administration. The education reform battles have divided each party, with both the Bush and Obama administrations seeking to nationalize education standards and support charter schools and each president facing opposition from both the left and the right.

According to Ravitch and other critics, recent education reforms are the pet projects of billionaire philanthropists like Bloomberg and Bill Gates: they are using their resources to disrupt public education and impose their untested ideas. The reformers, in turn, say teachers' unions have controlled local education policy making for too long, blocking competition and protecting bad teachers. In other words, both sets of interest groups claim to be fighting the special interests — they are willing to intervene in many types of election campaigns to change policies in their favor while decrying their opponents' efforts to do the same.

is likely to spend millions on a single presidential campaign, they may be less likely to criticize gambling or look for other ways to impress him; at a gathering in Las Vegas Adelson led, potential 2016 presidential contenders were careful to emphasize their positions in favor of military support for Israel and trade with China, two issues about which he cares deeply. Perhaps the downsides of interest group campaigning will not show up in campaigns at all, but in one-sided policies advanced by parties or candidates trying to curry their favor.

Conclusion

Citizens are not kind to the "special interests" they believe are corrupting campaigns. Candidates encourage their condemnation by christening their opponents as supporters of nefarious groups. But one person's special interest is another person's professional association, advocacy group, workplace, or church. Interest groups can help to make campaigns about policies designed to solve people's problems, rather than vacuous debates about personality and patriotism.

Interest groups regularly donate to candidates, air advertisements, and mobilize their followers. If the last election is any guide, they are likely to play increasingly important roles in driving campaigns. Voters in competitive districts may see more ads from interest groups than from the candidates. Although many groups that lobby still steer clear of campaigns, changes in campaign finance law and regulation are enabling more groups to play in campaigns—including many groups created for that express purpose.

In 2012 and 2014, some ideological interest groups considerably upped their ante, waging millions on the candidates they support and advertising nationwide. The Koch brothers alone helped create new organizations and funneled millions through their network of supportive groups. After running attack ads, they became the subject of competing ads run by Democratic interest groups. Harry Reid lashed out against their undue influence, but also helped to build groups that could play similar roles in favor of his candidates.

Some interest groups are extensions of the political parties, raising similar concerns but also playing similarly important roles in voter mobilization and education. Other groups play unique roles in ballot initiative campaigns, in representing ethnic or religious constituencies, or in making sure that the candidates address their issues. They all see elections as an important method of advancing their policy goals, but not always the only method; even Koch Industries is still spending money on traditional lobbying.

As interest groups spend considerable sums on campaigns, there is some fear that candidates may lose control of their own messages. The experience so far suggests that interest group campaigning looks a lot like candidate campaigning. Where candidate and interest group goals diverge, we should expect some different emphases. However, because winning elections still requires convincing the same voters, no matter who is running the campaign, interest groups are subject to the same constraints as candidates in convincing the voters to support their side.

KEY TERMS

interest group (p. 180)   ballot initiative campaigns (p. 190)

constituencies (p. 189)   campaign agenda (p. 197)

FOR DISCUSSION

1. Would American elections improve if interest groups left campaigning to the candidates? How would elections change if they donated less to candidates or spent less directly in campaigns?

2. If you were working for an interest group, how would you suggest attempting to influence elections in your state? Would you provide money to their campaign, work to mobilize your own membership, or seek to influence voters directly through an advertising campaign? What are the advantages and disadvantages of each approach?

3. Should interest groups act as adjuncts to the campaign, funding the same types of advertisements and voter contact efforts as candidates, or should they focus more on the issues that most concern them and target their resources on the voters most sympathetic to their specific positions? How would each strategy help advance interest group goals?

4. Is it better for voters to only hear directly from the candidates about their positions on the issues, or do interest groups help force candidates to take clear positions and better inform the voters about which candidates support their views?

CHAPTER 8

Media

At a private fund-raiser in May 2012, Mitt Romney described an electoral dilemma that he believed he was confronting:

> There are 47 percent of Americans . . . who are dependent on government, who believe that they are victims, who believe the government has a responsibility to care for them, who believe that they are entitled to health care, to food, to housing, to you-name-it. That's an entitlement. The government should give it to them. And they will vote for this president no matter what.[1]

His remarks would have gone unnoticed by the public were it not for three people: Scott Prouty, a bartender at the event who surreptitiously recorded the remarks on his personal camera; James Carter, a Democratic researcher (and the grandson of former president Jimmy Carter) who tracked down Prouty using YouTube and Twitter; and David Corn, a reporter for the liberal magazine *Mother Jones* who obtained the tape and wrote about it on the magazine's website. After the *Huffington Post* reported that Corn had the tape, he rushed out his scoop with accompanying videos on September 17.

A huge uproar followed. The story made that evening's news on NBC and ABC and was eventually referenced on television nearly 8,000 times before Election Day.[2] Romney twice apologized for the remark and the Obama campaign used it in debates and campaign ads.

Unfortunately for Romney, his comments matched a narrative about his candidacy promoted by the Obama campaign and discussed by reporters: that he was an out-of-touch rich man. In a series of prior gaffes, Romney had helped advance the storyline: he said his wife drove "a couple of Cadillacs," claimed he

---

[1] The video is available at www.youtube.com/watch?v=XnB0NZzl5H (accessed 1/19/15).

[2] David Corn. 2012. "The Story Behind the 47 Percent Video." *Mother Jones.* www .motherjones.com/politics/2012/12/story-behind-47-video (accessed 5/22/14). The video counts are from the Internet Archive television news archive at https://archive.org/details/tv (accessed 5/22/14).

enjoyed being able to "fire people," characterized hundreds of thousands of dollars in speaker's fees as "not very much," off-handedly suggested a $10,000 bet with his primary opponent Rick Perry, accidentally said he was "not concerned about the very poor," and tried to relate to NASCAR fans by citing his friendship with team owners.[3] All of these incidents as well as Romney's wealth and private equity career were widely believed to undermine voters' sense of his empathy.

And yet there is little evidence that the coverage of any of these gaffes — even what became known as the "47 percent video"—made much difference. The polls barely budged after the video's release. Some voters did momentarily shift from supporting Romney to declaring themselves undecided, but they returned to Romney within a few weeks. There was also little change in voters' perceptions about whether Romney cared about them: Obama consistently held the same small lead on this indicator.[4]

The coverage of Mitt Romney's "47 percent" comments highlights several important features of the news media and their role in contemporary American campaigns. First, the media's interest illustrates their news values, or the criteria by which they judge stories to be newsworthy. In this case, this story had video of the candidate — an inside look at a private event — and fit with a preexisting narrative about Romney's wealth and business career. Although Republicans assume that the news media targeted Romney to derail his candidacy, in 2008 reporters were similarly attracted to a video that many observers believed was

---

Core of the Analysis

- The news media typically seek to be objective but also to generate stories that will interest their audience.
- Candidates seek to persuade the public by influencing news content.
- The incentives of candidates and the news media often diverge, creating conflict between them.
- Media coverage can affect citizens, but its impact is often limited because citizens' attitudes are difficult to change.
- The news media do not always live up to democratic ideals, but citizens share some of the responsibility for the shortcomings in media coverage of campaigns.

---

[3] The media coverage of all of these events is covered extensively in Mark Halperin and John Heilmann. 2013. *Double Down: Game Change 2012*. New York: Penguin.

[4] The evidence is covered in John Sides and Lynn Vavreck. 2013. *The Gamble: Choice and Chance in the 2012 Presidential Election*. Princeton, NJ: Princeton University Press.

detrimental to Obama: the remarks of Obama's retired pastor, Jeremiah Wright, that included the words "God damn America." The news media do not so much champion one candidate or party as seek out stories that they deem newsworthy, especially ones that include video content ready for television or the Web.

Second, the media's coverage diverged sharply from what the implicated candidate, Mitt Romney, wanted to discuss. Although candidates attempt to shape media coverage to benefit themselves, media outlets often pursue a different agenda. Reporters view their job as sharing useful information and analyzing factors that may affect elections or government, rather than passing along unfiltered campaign messages. By contrast, candidates repeat their campaign messages again and again, frustrating reporters who want new information. These conflicting agendas create tension between the candidates and news media.

Third, candidates often feel forced to respond to media coverage, no matter how much they may want to repeat their preferred message. Candidates believe that the news media are an important source of information for the public and thus a platform that they must use to deliver their message. So rather than ignore the media, candidates attempt to reshape media coverage.

Fourth, the 47 percent episode suggests an irony: despite the media's extensive coverage of the story, it is unclear that this episode had much effect on the public. This lack of impact reflects two key facts: many citizens do not pay close attention to politics in the news, and it is often difficult to change the minds of those who do.

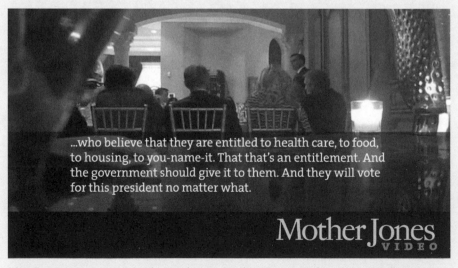

...who believe that they are entitled to health care, to food, to housing, to you-name-it. That that's an entitlement. And the government should give it to them. And they will vote for this president no matter what.

Mother Jones VIDEO

Mitt Romney's controversial remarks at a fund-raiser, as replayed repeatedly in news coverage of the 2012 presidential campaign.

Fifth, the episode raises important questions about the news media's role in campaigns and whether it is conducive to democratic values. One might easily criticize the media's focus on this story as excessive. Aren't there more important issues than what Romney said at a private fund-raiser? On the other hand, perhaps the story was useful, if one believes it revealed the "real" Romney in an unguarded moment. The incident raises the broader question of whether the news media uphold or undermine the ideals we have for campaigns.

In this chapter, we begin by discussing the different types of news media outlets and comparing the size of their audiences. We then describe how both rules and reality structure the campaign coverage that the news media produce. We emphasize how the economics of the news business shapes the content of the news. We next consider how the news media and candidates interact, noting the necessity of this relationship for both but also the tensions within this relationship. We then evaluate how much news coverage actually affects public opinion. The central point here is that the media's impact is constrained by the public's interest in the news and willingness to believe what they read, see, or hear. Finally, we examine how well the news media help campaigns meet democratic values.

Who Are the News Media?

Most people learn about political campaigns from the **news media**: regular communicators of information designed to reach large audiences. Historically, the daily newspaper was the primary source of news for most Americans. Newspaper stories allow regular and in-depth coverage of candidates, issues, and campaign events. Although newspapers are still a popular source of information, especially for older Americans, the audience for the printed product has been shrinking. In 2012, on average 44.3 million copies of print newspapers were distributed every day, compared to a peak of 63.3 million in 1984.[5] Newspapers' websites are still among the most popular online news sources. The top three American newspapers, the *Wall Street Journal*, the *New York Times*, and *USA Today*, claim hundreds of thousands of paid online subscribers. Even if newspapers no longer dominate campaign news coverage, they are still a source of information for citizens, politicians, and journalists and often shape the coverage of other media outlets. Newspapers are also the main source of coverage for many smaller campaigns. A nice illustration of this point comes from a study of Pittsburgh during a 1992 newspaper

---

[5] The data derive from the Newspaper Association of America and are available via the PewResearch Journalism Project at www.journalism.org/datasets/ (accessed 5/22/14).

strike. Without access to a newspaper, Pittsburgh residents did find other sources of information on that year's presidential and Senate elections, but they lacked information on congressional races.[6]

The most popular source of news today is television newscasts. Local news averages almost 23 million viewers per day in its early evening time slot (between 5 and 7:30 P.M.), more than 24 million viewers in its later time slot (10 P.M. to 12 A.M.), and nearly 12 million in the mornings. Sports and weather account for a larger share of local news, which offers only limited campaign coverage—but it is still the main news source for many Americans. National network television news also reaches a large audience, although its size has declined. In 2013, the nightly news on ABC, CBS, and NBC together averaged 22.6 million viewers per day, down from more than 50 million in 1980. Morning news shows, such as NBC's *Today* and ABC's *Good Morning America*, averaged a total of 13.4 million daily viewers.[7] Network news coverage favors stories with better visuals and less depth than newspapers. In 2008, the average **sound bite** from presidential candidates broadcast on television news was only 9 seconds long.[8] The public television channel PBS, funded in part by government and its viewers, offers more coverage and longer sound bites.

Cable news viewership is smaller on average but offers hours of continuous coverage. The average prime-time (8 to 11 P.M. Eastern) audience reached 3 million in 2013, with daytime viewership exceeding 2 million. Fox News Channel dominates CNN, HLN, and MSNBC in each time period throughout the day, in part because many Fox News viewers watch repeatedly. Fox News Channel's average evening viewership, 1.7 million per night, is larger than all of the other cable news networks combined.[9] During the daytime, cable networks repeat top stories, with content usually similar to network news shows. In the evenings, cable news channels are dominated by punditry, with Fox News offering mostly conservative commentators and MSNBC offering mostly liberals. Since many of the same viewers watch repeatedly,

---

[6] Jeffrey Mondak. 1995. *Nothing to Read: Newspapers and Elections in a Social Experiment.* Ann Arbor: University of Michigan Press.

[7] These figures are based on Nielsen ratings for ABC, NBC, CBS, and Fox and their affiliates. All viewership numbers are available from the PewResearch Journalism Project at www.journalism.org/datasets/ (accessed 5/22/14).

[8] Stephen J. Farnsworth and S. Robert Lichter. 2010. *The Nightly News Nightmare: Television Coverage of U.S. Presidential Elections: 1988–2008.* Lanham, MD: Rowman & Littlefield Publishers.

[9] These figures are based on Nielsen ratings for ABC, NBC, CBS, and Fox and their affiliates. All viewership numbers are available from the PewResearch Journalism Project, at www.journalism.org/datasets/ (accessed 5/22/14).

the cable audience is larger in terms of total minutes watched, but cable networks reach fewer people overall than network broadcasts. Only approximately 7 percent of Americans watch Fox News at least one hour per week; even fewer watch MSNBC (4 percent) or CNN (5 percent).[10]

Radio news also serves a niche audience. The United States has more than 1,500 commercial news or talk radio stations and 268 National Public Radio (NPR) member stations, which are partially funded by listeners. NPR's two daily news shows, *Morning Edition* and *All Things Considered*, average between 12 and 13 million listeners per week, while a total of 53 million listeners per week tune in to commercial news and talk radio.[11] (Because these numbers are weekly, rather than daily, and include people who listen only sporadically, they cannot be compared directly to the television audience estimates.) In 2014, the top talk radio hosts were all conservatives: Rush Limbaugh and Sean Hannity topped the list. Commercial radio news features content similar to cable television, especially in its commentary and its regular updates of news headlines. NPR, by contrast, is known for in-depth coverage and longer interviews; its audience is more liberal.

The Internet has also become an important source of news, but most of it originates from traditional news providers. Newspapers and television networks constitute 20 of the 25 most visited news websites.[12] Some online-only news outlets, like the Huffington Post, are becoming just as prominent, but some of their content recycles or adds commentary to stories originally reported by newspapers or television networks. Political blogs are likewise mostly sources of opinionated commentary (see Box 8.1). News stories posted on social networking sites also usually point to news that originates in traditional reporting. Facebook, Pinterest, and Twitter have become major sources of traffic for news sites, but a majority of original political news stories, especially about state or local campaigns, still come from newspapers.[13]

Beyond official news outlets, some entertainment programming also offers political content. During his career at *The Tonight Show*, Jay Leno made more than 20,000 jokes about politicians, with Bill Clinton and George W. Bush

---

[10] Markus Prior. 2013. "Media and Political Polarization." *Annual Review of Political Science* 16: 101–27.

[11] These figures are based on Arbitron ratings. Listenership numbers are available from the PewResearch Journalism Project, at www.journalism.org/datasets/ (accessed 5/22/14).

[12] This figure is from comScore Media Metrix. Data are available from the PewResearch Journalism Project, at www.journalism.org/datasets/ (accessed 5/22/14).

[13] Robert W. McChesney and John Nichols. 2010. *The Death and Life of American Journalism: The Media Revolution Will Begin the World Again*. New York: Nation Books.

BOX 8.1

Political Blogs

Blogs, which are websites with regularly updated news in reverse chronological order, have been touted as a form of "citizen media" in which individuals can become reporters and commentators. But the universe of blogs, or the blogosphere, is dominated not by ordinary citizens but by traditional media organizations. Relatively few blogs generate large audiences, and many of those that do are hosted by large news outlets, such as the *Washington Post* or the *New York Times*. By adding blogs to their sites, traditional media outlets have imitated the behavior of new outlets and blurred the boundaries between journalism by individual citizens and media companies.[1]

Some commentators hoped that blogs would become alternative sources of news, challenging the dominance of the big newspapers and television networks. This has happened from time to time, particularly when blogs pushed a story first, leading traditional media to report on it. During the 2004 presidential campaign, Dan Rather of CBS News questioned the U.S. National Guard service record of George W. Bush, holding up memos that supposedly came from Bush's superiors at the time of his service. Conservative blogs questioned the authenticity of those memos, arguing that their typeface was not available on typewriters used by the military at the time. CBS News eventually retracted the report and asked Rather to leave the show.[2]

Such cases are the exception, however. Blogs rely on newspapers and television stations for news, in part because few bloggers have the resources to report their own stories. In fact, most political blog posts are links to articles from other outlets with limited commentary.[3] Moreover, to gain traction for their stories, bloggers need them to be picked up by television and newspapers. The influence of blogs is tied not to their readership among the public but to their influence on reporters from traditional media outlets.[4]

Bloggers make a unique contribution not so much as news reporters but as commentators and activists. Many of the most prominent political blogs are ideological or partisan in nature. Political bloggers tend to self-segregate, with both liberal and conservative bloggers linking and responding mainly to bloggers with similar views.[5] Their audiences are also self-segregated, with people reading blogs they agree with. Few people read both conservative and liberal blogs.[6] Thus, blogs are more effective at reinforcing people's existing political beliefs and perhaps spurring them to act on them than they are at changing anyone's mind.

---

[1] Hindman. *The Myth of Digital Democracy*.

[2] Associated Press. 2005. "CBS Ousts Four for Roles in Bush Guard Story," January 10. www.msnbc.msn.com/id/6807825/ (accessed 9/29/10).

[3] Laura McKenna and Antoinette Pole. 2008. "What Do Bloggers Do: An Average Day on an Average Political Blog." *Public Choice* 134, 1, 2: 97–108.

[4] Henry Farrell and Daniel W. Drezner. 2008. "The Power and Politics of Blogs." *Public Choice* 134, 1, 2: 15–30.

[5] Eszter Hargittai, Jason Gallo, and Matthew Kane. 2008. "Cross-Ideological Discussions among Conservative and Liberal Bloggers." *Public Choice* 134, 1, 2: 67–86.

[6] Eric Lawrence, John Sides, and Henry Farrell. 2010. "Self-Segregation or Deliberation? Blog Readership, Participation, and Polarization in American Politics." *Perspectives on Politics* 8, 1: 141.

the most frequent targets.[14] Political satirist Jon Stewart, who was watched by 2.5 million viewers per night on Comedy Central, devoted substantial coverage to political campaigns.

These aggregate statistics in the audience for media largely comport with surveys that ask individuals where they get their news (although Americans do tend to overreport how much news they watch and read). Figure 8.1 shows the percent of people who said they "got news yesterday" from television, newspapers, radio, and the Internet. Reported newspaper readership and radio listenership declined throughout the 1990s and 2000s, while television news viewership declined and then stabilized—in part because the decline in the audience for network news was offset by the increase in the audience for cable news. At the same time, the number of people receiving news online is increasing rapidly. This is particularly true among young people. Although those under 30 are only half as likely as those over 60 to report that they generally follow the news, the median age of the online news consumer is 20 years younger than the general population.[15] Younger people are also more likely to share and receive news via social networks. But this does not mean that online news consumers are ignoring newspapers or television: they are primarily seeing the same stories in a repackaged or redistributed format. Elite media outlets stimulate the bulk of online political discussion.[16]

Americans vary greatly in their news consumption. Some citizens follow news regularly, reading a newspaper, watching cable news, and sharing news stories online. But this is far from the norm: most Americans, when given the option, prefer sports and entertainment to news.[17] As Election Day approaches, citizens do watch more news, but the levels are still relatively low. During the 2006 cycle, the proportion watching at least a half-hour of news per day doubled from one-in-eight to one-in-four from August to November.[18] Americans who are news junkies tend to be stronger partisans. For politicians, this means it is hard to reach potential voters who are not

---

[14] Center for Media and Public Affairs. www.cmpa.com/study-lenos-top-joke-target-was-bill-clinton/ (accessed 5/22/14).

[15] PewResearch Journalism Project.

[16] Matthew Hindman. 2008. *The Myth of Digital Democracy*. Princeton, NJ: Princeton University Press.

[17] Markus Prior. 2007. *Post-Broadcast Democracy: How Media Choice Increases Inequality in Political Involvement and Polarizes Elections*. New York: Cambridge University Press.

[18] Michael J. LaCour and Lynn Vavreck. 2014. "Improving Media Measurement: Results from the Field." *Political Communication* 31(3): 408–420.

FIGURE 8.1 Where People Get Their News

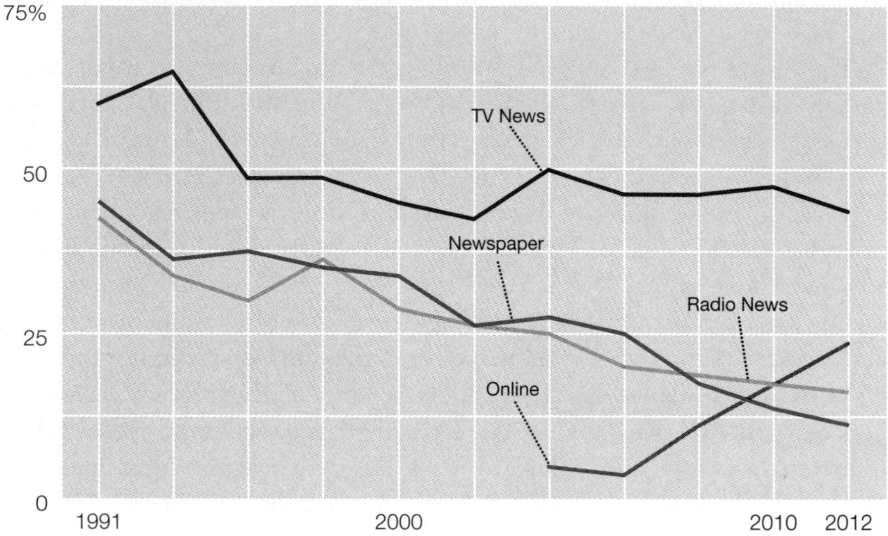

Source: Pew Research Center for the People and the Press. 2012. "In Changing News Landscape, Even Television Is Vulnerable." www.people-press.org/2012/09/27/in-changing-news-landscape-even-television-is-vulnerable/ (accessed 3/26/13).

already on their side via news media coverage. For media outlets, it means their regular customers are a minority with stronger views on politics.

Trends in media consumption demonstrate how both the media and their audience have changed in recent years. They also hint at some of the challenges that the news media face today, particularly declining audiences for some types of media. The need to attract an audience is crucial and, as we will see, profoundly affects how the media cover campaigns.

Government's Limited Oversight of the News Media

Like other actors in campaigns, such as candidates, parties, and interest groups, the news media are influenced by rules. In this case, rules involve constitutional doctrine and government policies that affect—or, more important, do not affect—the content of media coverage. The First Amendment's guarantee of a free press means that there are relatively few rules that constrain media coverage. Given that Supreme Court interpretations of the First Amendment have allowed the media to publish stories about classified government programs, where the stakes are much higher than in political campaigns, the media can largely report on political campaigns as they see fit.

The restrictions that do exist pertain mainly to broadcast radio—radio that uses the AM/FM spectrum—and broadcast television, which includes the major networks (ABC, NBC, CBS, and Fox) and their affiliates but not cable television networks. The Federal Communication Commission (FCC) regulates broadcast radio and television because there is limited space on the broadcast spectrum—think of the FM radio dial, which has space only between 87.5 and 108.0 megahertz.

The FCC rule that is most relevant to political campaigns is the **right to equal time**. Stations with FCC licenses are required to provide "equal time" to all candidates for office. In other words, they cannot simply devote attention to a favored candidate and ignore the others. This means that if a station sells time to a candidate who wants to air television advertisements on that station, it must make the same opportunity available to all candidates for that office.

However, there are important loopholes that allow unequal time. The FCC has declared that certain events are exempt from this rule, including news interviews and on-the-spot news events, like a presidential press conference. The incumbent president, whether or not he is running for reelection, gets news coverage simply for doing things like giving press conferences and traveling to foreign countries. The FCC also exempts presidential debates from the equal time rule. Debate organizers, who include representatives of the major parties and media companies, can thus exclude third-party candidates without breaking the rule.

One interesting application of the right to equal time involved the former Denver Bronco offensive lineman Dan Neil, who decided to run for the Texas state legislature in 2010. Neil was co-hosting a local sports talk show in Austin, Texas, from 6 to 9 A.M. every weekday morning. His opponent's campaign formally requested that the station either remove Neil from the airwaves or give their candidate three hours of free air time every weekday. Although Neil's show was apolitical—mostly focusing on the University of Texas's football program—the station asked that Neil take a "vacation" until after the election.

Note, however, that the right to equal time does not require media outlets to broadcast coverage of campaigns or political news generally. In some situations, television news outlets have not carried presidential speeches or presidential debates. During the 2000 presidential election, for example, Fox and NBC did not broadcast the first debate between Al Gore and George W.

Bush. Instead, NBC aired a World Series baseball game and Fox aired an episode of a science fiction program called *Dark Angel*.

Media regulation is much weaker in the United States than in other democratic countries. Many nations have strong and well-funded public media outlets and more requirements for private media companies that are also covering campaigns. One consequence is that other countries tend to provide more free time for parties and candidates to speak directly to voters.[19]

The Business of News and the Norm of Objectivity

The minimal requirements that the government places on news media outlets mean that these outlets can largely cover—or not cover—politics and campaigns as they see fit. News outlets are thus free to base decisions about coverage on other factors. Because of this, coverage of campaigns is powerfully shaped by the prevailing reality or context in which the media operate. News outlets have practical constraints of time, space, and personnel. They cannot cover every potentially newsworthy event and must make choices. These choices are guided by two aspects of their reality: the profit motive of business and the norm of objectivity.

News as a Business

The economics of the news business demand that the news be profitable, first and foremost. The need to turn a profit is not new, but it has grown more imperative with time. Today, large corporations traded on public stock exchanges own many news outlets; these firms do not have the same personal investment in the news product as a family that owns a newspaper might have had (and families owned most of the country's major newspapers until recently). Corporations are not content to lose money maintaining a news operation simply for the satisfaction of creating a quality news product. Thus, news outlets are expected to generate revenue and keep costs down.

This is a significant challenge. Many of the most prestigious news outlets—including major newspapers and television networks—are losing audience share and thus losing advertising dollars. Newspapers in particular are suffering, as their classified advertising revenue has declined sharply due in part to the advent of websites like Craigslist. Online audiences for newspapers

---

[19] Shanto Iyengar and Jennifer McGrady. 2015. *Media Politics: A Citizen's Guide, Third Edition*. New York: W. W. Norton.

FIGURE 8.2 Newspaper Advertising Revenue

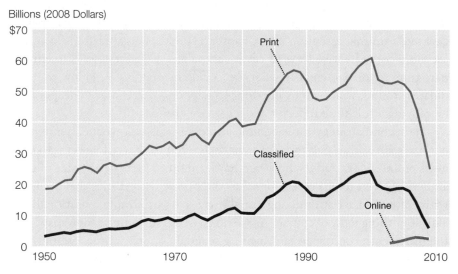

Source: Newspaper Association of America.

are growing, but, as yet, newspapers have not figured out a way to make as much money from their online content as they did from their print editions (Figure 8.2). At the same time, covering political campaigns is not cheap. The length of many American campaigns means that news outlets must commit significant resources if they want to provide continuous coverage.

Faced with these challenges, news outlets can either cut costs or raise additional revenue. Newspapers and television news organizations have cut costs by eliminating reporting positions and other staff, and newspapers have cut back on the size of their print editions. Some newspapers, such as Denver's *Rocky Mountain News*, have closed outright, and others, such as the *Seattle Post-Intelligencer*, now publish only online editions. News outlets have also changed the kinds of news they gather firsthand. Many have closed news bureaus, reducing the number of reporters who are based in places outside of the outlet's hometown. They are also reconsidering whether to use resources for relatively "expensive" stories—for example, whether to send reporters with the president on his travels.[20]

---

[20] Brian Selter. 2010. "When the President Travels, It's Cheaper for Reporters to Stay Home." *New York Times*, May 23. www.nytimes.com/2010/05/24/business/media/24press .html (accessed 5/22/14).

These sorts of cuts can affect coverage of campaigns. News outlets may simply devote less time to covering campaigns. Presidential campaigns continue to command vast resources, but state and especially local campaigns generate minimal attention (see Chapter 11). News organizations also look for more cost-effective ways to cover campaigns. One strategy is to employ part-time reporters who carry handheld video cameras and follow the candidates around, waiting for something to happen. This is much cheaper than employing a full-time reporter and a camera crew.

The second strategy for economic success is raising revenue. Some news outlets, such as the *New York Times*, have decided to charge for access to their news online. Most outlets, however, have sought to increase the size of their audience. News media often appeal to the public with stories that are laden with emotion, have stimulating visual images, or are simply sensationalistic. This is nothing new, of course. As we discussed in Chapter 3, newspapers in the nineteenth century began covering scandals, sports, crime, politics, and other stories in an often lurid way. But the continued rise of **infotainment**—a combination of informational and entertainment programming—is evident today. For example, the nightly news broadcasts have increased their coverage of celebrities, athletes, and famous criminals but not their coverage of business leaders and political figures. They have decreased the fraction of important congressional votes that they cover.[21] It is easy to criticize the news media for this, but news consumers may also bear some responsibility. These sorts of decisions often reflect careful monitoring of what the audience reads, watches, or hears. News outlets also pay close attention to what stories are shared on Facebook and Twitter, leading to a proliferation of funny lists, heartwarming stories, and coverage of gaffes.

The news media sometimes establishes new outlets. Internet technology means that content can be produced with lower distribution costs. Several recent news innovators seek to capitalize on the use of data, statistics, and background information to better explain the news. Traditional media companies have established separate brands such as FiveThirtyEight at ESPN and The Upshot at Nytimes.com to play this role, as have new upstarts like Vox.com. During campaigns, political junkies can now consume even more polling data and demographic analysis, even as most citizens ignore it.

---

[21] James T. Hamilton. 2004. *All the News That's Fit to Sell*. Princeton, NJ: Princeton University Press.

The Norm of Objectivity

Economic pressures are not the only influence on the contemporary news media. Most reporters, editors, and other news professionals subscribe to a set of norms that inform how they do their jobs. The most important is objectivity, a relatively recent feature of the news media. In Chapter 3, we described how the American print media were largely partisan until well into the twentieth century. Newspapers used to be directly allied with political parties, who in turn helped to fund their costs of production.

The decline of the partisan press and the rise of objectivity came about partly because newspaper owners sought to build a larger and broader audience by producing an objective news product that would appeal to many different kinds of readers. They sent journalists to report on events firsthand by seeking out information and interviewing sources.

Journalists then began to see it as their job to report on events fairly and accurately, with appropriate attention to all sides of controversial issues. The norm of objectivity became codified in the guidelines of news organizations. For example, the code of the American Society of Newspaper Editors, which was founded in 1922, included a principle of "impartiality": "News reports should be free from opinion or bias of any kind." This principle was taught to aspiring journalists in newly founded journalism schools; the first, at Columbia University, was founded by Joseph Pulitzer in 1902. Technology also enabled the spread of more objective journalism. The development of the telegraph in the 1830s led to the creation of **wire services** like the Associated Press. Wire services—named for the wires used to send messages via telegraph—produce content that is shared among news outlets. Thus, stories could be disseminated quickly to many outlets. A similar pattern evolved in radio and television news, where local stations chose to affiliate with national networks and reuse their news products.

An autonomous and impartial press also began scrutinizing the government and politicians more closely. Often this meant looking for evidence of scandal and malfeasance. Events such as the Vietnam War and the Watergate scandal weakened trust in political leaders and fueled the rise of investigative reporting. Some things that journalists knew about but did not report on—such as the extramarital affairs of Presidents Franklin Roosevelt and John F. Kennedy—became fair game for later generations of journalists.

This talk of objectivity might seem dated to today's media consumers. After all, with the proliferation of cable news talk shows and blogs, is objective journalism not a thing of the past? The short answer is "no." There is a larger audience for traditional news outlets, which generally strive to be ideologically neutral, than for outlets with an ideological or partisan agenda. Reporters dedicated to appearing impartial are even sometimes criticized for "false balance," the tendency to treat statements from each candidate's campaign equally even when one side is clearly stretching the truth.

Nevertheless, ideological and partisan outlets are clearly flourishing, as the growth in the audience for Fox News, MSNBC, and others suggests. One reason has to do with economic incentives, which can take precedence over the norm of objectivity. With news outlets seeking to appeal to an audience, it is natural that some may choose an ideological approach. This strategy will not earn them the loyalty of the majority of news consumers, some of whom are on the opposite side ideologically and others of whom prefer impartial news. But it can earn them a niche audience that is sizable enough to produce subscription and advertising revenues. Furthermore, advances in technology make niche broadcasting—sometimes called **narrow-casting**—financially viable. Many niche media products, such as blogs, can be produced relatively cheaply.

In sum, the rules and reality that affect the news media present something of a paradox. On the one hand, the government does relatively little to regulate the media, which gives them considerable discretion to write and publish what they wish. On the other hand, the news media face significant constraints of time and resources, even with the Internet providing essentially infinite space for news. Indeed, those resources have been shrinking for many outlets. The news media must therefore continue to find ways to cut costs or increase revenue by attracting a larger audience, or at least an audience that is desirable to advertisers. This has lead to an increasingly diverse media landscape, with most outlets continuing to observe the traditional norm of objectivity but other outlets pursuing a partisan or ideological agenda for a smaller but loyal audience. These constraints affect how the news media covers campaigns.

What Gets Covered, and How?

A top priority for most campaigns is to get the news media to cover their candidate and her message. This is often easier said than done. Campaigns vie with other candidates, other races, and the events of the day for the media's attention. Getting the media to communicate the campaign's message is partly a matter of skill and partly a matter of conditions, luck, and what we have been calling "reality."

Which Races Get Covered?

In deciding which campaigns to cover, the media must allocate their limited resources while stimulating interest among their audience. The media are more likely to cover a campaign when the race is competitive. Races where one candidate cruises to easy victory rarely generate stories that the media consider newsworthy. The front-runner can campaign conservatively, never risking an event where she might slip up and say something controversial. The challenger, if there is one, lacks the resources to promote his candidacy or draw unfavorable attention to the front-runner. If new polls are conducted and released, they show little change. In sum, nothing dramatic happens. Of course, the race might be more competitive if voters learned about the challenger through news coverage.

The media is also more likely to cover a campaign when the office at stake has more authority. The national news media cover the presidential campaigns extensively, as well as a few campaigns for governor and senator. They rarely cover campaigns for state legislature or local offices, or even the House of Representatives. To the extent that they cover House races, the national news media focus on the broader competition between Democrats and Republicans for majority control, rather than the particular candidates or issues in each race. Local media, especially newspapers, cover more state and local elections, but they also report on the presidential campaign and the battle for control of Congress.

When the media do cover a campaign other than the presidential campaign or a particularly competitive race, it is often because it has some feature that appeals to the audience. Media outlets are more likely to cover a congressional race when more of their readers live in that particular congressional district and can vote in that election.[22] The media are also drawn to celebrity candidates, like former California governor Arnold Schwarzenegger. They are drawn to scandals, particularly if sex or money—or, even better, money for sex—is involved. Reporters covered Anthony Weiner's long-shot bid for New York mayor in 2013 because he had resigned from Congress following the release of sexually suggestive photos he had sent to several female Twitter followers. He went on to place only fifth in the Democratic primary but not before generating yet more news coverage: he admitted that—after apologizing for the earlier incidents—he had sent lurid pictures to another woman, this time calling himself "Carlos Danger."

---

[22] James Snyder and David Stromberg. 2010. "Press Coverage and Political Accountability." *Journal of Political Economy* 118, 2: 355–408.

Which Aspects of Campaigns Get Covered?

When news media do cover election campaigns, what do they cover? Although newspapers typically run general profiles of the candidates and the campaign, the vast majority of news is driven by events. What kinds of events do the media judge to be particularly newsworthy? We speak of their criteria for newsworthiness as **news values**.

The first and most important news value is *novelty*. The term *news* does contain the word *new*, after all. Typically, this means that the news follows what happened recently—that is, since the last edition, newscast, or online update. Candidates and their advisers know this, of course, so they organize a continuous stream of new events to gain the media's attention. Consider the events that take place before the actual campaign begins. Potential candidates coyly suggest that they might enter the race in order to generate speculation in the media. When a politician formally announces her candidacy, it is treated as news, even when it is a foregone conclusion that she will be running. Politicians sometimes even hold multiple "announcements" in different media markets, as well as issuing press releases and online videos.

The media also value *personality*. Newsworthy stories often involve compelling people, and news audiences are presumed to be engaged by the "characters" in the campaign—whether they are good or bad. During the campaign, the news media will repeatedly dwell on the biographies of candidates in an attempt to understand what they are "really like." There are stories about where the candidates grew up, whether they were popular in high school, and so on. During the 2004 presidential campaign, a *New York Times* reporter wrote a profile of John Kerry, focusing on the views of his former classmates. The reporter argued that "the personal qualities that propel him—and daunt him—are the same ones that buoyed and bedeviled him when he was 16."[23]

The media also attempt to characterize a candidate's personality. Journalists play amateur psychologist, looking for evidence of candidates' personality traits in their words and deeds. Al Gore was repeatedly characterized as stiff and awkward and, in a different vein, dishonest. George W. Bush was characterized as dumb and resentful of his more successful father and older brother. Barack Obama was portrayed as intellectual and emotionally unflappable. John McCain was described as angry. Here is one example, from a *Washington Post* story published during the 2008 presidential campaign:

---

[23] Todd Purdum. 2004. "Prep School Peers Found Kerry Talented, Ambitious, and Apart." *New York Times*, May 16.

Some depict McCain . . . as an erratic hothead incapable of staying cool in the face of what he views as either disloyalty to him or irrational opposition to his ideas. Others praise a firebrand who is resolute against the forces of greed and gutlessness.[24]

Mitt Romney, as we noted, was regularly characterized as out of touch as a result of his wealth, an elitist image that was only reinforced by the 47 percent video.

All of these characterizations may have some truth to them, and clearly reporters try to document them with information from sources—although the sources are often described simply as "some" or "observers" so that reporters do not appear to be passing judgment themselves. But regardless of their accuracy, stories about personality are endlessly fascinating to the news media.

Another news value in campaign coverage is *conflict*. It is easier to generate newsworthy stories when the candidates, their surrogates, the parties, interest groups, and other campaign actors are at each other's throats. (Fortunately, all of these actors often comply.) The media's emphasis on negativity is evident in how it portrays campaign advertisements: negative ads, and especially ones with outlandish claims, are discussed to a far greater extent than positive ads—even when positive ads are actually more numerous.[25] Candidates can sometimes get the media to cover negative ads simply by releasing them on the Internet, without ever paying to air them on television. In 2008, an Obama Web video criticized McCain for his inability to use computers; it never ran, but it prompted several news stories. The same was true of a McCain ad criticizing Obama for allegedly supporting "comprehensive sex education" for kindergartners. It is easier to elicit emotion and tell dramatic stories if reporters focus on the dueling accusations of candidates. The media also focus on internal conflict within the Democratic and Republican parties, highlighting dissenters even when most party members are in agreement.[26]

The media cover candidate debates or other joint appearances with a similar hope for conflict. When the candidates do not disagree, the event is less newsworthy, perhaps frustratingly so from the media's perspective. In

---

[24] Michael Leahy. 2008. "McCain: A Question of Temperament." *Washington Post*, April 20, p. A01.

[25] Travis N. Ridout and Glen R. Smith. 2008. "Free Advertising: How the Media Amplify Campaign Messages." *Political Research Quarterly* 61, 4: 598–608.

[26] Tim Groeling. 2010. *When Politicians Attack: Party Cohesion in the Media*. New York: Cambridge University Press.

Covering a Potential Celebrity Candidate

Real estate mogul and reality television star Donald Trump spoke to the Conservative Political Action Conference, a traditional venue for potential Republican presidential candidates, on February 10, 2011. Media outlets began including him in lists of potential candidates and assessing his support in public opinion polls. In a March 17 interview on *Good Morning America*, Trump criticized potential rival candidates and questioned whether Barack Obama was born in the United States. Reporters regularly corrected Trump's claims, but Trump refused to drop the issue and claimed to have hired investigators to research Obama's birth certificate in Hawaii. He took advantage of nearly every invitation to be interviewed on television, hurling accusations—not only at Obama but at his potential primary opponents. He spoke at a Tea Party event, calling Obama the worst president in history. By April, several polls showed Trump leading the Republican field of potential presidential candidates.

The media had to decide whether to take Trump's candidacy seriously and whether to repeat and analyze his allegations. After all, he had voter support and was making newsworthy statements. In 2000, Trump had explored a third-party candidacy for president, but he advocated liberal policy positions such as support for national health care and a large wealth tax. Strangely for a Republican candidate, he had recently donated to Democratic candidates and rarely voted in primary elections. Some reporters suggested that his proto-campaign was an elaborate publicity stunt designed to increase ratings for *The Celebrity Apprentice*, his television program. Reports even hinted that he would announce his candidacy on the season finale.

Reporters expected that interviews with Trump would generate high ratings. To justify their coverage as news, they only needed to cite his support in the polls and argue that the media should correct his misstatements. Yet many were clearly skeptical of his candidacy. These mixed feelings produced news stories about the news coverage itself, focusing on the issue of whether the media should take Trump seriously.

Meanwhile, other candidates had to decide how to respond to Trump's sudden rise. Trump chided Mitt Romney as a "small business guy," literally arguing that his bigger bank account was a credential for his candidacy. That Trump could outpoll other candidates did not look good for them — but the other candidates did not know whether he was running and did not expect him to be a serious competitor. Many Republicans were concerned that Trump, and not more electable candidates, was dominating coverage of the presidential campaign. Obama eventually decided to respond to Trump's allegations, releasing his long-form birth certificate on April 27, 2011.

Even when reporters suspect that a potential candidate is engaged in a publicity stunt, they rarely turn away. If politicians produce material that appeals to news values, they can take advantage of the enhanced coverage. This puts their competitors in a quandary: should they attempt to make crazier statements to generate attention or toil at traditional campaign forums away from the spotlight?

February 2008, a debate between Hillary Clinton and Barack Obama was billed as "fight night" on CNN. CNN commentator Jack Cafferty previewed the debate by saying: "Remember last week, the heated debate in South Carolina? Tonight could make that seem like a garden party." But Clinton and Obama, fearful that the South Carolina debate was too rancorous, came out and played nice, much to the media's disappointment. A *New York Times* reporter who was behind the scenes with CNN staff observed their exasperation.[27] One CNN producer complained that the debate was "like a press conference" rather than the brawl they apparently wanted to see. Rarely does one see reporters and producers reveal news values so explicitly.

A fourth news value is *skepticism*. Today's professional journalists are trained to be dubious about the claims that politicians make, and perhaps for good reason. Thus, what candidates say is rarely taken at face value. At a minimum, the norm of objectivity requires news outlets to engage in "he said, she said" journalism, pairing claims by one candidate with responses by the opponent. Reporters sometimes engage in fact-checking, evaluating candidates' claims in advertisements and elsewhere for their accuracy. Some news outlets have even created fact-checking websites, like the *Tampa Bay Times'* PolitiFact.com, which regularly monitors the statements of politicians and ranks them on a scale from "true" to "pants on fire."

Perhaps the preeminent focus of campaign coverage, however, is *strategy*. This kind of campaign coverage is sometimes known as **horse race journalism**. Horse race campaign coverage focuses on which candidate is ahead or behind, who is gaining or losing ground, and what the candidates are trying to do to win (their strategies), much the way the announcer at a horse race describes which horse is winning, surging, or faltering. A study of print, broadcast, and Internet news outlets during September and October 2008 found that 53 percent of coverage of the presidential campaign was about the horse race, while only 20 percent dealt with policy issues. In the 2012 campaign, horse race coverage declined to 38 percent of coverage and policy coverage increased slightly to 22 percent.[28] It is easy to see why horse race coverage is so appealing. For one, there are many ways to determine who is ahead or behind: fund-raising, endorsements, polls, the size of rallies, and so on. These indicators can be frequently updated, as candidates release fund-raising numbers or as media outlets field new polls, creating

---

[27] Brian Stetler. 2008. "Even as the Candidates Make Nice, the TV Crew Hopes for a Fight." *New York Times*, February 4, p. 1.

[28] Project for Excellence in Journalism. 2012. "Winning the Media Campaign 2012," November 2. www.journalism.org/2012/11/02/winning-media-campaign-2012/ (accessed 5/22/2014).

fresh grist for a story. Similarly, candidate debates are scored in terms of who "won" or "lost." Stories about undecided voters also generate horse race coverage, as these voters can be canvassed again and again to see if they have moved toward a candidate. Television networks sometimes convene small groups of undecided voters to watch presidential debates and then interview them after the debate. One experiment, however, showed that viewers' opinions of a debate are often more influenced by the media's tone following it rather than their own interpretation of the candidates.[29]

Within the context of horse race coverage, the media's discussion of strategy allows them to engage in what is sometimes called **interpretive journalism**. Reporters do not simply report on what the candidates do and say. They provide further analysis and interpretation. That is, they attempt to tell their audience why the candidates are doing what they are doing and thereby reveal the candidates' underlying strategy. This type of coverage grows out of how journalists see their obligations as professionals. Their job is not to narrate events but to provide context. Reporters draw on their perceived expertise to read between the lines and to help their audience understand what is "really going on."

Is Campaign Coverage Biased?

Thus far, we have focused on how news values shape campaign coverage. But the most frequent public criticism of campaign coverage is that it is ideologically biased. One version of this complaint singles out specific news outlets as biased. Some of these complaints may have merit, as newspaper coverage tends to favor incumbent candidates that the newspaper supports on its editorial page.[30] But it is difficult to know whether this kind of bias simply reflects the preferences of that newspaper's audience. Any bias may be coming from the "demand side," which is based on what the audience wants, rather than the "supply side," which is based on what the news media provides. Some of the programming decisions on the more conservative Fox News and the more liberal MSNBC may be driven by the partisan biases of each network's audience.

The more important complaint about bias targets all news outlets. Supporters of each candidate complain that "the media" as a whole favor a different candidate. President George H. W. Bush's 1992 campaign made this

---

[29] Michael Norton and George Goethals. 2004. "Spin and Pitch Doctors: Campaign Strategies in Televised Political Debates." *Political Behavior* 26(3): 227–248.

[30] Kim Fridkin Kahn and Patrick J. Kenney. 2002. "The Slant of the News: How Editorial Endorsements Influence Campaign Coverage and Citizens' Views of Candidates." *American Political Science Review* 96: 381–94.

claim, producing bumper stickers that said "Annoy the Media: Re-Elect Bush!" Some people even assert that this bias is chronic and that the media favor the Republican or Democratic party in election after election. Of course, it is easy to find examples of news coverage that seem more favorable to one candidate or the other. Yet it has been difficult to prove that candidate coverage is consistently biased toward one party or ideology. Despite persistent claims of many conservatives, news coverage is not consistently more favorable toward liberal or Democratic candidates. Although journalists tend to be more liberal than the general public, studies examining the actual content of that coverage have found little evidence of consistent bias in either direction.[31] This is likely because the norm of impartiality is so strongly ingrained in journalists. Instead, most partisan bias is in the minds of citizens, rather than in the news. Even when members of the two parties are watching the same coverage, Democrats believe that media coverage is more favorable toward the Republican candidate and vice versa.[32] Nonetheless, Republican politicians and activists have repeatedly characterized the news media as liberal and raised concerns about its role in helping Democrats. This challenge has reduced public confidence in the press, especially among Republicans, and made it harder for citizens to learn facts from media coverage.[33]

This is not to say that the media are not biased in other ways. Most important, news coverage tends to be more favorable to candidates who are ahead in the polls. Reporters write stories about how the losing campaign is "in disarray" and "floundering," while extolling the strategic prowess of the winning campaign. This bias was evident during the 2012 presidential campaign. There were four negative stories about Mitt Romney for every positive story from late August to early October. Following Obama's poor performance in the first presidential debate, coverage of Obama turned much more negative and coverage of Romney was more positive. The same trends were evident in 2008: coverage was more positive toward Obama, except when

---

[31] David H. Weaver, Randal A. Beam, Bonnie J. Brownlee, Paul S. Voakes, and G. Cleveland Wilhoit. 2006. *The American Journalist in the 21st Century: U.S. News People at the Dawn of a New Millennium.* New York: Routledge; D. D'Alessio and M. Allen. 2006. "Media Bias in Presidential Elections: A Meta-Analysis." *Journal of Communication* 50, 4: 133–56.

[32] William P. Eveland and Dhavan Shah. 2003. "The Impact of Individual and Interpersonal Factors on Perceived News Media Bias." *Political Psychology* 24, 1: 101–17.

[33] Jonathan Ladd. 2012. *Why Americans Hate the Media and Why It Matters.* Princeton, NJ: Princeton University Press.

McCain was gaining in the polls.[34] In both years, stories about polling and strategy were especially more positive toward Obama.

In other words, horse race coverage was more favorable to the candidate winning the horse race. The moral of the story is that whatever their personal political preferences, reporters have an incentive to appear balanced while favoring dramatic coverage of the changing fortunes of each candidate.

How Do Candidates and the News Media Interact?

Campaigns seek to influence news media coverage and to use the news media to reach potential voters. Political consultants speak about "earned media" or "free media," meaning news coverage given to the candidates, as distinct from their "paid media," or advertising. There are many ways in which candidates seek to transmit messages via the news media. They interact directly with the media in interviews, meetings with newspaper editorial boards, and press conferences. They hold public events and give speeches, and invite reporters to attend. They issue press releases, report polling data, publish policy position papers, and announce endorsements. They also leak stories to selected reporters. Nearly everything a candidate does is designed to be picked up in the next day's newspaper, the night's television broadcast, the next hour's update to a website, or the next minute's tweet.

Candidates want every interaction with the news media to be on their terms. They seek to control when and where the interaction takes place, whom they interact with, and what they talk about. Thus, candidates often prefer to avoid the unexpected. For example, candidates cannot anticipate every question that will be asked at a press conference or television interview, and unexpected questions are more likely to trip them up and lead to some misstatement or gaffe. In 2008, Sarah Palin, the Republican vice presidential nominee, had a disastrous interview with CBS News anchor Katie Couric. Palin seemed unable to answer simple questions—such as which newspapers she read—and generally appeared hesitant and apprehensive. In 2012, Missouri congressman Todd Akin, a candidate for U.S. Senate, claimed that women's bodies could spontaneously end their pregnancies if they suffer a "legitimate rape." The comments led to near universal condemnation, including calls by fellow Republicans for him to exit the race. Occasionally, these episodes can be enough to change voters' minds. Candidates fearful of negative news coverage sometimes eschew interviews or press

---

[34] Project for Excellence in Journalism, "Winning the Media Campaign 2012."

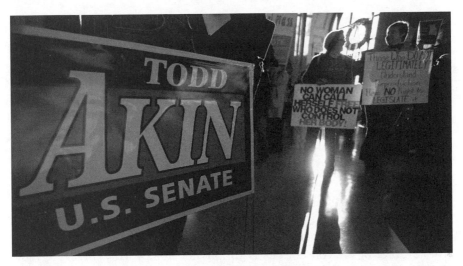

Todd Akin's comments about rape and pregnancy incited widespread outrage during his 2012 campaign for the U.S. Senate. Here, protesters at one of his campaign stops hold signs condemning Akin's remarks.

conferences, limiting their interactions with reporters and confining their public appearances to rallies and speeches. Campaigns sometimes take further steps to ensure that rallies and speeches lead to good media coverage— for example, by screening the attendees to guarantee that only cheering supporters, and not jeering opponents, are in the audience.

Candidates also plan their advertising around its anticipated media exposure. Many ads are shown much more by news shows, at no cost to candidates, than as a result of air time that candidates purchase. President Lyndon Johnson's 1964 "Daisy" ad, which featured a little girl counting flower petals before seamlessly shifting to a countdown for the detonation of a nuclear weapon, aired only once but generated significant media coverage and controversy because of the implication that Johnson's opponent, Barry Goldwater, would lead the country into nuclear war. The original anti-Kerry ads purchased by the Swift Boat Veterans for Truth in 2004 were aired sparingly but became fodder for newscasts. After the initial flurry of coverage, the group was able to raise enough money to run the ads more widely.

The media strategies of campaigns can help reporters do their jobs. The media want to tell their audience how day-to-day events might affect election outcomes, and campaigns strive to provide something eventful every day. The media are also looking for a good story, preferably one with drama and conflict. The candidates are often only too happy to leak scandalous tidbits of information about each other.

However, there are fundamental conflicts between the agendas of candidates and the news media. Candidates may schedule new events every day, but the content of those events is often repetitive. Because candidates want to present a consistent message, they repeat the same speech over and over. The audience at the speech will not have heard it—in fact, the candidate will have just flown into their town an hour before. But the reporters who traveled with the candidate on that plane have been to dozens of towns and heard the speech dozens of times. The day-to-day routine of a campaign does not satisfy the media's desire for fresh new story lines every day.

Moreover, when candidates attempt to turn every public appearance into a rally, this rarely supplies the sort of drama and conflict that the media want. If everybody is cheering for the candidate, nobody is arguing. The national party conventions are a good example. The media have long complained that live coverage of the conventions is simply not newsworthy. In 1996, ABC News anchor Ted Koppel actually left the Republican convention midway through the proceedings, declaring, "This convention is more of an infomercial than a news event. Nothing surprising has happened; nothing surprising is anticipated."[35] From the perspective of the party, this is what is supposed to happen. Parties would like the media to report that conflict is limited and the party has a consistent message—but that does not make for much of a news story.

Perhaps the most fundamental conflict between reporters and campaign organizations is that reporters do not have to deliver the candidate's message and often do not want to. This is what a professionalized press does: it makes its own decisions about what is important, rather than simply repeating what the candidate thinks is important. For example, although candidates spend most of their speeches talking, even if vaguely, about their policy agendas and goals, the media often talk about the horse race, especially when polls suggest that the race is becoming more competitive.[36] Even when journalists and commentators focus on what the candidates are talking about, they typically subject the candidates' messages to their own analysis. They comment on a candidate's statement or compare it to previous statements or opposition views. Often, the story the reporter writes is not the same one that the candidate hoped she would write.

Reporters are influenced by factors other than the candidates' messages. Newsworthy events such as the financial crisis of 2008 drive the news media's agenda and force candidates to respond accordingly. Frequently, reporters

---

[35] *Nightline.* 1996. Transcript, August 13.

[36] Danny Hayes. 2009. "The Dynamics of Agenda Convergence and the Paradox of Competitiveness in Presidential Campaigns." *Political Research Quarterly* 63, 3: 594–611.

follow the story lines developed by other reporters or commentators. This is the phenomenon of **pack journalism**. Reporters who cover campaigns tend to travel together, talk to each other, and read each others' stories. Because they fear missing an important story, they tend to converge on similar ideas and themes. Beltway denizens like Mark Halperin and daily digests like Politico's "Playbook" summarize what reporters are thinking and talking about and are read widely within the media. On a day-to-day basis, even MSNBC and Fox News generally highlight the same campaign events and candidate statements. Needless to say, candidates are not convinced that these insiders get the story right: "If Politico and Halperin say we're winning, we're losing," Obama's campaign major David Plouffe said repeatedly during the 2008 campaign.[37]

As a result of these differences, the relationship between candidates and the media is a lot like a marriage: sometimes cozy and sometimes combative. In *Journeys with George*, a documentary about George W. Bush's 2000 presidential campaign, Bush is depicted playing games with the reporters covering him. He gives them nicknames, spends time in their section of the plane, and attempts to make friends with many of them. He even kisses the cheek of the movie's producer, who happens to be the daughter of Representative Nancy Pelosi (D-CA). But Bush's relations with the news media were sometimes more frosty. At one campaign event, he was overheard telling Vice President Dick Cheney, "There's Adam Clymer—major league asshole—from the *New York Times*." This contradictory behavior reflects the tension in the relationship between candidates and the news media. They need to stay on good terms with one another but they have differing goals and incentives.

The Effects of Media Coverage on Citizens

Campaigns seek to influence media coverage because they believe it will influence what the public thinks about the candidates and thus the election's outcome. But the effects of media coverage are often not that dramatic. The media cannot easily move public opinion.

Although many observers fear that partisan media outlets are contributing to political polarization, the research evidence is mixed.[38] In experiments, some consumers do gravitate to news sources associated with their partisan

---

[37] Mark Leibovich. 2008. "Between Obama and the Press." *New York Times Magazine*, December 17. www.nytimes.com/2008/12/21/magazine/21Gibbs-t.html (accessed 9/24/10).

[38] Prior, "Media and Political Polarization."

slant, but others seek information from both sides. A study of Web browsing found that ideological and partisan segregation in online media is limited in comparison to face-to-face interactions: conservative Republicans talk mostly to others that share their views but visit some liberal websites (and vice versa).[39] Most MSNBC viewers watch some Fox News, though the most dedicated Fox viewers rarely watch a full MSNBC or CNN program.[40] Cable news watchers also tend to watch considerable local news, which usually lacks an ideological or partisan slant.

It is particularly difficult for information presented by the media to *persuade* people to change their opinions. For example, as news coverage of a candidate became more favorable, one might expect the public's view of that candidate to become more favorable as well. This is not so common for two reasons. First, many people do not follow politics very closely. They are unlikely to read, see, or hear much about a political campaign, and thus their opinions about the candidates, if they have any opinions, will not change.

Second, among those who do follow politics, relatively few people are undecided about political candidates, especially at higher levels of office, such as the presidency. Instead, these people tend to interpret information from the news media in ways that support the choice they have already made.[41]

Because of this, a much more common effect of media coverage is to strengthen or *reinforce* people's preexisting views. This happens not so much because people deliberately ignore contrary news. Instead, people simply interpret information in ways that confirm what they already think. Supporters of two different candidates who see a news report on the campaign will each see yet more reasons to support their favored candidate and oppose the other candidate. Even a news report that is highly unfavorable to a particular candidate is unlikely to change the opinions of that candidate's supporters. People have an impressive ability to ignore, rationalize, or argue against information that is contrary to their views.[42] They find reasons to dispute such a report or dismiss its importance. Fact checking can provoke a similar reaction. By repeating false claims, even to debunk them,

---

[39] Matthew Gentzkow and Jesse Shapiro. 2011. "Ideological Segregation Online and Offline." *Quarterly Journal of Economics* 126: 1799–839.

[40] Natalie Jomini Stroud. 2011. *Niche News: The Politics of News Choice.* New York: Oxford University Press.

[41] David O. Sears and Richard Kosterman. 1994. "Political Persuasion," in *Persuasion: Psychological Insights and Perspectives*, ed. Sharon Shavitt and Timothy C. Brock. Boston: Allyn & Bacon, pp. 251–78.

[42] Michael F. Meffert, Sungeun Chung, Amber Joiner, Leah Waks, and Jennifer Garst. 2006. "The Effects of Negativity and Motivated Information Processing during a Political Campaign." *Journal of Communication* 56, 1: 27–35.

fact-checkers may only reinforce misperceptions among those predisposed to hold them.[43]

Persuasion is thus more common when people do not have strong pre-existing opinions and are more susceptible to new information. A good example is presidential primaries. In primaries, voters are choosing among candidates in a single party, so whether voters are Democrats or Republicans themselves does not help them make a choice. Moreover, many primary candidates are not familiar figures, and so voters know less about them to begin with. Under these conditions, media coverage can affect opinions. For example, throughout the 2012 Republican presidential primary, there were sudden increases in media coverage of several different candidates, usually following the sort of novel or dramatic event that attracts media attention. In one case, news coverage of a candidate that few observers believed viable, businessman Herman Cain, increased after he won a nonbinding straw poll among Republican activists in Florida. This media coverage then increased the candidate's standing in the polls.[44]

Although the media are often less effective at persuasion—or changing what people think—they are more effective at changing what people think about. One way in which the media does this is **agenda setting**. The idea is simple: the more the media report on something, the more the public regards it as important. If the media talk a lot about health care, citizens are more likely to cite health care as an issue of concern. In one of the earliest studies of agenda setting, researchers measured the amount of attention to various issues in newspapers in Chapel Hill, North Carolina, during the 1968 presidential campaign.[45] At the end of the campaign, they conducted a survey of Chapel Hill residents. The issues emphasized in the newspapers were those that the public considered important. Subsequent studies that use experimental manipulations of media coverage have demonstrated the same finding: people who are randomly assigned to view newscasts with several stories about an issue will believe that issue to be more important than people who watch newscasts with no stories about it.[46] These findings provide candidates even more reason to try to shape the media's agenda.

---

[43] R. Kelly Garrett, Erik C. Nisbet, and Emily K. Lynch. 2013. "Undermining the Corrective Effects of Media-Based Political Fact Checking? The Role of Contextual Cues and Naïve Theory." *Journal of Communication* 63, 4: 617–37.

[44] Sides and Vavreck, *The Gamble.*

[45] Maxwell E. McCombs and Donald L. Shaw. 1972. "The Agenda-Setting Function of Mass Media." *Public Opinion Quarterly* 36, 2: 176–87.

[46] Shanto Iyengar and Donald R. Kinder. *News That Matters.* 1987. Chicago: Chicago University Press.

Related to agenda setting is a process called **priming**. The media influence or "prime" the criteria citizens use to make judgments by the degree of emphasis issues receive, even if the media are not explicitly telling the public to make judgments in this manner. In fact, priming occurs even when media reports do not mention the candidates in the context of discussing an issue. The more reporters discuss an ongoing war, the more the public will judge the president for his performance on the war, even if reporters do not explicitly credit or blame the president for the war.

An example of priming during a political campaign involved Senator Gary Hart (D-CO), who ran in the 1988 presidential primary. Hart, who was married, was caught having an affair with a young woman named Donna Rice. Reporters discovered a picture of Rice sitting on Hart's lap aboard a yacht named, appropriately enough, *Monkey Business*. Because of this scandal, people's own moral values became stronger predictors of their attitudes toward Hart as the campaign progressed, with those who were morally conservative being less favorable to Hart. In other words, news media coverage of Hart's affair "primed" moral values, making them an important factor in the public's judgments of Hart.[47]

Finally, the news media affect citizens by *informing*. News coverage of campaigns can help citizens learn relevant facts about the candidates, including candidate biographies and issue positions (even if issues are generally not the main focus of campaign coverage). As campaigns attract more media coverage, citizens are more likely to recognize and recall the names of the candidates and to identify the issues that the candidates are discussing.[48] Although it can be difficult to separate the informing effect of the media from that of other information sources, such as campaign advertising, media coverage plays an important role.

None of these effects are mutually exclusive. The information conveyed in the news media could simultaneously educate people about a candidate's position on an issue (informing), make them feel that issue is an important problem (agenda setting), and lead them to draw on that issue when deciding whom to vote for (priming). Candidates' attempts to influence news media coverage, if they are successful, might also have multiple effects simultaneously.

---

[47] Laura Stoker. 1993. "Judging Presidential Character: The Demise of Gary Hart," *Political Behavior* 15, 2: 193–223.

[48] Kim Fridkin Kahn and Patrick J. Kenney. 1999. *The Spectacle of U.S. Senate Campaigns.* Princeton, NJ: Princeton University Press.

There are, however, inherent limits to how much the media influence opinions. Many people do not pay attention to political news or already have well-defined viewpoints that are unlikely to change. Since the rise of cable television and the Internet, Americans who do not want to watch news have been able to choose from an increasing array of other programming, such as sports, cooking shows, and movies. With more channels, most people can avoid the news. The result is an increasingly divided electorate, where some people pay attention to news, learn about politics, and participate in political activities while the rest of the population largely tunes out and is less likely to vote.[49] Giving people more media choices has led to a citizenry that may be less susceptible to any political messages in the news media.

Evaluating the News Media's Role in Campaigns

How well do the news media uphold the standards of free choice, equality, and deliberation by which we might judge political campaigns? In some ways, the media meet the standard of free choice, which highlights the needs of citizens to learn about the candidates in order to cast an informed vote. Coverage of campaigns can help citizens learn who the candidates are and what they stand for. But news coverage is not created with education in mind. It is designed by companies trying to maximize the attention of the audiences coveted by advertisers. As a result, most campaigns receive little attention from the news media. For those that do get attention, media coverage often emphasizes what is new, dramatic, or scandalous. This is not due to any partisan or ideological biases. Unlike the candidates themselves, the news media — or at least those outlets that strive for objectivity — are not seeking to manipulate citizens into voting for particular candidates. Instead, they are seeking to build and maintain an audience. If juicy revelations surrounding a candidate's divorce emerge, then the media will feature these revelations regardless of whether this is the most important information for citizens to learn.

We can also ask whether news media contribute to equality. A central question here is whether news media coverage helps to address information inequality, whereby those citizens who are habitually attentive to politics learn a great deal but those who are inattentive to politics learn very little. There is always the potential for information in the news media to reach a wide and diverse audience. But this happens rarely — usually when a big story breaks and receives nonstop coverage by multiple outlets. More often, the many channels and websites available to consumers encourage segmentation,

---

[49] Prior, *Post-Broadcast Democracy.*

with political junkies getting their fill of campaign news, and most other people watching entertainment and sports programming. This information inequality reflects and may reinforce a broader economic inequality: people with lower incomes and education levels are less likely to see political news.

A third standard is deliberation. In a large democracy, deliberation must be mediated: Americans cannot all talk to one another or to the candidates face-to-face. Thus, it is up to the media to convey information that clarifies the views of each side. The media's interest in conflict means that they will often report on the differences among the candidates. At times they play referee, intervening as if moderating a debate, investigating the claims that candidates make, and helping citizens understand what the candidates are saying, and whether it is truthful. Of course, the news media's ability to serve as a watchdog depends in part on the economic prospects for the news business. Cuts in newsroom budgets tend to limit investigative journalism and lead outlets to rely on less experienced journalists.

If we conceive of deliberation as involving face-to-face conversation among citizens, there is less evidence that media facilitate this. Blogs, online communities, and social networks have the potential to allow millions to communicate and respond to one another's views. Yet partisans may be speaking mainly to one another, and disinterested citizens are mostly opting out of the conversation. Online communities can still promote involvement in campaigns: a large experiment on Facebook during the 2010 elections found that users who saw photos of their friends who reported voting were themselves a little bit more likely to turn out to vote.[50] But there is also evidence that offering token public support for a cause on Facebook or Twitter may make one less likely to be involved in offline campaign activities.[51]

Commentators raise other ethical concerns about media coverage. Some argue that the media are too adversarial and thus too quick to criticize candidates or seize on any hint of scandal, no matter how minor.[52] Some fear that negative media coverage of campaigns may have made people more cynical about politics generally.[53] But there is a delicate balance here. In a

---

[50] Robert M. Bond, Christopher J. Fariss, Jason J. Jones, Adam D. I. Kramer, Cameron Marlow, Jaime E. Settle, and James H. Fowler. 2012. "A 61-Million-Person Experiment in Social Influence and Political Mobilization." *Nature* 489: 295–98.

[51] Kirk Kristofferson, Katherine White, and John Peloza. 2014. "The Nature of Slacktivism: How the Social Observability of an Initial Act of Token Support Affects Subsequent Prosocial Action." *Journal of Consumer Research* 40, 6: 1149–66.

[52] Thomas E. Patterson. 1993. *Out of Order.* New York: Knopf.

[53] Joseph N. Cappella and Kathleen Hall Jamieson. 1996. "News Frames, Political Cynicism, and Media Cynicism." *Annals of the American Academy of Political and Social Science* 546: 71–84.

democracy, we also need the news media to hold candidates accountable, and certainly many media outlets see this as one of their roles. So is critical coverage of candidates necessary? Does it go too far? There is no easy answer to these questions. Often it is in the eye of the beholder where accountability ends and cynicism begins.

Furthermore, blaming the media gets us only so far. Consider a study conducted during the 2000 presidential campaign.[54] Participants in the study were sent a CD containing a variety of information about the candidates, Al Gore and George W. Bush, which was culled from various news reports. There were stories about the candidates and their biographies, their views on issues, strategy and the horse race, and a few other topics. Participants could read whatever they wanted on this CD, and their decisions were tracked by researchers. What did people gravitate to? Stories about candidates and strategy—precisely the kinds of topics that the news media are so often criticized for emphasizing. In fact, people who pay a lot of attention to politics, and are thus likely to be regular readers of the news, are more likely to read these kinds of stories. Thus, the news media's focus on campaign strategy and the horse race may simply give consumers the information they want. This is what we would expect when news organizations need to maintain and build an audience in order to sell advertising. Of course, we should not simply shift our blame from the news media to news consumers: it is not always easy to tell how much blame each deserves.

Conclusion

The media play an important role in communicating information about campaigns, determining the issues discussed in them, and shaping the images that voters develop of each candidate. The frenzy surrounding the video of Mitt Romney's "47 percent" remarks illustrates how the news media cover campaigns, as well as the potential for and the limits on their influence on voters. The attention to the video reflected the news values of journalists. The story was new. It involved drama and controversy. It had inflammatory rhetoric. This is why it featured so heavily in news coverage.

The story's salience demonstrates how the news media's agenda may diverge from the candidate's agenda. Certainly Mitt Romney did not want to talk about his remarks. But he was forced to engage nonetheless. Candidates cannot avoid interacting with the media because it is an important way

---

[54] Shanto Iyengar, Helmut Norpoth, and Kyu S. Hahn. 2004. "Consumer Demand for Election News: The Horse Race Sells," *Journal of Politics* 66, 1: 157–75.

in which they speak to the public. Romney did not react by simply criticizing the media. He had to apologize, provide an explanation, and attempt to change the subject.

Technological and commercial changes in the news media also played a role in the video's release. An individual citizen created the video and made contact with reporters and activists in online communities. A reporter for a left-leaning magazine and website generated the initial attention. Yet the story gained traction after the video garnered attention from more traditional media. The story fit the profile of Romney prominent in news coverage of the campaign, thanks in part to the Obama campaign's advertising and Romney's public gaffes.

The episode also shows us how difficult it is for the news media to affect public opinion. When the video first appeared, the campaign had been under way for months. Those paying attention to politics had already formed opinions of Obama and Romney. News coverage of political campaigns often implies that campaign events have a powerful impact on the public. In essence, the news media seem to believe in their own power. In reality, their effect on the attitudes of Americans is much more limited.

At their best, the news media can uphold the ideals we would like political campaigns to embody. Journalists can convey the messages from candidates while also serving as watchdogs. News coverage can contrast the views of the parties, correct untruths, and direct attention to important issues and to the candidates' strengths and weaknesses. At the same time, the coverage also focuses on sideshows and horse race trivia, while ignoring the bigger picture—a fact that must be blamed not only on the news media themselves but on citizens who consume news. Campaigns show us the best and worst of the contemporary news media.

KEY TERMS

news media (p. 205)

sound bite (p. 206)

blogs (p. 208)

right to equal time (p. 211)

infotainment (p. 214)

wire services (p. 215)

narrow-casting (p. 216)

news values (p. 218)

horse race journalism (p. 221)

interpretive journalism
   (p. 222)

pack journalism (p. 227)

agenda setting (p. 229)

priming (p. 230)

FOR DISCUSSION

1. Who is more responsible for the weaknesses of campaign coverage in the American news media: reporters or consumers? Do citizens get the news they ask for?

2. If you were starting a blog about campaigns in your state, what would you cover? Would you repeat candidate messages or independently analyze the strengths and weaknesses of each side? How would you generate an audience? Would the need to build your audience change the types of stories that you covered?

3. How should the media have covered the release of the Romney fund-raising video? Could they have ignored it? Was it a legitimate campaign issue?

4. What changes will online-only media outlets bring to campaigns over the next few election cycles? Will bloggers ever replace newspaper and television reporters as important actors in campaigns? How will the candidates change their behavior in response?

CHAPTER 9

Presidential Campaigns

In late August 2000, the Bush campaign team watched on television as the Democratic nominee, Al Gore, and his running mate, Joe Lieberman, boarded a boat in Wisconsin for a quick trip down the Mississippi River. The general reaction was mild contempt. "What are they doing? Another boat trip? Been there, done that," someone said, pointing out that George H. W. Bush and his vice-presidential nominee, Dan Quayle, had taken a riverboat trip in 1988 before the Republican convention. Bush's senior strategist, Karl Rove, was not so dismissive: "Somebody get me an atlas!" he shouted. After examining the Democrats' planned route, Rove quickly realized that Gore and Lieberman would be visiting places that were inaccessible to Bush. Bush's airplane was too big to land in any Iowa airfield east of Des Moines. The only alternative for reaching the critical swing counties of southwest Wisconsin and eastern Iowa along the Mississippi was for Bush to fly to Des Moines or Milwaukee and do a two- to three-day bus tour. Rove opted not to do this, using direct mail, paid phone calls, and prominent Republican officials to reach out to potential voters in the places that Gore and Lieberman visited by boat. On Election Day, Gore won Iowa and Wisconsin by a combined total of 11,000 votes. Exit polls and election returns showed that Gore did especially well in the parts of these states along the Mississippi River.

It is far from clear, however, that Gore's riverboat trip won him these two states. In fact, it is far from clear that this trip was even the best use of the candidate's time and energy. One might argue, for instance, that this time would have been better spent in Florida, which Gore lost by a mere 537 votes, thus losing the election. Still, the Democrats' decision to make the trip and the Republican's decision not to directly match it illustrates the strategic choices that animate modern presidential campaigns. And in close elections, these strategic choices might be critical.

The phrase *"might be critical"* reflects the skepticism among political scientists about the extent to which presidential campaigns affect election outcomes. This is not to say presidential campaigns do not matter. They do reinforce citizens' underlying partisan loyalties and raise the salience of fundamental factors such as the state of the economy. But campaigns do not necessarily decide who wins; broader political and economic realities may be more significant. Campaign consultants, by contrast, are much more confident that presidential campaigns affect public opinion and therefore the outcome of the election. Consultants tend to believe that campaign strategy is often decisive in who wins.

In this chapter, we explain how political scientists and campaign strategists understand the role of presidential campaigns in the electoral process, and seek to reconcile their somewhat different views. We argue that campaigns act strategically to maximize the chances that they will win the White House. In developing strategies, presidential campaigns are influenced by two institutional arrangements. First, there is the series of statewide nominating contests — primaries and caucuses — during the first five months of a presidential election year. Second, there is the Electoral College, in which electors cast the deciding ballots for president. The electors are determined largely by winner-take-all statewide popular vote outcomes. Both arrangements demonstrate how electoral rules affect campaign strategy. Maximizing the prospects for victory also means acknowledging the political reality of a given presidential election cycle. Candidates are likely to pursue different strategies depending upon whether the economy is strong or weak, whether the country is at war or peace, and which party presently holds the White House.

We first examine a presidential campaign's basic goals. We then turn to the three major stages of presidential elections — the nomination contest, the

Core of the Analysis

- Presidential candidates have two goals: to secure their party's nomination and then to win a majority of Electoral College votes.
- Electoral rules structure the presidential nominations process, and as candidates campaign for their party's nomination, they encounter a variety of election formats in different states.
- Nominating conventions provide critical boosts to the presidential candidates, while events that occur later in the campaign tend to have a smaller impact.
- The Electoral College structures the general election campaign, and candidates target particular states in order to win the necessary electoral votes.
- Political reality — especially the state of the economy — has an enormous influence on presidential elections.

In September 2000, Al Gore and Joe Lieberman took a boat trip down the Mississippi River to campaign in the battleground states of Wisconsin and Iowa. This trip may have increased support for the Democratic ticket in rural areas of these states.

national convention, and the general election—taking care to consider the important rules and broader realities that affect strategy at each stage. We also discuss the effects that conventions and debates typically have on public opinion. We conclude by considering how well modern presidential campaigns serve American democracy.

Goals of Presidential Campaigns

Two goals have to be met to win the White House. The first goal is to amass a sufficient number of **delegates** to secure a party's nomination at the national convention. Most delegates (roughly 75 percent) are selected in statewide primary elections, caucuses, and conventions. Of these methods, primary elections are the most common.

The second goal is to win enough states in the general election to garner at least 270—a majority—of the 538 available Electoral College votes and thus win the presidency. Note that the goal is *not* to win a majority of the popular vote; this is usually necessary to claim enough states to win 270 electoral votes, but not always. In fact, there have been presidents who lost the popular vote but still won the election: John Quincy Adams (1824), Rutherford B. Hayes (1876), and George W. Bush (2000). There is even some evidence that John F. Kennedy lost the popular vote in 1960.[1]

The problem is that these two goals can be somewhat incompatible. To win the nomination a candidate must win the votes of a plurality of partisans. But partisans, whether Republican or Democrat, tend to be more ideological than the average voter in the general election. This gives candidates the incentive to move away from the political center in order to cater to ideologues and win the nomination, and then back toward the center to win the election. (More will be said about this spatial theory of voting in Chapter 13.) One could certainly argue that this is what happened to the campaigns of Bob Dole (1996), John Kerry (2004), John McCain (2008), and Mitt Romney (2012), all of whom shifted their positions on certain issues between the primary and general elections. Some recent candidates have sought to avoid the inconsistency of following strident partisan appeals during presidential primaries with more inclusive, moderate policy appeals. George W. Bush (2000) and Hillary Clinton (2008) were careful not to embrace primary strategies that were inconsistent with their longer-term plans for the general election. But this strategy is risky too: appealing to more centrist general election voters can alienate hard-core partisans who play a major role in primaries and caucuses.

---

[1] Brian J. Gaines. 2001. "Popular Myths about Popular Vote–Electoral College Splits." *PS: Political Science and Politics* 74: 70–75.

Winning the Nomination

Before the convention and the general election campaign, presidential candidates have several important tasks to accomplish. We focus on two of the most important: contesting the party's primaries and caucuses, and selecting a vice-presidential candidate to be the running mate.

Primaries and Caucuses

In Chapters 3 and 6, we discussed how the political parties no longer directly control the nominating process.[2] As a consequence, individual candidates must campaign state by state, in primary elections and party caucuses. These elections determine who the state party will send to represent the state at the national party nominating convention. These representatives are called *delegates*. To win the nomination at the convention, a candidate has to accumulate delegates by winning an array of statewide elections, each with distinct rules, over a period of several months. This makes four different kinds of rules important: how states structure these elections, how delegates are allocated to candidates, how delegates are selected to attend the national convention, and the order in which states hold their elections.

States typically employ either caucuses or primary elections to determine who their delegates will be. **Caucuses** are relatively closed affairs in which registered partisans attend meetings at election precinct locations and vote to select delegates to the county or state party conventions. Typically, these delegates are "pledged" to support a particular presidential candidate at the next level. The actual delegates to the national convention are then selected at the state convention. To be successful in a caucus state, a candidate must have a committed group of followers and an organization that can deliver these followers to the caucus locations. The first contest of the presidential nominations process is the Iowa caucuses.

More commonly, states use some form of **primary election** to determine delegates to the national convention. The form of the primary election affects the kinds of voters who can participate. As we discussed in Chapter 2, primaries can be closed, open, or semi-closed. In closed primaries, only registered partisans can vote. That is, only registered Democrats can vote in the

---

[2] Although most scholars agree that the political parties no longer control the presidential nomination process, Cohen and his colleagues contend that higher-level party officials and donors remain the dominant forces in the selection of candidates. Their analysis features a case study of George W. Bush's rise in 1999 based on the preferences of the Republican Party's power-brokers. See Marty Cohen, David Karol, Hans Noel, and John Zaller. 2008. *The Party Decides: Presidential Nominations Before and After Reform.* Chicago: University of Chicago Press.

Democratic primary, and only registered Republicans can vote in the Republican primary. In open primaries, voters can choose the primary in which they will vote, regardless of their party, but they may only vote in one party's primary.[3] In semi-closed primaries, both unaffiliated voters and those registered as members of a party can vote in that party's primary—so, for example, registered Republicans and independents may vote in the Republican primary. Candidates will thus face more or less ideological electorates depending on the type of primary. For example, a socially conservative candidate who appeals to the Republican base would stand a better chance in a closed primary state than in an open primary state in which independents and Democrats are allowed to vote. The first primary of the presidential election year, in New Hampshire, is a semi-closed primary.

Most states allocate delegates in proportion to the percentage of the vote won by a candidate in the primary or caucuses. Under this system, a candidate with 40 percent of the vote in a state's primary gets 40 percent of the delegates from that state. The Democratic Party mandates a proportionality rule for its nomination process. In the Republican nomination process, some states have historically used a winner-take-all rule, allocating all delegates from the state to the winning candidate regardless of the vote margin. However, the winner-take-all rule is being phased out and will likely be replaced with a proportional rule.

To select the individual delegates, some states (such as New York) use a direct vote, others (such as California) allow the candidates to select as many delegates as they are entitled to based on the primary or caucus results, and still others (such as Texas) allow delegates to pledge themselves to candidates and then stand for election at the state convention. These differing arrangements affect what a campaign must do to maximize the number of delegates it can obtain. For example, in Texas, delegates are allocated in proportion to the vote a candidate gets statewide and by the proportion won in each of the state's congressional districts. Delegates to county conventions are then selected in precinct caucuses; delegates to the state convention are selected at the county conventions; and delegates to the national convention are selected at the state convention. This multistage process (known as the "Texas two-step") means that candidates need committed supporters in as many parts of the state as possible. In 2008, the Obama campaign was able to maximize delegate totals in several states through a mastery of complex caucus and convention selection processes.

---

[3] In fact, most open primary states do not have registration by party.

In addition to the delegates selected through the competitive processes of these statewide nomination contests, roughly one-quarter of delegates to the national nominating conventions achieve that status because they are officeholders or occupy certain positions within the party. These are referred to as *at-large* delegates (or *superdelegates*) and are not pledged to support any particular candidate based on a statewide vote. They are free agents who must be persuaded, one by one, by the candidate and campaign. Hillary Clinton's 2008 campaign worked long and hard to convince the at-large delegates to ignore Obama's edge in pledged delegates and to vote for her at the convention. In the end, however, at-large delegates sided with Obama, who had won more total votes in all the primaries and caucuses and thus more pledged delegates.

The primaries and consequent delegate selection occur in a sequence, with some states' primaries or caucuses held as early as January and others as late as June (Table 9.1). The early contests—especially the Iowa caucuses and the New Hampshire and South Carolina primaries—can have an effect on the process that is disproportionate to the actual number of delegates from those states. This is because their results are seen by both the news media and citizens as conveying important information about the **viability** of the candidates, or their chances for winning the nomination.[4] Because complex choices require more resources than they are willing or able to invest, the news media and citizens seek ways to simplify the choice, especially when many candidates are running for a party's nomination. The early races thus serve to winnow (that is, narrow) the field. Some candidates drop out because their performance in Iowa, New Hampshire, or South Carolina indicates they have no chance of winning the nomination. In 2008, 10 Democrats and 11 Republicans sought their parties' nominations; one week after the South Carolina primary on January 19, only 8 remained in the running: Barack Obama, Hillary Clinton, and John Edwards on the Democratic side, and John McCain, Rudy Giuliani, Mitt Romney, Mike Huckabee, and Ron Paul on the Republican side. In 2012, 11 Republicans were on the ballot in at least three presidential primaries, but by January 19, 2012, 5 had dropped out (Michele Bachmann, Herman Cain, Rick Perry, Jon Huntsman, and Gary Johnson); two others were never a factor (Fred Karger and Buddy Roemer).

---

[4] John Aldrich. 1980. *Before the Convention.* Chicago: University of Chicago Press; Larry Bartels. 1988. *The Dynamics of Presidential Primaries.* Princeton, NJ: Princeton University Press.

TABLE 9.1 2012 Republican Presidential Primary Calendar

Date	State	Contest	Rules
Tuesday, January 3	Iowa	Caucus	Closed
Tuesday, January 10	New Hampshire	Primary	Semi-closed
Saturday, January 21	South Carolina	Primary	Open
Tuesday, January 31	Florida	Primary	Closed
Saturday, February 4– Saturday, February 11	Maine	Caucus	Closed
Saturday, February 4	Nevada	Caucus	Closed
Tuesday, February 7	Colorado	Caucus	Closed
	Minnesota	Caucus	Open
Saturday, February 11– Wednesday, February 29	Wyoming	Caucus	Closed
Tuesday, February 28	Arizona	Primary	Closed
	Michigan	Primary	Open
Saturday, March 3	Washington	Caucus	Closed
Tuesday, March 6	Alaska	Caucus	Closed
	Georgia	Primary	Semi-closed
	Idaho	Caucus	Closed
	Massachusetts	Primary	Semi-closed
	North Dakota	Caucus	Closed
	Ohio	Primary	Semi-closed
	Oklahoma	Primary	Closed
	Tennessee	Primary	Open
	Vermont	Primary	Open
	Virginia	Primary	Open
Saturday, March 10	Kansas	Caucus	Closed
Tuesday, March 13	Alabama	Primary	Open
	Hawaii	Caucus	Closed
	Mississippi	Primary	Open
Tuesday, March 20	Illinois	Primary	Open
Saturday, March 24	Louisiana	Primary	Closed
Tuesday, April 3	District of Columbia	Primary	Closed
	Maryland	Primary	Closed
	Wisconsin	Primary	Open

(continued)

TABLE 9.1 (continued)

Date	State	Contest	Rules
Tuesday, April 24	Connecticut	Primary	Closed
	Delaware	Primary	Closed
	New York	Primary	Closed
	Pennsylvania	Primary	Closed
	Rhode Island	Primary	Semi-closed
Tuesday, May 8	Indiana	Primary	Open
	North Carolina	Primary	Semi-closed
	West Virginia	Primary	Semi-closed
Tuesday, May 15	Nebraska	Primary	Semi-closed
	Oregon	Primary	Closed
Tuesday, May 22	Arkansas	Primary	Open
	Kentucky	Primary	Closed
Tuesday, May 29	Texas	Primary	Open
Tuesday, June 5	California	Primary	Closed
	Montana	Primary	Open
	New Jersey	Primary	Closed
	New Mexico	Primary	Closed
	South Dakota	Primary	Closed
Tuesday, June 26	Utah	Primary	Closed

Source: http://elections.nytimes.com/2012/primaries/calendar (accessed 4/16/15).

The importance of early contests gives state legislatures the incentive to move their primaries and caucuses earlier in the calendar so that they will exert greater influence on the nominating process. This is known as **front-loading**. The national party organizations, aware that a system in which all states hold early primaries might help a charismatic but still relatively unknown and flawed candidate win the nomination, have discouraged front-loading in order to provide additional time for citizens to learn about the candidates. The Republican National Committee (RNC), for example, adopted a "preferred" calendar for 2012, with no primaries or caucuses scheduled before February 1 and some penalties for states that jumped to the front of the calendar. But the actual calendar in Table 9.1 demonstrates that the RNC's preferences were not realized, as state legislatures remain the ultimate authorities for election dates.

Taken together, these features of the presidential nominating process have important implications for campaign strategy. Candidates face a demanding task. They must develop a campaign organization that can compete in a rapid-fire sequence of contests with different eligible voters and different rules: the precinct caucuses in Iowa, the semi-closed primary election in New Hampshire a week later, the open primary election in South Carolina two or three weeks after that, and then the numerous primaries (including Georgia, Ohio, and Virginia) that mark "Super Tuesday." It is a significant test and one that requires money, attention from news media, and the support of at least some within the party organization.

Thus, the first strategic decision we discussed in Chapter 5—whether to run in the first place—entails a calculation about whether the candidate can muster the needed resources. Candidates must ask themselves whether they can raise the money necessary to assemble campaign organizations across the many states holding nominating contests. If they cannot, then they must answer a different question: whether they can convince enough voters in one of the early states to support them, thereby earning greater attention and ensuring that they remain relevant in subsequent contests. At this early stage of the election season, some lesser-known candidates craft issue-based or ideological appeals and hammer their message home, hoping to attract wider attention. For example, in 2008 Ohio congressman Dennis Kucinich presented himself as more liberal and more vehement in his opposition to the Iraq War than the other Democratic contenders. In the 2008 and 2012 Republican primaries, Texas congressman Ron Paul presented himself as the only truly Libertarian candidate, one distrustful of government intervention both in the economy and in people's personal lives. Both candidates generated enough support and attention early on to sustain lengthy campaigns.

For candidates that do run, subsequent decisions will depend on their level of prominence. **Front-runners**—candidates with a lot of money and who are well known by the electorate—must decide how much time and money to spend in the early states, since some of them are small and thus have fewer delegates than the large states whose primaries fall on Super Tuesday and later in the calendar. Hillary Clinton's national campaign in 2008 emphasized the early contests in Iowa and New Hampshire, which was a controversial strategy. She could have ignored Iowa, for example, and perhaps minimized the significance of an upset victory by Barack Obama or John Edwards, who both campaigned and organized tirelessly there. But ignoring Iowa would have raised questions about her front-runner status: Was she afraid of losing? How dominant was she really? The 2008 primary race was made even more complicated by the fact that two major states—Michigan and Florida—had moved their primaries up to January even though the national parties threatened not to seat either state's delegates at the national conventions. How were candidates to respond to this situation? Clinton chose not to campaign in those states but left her name on the ballot. Obama honored the ruling of the national party by staying out of Florida and Michigan, and not working to have his name placed on the ballot on those states—a decision made easier by the fact that Clinton was favored to win both states.

As alluded to earlier, lesser-known candidates face a different strategic challenge: Which of the early contests are the most promising targets for pulling off an upset and thereby generating important publicity for the campaign? Surpassing low expectations and thereby triggering favorable media coverage generates momentum. Candidates with momentum can build on early victories to win later primaries and ultimately the nomination. Candidates who benefited from momentum include Jimmy Carter in 1976, George H. W. Bush in 1980, Gary Hart in 1984, Pat Buchanan in 1992, John McCain in 2000, Howard Dean in 2004, Barack Obama in 2008, and Rick Santorum in 2012. Only one of these candidates won the nomination, however, illustrating that early victories are usually not enough.

In 2012, several Republican candidates sought to generate momentum by winning early caucuses or primaries on favorable terrain. Rick Santorum targeted Iowa (skipping New Hampshire), while Jon Huntsman targeted New Hampshire (skipping Iowa), and Newt Gingrich targeted South Carolina (largely bypassing New Hampshire). By way of contrast, in 2008 Barack Obama was able to pursue something of a hybrid strategy. While he was clearly an underdog relative to Clinton, he was also very well financed. He could thus afford to be more selective than Clinton in allocating resources to states, but he did not narrow his focus to a few early states. Obama began to build organizations in several states—especially those with caucuses, where organization often matters more than money. He also fought vigorously in the early contests. Indeed, his early victories in Iowa and then South Carolina were arguably essential to generating the money and support necessary to mount efforts in the later contests and ultimately to win the nomination.

Given the importance of fund-raising, primary contenders must also decide whether to accept public funds. As we discussed in Chapter 4, the Federal Election Campaign Act (FECA) provides public money for presidential candidates who meet fairly attainable thresholds—$5,000 in contributions of $250 or less across at least 20 states. But the money comes with conditions: the recipient must abide by state-by-state as well as overall spending limits. In 2012, the overall limits were about $45.6 million. Ever since multimillionaire Steve Forbes targeted Bob Dole with millions of dollars in negative ads in the 1996 New Hampshire Republican primary, some candidates have been reticent to accept public funds and the limits they entail. George W. Bush in 2000; Bush, John Kerry, and Howard Dean in 2004; Barack Obama, Hillary Clinton, John McCain, Mitt Romney, Mike Huckabee, and Rudy Giuliani in 2008; and Barack Obama, Mitt Romney, Rick Santorum, Newt Gingrich, Ron Paul, Rick Perry, Herman Cain, Michele Bachmann, and Jon Huntsman in 2012 all declined public funds and continued fund-raising throughout the primary season. This made these candidates' nomination contests far more expensive than their predecessors'.

For all intents and purposes, the nominating contest is over when one candidate has earned a sufficient number of delegates to claim a majority at the convention. Oftentimes, this threshold is determined by the news media, or even the candidates themselves, who update their "delegate counts" after every contest. The result, of course, is not official until the **roll-call vote** at the convention. Still, there is pressure on the other candidates to drop out and rally behind the winner after the result begins to look clear.

Choosing a Running Mate

After the nominations are clinched, the presidential campaign enters the pre-convention phase. The 2008 Democratic contest was unusual because it lasted so long; typically, the delegate contest is decided by the end of March and the nominee has until mid- or late summer to prepare for the convention. An important part of this phase is the selection of the vice-presidential nominee. Despite the fact that there is little evidence that the vice president has any direct effect on the outcome of the general election, this decision drives media coverage before and during the convention. There are at least five strategic options for the vice-presidential pick. The first is to select someone whose knowledge and expertise compensate for the shortcomings of the presidential candidate. In 2008, Barack Obama, a first-term senator from Illinois with almost no foreign policy experience, selected Joe Biden, a six-term senator who served as chairman of the Foreign Relations Committee. In 2000, Texas governor George W. Bush also sought to bolster the foreign policy credentials of his presidential campaign by selecting former defense secretary Dick Cheney.[5]

A second option is to choose someone who can help the candidate carry a state or region. For example, John F. Kennedy's selection of Texas senator Lyndon Johnson in 1960 helped win the state for the Democrats and bolster their standing with conservative white party members. More generally,

---

[5] Lee Sigelman and Paul J. Wahlbeck. 1997. "The 'Veepstakes': Strategic Choice in Presidential Running Mate Selection." *American Political Science Review* 91, 4: 855–64.

presidential nominees often select running mates from large states, like Texas, where there are more electoral votes in play.

A third option is to select someone from a political or demographic group whose support the candidate needs. In 2012, Mitt Romney was viewed unenthusiastically by conservatives due to his support of health care reform in Massachusetts and his formerly pro-choice position on abortion. To win over conservatives, he selected Wisconsin representative Paul Ryan, who was the architect of the House Republicans' aggressive deficit reduction plan.

A fourth option is to select someone to heal intraparty wounds. In 1980, Ronald Reagan reached out to his chief rival from the primaries, George H. W. Bush. In 1976, Gerald Ford almost asked Reagan to be his running mate even though the two had had a bruising struggle for the nomination. In 2008, many Democrats urged Obama to ask Hillary Clinton to join the ticket despite their nomination fight. In the end, however, both Ford and Obama saw more downside than upside to this strategy.

Finally, a fifth option would be to select someone who reinforces the image of the candidate. Although it may seem counterintuitive, the vice-presidential selection need not always be about shoring up weaknesses. In 1992, Bill Clinton asked Tennessee senator Al Gore to be his running mate. Both were young, white, and southern. But Clinton's campaign strategists saw the virtue of reinforcing their candidate's image as a new, fresh face.

Presidential candidates must also decide when to announce their choice of a running mate. Announcing several weeks before the convention maximizes the time that both the presidential and vice-presidential nominees are on the trail and ensures that there will be two media "hits" (the announcement plus the convention). In contrast, announcing the pick right before the convention helps to maximize the impact of the convention. In recent years, major-party candidates have typically opted for the second strategy. In 2008, both Obama and McCain, for example, named their running mates within the week before their nominating conventions.

The National Conventions

The Republican and Democratic national conventions mark the formal transition from the nominating process to the general election campaign, even though the general election is always the ultimate goal as the nominating contest unfolds. Like the nominating process, today's conventions are quite different than they were through the 1960s. Before 1972, the political parties exercised a great deal of control over the nomination, and the conventions were deliberative bodies where party officials and state delegates bargained and cut deals to arrive at a consensus choice for the nomination. Today, conventions are essentially four-day public relations spectacles, during which the nominees present themselves to the American electorate.

Conventions as Showcase Events

The candidate's travel to the convention is itself a part of the convention process. Candidates publicly preview the message of their nomination acceptance speech, as well as the entire fall campaign. In 2008, John McCain spent the days before the Republican convention talking about reforming Washington, and seeking to reassert his image as someone who would challenge entrenched interests. Candidates also reveal the constituencies and states that they believe are critical to victory. As noted earlier, George H. W. Bush campaigned from a Mississippi riverboat in the days leading up to the 1988 Republican convention in New Orleans, visiting Missouri, Arkansas, and Louisiana. Al Gore visited a series of battleground states in the Rocky Mountains just before the 2000 Democratic convention in Los Angeles.

Despite the attention the campaigns and the news media give to these appearances, their impact is minimal. Both the timing and the location of

National conventions used to be the setting in which the party's presidential nominee was selected. Today, the nominee is almost always determined in advance of the convention, through primary elections and caucuses, as was the case for Mitt Romney and his running mate, Paul Ryan, in 2012.

the conventions have greater potential influence. Unfortunately for the candidates, the parties choose the location well in advance of the actual campaign, after a selective bidding process. Parties also set the timing in advance. Traditionally, the party that is not in power holds its convention first, and sometimes there is a significant gap between the two conventions. For example, in 1992, seven weeks separated the conventions—the Democrats held theirs in mid-July and the Republicans held theirs in late August. More recently, both parties have attempted to hold their conventions as late as possible in order to maximize television audiences and the presumed impact of coverage on voters: after the Summer Olympics but before Labor Day.

Campaign strategists have three goals at the convention: tell voters what the past four years have been about, identify how the current candidates are different, and offer a vision for the country. Most conventions thus begin with a narrative of what has happened over the past four years. Speakers at the convention of the party out of power (the "out-party") talk about what has gone wrong and why there is a need for change. Speakers at the convention of the incumbent party talk about what has been successfully accomplished and how it occurred. These contrasting narratives are usually conveyed by well-known politicians on Monday and Tuesday nights of the convention week. Then conventions tend to focus on the contrasts between the candidates, with convention speakers describing the choice before the nation: What are the stakes and options the party faces? What would the party's candidate do, and how does that differ from the opposing candidate? This is usually accomplished in the Wednesday speech of the vice-presidential nominee. Last, the party and its candidate have to offer a vision for the future: Where is the country headed, and how will it get there? This is the goal of the presidential nominee's speech on Thursday night.

Convention Effects

Do conventions actually affect what the public thinks of the two candidates? Yes, they do. Each party's nominee garners additional support from the public after the convention. This is commonly referred to as the **convention bump** (or **convention bounce**). More precisely, the convention bump is defined as the candidate's share of the two-party vote in trial-heat polls conducted 1 to 7 days after the convention minus his share of the two-party vote in polls conducted 1 to 7 days before the convention. The average convention bump is about six points, as measured by polling data from Gallup (see Table 9.2). As we will see, conventions have a much larger effect than other presidential

TABLE 9.2 Convention Bumps, 1964–2012

Year	Candidate	Democratic Convention City	Bump	Candidate	Republican Convention City	Bump
2012	Obama	Charlotte	+3	Romney	Tampa	−1
2008	Obama	Denver	+4	McCain	St. Paul	+6
2004	Kerry	Boston	−1	G. W. Bush	New York City	+2
2000	Gore	Los Angeles	+8	G. W. Bush	Philadelphia	+8
1996	Clinton	Chicago	+5	Dole	San Diego	+3
1992	Clinton	New York City	+16	G. H. W. Bush	Houston	+5
1988	Dukakis	Atlanta	+7	G. H. W. Bush	New Orleans	+6
1984	Mondale	San Francisco	+9	Reagan	Dallas	+4
1980	Carter	New York City	+10	Reagan	Detroit	+8
1976	Carter	New York City	+9	Ford	Kansas City	+5
1972	McGovern	Miami Beach	0	Nixon	Miami Beach	+7
1968	Humphrey	Chicago	+2	Nixon	Miami Beach	+5
1964	Johnson	Atlantic City	+3	Goldwater	San Francisco	+5

Source: www.gallup.com/poll/109702/conventions-typically-result-fivepoint-bounce.aspx (accessed 5/5/11). 2012 estimates calculated by authors using Gallup Poll figures; see www.gallup.com/video/109906/obama-sees-convention-bounce.aspx (accessed 5/5/11).

campaign events, such as the debates. Political scientists believe that this effect is larger for two main reasons. First, conventions occur relatively early in the general election campaign, when there are a larger number of citizens who are undecided or only weakly committed to a candidate. There is thus a greater potential for persuasion. Later in the campaign, with fewer undecided voters, events serve mainly to strengthen preexisting opinions about the candidates—the phenomenon of reinforcement that we discussed in Chapter 7. Second, conventions produce news stories that tend to be favorable to the candidate being nominated. This is what the hoopla of conventions is designed to do. This effect is amplified by the fact that the candidate from the opposition party is likely to campaign less vigorously during this period, knowing that it is not easy to compete with the speeches and images of the other party's convention.

Of course, not all conventions give candidates the same size bump. Bill Clinton's 1992 convention stands out as the most effective since 1964, although it was due mostly to an unusual occurrence: on the last day of the Democratic convention, Ross Perot, who had run as an independent candidate, dropped out of the race, thus leaving his supporters, about one-third of likely voters, looking for a new candidate to support. More often, the size of the convention bump depends on how well the candidate is doing given prevailing political realities, such as the state of the economy and approval of the incumbent president.[6] Candidates who are favored by these realities but are for other reasons underperforming in the polls will tend to get a larger bump—in part because convention messages often include messages about the economy and the incumbent president.

The General Election

After the convention balloons have popped and the confetti has been swept up, the presidential candidates and their running mates hit the campaign trail, followed by a gaggle of reporters. At the same time, the campaigns blanket the airwaves with radio and television advertisements. But the states and media markets where the candidates travel and broadcast advertisements are not chosen at random. Moreover, candidates assiduously court some citizens more than others. Understanding contemporary presidential campaigning requires an understanding of the rules and reality that govern it. The resulting system, though often criticized, has positive as well as negative implications for democratic values.

The Electoral College

The strategic context of the general election is dominated by the institutional reality of the Electoral College. According to Article II of the Constitution, each state has a number of electoral votes equal to its total number of representatives to the U.S. Congress—that is, its members in the House plus its two senators. The passage of the Twenty-third Amendment gave the District of Columbia three electoral votes. In sum there are 538 electors (based on 435 House members plus 100 senators plus three electors from

---

[6] Thomas Holbrook. 1996. *Do Campaigns Matter?* Beverly Hills, CA: Sage Publications.

DC).[7] As noted earlier, the strategic goal is thus to win some combination of states whose electoral votes total at least 270.

The Constitution originally called for the candidate winning the second-most electoral votes to be the vice president. This situation became untenable with the emergence of political parties. In the 1800 election, the Democratic-Republicans and the Federalists ran two candidates each in an effort to win the presidency and vice presidency. The simultaneous election of these different positions meant that the parties had to ensure that their "top" candidate would win a majority while their second candidate would get the second-most votes. But the victorious Democratic-Republicans miscalculated, and Aaron Burr, their second choice, wound up with the same number of votes as their first choice and presumptive presidential candidate, Thomas Jefferson, sending the election to the House of Representatives to break the tie. To add insult to injury, the defeated Federalists considered throwing their support behind Burr in a potential House vote, although key Federalists, including Alexander Hamilton, ultimately sided with Jefferson, making him president. The Twelfth Amendment was soon passed in 1804 to "fix" the system.

The Electoral College has often been the subject of controversy. One criticism involves the method for determining electoral votes. The formula—the total number of representatives plus the total number of senators—was derived to secure the support of small states in the fight over the ratification of the Constitution; it creates a bias in favor of those smaller states. For example, Wyoming has one elector for every 165,000 residents, while California has one for every 617,000. However, some argue that the Electoral College actually benefits large states because carrying a large state by a tiny margin creates an Electoral College windfall due to the winner-take-all rule. For example, Bill Clinton won 70 percent of the electoral vote despite only getting 49 percent of the popular vote in 1996.

Concern about the representation of states has led to various attempts for reform. For instance, a group called National Popular Vote has called for state legislatures to commit their state's electoral votes to the candidate who receives the most popular votes nationwide. These bills would take effect

---

[7] Most states use a winner-take-all rule in assigning Electoral College votes to candidates: the candidate with the most votes in the state gets all of the state's electoral votes. This is a matter of state law, however, and Maine and Nebraska allocate two votes based on the statewide vote and then allow votes in the congressional districts to determine the remaining electors. In 2004, Colorado voters considered a ballot proposition that would have awarded presidential electors based on district-by-district results; this complicated things for the presidential campaigns, as this Election Day vote could have significantly affected the simultaneous awarding of electors. Ultimately, voters rejected the plan and Bush won all eight of Colorado's electoral votes.

only when enough states passed them to represent a majority of electoral votes—that is, sufficient votes to elect a president. As of 2015, eleven states (plus DC) have passed such bills into law and another four have bills pending in the current legislative session. The laws would in effect create a system under which the president wins by a plurality of the popular vote. Support for this proposal is buttressed by public opinion polls, which indicate that Americans would prefer to have the president elected via a simple national vote, and by controversies like the one after the 2000 presidential election, when some questioned the legitimacy of George W. Bush's victory, given that Al Gore won more popular votes. The reform is also designed to circumvent the difficulties in actually amending the Constitution to replace the Electoral College with another system. However, at this point in time, National Popular Vote bills seem unlikely to pass in enough states to affect presidential elections in the near future.

Recent Trends in Electoral College Outcomes The Electoral College's role makes it important for presidential candidates to understand the partisan complexion of individual states. Some states tend to produce close presidential elections, while others are predictably Republican or Democratic. Furthermore, some states are more likely to actually swing from one party to the other in different presidential elections. Table 9.3 shows how states might be categorized based on the 2000, 2004, 2008, and 2012 elections, with states that voted the same way every time ("base states") distinguished from those that produced mixed results ("battleground states"; see also Figure 9.1). The Democrats start off with a near majority in the Electoral College because they dominate large states such as California, New York, Pennsylvania, New Jersey, and Illinois, which together have 138 electoral votes. In these elections, Democrats have dominated the northeastern, upper midwest, and Pacific coast states. Republican candidates have dominated in the southern and mountain west states, creating what analysts call the **Republican L**.

The outcomes of recent elections have thus hinged upon the results in a handful of states. As shown in Table 9.3 and Figure 9.1, 40 states (and DC) voted for the same party in the 2000, 2004, 2008, and 2012 presidential elections, while 10 states did not: Colorado, Florida, Indiana, Iowa, Nevada, New Hampshire, New Mexico, North Carolina, Ohio, and Virginia. These **battleground** (or **swing**) **states** combined for 116 electoral votes in 2012, and when they have favored a single candidate, as they did Obama in 2008, they provide that candidate with a comfortable margin of victory. Other states, such as Michigan, Missouri, Oregon, Pennsylvania, Washington, and

TABLE 9.3 Classification of States Based on Presidential Votes, 2000–2012

Base Democratic States (18 states + DC, 242 electoral votes)	Battleground States (10 states, 116 electoral votes)	Base Republican States (22 states, 180 electoral votes)
California (55)	Colorado (9)	Alabama (9)
Connecticut (7)	Florida (29)	Alaska (3)
Delaware (3)	Indiana (11)	Arizona (11)
District of Columbia (3)	Iowa (6)	Arkansas (6)
Hawaii (4)	Nevada (6)	Georgia (16)
Illinois (20)	New Hampshire (4)	Idaho (4)
Maine (4)	New Mexico (5)	Indiana (11)
Maryland (10)	North Carolina (15)	Kansas (6)
Massachusetts (11)	Ohio (18)	Kentucky (8)
Michigan (16)	Virginia (13)	Louisiana (8)
Minnesota (10)		Mississippi (6)
New Jersey (14)		Missouri (10)
New York (29)		Montana (4)
Oregon (7)		Nebraska (5)
Pennsylvania (20)		North Dakota (3)
Rhode Island (4)		Oklahoma (7)
Vermont (3)		South Carolina (9)
Washington (12)		South Dakota (3)
Wisconsin (10)		Tennessee (11)
		Texas (38)
		Utah (5)
		West Virginia (5)
		Wyoming (3)

Note: 2012 electoral votes in parentheses.

FIGURE 9.1 Presidential Election Results, 2000–2012

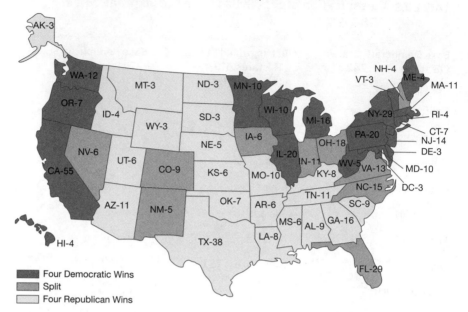

Note: 2012 electoral votes presented after state abbreviation.
Source: Rhodes Cook, Alice V. McGillivray, and Richard M. Scammon. 2010. *America Votes 28: Election Returns by State, 2007–2008*. Washington, DC: CQ Press.

Wisconsin, are sometimes considered battleground (or swing) states by campaign experts even though they have consistently (but narrowly) favored one party or the other. Although knowledgeable people may differ with respect to which states are battleground states, the main point is that battleground states are targeted in presidential campaigns.

The decennial U.S. census can change the playing field. As mandated by the Constitution, House seats, and therefore electoral votes, are reapportioned according to changes in state populations. Based on the 2010 census, states that were safely Democratic in 2008 lost six seats and those that were safely Republican gained six seats (Table 9.4). This will not help Democratic candidates in the next decade and beyond, but it might not hurt them very much either. In 2008, for example, Barack Obama would have won by a healthy margin even if that election had been conducted with the new allocation of electoral votes.

Strategic Impact of the Electoral College We have emphasized the effects of rules on campaign strategy, and the presidential election is an obvious example. In particular, the Electoral College affects how and where candidates

TABLE 9.4 Electoral Vote Changes Based on the 2010 Census

Safe Democratic States	Battleground States	Safe Republican States
Illinois (–1)	Florida (+2)	Arizona (+1)
Massachusetts (–1)	Iowa (–1)	Georgia (+1)
Michigan (–1)	Nevada (+1)	Louisiana (–1)
New Jersey (–1)	Ohio (–2)	Missouri (–1)
New York (–2)		South Carolina (+1)
Pennsylvania (–1)		Texas (+4)
Washington (+1)		Utah (+1)
Overall: –6	**Overall: no change**	**Overall: +6**

campaign. Presidential campaigns begin with a list of targeted states that are necessary for them to get 270 electoral votes. Whether (and how much) to campaign depends not only on how competitive a state is and whether it is critical to achieving 270 votes but also on the relative cost of campaigning in that state compared to other target states. Thus, candidates concentrate their television ads and in-person visits on the most cost-effective states and media markets on their list.[8]

In 2012, both the Obama and the Romney campaigns focused on television advertising and visits to states the campaigns determined to be critical to the election outcome. Obama spent 56 percent of his total advertising budget, an estimated $225 million, on ads in 10 media markets that his campaign deemed crucial. Romney spent approximately 53 percent of his total television advertising budget, an estimated $263 million, on his top 10 markets (Table 9.5). Their visits were also concentrated on battleground states, with the top 5 most-visited states receiving 66 percent of all presidential visits (Table 9.6). Furthermore, visits to nonbattleground states were typically to hold fund-raising events.

In 2012, the presidential candidates were roughly equal with respect to resources. In 2008, however, Obama was much better financed than McCain. Indeed, the data show that while Obama and McCain made roughly equivalent numbers of campaign visits overall, Obama and the Democratic Party

---

[8] Daron Shaw. 2006. *The Race to 270*. Chicago: University of Chicago Press.

TABLE 9.5 Romney and Obama TV Ad Spending: The Top Ten Media Markets

Romney and Republican Groups		Obama and Democratic Groups	
Washington, DC	$41 million	Washington, DC	$34 million
Denver, CO	$29 million	Denver, CO	$30 million
Cleveland, OH	$28 million	Cleveland, OH	$27 million
Tampa, FL	$27 million	Orlando, FL	$22 million
Charlotte, NC	$27 million	Tampa, FL	$21 million
Las Vegas, NV	$25 million	Las Vegas, NV	$21 million
Orlando, FL	$23 million	Charlotte, NC	$17 million
Miami, FL	$21 million	Miami, FL	$16 million
Columbus, OH	$16 million	Columbus, OH	$15 million
Cincinnati, OH	$14 million	Boston, MA	$12 million
Boston, MA	$12 million	Cincinnati, OH	$10 million
TOTAL	**$263 million**	**TOTAL**	**$225 million**

Source: Data are from the *Washington Post*, as provided by Kantar Media/CMAG. Updated on 11/14/12 and inclusive of all TV ad buys from 5/11–11/5/12.

vastly outspent McCain and the Republicans on television advertising. This disadvantage made it imperative for McCain to deploy his resources as strategically as possible. Conversely, this advantage allowed Obama to advertise in places normally considered out of reach for Democratic candidates, such as Virginia, Indiana, and North Carolina—states that he ultimately carried.

Although all presidential campaigns target battleground states, they differ in how ambitious their targeting is. Some campaigns, such as George H. W. Bush's 1988 campaign, play "offense" by targeting a number of states that usually vote for the other party. Other campaigns, such as Bill Clinton's in 1996, play "defense" by looking to solidify states that voted for them last time or that look "safe" in the current election. Still other campaigns, such as Al Gore's in 2000, concentrate on a very small number of highly competitive battleground states in an attempt to create a narrow Electoral College

TABLE 9.6 Romney/Ryan and Obama/Biden Appearances: The Top Ten States

Romney/Ryan		Obama/Biden	
Ohio	69	Ohio	55
Florida	46	Florida	44
Virginia	42	Virginia	30
Iowa	26	Iowa	29
Colorado	25	New York	21
California	21	District of Columbia	20
New York	18	California	18
Pennsylvania	16	New Hampshire	18
Nevada	15	Colorado	17
Wisconsin	14	Wisconsin	17
New Hampshire	13	Nevada	15
TOTAL	**305**	**TOTAL**	**284**

Source: *Washington Post*. Candidate appearances include all events, including fund-raisers, 5/29–11/6/12.

majority—a tactic referred to as "threading the needle." Finally, campaigns can employ a "mixed" strategy—emphasizing defensive campaigning at one stage of the campaign, and then offensive campaigning at another stage. George W. Bush's campaign organization did this in 2000, casting a very broad net early and then narrowing it considerably when data showed progress in some states but not in others.[9]

Electoral College strategies are not set in stone, however. Campaigns may adjust these strategies during the campaign itself. By the month before the general election, the campaigns should have enough polling information to abandon some states, add others, or simply narrow the battlefield to those states that are absolutely essential to victory. In 2008, the Obama campaign added Indiana and North Carolina to their list of targets based on late September polling that showed Obama was ahead in those traditionally

[9] Shaw, *The Race to 270*.

Putting Together an Electoral College Plan

I n the 2008 presidential election, Barack Obama won 52.9 percent of the national popular vote to John McCain's 45.6 percent. More important, Obama won 365 electoral votes to McCain's 173. Obama's electoral coalition included Democratic strongholds, such as California, New York, and Massachusetts, as well as traditionally Republican states, such as Indiana and North Carolina. These results — and the issues and attitudes that drove them — will fascinate political scientists for years. But for Team Obama, the results of the 2008 election (and, to a lesser degree, those of 2004) became the baseline for drawing up the 2012 battle plan. Presidential campaign strategists, like meteorologists, assume that tomorrow will look a lot like today, with modest changes driven by factors such as the Census, the performance of the incumbent president, and the particular candidates. Understanding how those changes influence the relative competitiveness of states compared to the last election is critical to a successful Electoral College plan.

In devising their plan for the 2012 election, the starting point for Obama's team was 2008 plus the fact that the 2010 census had changed the map. For the 2012 election, 18 states saw a change in their electoral votes because of the decennial census. Obama's 2008 coalition was worth 6 fewer points in 2012 — 359 electoral votes — because of these adjustments. Compared to Bush's reelection campaign, Obama was also defending more turf. This was because Obama's victory in 2008 was much larger than Bush's in 2000. In all, there were six states decided by fewer than five percentage points in 2008: Florida, Indiana, Missouri, Montana, North Carolina, and Ohio. Obama carried four of the six, losing only in Missouri and Montana. Factoring all of this into its plans, Obama's 2012 campaign used Kerry's 2004 coalition (which they viewed as the "baseline" for a competitive Democratic candidate in the new millennium) as its starting point and identified five potential paths to 270 electoral votes. First, there was the "West Path." If Obama won Colorado (9 electoral votes), New Mexico (5) and Nevada (6), and added them to Kerry's 246 electoral votes, he would have 266. Add in the 6 electoral votes from Iowa, and he'd have 272. The second path for Obama was the "Florida Path," which meant winning the Sunshine State and its 29 electoral votes. That total added to Kerry's 246 electoral votes would equal 275. The third path was the "South Path," which involved adding North Carolina (15 electoral votes) and Virginia (13) to Kerry's total to reach 274. The fourth path was the "Midwest Path," which involved adding Ohio (18 electoral votes) and Iowa (6) to Kerry's total to get to 270 on the nose. Finally, there was the "expansion path," which had the president losing critical states but still winning the election by bringing others into the fold. Under this scenario, the reelection campaign wouldn't hold on to Kerry's wins in Pennsylvania and New Hampshire, losing their 20 and 4 electoral votes, respectively. He would also fail to win Ohio and Florida. But by rewinning Colorado, Nevada, New Mexico, and adding Arizona (11 electoral votes), a more likely proposition than in 2008 when John McCain (R-AZ) was running, Obama would get to 272. In the end, the campaign kept the "West," "Florida," "South," and "Midwest" paths on the table, committing resources to all relevant states. Only the "South" path proved beyond their reach, as Romney carried North Carolina by two points.

Of course, Obama's campaign monitored the movements of the Romney campaign, which had its own Electoral College strategy. The Romney team adopted what many called the "3-2-1" strategy. Start with McCain's 2008 coalition. From there, the "3" refers to winning back the three states that had traditionally gone Republican but went for Obama in 2008: Indiana, Virginia, and North Carolina. The "2" refers to winning the critical battleground states of Ohio and Florida. And the "1" refers to winning one state from the following menu: Colorado, Nevada, New Mexico, Michigan, Pennsylvania, Wisconsin, or New Hampshire. Again, in the end, Romney was unable to attain any of the three points to his Electoral College plan. But both he and Obama followed their plans, allocating personal appearances and advertising dollars in a handful of states as they fought to win the White House.

Republican states. In 2000, George W. Bush decided to make a concerted effort to win Tennessee (the home state of his opponent, Al Gore) and West Virginia (which had not voted for a Republican presidential candidate since 1964) after early October polls revealed competitive contests.

The targeting strategies of presidential candidates create a self-fulfilling prophecies; the perceived structure of the election causes campaigns to target their resources to a handful of states such that most recent presidential elections have been decided (as predicted!) by voters in these states. Is this smart? Perhaps other states could have become competitive if resources had been allocated on their voters. Is this fair? Might it be that certain states—Ohio, Florida, and Nevada, for example—receive disproportionate public policy commitments and advertising revenue, resources that distort a supposedly representative system? Advocates of Electoral College reform certainly think so. In any case, criticism of the candidates or their campaigns for this reality is misplaced: they are simply responding to the rules of the current system.

Political and Economic Realities

Presidential campaigns are substantially constrained not only by the rules of the elections but also by political reality. In any given election, a campaign is dealt a deck of cards. How the campaign plays the cards is important, but the luck of the draw has a major impact on who wins the hand. Three factors in a presidential election are particularly important: incumbency, war, and the economy. Of these, the economy is usually considered paramount.

Incumbent presidents have natural advantages. They have the advantage of experience, having run a previous presidential campaign. They have the trappings of the office of presidency, including the pomp and circumstance and an enhanced ability to make news, communicate with the public, and shape the national agenda. They also have an easier road to the party's nomination, with typically no opposition or only token opposition. It is no surprise, then, that two-thirds of incumbent presidents who seek reelection win. Typically, they begin the campaign with a larger lead than nonincumbent candidates and hold on to a larger portion of this lead during the campaign.[10]

Ongoing wars matter in both positive and negative ways. An incumbent president up for reelection at the outset of a war will likely benefit from the public's tendency to rally behind the president in times of crisis. But it has been rare for an election to occur just as a conflict is getting under way. At the same time, it is often thought that presidents will seek to create such a crisis right before the election—sometimes referred to as an "October Surprise." This, too, is rare, in fact. Historically, wars have more often had a negative impact on the incumbent president's reelection bid. The number of American military personnel killed in action during war tends to sour voters on the mission, producing more negative evaluations of the president's job performance, and reducing his support at the polls.[11] This was particularly consequential for the Democratic Party in both 1952 and 1968, when Presidents Truman and Johnson were presiding over the wars in Korea and Vietnam, respectively.

The economy is the most powerful influence on presidential elections. The candidate of the incumbent party, and especially an incumbent president, is much more likely to win if the economy is growing strongly. In recent presidential elections, there is a powerful relationship between the incumbent party's share of the vote and economic indicators like the growth in average disposable income in the year before the election. The upward sloping line of Figure 9.2 captures the trend: as economic growth increases, so does the incumbent party's share of the vote. Jimmy Carter, who ran for reelection when incomes were shrinking, won only 45 percent of the two-party vote. But his successor, Ronald Reagan, was reelected easily, thanks to the booming economy of 1984.

The powerful impact of the economy creates strategic imperatives for the candidates. Candidates who benefit politically from the state of the economy tend to make it the central issue of their campaign. Thus, an incumbent president or incumbent party candidate will emphasize the economy during

---

[10] James E. Campbell. 2000. *The American Campaign: U.S. Presidential Campaigns and the National Vote.* College Station: Texas A&M University Press.

[11] Douglas A. Hibbs, Jr. 2000. "Bread and Peace Voting in U.S. Presidential Elections." *Public Choice* 104: 149–80.

FIGURE 9.2 **Election Year Income Growth**

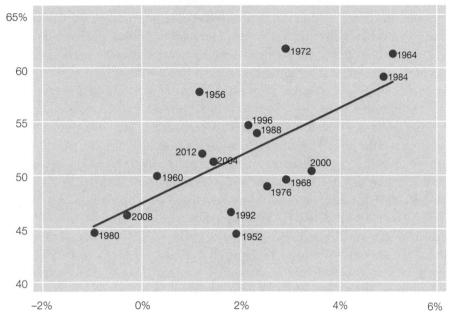

Incumbent Party's Share of Two-Party Vote

Income Growth in Year Before Election

periods of economic growth. Conversely, the opposition party will emphasize the economy during an economic downturn. Candidates who are not
favored by the economy need to change the subject by emphasizing other
issues.[12]

The Fall Campaign

As the campaign gets under way after the conventions, candidates must make
a series of strategic decisions within the context of Electoral College math
and broader realities. We discuss several important parts of that process: message development, the timing of campaign activity, the candidate debates,
and mobilizing supporters to vote.

Message Development As presidential candidates shift from the primary
campaign to the general election campaign, they often refine their message,
particularly to address contrasts with their opponent. As we discussed in

---

[12] Lynn Vavreck. 2009. *The Message Matters: The Economy and Presidential Campaigns.*
Princeton, NJ: Princeton University Press.

Chapter 5, campaign messages are designed to appeal to undecided voters or mobilize sympathetic partisans. Typically, campaigns rely on polls and focus groups to discern which issues are salient to the public, which issue positions are most popular, and how issues can be framed to improve the campaign's chances for success. Candidates have their own ideas about political issues, of course, but no serious presidential campaign makes a move without surveying public opinion. Campaigns do not always follow the results of their polls, but they need to know how the public will likely react to the campaign's message.

As candidates decide what issues to emphasize, they are thinking not only about the broader political realities but about any other factor that might advantage or disadvantage them. One factor is the political reputation of their party. In 1988, George H. W. Bush's campaign manager, Lee Atwater, decided that his candidate would do best if the election were about crime, taxes, and national defense. He was confident that Americans would trust his candidate to handle these issues more effectively than the Democratic candidate, Massachusetts governor Michael Dukakis. A second factor is the particular positions of "swing voters." As we discussed in Chapter 5, campaigns have an incentive to locate themselves close to the so-called median voter, so that candidates will maximize their appeal to the public. In the United States, this incentive pushes candidates to the center of the political spectrum because many Americans hold fairly centrist positions on political issues.

But calculations about issue agendas and positions are fraught with difficulties. What if a candidate would prefer to ignore an issue that is a top priority of the party's base? What if a candidate's position appeals to a slim majority of voters overall but is unpopular with the base? And what if the popular position contradicts the candidate's previous position? Candidates naturally want to avoid contradicting themselves. In 2004, for example, Democrat John Kerry attempted to explain how in 2003 he had supported a bill allocating $87 billion for the troops fighting the Iraq War, but then ended up opposing the funding bill that ultimately was passed. He famously said, "I actually did vote for the $87 billion before I voted against it." This quote was later used by the Bush campaign to portray Kerry as a flip-flopper.

Presidential campaigns can sometimes finesse the challenges of message development by delivering different messages via different media. In television ads and public speeches, candidates focus on broadly salient issues and popular positions. In direct mail, phone calls, and e-mails, candidates focus on issues and positions popular with their party's base. This is because they can use **narrow-casting**, targeting a smaller audience using these media, without the visibility that mass media entail. In 2008, for example, John McCain used direct mail to Republican households to emphasize his pro-life position on abortion, even as he made no mention of this issue in his television advertising. Similarly, Obama never mentioned race in his television or radio advertising; telephone calls to black households, though, focused on his being the first black major-party candidate.

When asked about his opponent's claim that he "had a plan" to defeat him, the former heavyweight boxing champion Mike Tyson said, "Everyone has a plan until they get hit in the mouth." This statement applies to every presidential campaign ever run. Despite all of the planning that goes into developing a message, life intervenes. Campaigns are particularly sensitive to the harsh judgments of the electorate, and they have up-to-the-minute feedback loops in the form of polls from all of their battleground states. By mid- to late September, they have enough information about public opinion to know whether they need to change course or not.

Front-runners have less need to make adjustments, unless their lead is shrinking. The trailing candidate, however, may decide to do something different. The most common major strategic adjustment is often to "go negative." In 1988, George H. W. Bush was trailing by double digits when his campaign made a strategic decision to attack Michael Dukakis's record as governor of Massachusetts. This was deemed easier and more effective than rebuilding Bush's image. After all, Bush had been in the public eye for over two decades, while Dukakis was a newcomer and had received little scrutiny during the Democratic primaries. In August, Bush strongly criticized Dukakis's record on crime and the environment. By early September, Bush had pulled ahead strongly, and the entire dynamic of the election had changed.

Timing Although the Electoral College dominates decision making about *where* campaign activity occurs, *when* that activity occurs is a separate question. Some campaigns prefer to stockpile their resources and end the campaign with a massive advertising blitz, presumably when more citizens are paying attention. In 2008, John McCain's campaign spent much of its resources in the final 10 days. His campaign strategists assumed that citizens are more affected by the last thing they see or hear, and that the best strategy was to match Obama's ad expenditures in the battleground states during the closing days. Other campaigns like to spend more of their resources earlier, hoping to define the race at the opening of the campaign. Still others expend resources during such high-profile events as the conventions and debates. For example, George W. Bush increased his television advertising during the 2000 presidential debates, while Al Gore significantly decreased his advertising on those days. Bush wanted to reinforce the themes he articulated during the debates, whereas Gore believed the debates and their attendant news coverage rendered additional campaigning superfluous.

There is no conclusive evidence that any particular timing strategy is best. The relatively large size of convention bumps are consistent with the notion that it is easier to influence the public's preferences early in the campaign when more people have yet to develop strong opinions of the candidates. In the 2004 and 2008 presidential elections, polling showed that citizens made up their minds about the candidates quite early in the campaign season, and much earlier than they had in 2000. However, other evidence suggests that many citizens do not pay attention to the campaign until late in the process and that the effects of a television advertisement or candidate visit usually dissipate after only a few days.[13]

Candidate Debates Every fall campaign has its share of important events. But televised candidate debates stand out as the only potentially significant events that a campaign knows are coming. These are the most watched events of the campaign, and underdog candidates often look to them with the hope that they will reshape a race.

The bipartisan Commission on Presidential Debates was established in 1987 to ensure that debates are a part of every presidential campaign. The commission sponsors the debates, varying their geographic location and format in an effort to engage as much of the public and to provide as much information as possible. After the major-party candidates accept their nominations, the commission produces a debate schedule and the campaigns are obliged to either accept or decline their recommendations. If they decline—or even suggest direct negotiations between the campaigns, as George H. W. Bush did in 1992 and George W. Bush did in 2000—they must explain their reasoning to the news media and the public. Any campaign that does not immediately accept the commission's recommendations will surely face the accusation that their candidate is dodging the debates, and so the standard in recent years has been to accept.

---

[13] Alan Gerber, James Gimpel, Donald Green, and Daron Shaw. 2011. "The Influence of Television and Radio Advertising on Candidate Evaluations: Results from a Large Scale Randomized Experiment." *American Political Science Review* 105, 1: 135–150; Daron Shaw and James Gimpel. 2012. "What If We Randomized the Governor's Schedule?" *Political Communication* 29, 2: 137–59.

During the debates, campaigns have several goals. The first and most obvious goal is to "do no harm"—that is, avoid the sort of gaffe that drives subsequent news media coverage and undermines the campaign's effort to control messaging. To minimize the chances of a major mistake, presidential candidates prepare well in advance, usually for an hour or two each week during the summer and early fall and then all day for three to four days before the debate itself. Campaigns run mock debates for the candidate, using stand-ins for the opposition and staging the aggressive questioning that sometimes occurs. These efforts are videotaped and then critiqued on the basis of style and substance. Campaign staff make sure the candidates absorb voluminous briefing books on issues; candidates are then quizzed and asked to redress substantive weaknesses.

During the debate, candidates essentially seek to implement a miniature version of their overall campaign strategy. They emphasize issues and appeals that benefit them, avoiding issues on which their opponent has the advantage. Viewers may not tune in to the debate for very long and may not be paying much attention, so candidates want to broadcast the strongest case for their candidacy. This is why candidates often seem to be answering questions besides the ones that were actually asked. When challenged, candidates tend to respond to every charge made by the opposition. They do this because it has been shown that viewers may assume that any charge, no matter how outrageous, is true if not contradicted.

Candidates also address their answers to the television audience and not to the other candidate or the audience in the hall (unless the debate is held in a town hall format, with actual citizens asking questions). The reaction of those in the auditorium is much less important than the reaction of those watching on television, and especially the news media. Media coverage of the debates is actually more important for influencing public opinion than the debates themselves.[14] For example, immediately after the first debate of the 2000 presidential campaign, Al Gore was judged to have scored a slight victory over George W. Bush, but subsequent media coverage of several questionable claims he made during the debate, as well as mocking coverage of his colorful makeup, turned opinion around. One week after the debate, Bush was judged to have been the winner. The lesson here reinforces the main goal of debates (do no harm) but also emphasizes the need for the campaign to defend its candidate's performance in order to shape news media interpretations.

---

[14] Richard Johnston, Kathleen Hall Jamieson, and Michael Hagen. 2004. *The 2000 Presidential Election and the Foundations of Party Politics.* New York: Oxford University Press.

Despite all the preparation and strategizing that goes into debates, and despite the public's opinions about who did or did not win a particular debate, there are rarely large changes in public support for the candidates after a debate. Simply put, most debates have little impact on the polls and on the election's outcome. Because debates occur relatively late in the campaign, most people have made up their minds. People then view debates through partisan lenses: the vast majority of partisans believe that their candidate won. In a CNN poll conducted after the first 2008 presidential debate, 85 percent of Democrats thought Obama had won and 64 percent of Republicans thought McCain had won. Moreover, whereas during each convention one party dominates the news, debates consist of opposing messages from both parties. In a sense, these messages tend to cancel each other out, making it difficult for either party's candidate to get much of a boost in the polls from the debate.

Even when debates do seem to move the electorate a point or two, as happened with the first presidential debate of 2012 when Mitt Romney scored a clear victory in the view of voters and the news media over Barack Obama, the effect is usually ephemeral. Sometimes the debate bounce simply fades and other times, as in 2012, subsequent debates even things out.

In the first presidential debate of 1960, John F. Kennedy delivered a surprisingly strong performance against the more experienced Richard Nixon.

Mobilizing Citizens At the end of the campaign, the candidate's staff works furiously to reach out to supporters and encourage them to vote. Complicating this effort is the rise of **convenience voting**, a term that includes a variety of ways in which citizens can vote without actually going to their polls on Election Day (Figure 9.3). Methods of convenience voting include early voting, voting by mail, and voting by absentee ballot. In 2012, close to 30 percent of Americans cast their presidential votes before Election Day. Presidential campaigns must therefore ensure that supporters get absentee ballot applications or information about early voting locations well in advance of the relevant deadlines.

Campaigns have to time their outreach appropriately. In 2012, 50 percent of Florida voters voted early, so it would have been foolish to launch an extensive get-out-the-vote operation in late October. Campaigns must also monitor early voting records from the states to see which of their targets have failed to vote (these individuals receive additional outreach) and which have voted (these individuals may be asked to contribute to or volunteer for the campaign).

As Election Day draws near, candidates visit the most critical locales and groups. In 2008, Barack Obama added last-minute stops in Indiana, a reliably

FIGURE 9.3 Convenience Voting across the States, 1992–2012

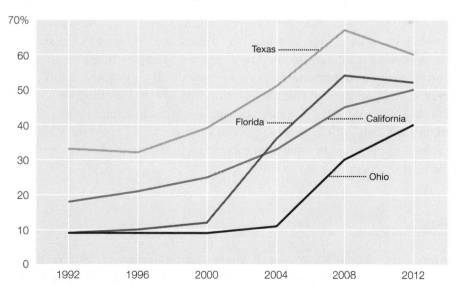

Note: Lines indicate convenience voting as a percentage of all votes cast in presidential elections from 1992 to 2012.
Source: The underlying data were compiled by the Associated Press and provided to members of the National Election Pool (NEP) for the 2012 elections.

Republican state that nonetheless looked to be leaning toward Obama (he ended up carrying the state by a single point). In an effort to drive more (and more favorable) coverage, they sometimes try gimmicks to get the news media's attention. In 2000, for example, Al Gore vowed to campaign without sleep for the final 72 hours of the campaign. His midnight and early morning events produced large crowds and extensive media coverage.

Gore's personal efforts and the perceived success of the Democratic Party's last-minute organizational outreach prompted a comparable effort by the Republicans in 2002 and 2004. This "72-hour plan" featured extensive door-to-door campaigning and phone calls in the three days before the election. It was credited with mobilizing the Republican base in key areas. Naturally, Democrats responded in kind. In 2008 and 2012, Obama and the Democrats flooded neighborhoods with volunteer workers and also used e-mail lists and social networking websites to greatly extend the range and scope of their outreach. Political science scholarship has confirmed that contact with a campaign does raise the likelihood of an individual turning out to vote.

On Election Day, citizens have to be contacted (via phone and e-mail) and mobilized to vote (using buses, cars, walks, and so on). As the day wears on, reports from precincts allow campaign staff to know where they are "light" (getting fewer targeted votes) and "heavy" (getting all or most targeted votes). Campaign attention can be refocused accordingly. Lawyers are also employed to file motions to keep the polls open in places where candidates expect to win and where there might be "irregularities," such as too few ballots or long lines. This has become a standard tactic in recent elections, especially among Democrats, who want to ensure that lower-income and minority precincts are properly equipped. Of course, the 2000 presidential election showed that the election may not end on Election Day. In 2004, 2008, and 2012, Democratic and Republican campaigns allocated money not only for election night parties for staff and supporters but also for media operations to influence news media reportage of close contests and for legal teams in case of recounts.

Conclusion

American presidential elections illustrate a crucial feature of elections everywhere: they depend a great deal on the rules and realities that candidates confront. For presidential candidates, the rules of the nomination process and the Electoral College strongly affect strategies—the decision to run, the states to target, and so on. Candidates are also constrained by the realities of whether an incumbent is running, whether the country is at war or at peace, and whether the economy is prospering or struggling. As a result, candidates will often find it difficult to persuade the public. Political scientists and campaign professionals have different perspectives on how much these factors constrain campaign effects: academics emphasize the limits to what electioneering can accomplish, while practitioners emphasize the small effects that a good campaign can produce—effects that could decide a close election.

Do American presidential elections meet democratic ideals? Both the nominations and the general election processes frequently elicit criticisms. For one, some claim that the nominating process produces unrepresentative candidates. Specifically, the complaint is that the sequence of primaries and caucuses allows small and ideologically extreme groups to exercise disproportionate influence by electing their favored candidates in states such as Iowa or New Hampshire. A cursory examination of the historical record casts doubt on this claim. Republicans John McCain, Robert Dole, George H. W. Bush, and Mitt Romney and Democrats Bill Clinton, Al Gore, John Kerry, and Barack Obama hardly seem out of the mainstream. One could argue that Ronald Reagan was more conservative than the average Republican or that Michael Dukakis was more liberal than the average Democrat, but their records as governors offer many examples of pragmatism. Moreover, this is consistent with political science research demonstrating that while presidential primary electorates tend to be older and slightly more ideological than the party electorate as a whole, they are not necessarily ideologically extreme.[15]

A second complaint is that the national conventions are just public relations events. There is no deliberation about the candidates and little meaningful debate about the parties' platforms. This complaint is undoubtedly justified. It is less clear, however, that conventions themselves are simply fluff. Conventions help to unify parties after divisive primaries. They also allow the candidates to present themselves and their campaigns to a wide swath of citizens. The nominees' speeches are often rich in information about their policy agendas and goals.[16] After the conventions, citizens typically express more interest in the campaign.[17] The television networks may claim that the

---

[15] John G. Geer. 1988. "Assessing the Representativeness of Electorates in Presidential Primaries." *Journal of Politics* 32, 4: 929–45.

[16] Marion Just, Tami Buhr, and Ann Crigler. 2000. "Shifting the Balance: Journalist versus Candidate Communication in the 1996 Presidential Campaign," in *Campaign Reform: Insights and Evidence*, ed. Larry M. Bartels and Lynn Vavreck. Ann Arbor: University of Michigan Press.

[17] For data from the 2000 campaign, see Richard Johnston, Michael G. Hagen, and Kathleen Hall Jamieson. 2004. *The 2000 Presidential Election and the Foundations of Party Politics.* New York: Cambridge University Press.

conventions are staged, but it may not be a bad thing to allow the parties to speak directly to the American people once every four years.

A third complaint is similar to the second: debates are uninspired and scripted. This may be true at times, but debates still have positive consequences. After the debates, citizens tend to be more interested in the campaign, feel more favorably about the candidates, and be more knowledgeable about the candidates in some ways.[18] However, the knowledge they've gained is not always about the candidates' positions on issues. Thus, it is quite possible that debates could be reformed to become more informative or empowering. Citizens seem especially impressed by the town hall debate format, suggesting that more direct citizen involvement in the debates would be desirable. There are also those who would like to see more debates, spread out over the entirety of the campaign.

A final set of complaints concerns the Electoral College. Perhaps the most prominent of these is that the Electoral College is not as democratic as a direct popular vote and can produce a winner who did not win the popular vote. Other complaints center on the perceived built-in biases of the Electoral College—most notably, that it favors smaller states and leads candidates to focus on battleground states and ignore others. In particular, critics fear that this focus on battleground states leads citizens in other states to be less motivated to vote on Election Day.

Defenders of the Electoral College respond that discrepancies between the Electoral College and popular vote are rare. They also note that battleground states are actually quite representative of the country as a whole.[19] Moreover, although citizens in battleground states, and particularly those with lower incomes, can be mobilized by campaign activity, citizens outside battleground states are not turned off.[20]

Would a new presidential election system have comparable or even greater drawbacks? A direct national vote may not stop candidates from campaigning selectively. For instance, Democrats would be tempted to spend a lot of

---

[18] Larry Bartels. 2000. "Campaign Quality: Standards for Evaluation, Benchmarks for Reform," in *Campaign Reform: Insights and Evidence*, ed. Larry M. Bartels and Lynn Vavreck. Ann Arbor: University of Michigan Press; Thomas Holbrook. 1999. "Political Learning from Presidential Debates." *Political Behavior* 21, 1: 67–89.

[19] Darshan J. Goux and David A. Hopkins. 2008. "The Empirical Implications of Electoral College Reform." *American Politic Research* 36: 857–79.

[20] James G. Gimpel, Karen M. Kaufmann, and Shanna Pearson-Merkowitz. 2007. "Battleground States versus Blackout States: The Behavioral Implications of Modern Presidential Campaigns." *Journal of Politics* 69, 3: 786–97; Keena Lipsitz. 2009. "The Consequences of Battleground and 'Spectator' State Residency for Political Participation." *Political Behavior* 31: 187–209.

time in major urban areas such as New York, Chicago, and Los Angeles, mobilizing reliably Democratic constituents. Republicans, meanwhile, would have incentives to concentrate in suburban areas around cities such as Dallas, Atlanta, and Phoenix. For candidates to campaign nationally, they might also have to work harder and spend more money than they currently do. This would make presidential campaigns even more arduous and expensive than they currently are—and the challenges and costs of campaigns are already criticized as discouraging potential candidates from running and allowing too much money into politics.

Of course, it is entirely possible that the presidential election system could be improved. But alternatives entail trade-offs among competing values, with any improvements creating new and even unforeseen problems. This is not an excuse for inaction; rather, it is a reminder that the words *perfection* and *democracy* rarely appear in the same sentence.

KEY TERMS

delegates (p. 239)

caucuses (p. 240)

primary election (p. 240)

viability (p. 242)

front-loading (p. 244)

front-runner (p. 245)

roll-call vote (p. 247)

convention bump/convention bounce (p. 250)

Republican L (p. 254)

battleground/swing states (p. 254)

narrow-casting (p. 265)

convenience voting (p. 269)

FOR DISCUSSION

1. Why do states want to move their primary dates up in the election calendar? What is this process called? What is the effect of this process on campaigning?

2. How are the national party conventions different today compared to conventions in the 1950s?

3. How does the Electoral College affect the strategies of presidential campaigns?

4. Why might a presidential candidate want to campaign relatively early in the fall? Why might she want to campaign relatively late?

CHAPTER 10

Congressional Campaigns

As the midterm election of 2014 got under way, Democrats knew that they faced an uphill battle. They had virtually no chance to win a majority in the House of Representatives. The Republicans controlled 234 of 435 seats after the 2012 election, and Democrats were hoping only to keep the Republican majority from getting much larger.

But in the Senate, Democrats had higher hopes. Including two independent senators who caucused with the Democrats, they had 55 of 100 seats. It was certainly likely that they would lose some seats, but they believed they could retain their majority. They even hoped to pick off a few Republican incumbents. Perhaps their biggest target was Senate Minority Leader Mitch McConnell.

McConnell had represented Kentucky for 20 years and had served as minority leader since 2006. It is rare for congressional leaders to lose elections — as Representative Eric Cantor's surprising defeat illustrates (see Chapter 6) — but McConnell seemed vulnerable. In a February 2014 poll, only 32 percent of voters in Kentucky approved of the job he was doing.[1] For this reason, he faced several challengers in the primary election, and was held to only 60 percent of the primary vote — the lowest for any Kentucky senator since 1938.

Meanwhile, the Democrats recruited Alison Lundergan Grimes to oppose McConnell. Grimes was young — 35 years old, whereas McConnell was 72 — and considered an up-and-coming political talent. She had been elected Kentucky's secretary of state in 2011. Early polls showed a tight race, and several election handicappers called the race a toss-up.

By October, the picture was substantially different. McConnell led in nearly every poll. The Democratic Senatorial Campaign Committee (DSCC) was no longer buying television advertisements to support Grimes. And Grimes herself was ridiculed when she refused to say how she had voted for president in 2008

---

[1] Sam Youngman. 2014. "Alison Lundergan Grimes Holds a Slim 4-Point Advantage over Mitch McConnell in Kentucky." *Lexington Herald-Leader*, February 6. www.kentucky.com /2014/02/06/3073014_alison-lundergan-grimes-holds.html?rh=1 (accessed 1/13/15).

or 2012 — presumably because admitting she had voted for Obama would not have helped her in a state where most people disapproved of the president.

On Election Day, the race was over even faster than observers anticipated. McConnell was declared the winner early in the evening. Although the average of the polls suggested he would win by 6 points, he actually won by 15 points. McConnell's victory was only one part of a very good night for Republicans, who ultimately picked up 9 Senate seats and 13 more House seats than they had after the 2012 elections.

But, in many ways, this outcome was not a surprise. The president's party typically loses seats in a midterm election. Moreover, Democrats were campaigning while Obama was relatively unpopular, with only about 42 percent job approval. On top of that, the Senate seats that were up for reelection in 2014 were disproportionately in Republican states — not only Kentucky but also South Dakota, West Virginia, Montana, and Georgia. Democrats also suffered because long-term Democratic incumbents retired in several of these states, making it harder for Democrats to hold onto those seats.

The 2014 election therefore illustrates an important truth about congressional elections: their outcomes are often driven by factors beyond candidates' control. In 2014, there was little Democratic Senate candidates could do about the fact that they had to compete in so many Republican-leaning states, or that voters were not so keen on the Democratic president. They also found that it was difficult to knock off a Republican incumbent like McConnell. As we will learn in this chapter, incumbents have an enormous advantage in congressional elections, so McConnell's victory was hardly unexpected.

Core of the Analysis

- The rules governing congressional elections and campaign finance directly shape the strategies of House and Senate candidates.
- The political fortunes of congressional candidates often hinge on factors beyond their control, such as the popularity of the president and the state of the economy.
- Potential congressional candidates are ambitious and are strategic about when they run.
- Voters typically know little about congressional candidates and especially about challengers.
- Incumbents have substantial advantages over challengers in congressional races.

Senator Mitch McConnell and his wife, Elaine Chao, acknowledge supporters on election night after McConnell's victory over Democratic challenger Allison Lundergan Grimes.

In this chapter, we explore the nature and effects of congressional campaigns. As with presidential campaigns, we find that the impact of congressional campaigns depends on the particular rules governing the elections. Constitutional provisions and campaign finance law are especially important. We also find that incumbents have a substantial advantage over challengers in most congressional races. Consequently, challengers typically need fortuitous circumstances and a strong campaign to beat incumbents. Recent elections illustrate this point: in 2010, an unusually large number of House incumbents were defeated, owing to voter frustration with the economy and President Obama. These conditions made it easier for the minority party to recruit and fund challenger candidates. At the same time, even in 2010, about 85 percent of incumbents who ran won reelection, signaling the advantages of incumbency even in potentially difficult conditions.

Rules, Reality, and Who Runs for Congress

If you decide to run for Congress, few legal obstacles stand in your way. As we discussed in Chapter 2, the constitutional requirements entail only a minimum age, U.S. citizenship for a period of years, and residency in the state that you want to represent. If you satisfy these requirements and can meet state requirements for having your name appear on the ballot, such as paying a filing fee or collecting a certain number of signatures, you can run for Congress. Because the bar for running is so low, one might assume that people from all walks of life can and do run for office. If this were the case, we would expect Congress to be representative of the electorate in terms of demographic characteristics, such as age, income, race, and gender. Yet, as we shall see, those who seek to run and those who eventually win share certain characteristics that make them unrepresentative of the broader electorate.

Most individuals who run for office are ambitious and strategic. Politicians are rarely content to hold one job for long and are always looking for opportunities to advance. Congressional candidates have usually held a lower political office that has provided them with experience and connections that are helpful to their campaign. Serious candidates are also strategic, which means they will enter a race only when their prospects of winning are good. If a candidate runs and loses, then the connections and resources that one has may dry up. Thus, individuals who are ambitious and strategic run for office only when they believe the odds of winning are good.

The person with the best odds of winning an election is the **incumbent**, or the person who already occupies the office. Figure 10.1 shows the percentage of House and Senate incumbents seeking reelection who then won. From 1946 to 2014, the average percent of House incumbents running who were reelected was 92 percent, while the average for Senate incumbents was 80 percent. Even in bad years for incumbents, they are much more likely to be reelected than defeated. As mentioned earlier, 2010 was one of the worst years for House incumbents, but even so, about 85 percent of the House incumbents who ran were reelected.

Because the odds of their winning are so high, only extraordinary circumstances such as poor health will keep incumbents from running for reelection. Incumbents may also step down because of scandal. Sixty-six members of the House decided to retire after the 1992 House banking scandal, in which many representatives had written checks from their House bank accounts without the funds to cover those checks.

FIGURE 10.1 **Percentage of House and Senate Incumbents Seeking Reelection Who Won, 1946–2014**

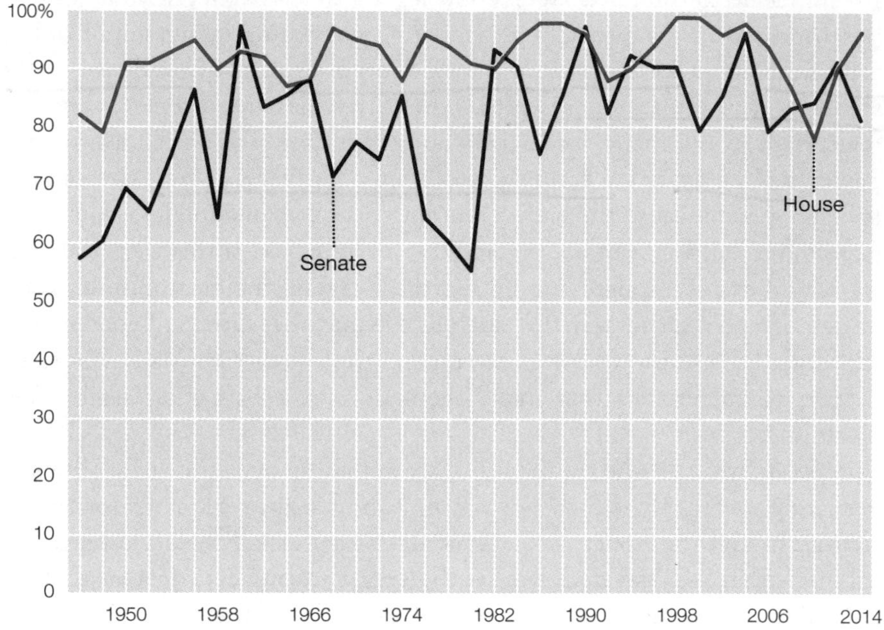

Source: Gary Jacobson. 2009. *The Politics of Congressional Elections.* New York: Longman, pp. 28–29. Additional data for 2008–14 collected by the authors.

House incumbents may also decide to retire when their districts change after redistricting and they face the prospect of courting a new or mostly new constituency. As we discussed in Chapter 2, districts are usually drawn in a manner that protects incumbents of both parties, but anti-incumbent redistricting can occur if a party that has been out of power for a while gains control of the redistricting process. In Chapter 2, we described an unusual mid-decade redistricting undertaken by Texas Republicans in 2003. Their plan targeted 10 Democratic incumbents, most of whom faced the prospect of competing in the 2004 election in substantially changed districts.[2] Although many of these incumbents decided to run in their new districts and lost, one incumbent—Congressman Jim Turner, a Democrat who had served Texas's 2nd District for six years—saw the writing on the wall. Republican state legislators had moved most of Turner's district into the 8th District, leaving him in the solidly conservative 6th District, which was

---

[2] Steve Bickerstaff. 2007. *Lines in the Sand: Congressional Redistricting in Texas and the Downfall of Tom DeLay.* Austin: University of Texas Press.

represented by a 10-term Republican incumbent, Joe Barton. As a result, Turner decided to retire rather than run for reelection in 2004.

House and Senate incumbents may also retire if they feel that the country is experiencing a wave of anti-incumbent sentiment or a wave of sentiment that favors the opposing party. For example, as noted earlier, in 2014 some key Senate Democrats decided to retire—including Tim Johnson in South Dakota, Jay Rockefeller in West Virginia, and Tom Harkin in Iowa. Given the challenges that Democrats faced in this election, these incumbents may have decided to retire rather than face tough reelection campaigns.

When incumbents decide to retire, their decision creates an open seat, or a contest between nonincumbents. Open seats are significant because they attract quality challengers who recognize that their chances of winning are higher with the incumbent out of the picture. A quality challenger is a candidate with the experience and backing necessary to run a competitive campaign. In contrast, political amateurs are candidates who have no political experience and are unlikely to win an election. Quality challengers are strategic candidates, basing their decision to run on whether the incumbent is running or is vulnerable because of a scandal or a national political tide. Quality challengers also assess the incumbent's ability to attract votes and money. For example, if an incumbent has been winning by smaller margins or is struggling to raise money, potential challengers may assume that the incumbent is vulnerable.

Challengers have to consider whether they will be supported by their own party. The clearest indication of the party's support is whether the party has recruited a person to run. The "**Hill committees**"—the National Republican Senatorial Committee (NRSC), Democratic Senatorial Campaign Committee (DSCC), National Republican Congressional Committee (NRCC), and Democratic Congressional Campaign Committee (DCCC)—encourage prospective candidates throughout the country to run for office. Much like scouts in sports, the parties are always looking for leaders who might make successful candidates for office. These individuals are courted by party leaders and sent to workshops to learn how to run campaigns. They may also be provided with lists of potential contributors. Without such support, an ambitious and strategic individual might make the rational calculation that it is better to keep her current job than to run for Congress.

Because winning a congressional election requires resources and connections, certain types of individuals are more likely to run than others. On average, those who choose to run are more educated and wealthier than most Americans. They are also overwhelmingly white and, as we discussed in Chapter 5, male. Quality challengers tend to work in business, the law, or

Witches, Action Figures, and Political Amateurs

The 2010 midterm election will be remembered for the "shellacking" Democrats received by the Republicans. The GOP picked up 6 seats in the Senate and a stunning 63 in the House, giving them control of that body. The election will also be remembered for its colorful cast of candidates, including a range of "witches, wing-nuts and wackos,"[1] many of whom were political amateurs—candidates without any prior political experience. Americans were angry with Washington in 2010 due to the economic recession and high unemployment. At such times, political amateurs can exploit their outsider status to make a run for Congress.

Among the most colorful amateurs of 2010 was Christine O'Donnell, a Tea Party–backed candidate who defeated the longest-serving congressman in Delaware history, Representative Mike Castle, in the primary. O'Donnell came under attack for allegedly using campaign funds to pay a portion of her rent. Her campaign took another hit when Bill Maher released footage from a 1999 *Politically Incorrect* show in which she admitted to having "dabbled" in witchcraft. Her response, a television advertisement that began "I'm not a witch," was spoofed on *Saturday Night Live* and became a Songify This sensation with more than 3 million hits.[2]

Odd political amateurs ran on the Democratic side as well. Alvin Greene, who challenged Senator Jim DeMint of South Carolina, attracted the most media attention of any 2010 campaign, according to a Pew Research Center study, because he appeared to win the primary without running a campaign and was charged with felony obscenity charges the day after his primary election. Greene's proposal to create jobs by hiring people to make Alvin Greene action figures also raised eyebrows.

Most political amateurs do not engage in such bizarre antics, but any election that promises to be a landslide for one party will attract candidates who know that their chances of winning—although in many cases still meager—are higher than they would be under normal circumstances. Some of these candidates are bound to be peculiar.

Elections that promise to be landslides also attract politically experienced challengers. These more experienced candidates tend to run in the most competitive races, however, while political amateurs run more often in uncompetitive ones. For example, in 2010, 93 percent of the Republican candidates who ran in safe Democratic districts were political amateurs, and 80 percent of the Democrats that ran in safe Republican districts were amateurs.[3] Thus, in many safe congressional districts across the country, the only alternative to the candidate of the dominant party is often a political amateur.

---

[1] David Canon. 2010. "The Year of the Outsider: Political Amateurs in the U.S. Congress." *Forum* 8, 4: Article 6.

[2] www.youtube.com/watch?v=44mqiBrB0zI (accessed 5/13/11).

[3] Canon, "The Year of the Outsider," p. 9.

politics, with large networks that can be tapped for campaign resources. Thus, members of Congress are unrepresentative of the nation in terms of their education, wealth, race, and gender because the people who run for office are unrepresentative of the nation.

Campaign Organization and Funding

Once candidates have decided to run for Congress, they need to put together a campaign staff. Because campaigns in the United States are candidate-centered, candidates, rather than parties, are almost entirely responsible for raising money and putting together a campaign organization. This is true even if a party has recruited the candidate. The party might provide the candidate with a list of political consultants who have worked with other party candidates, but the candidate still must choose consultants that she feels will best help her win. And many candidates are left entirely to their own devices. They have to piece together a campaign staff as best they can.

Congressional campaign organizations range widely from bare-bones operations that are run by unpaid volunteers to big organizations that are run by paid professional consultants. Amateurs with no prior political experience, and thus fewer contacts and resources, are more likely to have the former, while incumbents often have the latter. A well-funded congressional campaign typically has a campaign manager, who oversees the day-to-day operations of the campaign and helps develop strategy. There may be a separate campaign strategist, as well as staff to deal with press relations, issue and opposition research, fund-raising, accounting, and grassroots organizing. The best-funded candidates, who include many House and Senate incumbents, may also hire consultants to conduct polls, develop radio and television advertisements, create direct mail pieces, and operate phone banks. An example of a campaign at this end of the spectrum was Hillary Rodham Clinton's 2006 Senate reelection bid in New York, in which she spent nearly $41 million despite having only token opposition. In addition to the tens of thousands of dollars paid each month to consultants, her campaign spent $27,000 on valet parking, $160,000 on private jet travel, and almost $750,000—more than the cost of most House campaigns—on catering and entertainment.[3]

The size and shape of congressional campaign organizations depends almost entirely on how much money they can raise. In 2014, the average

---

[3] Anne Kornblut and Jeff Zeleny. 2006. "Clinton Won Easily but Bankroll Shows the Toll." *New York Times*, November 21. www.nytimes.com/2006/11/21/us/politics/21donate.html ?pagewanted=all&_r=0 (accessed 1/13/15).

House incumbent raised $1.6 million, while the average House challenger raised $258,000; the average Senate incumbent raised $12 million, while the average Senate challenger raised $1.2 million.[4] Congressional candidates differ greatly in how much they raise and spend, however. For instance, in 2014, incumbent senator Mike Lee (R-UT) easily won reelection after spending just under $4 million. In contrast, Kay Hagen, the Democratic senator from North Carolina, lost her race in 2014 despite raising nearly $25 million in the two years before the election.[5]

The funding sources for congressional candidates are different from those for presidential candidates. First, unlike presidential candidates, congressional candidates are not eligible for public financing. They have no option but to raise money from individuals and political action committees (PACs). Congressional candidates differ in this respect from even Barack Obama and Mitt Romney, the only two opposing presidential candidates who have declined public funding for their campaigns. Figure 10.2 shows that House candidates in 2012 raised 58 percent of their funds from individual contributions and 36 percent of their funds from PACs. The comparable figures for Senate candidates were 71 percent and 13 percent, respectively. In

FIGURE 10.2 Comparison of House, Senate, and Presidential Candidate Funding Sources in 2012

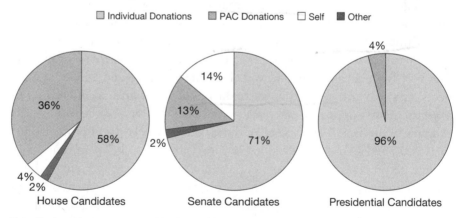

Note: Pie charts depict percentage of funds raised from each source during the general election campaign.
Source: Federal Election Commission.

---

[4] Center for Responsive Politics. 2015. "Incumbent Advantage." www.opensecrets.org /overview/incumbs.php (accessed 1/13/15).

[5] Center for Responsive Politics. 2015. "Who's Raised the Least." www.opensecrets.org /overview/btmraise.php?Display=A&Memb=S (accessed 1/13/15).

contrast, Obama and Romney raised nearly all of their funds from individuals and virtually nothing from PACs. PACs are limited to a contribution of $5,000 per candidate for each election cycle, making total PAC contributions a drop in the bucket for a presidential campaign but a more significant amount for congressional candidates.

Despite these differences, congressional candidates, like presidential candidates, raise the bulk of their funds from individuals. But these individual contributions do not necessarily come from the candidates' districts or states, especially in competitive races. For example, House candidates in 2004 received an average of two-thirds of their individual contributions from non-residents.[6] Citizens who give to out-of-district (or out-of-state) candidates appear to be chiefly motivated by partisanship, seeking to increase their party's share of congressional seats.

Beyond individual and PAC contributions, it is becoming more common for House and Senate candidates to self-finance their campaigns and to rely on the help of outside groups, such as the Super PACs and 501(c)4's discussed in Chapter 4. Whereas only 30 House and Senate candidates wrote themselves checks of $500,000 or more in 2004, 50 did so in 2012.[7] As we discussed in Chapter 4, self-financed candidates do not always win, but they can give their opponents a run for their money. In 2014, outside groups unaffiliated with the parties spent $565 million on campaign contributions. This was approximately 60 percent of the amount that all House candidates spent on the election and 89 percent of the amount Senate candidates spent.[8] Like candidates, outside groups are strategic, however, which means they target races where their money is likely to make a difference. For example, with control of the Senate at stake in 2014, outside groups focused their spending on the closest races, spending $82 million in North Carolina, $69 million in Colorado, $62 million in Iowa, and $35 million in Kentucky.[9]

---

[6] James G. Gimpel, Francis E. Lee, and Shanna Pearson-Merkowitz. 2008. "The Check Is in the Mail: Funding Flows in Congressional Elections." *American Journal of Political Science* 52, 2: 373–94.

[7] Center for Responsive Politics. 2013. "Millionaire Candidates." www.opensecrets.org /bigpicture/millionaires.php (accessed 2/13/15).

[8] Center for Responsive Politics. 2015. "Outside Spending." www.opensecrets.org /outsidespending/fes_summ.php (accessed 2/13/15); Center for Responsive Politics. 2014. "Estimated Cost of Election 2014." www.opensecrets.org/overview/cost.php (accessed 2/13/15).

[9] Center for Responsive Politics. 2015. "2014 Outside Spending, by Race." www .opensecrets.org/outsidespending/summ.php?disp=R (accessed 2/13/15).

The Primary Election

Like all candidates who run for a partisan office in the United States, congressional candidates must first compete for their party's nomination in a primary election. In the United States, it is not uncommon for congressional primaries to be uncontested. Such primaries usually feature a popular incumbent, whose seniority, power, and connections discourage would-be challengers. When incumbents do face primary challenges, they usually win for the same reasons. Thus, recent high-profile challenges to congressional incumbents — some of which were successful, like the challenge to Representative Eric Cantor in 2014—do not suggest a broader trend. There has not been an increase in the number of incumbents drawing challengers or in the number of successful primary challenges. In 2014, for example, no incumbent senator lost his or her primary.[10]

Open-seat primaries occur when a party's incumbent has retired or when the party that is out of power chooses a candidate to challenge the incumbent in the general election. These are typically the most competitive primaries and the most likely to attract quality challengers. In such contests, the party normally remains neutral and lets the voters decide who the party should back in the general election. From time to time, however, party leaders back an open-seat primary candidate who they believe has a good chance of winning the general election. For example, in 2014, Democrats saw an opportunity in Virginia's 10th District, where there was an open seat after the retirement of Republican representative Frank Wolf. So Democrats worked to "clear the field" for Fairfax County supervisor John Foust, leading another Democratic candidate to suspend his campaign.[11] Party leaders likely wanted to save Foust from a bruising primary so that he would have sufficient standing and resources to run in the general election. Regardless, Foust lost to Republican Barbara Comstock. This example is more the exception than the rule, however. Parties rarely get involved in congressional primaries because they have limited resources and prefer to save them for the general election.

Just like candidates in presidential primaries, candidates in House and Senate primaries must compete for votes from an electorate that is more

---

[10] Robert Boatright. 2013. *Getting Primaried*. Ann Arbor: University of Michigan Press. See also Robert Boatright. 2014. "Who Won the Republican Civil War?" *Monkey Cage*, August 13. www.washingtonpost.com/blogs/monkey-cage/wp/2014/08/13/who-won-the-republican-civil-war/ (accessed 2/13/15).

[11] Emily Cahn. 2014. "Democrats Clear Primary Field in Competitive Virginia House Race." *Roll Call*, March 14. http://atr.rollcall.com/democrats-clear-primary-fieldr-competitive-virginia-house-race/ (accessed 2/13/15).

ideological than the electorate in a general election. Thus, they must appeal to party stalwarts without jeopardizing their ability to attract the votes of moderates in the general election. One way to do this is to emphasize issues in the primary election that are ideological in nature—issues on which they can adopt positions that might be described as "modestly extreme," positions that appeal to ideological primary voters but are not as extreme as the views of some primary voters.[12] Then, in the general election, candidates move toward the center by emphasizing nonideological issues, such as personal character. They must be careful, however, not to change their agendas or positions too dramatically or else they might be criticized for "flip-flopping" or "waffling." This possibility encourages primary candidates to adopt only modestly extreme positions, since these positions will be easier to moderate in the general election, if necessary.

Republican Barbara Comstock, mentioned above, provides a good example of how a candidate may try to appeal to primary voters but not necessarily turn off general election voters. The 10th District is located in northern Virginia and tilts only slightly Republican, which makes appealing to moderate voters more important. Comstock's position on reproductive rights therefore reflects a balancing act. She takes a more conservative, but not the most conservative, position on abortion: allowing it only in cases of rape, incest, and danger to the mother's life. At the same time, she takes a more liberal position on birth control, supporting the sale of contraceptives over the counter without a prescription.

On the other hand, the fate of Todd Akin, the Republican Senate candidate in Missouri in 2012, illustrates the potential difficulty of shifting from a primary to a general election constituency, and on this same issue of reproductive rights. As we mentioned in Chapter 8, Akin brought on the ire of Democrats and even some Republican leaders when, shortly after defeating more moderate GOP candidates in the primary, he explained in an interview that he opposed allowing women who have become pregnant as the result of rape to have an abortion because such pregnancies are "really rare." They are rare, he explained, because "if it's a legitimate rape, the female body has ways to try to shut that whole thing down."[13] Although Akin apologized

---

[12] Barry C. Burden. 2004. "Candidate Positioning in U.S. Congressional Elections." *British Journal of Political Science* 34, 2: 211–27; Samuel Merrill III and Bernard Grofman. 1999. *A Unified Theory of Voting: Directional and Proximity Spatial Models.* New York: Cambridge University Press.

[13] John Eligon and Michael Schwirtz. 2012. "Senate Candidate Provokes Ire with 'Legitimate Rape' Comment," *New York Times*, August 12. www.nytimes.com/2012/08/20/us /politics/todd-akin-provokes-ire-with-legitimate-rape-comment.html (accessed 2/13/15).

In another example of the difficulties of taking ideological issues to a general election constituency, Republican Richard Mourdock lost his bid for an Indiana Senate seat in 2012 in part because he claimed a pregnancy occurring from rape was a "gift from God" and should not be terminated. Mourdock, a staunch conservative, had knocked off a popular centrist Republican in the primary due in large part to Tea Party support. The Indiana seat was crucial for the GOP to take control of the Senate.

for his comments and claimed he "misspoke," he forfeited his lead in the polls and ultimately lost to Democratic senator Claire McCaskill, who was one of the most vulnerable Democratic incumbents in 2012.

The General Election

Once candidates have secured their party's nomination, they must quickly turn their attention to the general election campaign. Some candidates who were uncontested in the primary or did not have any serious challengers can even start their general election campaign earlier if they have the resources to do so. Incumbents typically have these resources, so challengers face a particularly difficult path: while they are battling for the nomination, the incumbent has already started appealing to the general election electorate.

Voters often know far less about House and Senate candidates than they do about candidates for president. According to a 2002 study, after an uncompetitive House election featuring an incumbent and a challenger, less than 15 percent of the people living in the district can remember the names of both candidates. After a competitive House election, approximately 40 percent of the electorate can remember the candidates' names. Citizens are typically more familiar with Senate candidates. Approximately one-third can remember their names after a noncompetitive election, while two-thirds can remember the names of both candidates after a competitive open-seat race.[14] These numbers suggest that many citizens vote for congressional candidates without knowing their names, let alone anything substantive about them. Congressional candidates and their political consultants are well aware of voters' lack of knowledge. Challengers, in particular, are well aware that people rarely vote for someone they do not know. Thus, many congressional candidates spend their entire campaign simply introducing themselves to voters. They do this by communicating with potential supporters and working to ensure that supporters turn out on Election Day.

Developing a Campaign Message

As we discussed in Chapter 5, a key to winning an election is knowing the electorate. Candidates need to know who their supporters are and where they live. They also need to know who the persuadable voters are in their district or state and how to get their message to these voters.

The next step is to develop a message that appeals to the target audience, which requires understanding the issues that are important to the potential voters in the district or state. Candidates acquire this knowledge in several ways. Congressional candidates are often community leaders or have prior political experience that has given them knowledge of the state or district in which they are running. They may be business leaders who know the state's economy, or state legislators who have passed bills designed to address problems in the state. Candidates also have extensive social and professional networks that can provide a sense of the issues affecting their communities. They also have help in developing their message from the organizations whose endorsements they seek. These groups not only help candidates contact their members but also provide the candidate with information about their members' concerns. Finally, if candidates have enough money they can also hire a pollster to conduct polls of voters. If the race is competitive, one of the congressional campaign committees or state party organizations may conduct polls and share them with their party's candidates.

Unlike presidential candidates, whose messages are focused almost exclusively on national politics, congressional candidates face the challenge of crafting a campaign message that addresses both local and national issues. The conventional wisdom is that local issues should predominate—a sentiment

---

[14] Paul S. Herrnson. 2004. *Congressional Elections: Campaigning at Home and in Washington.* Washington, DC: CQ Press, p. 190.

best captured by former speaker of the House Thomas "Tip" O'Neill's famous assertion that "All politics is local." Yet, when local issues dominate a campaign, then both the Democratic and Republican candidates may end up taking very similar positions. For instance, candidates from a rural House district whose economy depends on farming may be united in their support of federal agricultural subsidies. When national issues dominate, candidates may have similar agendas—such as the need for jobs in a weak economy—but may take quite different positions. For example, to create jobs, Republican candidates may emphasize the need to cut taxes on businesses to encourage them to hire workers, while Democrats may emphasize the need for government spending to stimulate job growth. The positions of individual congressional candidates will often be similar to the positions of their respective national parties. Studies of congressional campaign messages have found that national issues are more prevalent than local issues. As a result, candidates often take different positions, in contrast to the median voter theorem discussed in Chapter 5.[15]

Communicating the Message

Once candidates have determined what they want to say to voters, they communicate that message in several ways. Like presidential candidates, congressional candidates rely on direct mail as well as newspaper, radio, and television advertisements to communicate with voters, but the extent to which they rely on each of these is different. For example, a typical presidential campaign spends approximately 75 percent of its entire budget on television advertising, while the typical Senate campaign spends one-third of its budget and the average House campaign spends just 20 percent of its budget on television ads.[16] House candidates rely the least on television advertisements because they are expensive and House candidates typically have less money to spend per voter than Senate candidates. In fact, many uncompetitive House races feature no television advertising whatsoever.

Another problem for House and Senate candidates is that television advertisements are purchased in predefined media markets. Large media markets often serve more than one congressional district, which means that a House candidate who purchases television advertisements may be paying for people in neighboring districts to see those ads. Media markets do not necessarily

---

[15] Stephen Ansolabehere, James M. Snyder, Jr., and Charles Stewart III. 2001. "Candidate Positioning in U.S. Congressional Elections." *American Journal of Political Science* 45, 1: 136–59; Burden, "Candidate Positioning in U.S. Congressional Elections."

[16] Herrnson, *Congressional Elections*, p. 85.

respect state borders either. If a state has a competitive Senate race, voters in neighboring states that share media markets with the competitive state may see advertisements in races in which they cannot vote. For example, New Jersey has no television media markets of its own. Its northern half lies in the New York City media market and its southern half in the Philadelphia media market. Thus, congressional candidates in New Jersey must purchase airtime in one or both of these extremely expensive media markets if they want to run television ads.

For all of these reasons, congressional candidates may rely less on television advertisements and more on radio and newspaper advertisements, billboards, and yard signs. Congressional candidates, especially House candidates, can also rely more than presidential candidates on communicating with citizens directly. Presidential candidates have no personal contact with most Americans; the population is simply too large. Citizens "experience" presidential candidates mainly as talking heads on their television screens.

In contrast, House candidates can have direct, unmediated contact with a larger portion of their constituency. They attend parades, sporting events, or any type of event where large numbers of potential voters gather. This kind of contact is intended to increase name recognition and to make a favorable impression, not to convey substantive information about policy agendas or proposals. House challengers, who have less money to purchase advertisements, rely heavily on personal contacts to get their name out. It is not unheard of for House challengers to literally walk across their district to meet voters and generate publicity. For example, in 2014 a Republican House candidate, Andrew McNeil, embarked on a walking tour of Indiana's 8th Congressional District as part of an unsuccessful primary challenge to Republican incumbent Larry Bucshon.[17] Though such tactics might seem gimmicky, they are often one of the few means by which an underfunded challenger can generate name recognition. (McNeil raised only $32,000, while Bucshon raised $1.2 million.) Although there are seven states that have only one representative, meaning that the state and congressional district have identical boundaries, Senate candidates usually have a much larger territory to cover than House candidates. As a result, it is often more practical for Senators to rely on television and radio than on personal contact with voters.

Congressional candidates also differ from presidential candidates in how much they depend on earned media. **Earned media** (or **free media**) is the

---

[17] "Congressional Candidate to Walk across 8th District." *City-County Observer*, March 12. http://city-countyobserver.com/congressional-candidate-to-walk-across-8th-district/ (accessed 2/14/15).

publicity that candidates get by engaging in promotional activities. For example, candidates frequently hold press conferences or give speeches hoping that these events will be covered by the local media. Candidate appearances, such as walking tours, have the same goal. Congressional candidates sometimes use gimmicks to attract news attention. In 2010, Van Irion, a Republican candidate from Tennessee's 3rd House District, always carried a pitchfork to symbolize his promise that he would clean up the "manure" in Washington. Irion also filed a lawsuit challenging the constitutionality of the health care reform legislation and personally traveled to Washington to give President Obama and congressional leaders a copy of the lawsuit. To be sure, presidential candidates also use gimmicks to generate free media, but the range of behavior that is considered appropriate or "presidential" limits both how much they can rely on gimmicks and how bizarre those gimmicks can be.

Mobilizing Voters

Congressional candidates use the same basic tactics that presidential candidates do to get their supporters to the polls on Election Day, including mailers, phone calls, and neighborhood canvassing. The main differences are the size and sophistication of their mobilization drives. Presidential candidates have vast resources at their disposal, which enable them to develop extensive field organizations. In presidential election years, congressional candidates benefit from the presidential campaigns' mobilization efforts because most voters who go to the polls to cast a ballot for the president usually cast a ballot for candidates in other races at the same time. In midterm election years, however, congressional candidates must turn out voters themselves, assisted by other organizations, including state and national party committees and interest groups. Despite those efforts, congressional campaigns rarely generate the kind of interest that presidential campaigns do. As a result, voter turnout in midterm elections is lower than in presidential elections.

The Role of the Parties and the Hill Committees

Political parties can play a significant role in congressional campaigns. The Hill committees defined earlier in this chapter focus exclusively on electing party members to Congress. They accomplish this by targeting the handful of House and Senate races that are closely contested in each election cycle and ignoring the rest. Their first priority is to protect incumbents who are in jeopardy of losing their seats. Their second priority is to defend the seats of members of the party who are leaving office. When national political and economic conditions favor a party, that party may also target seats that have been controlled by the other party. In 2014, for example, the National Republican Campaign Committee launched a "Drive to 245" campaign, which reflected their goal of picking up enough seats to control 245 seats in the House (they eventually won 247).

The Hill committees do not rigidly adhere to campaign plans. In response to campaign events, they redirect resources to crucial races. They typically begin the election season with a longer list of competitive races and whittle that number down as the campaigns evolve and it becomes clear which ones will be the most fiercely contested. They may decide some races are not worth their involvement, as was the case for the Democratic Senatorial Campaign Committee in the 2014 Kentucky Senate race. In the races where they are involved, the committees can make a direct contribution, coordinate expenditures with the candidate, or make an independent expenditure without a candidate's involvement. **Coordinated expenditures** involve collaboration between the committee and the candidate or a representative of the candidate. They are usually spent on services that are given to a candidate directly or performed by a political consultant on behalf of a candidate. The services might include the purchase of airtime on television and radio, direct mail, polling, or the organization of fund-raising events. Campaign finance law treats coordinated expenditures the same way it treats direct contributions to a candidate, which means they are subject to strict limits.

As a result, the Hill committees usually rely on **independent expenditures** to fund their campaign efforts. These expenditures are made without consulting or coordinating with a candidate. According to *Buckley v. Valeo*, the landmark campaign finance case discussed in Chapter 4, these expenditures cannot be limited in any way, allowing the committees to spend large sums of money on a race. For example, in 2012 both the DCCC and the NRCC spent heavily in Arizona's 1st District. The NRCC spent $4.3 million to support its candidate, Andy Tobin, while the DCCC spent $3.1 million to support its candidate, incumbent Rep. Ann Kirkpatrick. To put this amount of money in perspective, consider that Tobin raised $1.4 million for his bid, while Kirkpatrick raised $3.4 million for hers. Thus, the DCCC and the NRCC collectively spent more than the candidates did in this race. (Kirkpatrick eventually won a close race, with 52 percent of the vote.)

While the Hill committees tend to help candidates purchase campaign communications and provide technical expertise, state and local party committees more often help candidates with grassroots activities, such as voter registration and mobilization drives designed to get voters to the polls. In addition, they organize phone banks and neighborhood canvassing campaigns to knock on doors and provide voters with campaign literature.

The Incumbency Advantage

A defining feature of congressional elections is the electoral advantage that incumbents enjoy over challengers. The **incumbency advantage** is defined as the vote share earned by an incumbent compared to what a nonincumbent would have earned if he or she had run.

The incumbency advantage can be attributed to several factors. For one thing, incumbents have greater political experience. They also have an easier time soliciting campaign donations than challengers do. Contributors like to back winners and are well aware that challengers lose most elections. Only challengers in competitive races or candidates in open-seat races can typically raise anything close to what incumbents raise. Similarly, parties and interest groups funnel resources to candidates who have a greater chance of winning. As a result, House incumbents typically raise about three times what their challengers do. Senate incumbents raise even more—approximately 10 times as much as challengers. Quality challengers fare better than the average challenger, but they typically cannot match incumbents dollar for dollar.

Another important source of incumbents' advantage is their familiarity to voters. For example, in the 113th Congress, the average House member had served 9 years and the average Senator had served 10 years.[18] Incumbents have had the chance to establish a relationship with the citizens they represent. Citizens see them in the news and around the district or state. Incumbents can also make use of certain perquisites of office to get publicity. For example, the **franking privilege**, which has existed since colonial times, allows members of Congress to send mail to constituents without postage. Although it cannot be used for campaigning purposes, to send holiday greetings, or to provide biographical information about representatives and their families, it can be used to send out newsletters and other informational mailings. The volume of franked mail increases in election years, suggesting that the mailings are being used for campaign purposes. In addition, members of Congress can employ staff for **casework**, which typically involves helping constituents deal with government bureaucracies. Whenever a staff member solves a constituent's problem, that constituent is likely to view the congressperson more favorably.

Contrast the situation of incumbents with that of challengers. Unless challengers are well known for other reasons, most citizens in their districts or

---

[18] Jennifer E. Manning. 2014. "Membership of the 113th Congress: A Profile." Congressional Research Service. www.senate.gov/CRSReports/crs-publish.cfm?pid =%260BL%2BR\C%3F%0A (accessed 12/15/14).

states will know little about them and may not even be able to recognize their faces or names. And challengers have only limited resources to make themselves better known. Moreover, even if an incumbent is unpopular, many voters may still feel it is better to cast a ballot for the devil they know than the devil they don't know. The **personal vote**—that portion of an elected official's vote share that can be attributed to their relationship with constituents—is one component of the incumbency advantage.

The size of the incumbency advantage is not, however, a constant. It has changed over time. The incumbency advantage increased substantially beginning in the 1960s and continuing through the 1980s—from about 2 points to 8 points in the House, and 1 point to nearly 10 points in the Senate.[19]

Why did the incumbency advantage increase during this period? There are several partial explanations. For one, the increase in House incumbents' advantage in the 1960s has been linked to the growth in local television stations across the country.[20] At that time, local news broadcasts were widely watched, and, unlike today's broadcasts, they emphasized news stories about politics. Local television stations even relied on members of Congress to produce reports about their activities, which the stations then inserted into their local newscasts. In the 1970s, local television news began to focus less on political stories, and in the late 1970s audiences began watching local news broadcasts less often as their attention shifted to emerging cable television stations. Despite these changes, local news stations continued to cover incumbent activities and to do so in a largely positive manner, which helped maintain the incumbency advantage. However, similar analysis of Senate elections has not found much connection between television and the incumbency advantage.[21]

Second, members of Congress have given themselves more official resources over the years, such as increased funds for franked mail, larger salaries for staff, and bigger travel budgets. These have allowed them to communicate more with their constituents and potentially increased their advantages over challengers.

Third, the Supreme Court decisions in the early 1960s that reformed the redistricting process may also have contributed to the incumbency advantage.

[19] Stephen Ansolabehere and James M. Snyder, Jr. 2002. "The Incumbency Advantage in U.S. Elections: An Analysis of State and Federal Offices, 1942–2000." *Election Law Journal* 1, 3: 315–38.

[20] Markus Prior. 2006. "The Incumbent in the Living Room: The Rise of Television and the Incumbency Advantage in U.S. House Elections." *Journal of Politics* 68, 3: 657–73.

[21] Stephen Ansolabehere, Erik C. Snowberg, and James M. Snyder, Jr. 2006. "Television and the Incumbency Advantage in U.S. Elections." *Legislative Studies Quarterly* 31, 4: 469–90.

These decisions require that virtually every district in the country change every 10 years through the processes of reapportionment and redistricting (which we discussed in Chapter 2). As a result, many candidates wait until the election following redistricting to determine whether they will run. Incumbents must decide how the new boundaries of their district affect their electoral prospects. Incumbents may decide to retire if their new districts are very different from their old districts.[22] Thus, the increase in the incumbency advantage for House members after the 1960s can be partly explained by changes in the reapportionment and redistricting processes and their influence on incumbent retirements.

At the same time, the incumbency advantage has waned somewhat since the 1990s.[23] This shrinking advantage may reflect the growing "nationalization" of congressional elections—whereby congressional elections are influenced less by local factors, such as the personal vote accrued by an incumbent, and more by the national political factors, like the popularity of the president. One consequence of nationalization is that voters are more consistently partisan—voting loyally for their party's candidates at all levels of offices, presidential and congressional.[24] If part of the incumbency advantage depended on appealing to voters in the other party—perhaps because incumbents could demonstrate the good work they had done in the district—then cross-party appeals have simply become harder in a more partisan electorate.

Although the incumbency advantage may have declined, it certainly still exists. Nevertheless, despite the many advantages incumbents have, they rarely act as if they are confident about winning. This creates a paradox in congressional elections: many incumbents are "running scared" even though incumbents rarely lose.[25] Why? For one, incumbents do occasionally lose—especially when they are vulnerable due to personal scandals or a national

---

[22] Gary W. Cox and Jonathan N. Katz. 2002. *Elbridge Gerry's Salamander: The Electoral Consequences of the Reapportionment Revolution*. Cambridge: Cambridge University Press.

[23] Andrew Gelman and Zaiying Huang. 2008. "Estimating Incumbency Advantage and Its Variation as an Example of a Before-After Study." *Journal of the American Statistical Association* 103: 437–51.

[24] Joseph Bafumi and Robert Shapiro. 2009. "A New Partisan Voter." *Journal of Politics* 71: 1–24; Marc J. Hetherington. 2001. "Resurgent Mass Partisanship: The Role of Elite Polarization." *American Political Science Review* 95: 619–31; Larry M. Bartels. 2000. "Partisanship and Voting Behavior, 1952–1996." *American Journal of Political Science* 44: 35–50; Alan Abramowitz and Kyle Saunders. 1998. "Ideological Realignment in the U.S. Electorate." *Journal of Politics* 60: 634–52.

[25] Anthony King. 1997. *Running Scared: Why American Politicians Campaign Too Much and Govern Too Little*. New York: Free Press.

political climate that is not favorable to their party. Moreover, the cost of losing is high. When incumbents lose elections, they also lose their jobs and the political power and reputation that they have amassed. The loss might even mean the end of their political careers.

Thus, despite the high chance of victory, incumbents in campaigns often behave as if they are fighting for their political lives. This is one reason that they are constantly raising money for their next election bid: amassing a huge war chest helps scare off serious competitors. They want to avoid sending any signal that they may be vulnerable. Serious competitors know better than to compete with incumbents under most circumstances, so they bide their time until the district boundaries are redrawn or the incumbent decides to retire. As a result, most congressional elections pit incumbents against political novices, and, unsurprisingly, incumbents tend to win.

The Declining Competitiveness of Congressional Elections

Since the middle of the twentieth century, competitive congressional elections have become somewhat rarer. A simple measure of competitiveness is the number of seats won by less than 10 percent (Figure 10.3).

The decline in electoral competitiveness is most visible from 1952–88. Two likely causes are the increased power of incumbency and increasing party loyalty. Electoral competitiveness has decreased only in House elections that feature an incumbent. It has not decreased in open-seat House races. This may stem in part from the increasing financial advantage of incumbents.[26] At the same time, as we have discussed, Americans have become less willing to vote for political candidates from a different party. To understand why this leads to declining competition, consider a district in which 60 percent of the voters are Democratic and 40 percent are Republican. If Democratic voters are willing to cross party lines, then a strong Republican candidate could make the election competitive. But if Democratic voters are unwilling to cross party lines, then this district would rarely have a competitive election. Interestingly, redistricting appears to play little role in declining competitiveness in House elections. There appears to be little change in competitiveness before and after redistricting cycles.[27]

---

[26] Jacobson, *The Politics of Congressional Elections*, p. 30; Alan I. Abramowitz, Brad Alexander, and Matthew Gunning. 2006. *Journal of Politics* 68: 75–88.

[27] Abramowitz, Alexander, and Gunning, "Incumbency, Redistricting, and the Decline of Competition in U.S. House Elections."

FIGURE 10.3 Number of House Elections Won by 10 Points or Less, 1952–2014

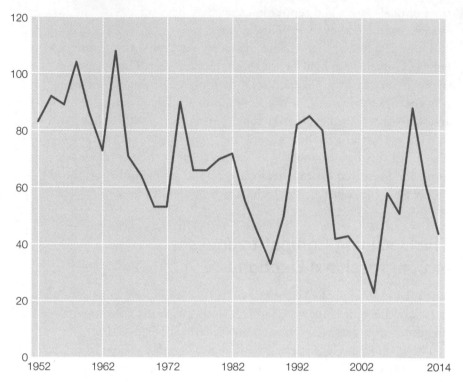

Source: Authors' data.

At the same time, there are clearly years in which a larger number of House elections are competitive—such as 1992, 1994, and 2010. In 1992, there was the previously mentioned scandal of House incumbents' over-drawing their House bank accounts. In 1994 and 2010, the national political climate produced conditions very favorable to one party—in this case, the Republicans—which gave them a good opportunity to defeat Democratic incumbents. This made many more seats competitive.

Nevertheless, there does appear to be a decline in competitiveness over-all, which raises at least three concerns about the American electoral system. First, a decline in competitiveness can undermine democratic accountabil-ity. In a representative democracy, the main way to ensure that politicians respond to citizens is to hold frequent elections; if the public is unhappy with a politician, voters can replace this person. But if representatives know that their reelection is virtually guaranteed, they respond less to citizens, relying more on their own views or on those of interest groups and lobbyists. Second, declining competitiveness can prevent the demographics of Congress from changing to reflect the electorate. This is a major problem for women and minorities, both of whom are underrepresented in Congress. Finally, the demographics of a state or district can change during an incumbent's tenure. If so, then incumbents may grow out of touch with constituents. Without a competitive election, incumbents have less incentive to bring their views into line with those of a changing electorate.

Because it can be difficult for challengers to defeat a well-known and well-funded incumbent, some incumbents run unopposed. For example, in Georgia's 5th District, Democratic incumbent John Lewis ran unopposed in both the primary and general elections in 2014.

At the same time, declining competition in congressional elections may not be a serious problem. It may be less important whether party control of a congressional district changes regularly than whether party control of Congress as a whole changes regularly. Despite the declining number of competitive districts, party control of Congress has changed frequently in the last three decades—and most recently in 2010. Naturally, critics of the current system have a response: that the framers of the Constitution did not want the legislature to represent parties—in fact, political parties did not exist in this country at that time—but to represent the diverse interests of the public. For example, the Constitution specifies that representatives are to be elected every two years so that they would be sensitive to the needs of their constituents. Thus, the rotation of power between the parties is irrelevant to critics, who believe that declining competitiveness undermines the theory of representation enshrined in the Constitution.

Another argument for why declining competitiveness may be of little concern is that even if incumbents almost always win the general election, they must fight for the party's nomination. Direct primaries were adopted precisely because they would introduce contested elections into jurisdictions that were dominated by a single party. And primaries do appear to provide some accountability for incumbents.[28] Critics of this argument point out that most primaries are closed, meaning that only registered members of the party can vote in them and independent voters or opposite partisans have no say in who will represent them. Moreover, most primaries are not competitive; in fact, most House incumbents do not face any primary opposition.

Among the reforms that have been proposed to improve the competitiveness of congressional elections are term limits, public financing, and redistricting. The most obvious reform—one that is embraced by many citizens[29]—is term limits, which require incumbents to leave office after having served a certain number of terms. But as we discussed in Chapter 2, the Supreme Court has ruled that term limits are unconstitutional for federal officeholders, so term limits could be adopted only through a constitutional amendment.

Public financing for congressional candidates would entail providing all federal candidates with a minimum amount of money to help them get their campaigns off the ground. As we noted in Chapter 4, public financing does appear to increase competitiveness. But it is not clear whether Congress or a majority of Americans would ever support public funding. Critics of public financing have noted that it can create "false" competitiveness, since some districts really are decidedly Republican or Democratic. Subsidizing candidates of the minority party in such districts seems unnecessary and perhaps even wasteful.

A third kind of reform involves redistricting. Proposed reforms include taking the redistricting process out of the hands of state legislatures and giving it to independent commissions. Although redistricting does not appear to explain the overall trend in competitiveness, there is some evidence that independent commissions create more competitive districts (see Chapter 2). States can also adopt guidelines for drawing districts that promote competition—for example, by requiring that competitive districts be created whenever possible. But it is unclear whether such guidelines are

---

[28] Shigeo Hirano and James M. Snyder. 2014. "Primary Elections and the Quality of Elected Officials." *Quarterly Journal of Political Science* 9(4): 473–500.

[29] Carol Weissert and Karen Halperin. 2007. "The Paradox of Term Limit Support: To Know Them Is Not to Love Them." *Political Research Quarterly* 60, 3: 516–30.

effective, and they can actually conflict with other priorities such as the imperative to create majority-minority districts under the Voting Rights Act. In 2000, Arizonans adopted a proposition that established an Independent Redistricting Commission, as well as a list of criteria for redistricting that included competitiveness. The redistricting commission found, however, that once Native American and Hispanic (heavily Democratic communities) districts had been drawn to comply with the Voting Rights Act, few Democrats were left in the state to spread around in the interest of creating competitive districts.[30] As a result, the districts created by the new commission were no more competitive than the districts that had been drawn by the state legislature in the past.[31]

Conclusion

The Congressional scholar David Mayhew has described members of Congress as being "single-minded seekers of reelection."[32] Although this statement may be somewhat unfair to public servants who are motivated by other purposes, it is true that members of Congress want to be reelected and spend a great deal of time pursuing reelection, engaging in a permanent campaign, as we discussed in Chapter 2. The two-year House election cycle means that House members are campaigning virtually all of the time, while senators have time to focus on governing before turning their attention to the next election. However, even those senators who are not up for election in a given cycle may campaign on behalf of other senators in their party who are running. Thus, elections are always central for members of Congress.

As a result of the permanent campaign, the lines between campaigning and governing have become blurred. Members of Congress have changed the rules and procedures of Congress to aid them in pursuing reelection. For instance, prior to the institution of electronic voting in 1973, many votes

---

[30] Michael McDonald. 2006. "Redistricting and Competitive Districts," in *The Marketplace of Democracy*, ed. Michael P. McDonald and John Samples. Washington, DC: Brookings Institution Press, pp. 222–44; Michael McDonald. 2008. "Reforming Redistricting," in *Democracy in the States: Experiments in Elections Reform*, ed. Bruce Cain, Todd Donovan, and Caroline Tolbert. Washington, DC: Brookings Institution Press, pp. 147–60.

[31] McDonald, "Reforming Redistricting," p. 150.

[32] David Mayhew. 2004. *Congress: The Electoral Connection*. New Haven, CT: Yale University Press, p. 17.

taken in the House and Senate were anonymous. Since then, it has become common to demand a recorded vote, which makes all votes public. This has made the legislative process more transparent, while forcing members of Congress to think of every vote as a potential campaign issue.[33]

In addition, senators increasingly resort to the filibuster, so much so that it is now assumed that 60 votes are needed to pass a bill because it takes 60 votes to end a filibuster. Filibusters provide senators with a very visible way of signaling to interest groups—many of which have campaign PACs—that they are looking out for their concerns.[34] Although such procedures might serve electoral goals, they can undermine the collegiality of Congress and contribute to legislative gridlock.

Ultimately, focusing on electoral goals can make it difficult for party members to work together. At the same time, focusing on electoral goals is what keeps representatives "running scared" and in contact with their constituents—even if they are almost certain to win their next race. This is an important trade-off inherent in the permanent campaign: it may improve the quality of representation even as it hurts the quality of governance.

---

[33] David Brady and Morris Fiorina. 2000. "Congress in the Era of the Permanent Campaign," in *The Permanent Campaign and Its Future*, ed. Thomas Mann and Norman Ornstein. Washington, DC: American Enterprise Institute, p. 141.

[34] Sarah A. Binder and Steven S. Smith. 1997. *Politics or Principle? Filibustering in the United States Senate*. Washington, DC: Brookings Institution Press.

KEY TERMS

incumbent (p. 277)

open seat (p. 279)

quality challenger (p. 279)

political amateur (p. 279)

Hill committees (p. 279)

earned media/free media (p. 289)

coordinated expenditures (p. 291)

independent expenditures (p. 291)

incumbency advantage (p. 292)

franking privilege (p. 292)

casework (p. 292)

personal vote (p. 293)

FOR DISCUSSION

1. What kinds of people make successful congressional candidates?

2. What roles do the parties play in congressional campaigns?

3. What are some of the causes and consequences of the incumbency advantage?

4. How does the goal of being reelected affect the ability of members of Congress to govern?

CHAPTER 11

State and Local Campaigns

On August 6, 2003, Arnold Schwarzenegger announced his candidacy for the governorship of California. The incumbent, Democrat Gray Davis, was subject to a recall election, wherein voters would determine first whether he would stay in or be recalled from office and then who would replace him if he were recalled. Schwarzenegger did not make his announcement at a rally or press conference, but on *The Tonight Show*, speaking to its host, Jay Leno. The ensuing campaign garnered no end of attention. One hundred and thirty-five candidates were on the ballot as alternatives to Davis, including Schwarzenegger, Lieutenant Governor Cruz Bustamante, State Senator Tom McClintock, and a host of colorful characters from outside politics: Gary Coleman, most famous for his role as a child actor on *Diff'rent Strokes*; Larry Flynt, the publisher of the pornographic magazine *Hustler*, whose campaign slogan was "Vote for a Smut-Peddler Who Cares"; and Mary Carey, an adult film actress whose movie credits include *Busty Beauties 3*. The California recall election had all of the trappings of a big, closely contested campaign. The candidates seeking to replace Davis raised over $37 million. There was national media attention, including 450 articles in the *New York Times* alone.[1] There were mini-scandals involving Schwarzenegger's alleged unseemly behavior toward women on some of his movie sets. In the end, 55 percent of voters chose to recall Davis, and Schwarzenegger was elected to replace him.

In August 2010, Greg David was mounting a campaign for another California political office: the city council of Mountain View. He pledged to spend no more than $1,000: $500 for a ballot statement and $500 for everything else. He said that he would make his campaign signs from recycled wood and leftover paint.[2] Across the country, in Wilkes-Barre, Pennsylvania, Terrence O'Connor ran for the

---

[1] A search for articles with the terms "California" and "recall election" turned up 450 articles in the *New York Times*.

[2] Daniel DeBolt. 2010. "Council Campaign on a Shoestring." *Mountain View Voice*, August 25. www.mv-voice.com/news/show_story.php?id=3272 (accessed 7/14/14).

state House of Representatives by doing little besides affixing large banners to his 1995 Ford Windstar minivan, donning a Revolutionary War–era costume that included a tri-cornered hat, and driving around the district to preach his message of lower taxes through a megaphone.[3] O'Connor's minivan might be called luxurious by some standards: Rory Allen, a candidate for the New York State Senate, often campaigned by driving a golf cart through the streets of his district.[4]

Our focus in this chapter is on state and local races — that is, elections other than those that occur at the federal level. Although these elections receive far less attention than federal elections, they comprise the lion's share — a whopping 96 percent — of all elections that take place in the United States. The victors of these elections have incredible power over our lives — they tell us where we can live, how we can act in public places and in our homes, and what our children will learn in school. State and local governments also spend $3.2 trillion a year, roughly one-fifth of our gross domestic product (GDP).[5] Thus, state and local governments comprise an enormous part of America's governing structure.

Core of the Analysis

- State and local political offices and election laws often differ from their federal counterparts, and these differences affect campaign strategies.
- National political realities shape both candidate strategy in and the outcomes of state and local races.
- State and local campaigns are increasingly adopting the techniques of national campaigns, and thereby becoming more expensive and professionalized.
- At the same time, many state and local campaigns attract scant media attention and require little fund-raising, thereby necessitating very different campaign strategies and tactics.
- Because state and local elections are largely invisible to most voters and to the media, small groups of activists may gain additional influence in these races.

---

[3] Michael Sadowski. 2010. "Candidate Gets Message Out in a Very Public Way." *Pocono Record*, August 14. www.poconorecord.com/apps/pbcs.dll/article?AID=/20100814/NEWS/8140335/-1/NEWS2205 (accessed 7/14/14).

[4] Mark Scheer. 2010. "Could 2010 be the Year for Political Outsiders? Allen Palladino Thinks So." *Niagara Gazette*, August 21. www.niagara-gazette.com/12/x865118062/Reversing-the-political-trend (accessed 7/14/14).

[5] Jeffrey Barnett and Phillip M. Vidal. 2013. "State and Local Finances Summary: 2011." Government Division Briefs, United States Census. www2.census.gov/govs/local/summary_report.pdf (accessed 6/17/14).

State and local elections involve a wide array of offices, but an easy way to think about them is in terms of the three traditional branches of government. At the state and local levels, voters select members of the executive branch (such as governors, lieutenant governors, attorneys general, mayors), members of the legislature (state senates and houses, city councils), and often members of the judiciary (judges and justices). In addition, Americans elect a variety of other non-governing officials, including auditors, road and highway commissioners, surveyors, assessors, and coroners. This entails a vast number of elections, simply because there are so many states and localities with governments — the 50 states, over 3,000 counties, over 19,000 cities or municipalities, and nearly 14,000 school districts.[6] In addition, many states and localities afford citizens an opportunity that does not exist at the federal level: the opportunity to vote on public policies, via ballot propositions, initiatives, and referenda.

The category "state and local" is very broad, as the contrast between the California recall election and the three examples above of local campaigns

In 2003, Arnold Schwarzenegger announced his candidacy for governor of California on *The Tonight Show*. His campaign generated massive media attention and millions of dollars in contributions.

---

[6] John P. Pelissero. 2003. "The Political Environment of Cities in the Twenty-first Century," in *Cities, Politics, and Policy: A Comparative Analysis*, ed. John P. Pelissero. Washington, DC: CQ Press, p. 10.

reveals. Within this category are races that vary dramatically in their resources and thus the visibility of the campaigns themselves. Expensive statewide races, such as those for governor, are essentially analogous to U.S. Senate races. They have features similar to campaigns for federal office: professional consultants, pollsters, television and radio advertising, and so on. But many other races — in fact, most state and local races — have little if any of these features. Many such campaigns are run on a shoestring budget. Family and friends replace paid consultants. Lawn signs replace television advertisements. If one imagines a spectrum running from "campaigns in a golf cart" to "campaigns on *The Tonight Show*," most state and local races are closer to the golf cart end of the spectrum.

At the same time, in recent years state and local campaigns have become more professionalized. The average sum spent on many types of state and local races has increased over time, and some of them now resemble more expensive campaigns in various respects. Professional campaigns have also become increasingly common for offices and issues that previously did not feature prominent campaigns, such as elections to state courts and ballot initiatives and referenda. This trend is being driven in large part by outside groups who have found influencing these kinds of elections to be a highly effective way of shaping policy and also by political consultants who are eager to sell their services. State parties also encourage their candidates to professionalize their campaigns to boost their chances of winning. Thus, the strategic calculations for state and local candidates are changing. At the least, serious state and local campaigns have come to rely less on megaphones and golf carts.

The shoestring nature of campaigns both reflects and perpetuates a simple fact about state and local elections: relative even to congressional elections, they are often profoundly uncompetitive. Incumbents frequently run without any challengers. The news media's attention is usually elsewhere. Citizens turn out to vote in lower numbers and have little information to use in making a choice. And, just as with congressional districts, local districts can be drawn so that only one party has a chance of winning. Under these circumstances, highly organized parties, activists, and interest groups can influence the campaign and election outcomes in ways that may not coincide with the preferences of most citizens in the district. Thus, state and local races — the ones that most affect schools, homes, roads, and many other aspects of citizens' daily lives — are often the ones that live up to ideals of political campaigns the least. This is particularly unfortunate because state and local elections have the potential to promote citizen participation far more than national elections. Not only do the sheer number of local and state elections offer citizens a vast number of opportunities to participate, but also people seem to be more comfortable getting involved in elections closer to home.[7] When they do participate, such elections move closer to the ideal.

We begin this chapter by discussing how local and state electoral rules affect these elections. We also consider how state and local elections depend on the prevailing political and economic winds—the "reality" that candidates must confront. How much do state and local officeholders find their fortunes bound up with broader trends—a weak economy, an unpopular party—that are beyond their control? We discuss the broader impact of rules and reality on the incumbency advantage—a feature of federal elections that is also important in state and local races and that strongly influences how competitive these races are.

We then describe how both rules and reality lead to differences among federal, state, and local campaign strategies, as well as the ways in which these strategies are becoming more similar, thanks to the creeping professionalization of state and local campaigns. We look at campaigns for state courts and ballot initiatives in particular. We also discuss how the uncompetitive features of state and local campaigns have historically advantaged, and continue to advantage, organized interests of various kinds, especially political parties. The concluding section considers the implications for democratic ideals.

Rory Allen ran for New York's State Senate by campaigning in a golf cart.

[7] Andrea McAtee and Jennifer Wolak. 2011. "Why People Decide to Participate in State Politics." *Political Research Quarterly*, 64, 1: 45–58.

Rules and Reality in Local Elections

Local elections typically operate under a very different set of rules than state and federal elections, and may also occur in a different context or "reality"— to use the term from the framework introduced in Chapter 1. Three important ways in which local electoral rules differ from the electoral rules that operate at other levels of government are the use of nonpartisan ballots, at-large elections, and off-cycle elections. The reality of local elections is shaped in large part by the small scale and limited power of local governments, as well as the fact that media largely ignore local elections.

Nonpartisan Elections

The use of nonpartisan ballots reflects a particular philosophy of governance, historically associated with the Progressive movement at the turn of the last century. At that time, as we discussed in Chapter 3, many localities, especially large cities, were governed by party machines. Progressives thought that this created corruption, and they promoted reforms that stripped power from parties. One feature of these reforms was the institution of nonpartisan elections, in which candidates are listed on the ballot without any party affiliations. This curtailed the ways in which party machines could work to choose candidates and help them get elected to office—although, as we discuss later, this does not make parties irrelevant in contemporary city politics. It was also intended to promote the election of city officials who were more concerned with the practical challenges of policy making than with partisan politics. Today, over 75 percent of city council and mayoral elections are nonpartisan—differentiating them from the vast majority of state races and all federal races.

At-Large Elections

A second way local elections differ is in the types of constituencies that elected officeholders represent. Recall from Chapter 2 that districts for the U.S. House of Representatives elect a single representative; they are single-member districts. Many state legislatures also feature single-member districts. City council elections, by contrast, have different methods of representation. Less than 20 percent of cities use districts, sometimes called wards, exclusively—although district elections are more common in the largest metropolitan areas, such as Los Angeles. Just over 20 percent use a mixed system, with some members elected from districts or wards, and other members elected at large—meaning that all voters in that city can vote for candidates for these seats. The majority of cities, however, use at-large elections exclusively; this is particularly true among small and medium-sized cities (that is, those with populations of less than 200,000).[8] Mayors, of course, are always elected in at-large elections.

Off-Cycle Elections

Local elections are often not held at the same time as state and federal elections—another change instituted as part of the broader attempts to reform city governments. For example, more than half of city council elections are held at different times than state and national elections.[9] This has two major consequences. First, off-cycle local elections have significantly lower turnout. Turnout in mayoral elections held off-cycle is 27 percentage points lower than in mayoral elections held at the same time as a presidential election and 15 percentage points lower than in elections that coincide with midterm elections.[10] Nevertheless, many cities hold off-cycle elections to insulate local candidates from some of the events and issues that may be prominent in elections for higher levels of office. As a result, local elections typically center on issues unique to a community, with voters holding local officeholders accountable for their handling of those issues. Some natural disasters become issues that can affect election outcomes. For example, in 2001, Tropical Storm Allison dumped as much as 37 inches of rain on Houston, Texas, causing massive flooding and 22 deaths. A survey conducted afterward found that nearly half of respondents gave credit or blame to the city or county governments for the handling of the flooding, while the state and federal governments were rarely mentioned. Those who blamed the city were less likely to vote for the incumbent mayor who had presided over the response to the storm.[11] This illustrates how local issues may be especially important in local elections.

The Reality of Small-Scale Democracy

Local elections also operate under different realities than state and federal elections. This is because local jurisdictions are small, their elected officials have limited power, and the services they provide are available to everyone

---

[8] Timothy B. Krebs and John P. Pelissero. 2003. "City Councils," in *Cities, Politics, and Policy: A Comparative Analysis*, ed. John P. Pelissero. Washington, DC: CQ Press, p. 172.

[9] Krebs and Pelissero, "City Councils," p. 170.

[10] Thomas M. Holbrook and Aaron C. Weinschenk. 2014. "Campaigns, Mobilization, and Turnout in Mayoral Elections." *Political Research Quarterly* 67(1): p. 8.

[11] Kevin Arceneaux and Robert M. Stein. 2006. "Who Is Held Responsible When Disaster Strikes? The Attribution of Responsibility for a Natural Disaster in an Urban Election." *Journal of Urban Affairs* 28, 1: 43–53.

rather than certain groups of constituents.[12] In small jurisdictions, elected officials can win with relatively few votes, which means their campaigns will revolve around personal connections and require less money. Smaller jurisdictions also have lower revenues and can offer fewer services than larger jurisdictions. For example, cities with less than 100,000 people rarely offer services beyond water, sewage, police, fire, parks, and street repair.[13] Because the mayors of these cities have such limited power, voters will judge them based on their managerial skills rather than their ideological leanings. Moreover, the services just described are typically offered to everyone living in a city. In larger jurisdictions, government services are distributed more unevenly— much like the federal government's social security program or its tax subsidies for farmers. Such particularistic government benefits give groups an incentive to organize and advocate for certain candidates in elections. In contrast, when a city or town offers universalistic services, groups have less of an incentive to mobilize, which makes their elections sleepier affairs.

Another reality of local elections is that they get very little television news coverage, especially if the contest is taking place in a large media market.[14] Because media markets often span large geographic areas encompassing multiple municipal, county, congressional, and even state boundaries, the media in larger markets tend to focus on higher-level races that interest a broader segment of their viewers. In fact, research has found that even in a midterm election year when there is no presidential contest to steal the spotlight, just 4 percent of local news stories concerned local races.[15] Newspapers can make up for this to a certain extent, but they have many of the same incentives the television media have.

If local elections are different from state and federal elections in these respects, they are quite similar in another: the advantages that accrue to incumbents. Indeed, with the nonpartisan ballot in place, voters are dependent on information other than party affiliation, especially their basic familiarity with the candidates. Small wonder, then, that incumbents typically do well in local elections. They are better positioned to have personal contact with voters. They are more likely to get endorsements from prominent

---

[12] J. Eric Oliver, Shang E. Ha, and Zachary Callen. 2012. *Local Elections and the Politics of Small-Scale Democracy.* Princeton, NJ: Princeton University Press.

[13] Oliver, Ha, and Callen, *Local Elections and the Politics of Small-Scale Democracy*, p. 25.

[14] Scott L. Althaus and Todd C. Trautman. 2008. "The Impact of Television Market Size on Voter Turnout in American Elections." *American Politics Research* 36, 6: 824–56.

[15] Martin Kaplan, Kenneth Goldstein, and Matthew Hale. "Local TV News Coverage of the 2002 General Election." The Norman Lear Center. www.learcenter.org/html/projects/?cm =news/pubs (accessed 6/18/14).

leaders and media outlets. They are better able to raise money. Research on city council races has found that incumbents get a far larger share of the vote than nonincumbents and tend to win elections at rates only a little below those of incumbent members of Congress.[16] Despite the very different rules under which local elections are conducted, incumbency remains "the 800-pound gorilla."[17] As a consequence, many local elections—much like many congressional elections—are not very competitive.

Rules and Reality in State Elections

Certain rules distinguish state elections from both local and federal elections. Many states use term limits, which have implications for both aspiring office-holders and incumbents. Variation in state laws concerning how long state legislatures are in session and how much state legislators get paid have consequences for how professionalized state legislatures are. This has consequences for state legislative elections as well. State elected officials also confront a distinct political reality that arises from variation in the strength of state party organizations and the kinds of people that live in their state. They must also deal with the reality that national forces beyond their control may affect their chances of winning. Despite all of these differences, however, incumbents still reign supreme in state-level contests just as they do in local and federal elections.

Term Limits

Many state elections are affected by a rule that members of Congress never confront: term limits. As noted in Chapter 2, most states limit the number of terms a governor can serve, and a substantial minority limit the terms of state legislators as well. The most common limit for governor, following the restrictions on presidents, is two consecutive terms. Statewide offices therefore see more turnover than either the U.S. House or Senate, where incumbents can accrue a considerable advantage from their years of service, as we discussed in Chapter 9. Term limits can change the calculus of both aspiring and current officeholders. Aspiring officeholders know they will be able to run for an open seat on a regular basis. Current officeholders know that their tenure is short-lived, and they may therefore be even more inclined to

---

[16] Timothy B. Krebs. 1998. "The Determinants of Candidates' Vote Share and the Advantages of Incumbency in City Council Elections." *American Journal of Political Science* 42, 3: 921–35; Jessica Trounstine. 2011. "Evidence of a Local Incumbency Advantage." *Legislative Studies Quarterly* 36, 2: 255–80.

[17] Krebs and Pelissero, "City Councils," p. 178.

position themselves to run for higher levels of office once, or even before, their term has expired.

The natural conclusion, then, would be that term limits make elections more competitive, by weakening the advantages of incumbents and increasing the number of open-seat races. However, the real story is more complicated. Term limits have been instrumental in reducing the number of incumbents running in elections, but this does not necessarily make elections as a whole more competitive.[18] Instead, what often happens is that when first-term officeholders run for reelection, they do so without a serious challenger. This is because serious challengers would rather wait until the incumbent leaves office at the end of the term limit than mount a long-shot challenge. Moreover, several factors often combine to make it difficult for more than one serious challenger to compete for a newly open seat. The district itself may be dominated by one party, due to its underlying demography or a prior redistricting. Leaders in this dominant party may work to promote one favored candidate and thereby avoid a hotly contested primary. As a consequence, term limits do not consistently result in closer races.

Legislative Professionalism

One category of rules concerns the **professionalism** of the legislature. The U.S. Congress is perhaps the most salient model of a professional legislature: it is a full-time job that comes with a substantial salary and staff support. Being a legislator in the national legislature is essentially a profession, like being a doctor or lawyer. But this model is hardly universal. State legislatures are often far less professional. Depending on state law, they may meet for only a few months every other year, as in North Dakota and Texas. Legislators in some states receive only small salaries. In fact, New Mexico state legislators receive no salary, only reimbursement for expenses. State legislatures also vary widely in the number of staff employed to assist legislatures. California's professionalized state legislature has several thousand staff, but New Mexico's has less than 100.[19] Legislatures that are not as professionalized are sometimes called **citizen legislatures**.[20]

---

[18] Seth E. Masket and Jeffrey B. Lewis. 2007. "A Return to Normalcy? Revisiting the Effects of Term Limits on Competitiveness and Spending in California Assembly Elections." *State Politics and Policy Quarterly* 7, 1: 20–38; Scot Schraufnagel and Karen Halperin. 2006. "Term Limits, Electoral Competition, and Representational Diversity: The Case of Florida." *State Politics and Policy Quarterly* 6, 4: 448–62.

[19] These examples come from Keith E. Hamm and Gary F. Moncrief. 2004. "Legislative Politics in the States," in *Politics in the American States*, ed. Virginia Gray and Russell L. Hanson. 8th ed. Washington, DC: CQ Press: 163–207.

[20] City councils also vary in their level of professionalization, although there have been fewer studies of how professionalization affects campaign strategies in local elections.

The professionalism of the legislature has a two-edged effect on the incumbency advantage. On the one hand, the more professionalized the legislature, the more its incumbents are likely to attract challengers. This is not surprising: jobs in a professionalized legislature are particularly attractive. But at the same time, incumbents in professional legislatures are actually *less* vulnerable even though they more often face a challenger. They have more resources at their disposal. Like members of Congress, they can claim credit for significant legislative accomplishments and serve their constituents' needs via casework. They can use the perquisites of their office to raise more money than incumbents in citizen legislatures. This helps explain why incumbents in professionalized legislatures are reelected at higher rates.[21]

Characteristics of the Electorate

One reason why state (and local) elections are so interesting is that state electorates can differ dramatically from one another. Consider the differences between a state like California, with its population of 38 million that is 39 percent white, and Iowa, a state of 3 million that is 88 percent white. State legislative districts can vary just as dramatically. These demographic differences affect election outcomes. For example, candidates running in state legislative districts with electorates that are older, whiter, and more educated, or districts with more farmers and government employees, will find it is easier to get voters to the polls because these groups vote at a higher rate than other groups.[22] Perhaps unsurprisingly, candidates who reside in districts with more independent voters will find there are more voters that can be persuaded.[23]

State Party Organizational Strength

State party organizations across the country vary dramatically in terms of their strength, with Republicans generally being stronger organizationally than Democrats.[24] State parties have adapted themselves to this era of

[21] John M. Carey, Richard G. Niemi, and Lynda W. Powell. 2000. "Incumbency and the Probability of Reelection in State Legislative Elections." *Journal of Politics* 66, 3: 671–700; Robert E. Hogan. 2004. "Challenger Emergence, Incumbent Success, and Electoral Accountability in State Legislative Elections." *Journal of Politics* 66, 4: 1283–1303.

[22] Robert Hogan. 1999. "Campaign and Contextual Influences on Voter Participation in State Legislative Elections." *American Politics Research* 27, 4: 403–33.

[23] Nicholas Seabrook. 2010. "Money and State Legislative Elections: The Conditional Impact of Political Context." *American Politics Research* 38, 3: 399–424.

[24] Thomas Holbrook and Raymond La Raja. 2012. "Parties and Elections," in *Politics in the American States: A Comparative Analysis*, ed. Virginia Gray, Russell Hanson, and Thad Kousser. 10th ed. Washington, DC: CQ Press, p. 73.

candidate-centered campaigns, by reinventing themselves as service organizations that provide candidates with important campaign resources. Strong state parties supplement their candidates' campaign organizations by providing financial support and a variety of campaign services, such as polling, media consulting, and voter mobilization programs. They also provide candidates with connections to interest groups allied with the party. Candidates running in states where their party organization is strong will have considerably more help than those running where their party organization is weak.

National Factors

Elections for state offices, like those for president or Congress, are strongly affected by fundamental factors such as the state of the economy. What is particularly striking about state elections is how they can be affected by conditions *outside* the state or locality. To be sure, we do not mean to suggest that individual states have no unique circumstances. One can often see clear differences between the dynamics of federal and state elections. For example, in the American South, the gradual shift from one-party rule by the Democratic Party to a strong tendency to support Republican candidates occurred much more quickly at the federal level than at the state level.[25] That said, the diverse characteristics of individual states do not make each governor's or state legislator's race independent from events in Washington or the country as a whole.

Incumbent governors and their parties can be judged not only on state economic performance but on national economic performance, even though there is almost nothing they can do to affect the national economy.[26] The effects of the national economy are stronger in citizen legislatures, as professionalized legislatures provide advantages to incumbents that make them less likely to be defeated when the economy is weak.[27]

Similarly, candidates for state and local offices are often judged based on the performance of someone who may be thousands of miles away: the

---

[25] Charles S. Bullock III. 2010. "Introduction: Southern Politics in the Twenty-first Century," in *The New Politics of the Old South*, ed. Charles S. Bullock III and Mark J. Rozell. Lanham, MD: Rowman & Littlefield, pp. 1–26.

[26] John E. Chubb. 1988. "Institutions, the Economy, and the Dynamics of State Elections." *American Political Science Review* 82, 1: 133–54; D. M. Simon. 1989. "Presidents, Governors, and Electoral Accountability." *Journal of Politics* 51, 2: 286–304; D. M. Simon, C. W. Ostrom, Jr., and R. F. Marra. 1991. "The President, Referendum Voting, and Subnational Elections in the United States." *American Political Science Review* 85, 4: 1177–92.

[27] William D. Berry, Michael B. Berkman, and Stuart Schneiderman. 2000. "Legislative Professionalism and Incumbent Reelection: The Development of Institutional Boundaries." *American Political Science Review* 94, 4: 859–74.

president. State and local candidates in the president's party often do better when the president is more popular. In fact, this is true regardless of whether a presidential election is occurring at the same time that local candidates are on the ballot. Thus, just as the president's party loses seats in Congress when the economy is weak and the president unpopular, it loses seats in, and sometimes control of, state legislatures. The year 2010 was a case in point: the Democrats not only lost seats in Congress, but they also lost control of six governorships and nearly 700 state legislative seats (including the control of 21 different legislative chambers).

Coattail Effects

Candidates for state and local office can be helped by the presence of higher-profile candidates on the ballot, such as candidates for president. Rules governing the timing of federal, state, and local elections mean that, in some years, state and local elections may occur alongside more visible federal elections. However, in some states, gubernatorial elections never occur in the same year as presidential elections. New Jersey and Virginia hold their gubernatorial elections off-cycle—just as many municipalities across the nation do—so that they do not compete with any federal elections.

What happens when more-visible candidates are on the ballot? They may create a **coattails effect**: less-visible candidates will "ride the coattails" of a more visible popular candidate of the same party who is on the ballot, and thereby do better at the polls. The presence of presidential and senatorial candidates on the ballot may help candidates for governor and state legislator. Similarly, the presence of gubernatorial candidates may help state legislative candidates. Coattails may matter more for challengers and open-seat candidates, who do not have the advantages of incumbency. Coattails also matter more in states where voters can cast a "straight-ticket" vote by pulling a single lever or punching a single button for all the Democrats or all the Republicans on the ballot. (Currently, 14 states allow straight-ticket voting, although that number has declined in recent years.)[28]

The advantages that accrue to incumbent presidents, members of Congress, and even city council members are equally visible in state elections. In fact, state elections are on average less competitive than federal races. This is less true in statewide races, such as those for governor, than in races for state legislatures, where candidates run in smaller districts. Indeed, in state

---

[28] National Conference of State Legislatures. 2011. "Straight-Ticket Voting." www.ncsl.org /default.aspx?tabid=16597 (accessed 7/14/14).

legislative elections, including both primary and general elections, substantial fractions of races are not even contested—meaning one candidate runs unopposed. There has been a striking decline in contested primaries for state legislative elections: from 1910 to 1938, 50 percent of primaries were contested, but from 1960 to 2000, only 25 percent were.[29] Large numbers of races are uncontested in the general election as well: in state legislative races in 2014, 43 percent of major-party candidates faced no major-party opposition (see Figure 11.1).[30] By contrast, in the 2014 U.S. House general election, this

FIGURE 11.1 **Percentage of General Election Candidates in 2014 State Legislative Races with No Major Party Opposition**

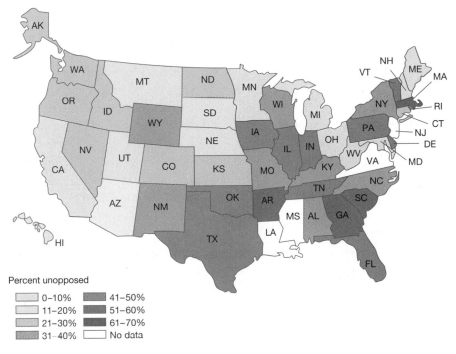

Percent unopposed

0–10%	41–50%
11–20%	51–60%
21–30%	61–70%
31–40%	No data

Source: Percentages calculated by the author.

[29] Stephen Ansolabehere, John Mark Hansen, Shigeo Hirano, and James M. Snyder, Jr. 2006. "The Decline of Competition in U.S. Primary Elections," in *The Marketplace of Democracy*, ed. Michael P. McDonald and John Samples. Washington, DC: Brookings Institution Press. Calculated from Table 4.1, p. 87.

[30] Ballotpedia. 2014. "Major Party Candidates with Major Party Competition in the 2014 State Legislative Elections." http://ballotpedia.org/Major_party_candidates_with_major _party_competition_in_the_November_2014_state_legislative_elections (accessed 2/4/15).

was true of only 14 percent of seats. Naturally, this lack of competitiveness tends to advantage incumbents. In these same state legislative races, 34 percent of incumbents ran unopposed in both the primary and the general elections—albeit with significant variation among states.[31] It is especially rare for incumbents to face challengers who have raised as much money as they have, or even anything close to it. This is one reason that a few states have adopted "clean elections" laws (see Chapter 4): they wish to provide funding to lesser-known challengers.

Campaign Strategies Big and Small

As the stories at the beginning of this chapter make clear, it is not easy to generalize about the strategies of state and local campaigns. At a minimum, of course, almost every candidate for any level of office wants the same thing: to win enough votes to win the election. Certain features of state and local governments, however, can shape candidate strategies for achieving that goal. In particular, the size of a jurisdiction, the powers of office, and the rules that govern election to that office all interact to shape a candidate's strategy.

Perhaps the most important feature is the size of a jurisdiction. In smaller cities and districts, candidates rely mainly on personal connections for campaigning. This is why many local and state campaigns are nearly invisible. Candidates raise little money. Their campaign organizations are composed of a few friends and family, not a stable of well-compensated consultants. They take no polls and air no ads. Instead, they rely on more cost-effective forms of communication, including mailings to voters, billboards and the occasional radio ad. Indeed, one prominent guide to local campaigns includes entire chapters on brochures and lawn signs, including a discussion of the importance of buying weatherproof paper stock for the latter.[32]

As the size of the jurisdiction grows, however, candidates need to develop strategies for reaching larger groups of voters. One of the most effective ways to do this is to reach out to local organizations, such as churches, local clubs, and civic organizations. Candidates hope these groups will mobilize their members on the candidate's behalf and provide volunteers for the campaign. Yet campaigns in even medium-sized jurisdictions still lack resources. This is particularly true for less professionalized political offices. For example, in

---

[31] Ballotpedia. "Major Party Candidates with Major Party Competition in the 2014 State Legislative Elections."

[32] Catherine Shaw. 2000. *The Campaign Manager: Running and Winning Local Elections.* 2nd ed. Boulder, CO: Westview Press.

Wyoming, which has a citizen legislature, the average candidate for the Wyoming State House spent only $7,345 in 2014.[33] That is less than what Terry McAuliffe spent on office supplies ($8,350) in his successful bid for governor of Virginia in 2013.[34]

In large cities and statewide races, personal connections and groups still matter, but candidates must use mass advertising on television and radio to reach more voters. They also raise large sums of money to hire campaign consultants and take polls. All this makes these campaigns resemble campaigns for federal office. A statewide campaign for governor, especially in a large state, is essentially a presidential campaign run on a somewhat smaller scale.

The size of a jurisdiction is related to the power its elected officials hold, which in turn affects the issues that candidates run on. For example, mayors of small towns focus almost exclusively on providing services such as fire and police protection, water, and sewage. A U.S. Senator, however, may focus on foreign affairs, monetary policy, and other federal issues. As a result, a candidate for mayor in a small town is likely to emphasize his or her managerial skills, while the candidate for Senate may express a larger vision for society that often involves taking liberal or conservative positions.[35] Candidates in larger jurisdictions also need to appeal to different groups in order to build a winning coalition. They may emphasize issues important to key groups—for example, by defending the Second Amendment to appeal to gun owners. A small-town mayor will find such group appeals less necessary.

We might also expect campaign strategies for state and local races to differ depending on the rules that govern them. A good example involves city council races, which may involve single-member district seats, at-large seats, or both. In cities with single-member districts, prevailing patterns of housing may mean that many districts are characterized by a large majority of one ethnic group. In turn, this means that candidates in any given district must appeal to voters from the dominant ethnic group. Washington, D.C., is one example. It has eight members elected from wards and five members, including the chair, elected at large. City council wards tend to be majority white or black and elect white or black city council members, respectively. Candidates for at-large elections may not need to appeal to smaller ethnic groups, however: a winning coalition can be built from the dominant or

---

[33] National Institute on Money in State Politics. www.followthemoney.org/election-overview?s=WY&y=2014 (accessed 4/8/15).

[34] The Virginia Public Access Project. www.vpap.org/committees/profile/money_out_services1/2577 (accessed 7/10/14).

[35] Oliver, Ha, and Callen, *Local Elections and the Politics of Small-Scale Democracy*, p. 33.

Travis County Clerk Elections Division

November 4, 2014 Joint General and Special Elections

División de Elecciones de la Secretaria del Condado de Travis

el 4 de noviembre de 2014 Elecciones Generales y Especiales Conjuntas

If you do not know your election precinct or need other election information, call the
Travis County Clerk Elections Division at (512) 238-VOTE (8683). www.traviscountyelections.org
Sí usted no sabe su precinto de elección o para más información sobre la elección, llame a la División de Elecciones
de la Oficina de la Secretaria del Condado de Travis (512) 238-VOTE (8683). www.traviscountyelections.org

---

Straight Party
(Partido Completo)
All precincts/Precintos enteros:

☐ Republican / Republicano
☐ Democratic / Democrático
☐ Libertarian / Libertariano
☐ Green / Verde

United States Senator
(Senador de los Estados Unidos)

All precincts / Precintos enteros:

☐ John Cornyn - REP
☐ David M. Alameel - DEM
☐ Rebecca Paddock - LIB
☐ Emily "Spicybrown" Sanchez - GRN
☐ Write-in / Voto Escrito

District 10, United States Representative
(Distrito Núm. 10, Representante de los Estados Unidos)

Precincts / Precintos: 103, 104, 105, 106, 108, 114, 118, 123, 125, 127, 131, 136, 138, 140, 141, 142, 146, 149, 150, 153, 154, 156, 200, 203, 211, 212, 217, 218, 222, 227, 228, 235, 236, 237, 239, 240, 241, 242, 243, 245, 246, 248, 249, 252, 253, 258, 260, 262, 266, 268, 273, 321, 323, 326, 327, 331, 333, 334, 335, 336, 337, 343, 374, 375

☐ Michael McCaul - REP
☐ Tawana Walter-Cadien - DEM
☐ Bill Kelsey - LIB

District 17, United States Representative
(Distrito Núm. 17, Representante de los Estados Unidos)

Precincts / Precintos: 102, 107, 109, 110, 111, 112, 113, 137, 145, 148, 160, 161, 163, 205, 207, 215, 216, 219, 225, 226, 229, 254, 259, 263, 267, 305, 328, 345

☐ Bill Flores - REP
☐ Nick Haynes - DEM
☐ Shawn Michael Hamilton - LIB

District 21, United States Representative
(Distrito Núm. 21, Representante de los Estados Unidos)

Precincts / Precintos: 250, 277, 301, 309, 310, 311, 314, 315, 329, 330, 332, 339, 340, 341, 342, 344, 349, 350, 351, 352, 354, 356, 357, 363, 365, 368, 406, 408, 409, 412, 416, 418, 419, 420, 421, 422, 424, 428, 430, 431, 433, 435, 437, 446, 454, 458, 460, 461

☐ Lamar Smith - REP
☐ Ryan Shields - LIB
☐ Antonio Diaz - GRN

District 25, United States Representative
(Distrito Núm. 25, Representante de los Estados Unidos)

Precincts / Precintos: 122, 124, 126, 129, 130, 132, 133, 135, 151, 152, 202, 206, 208, 210, 213, 214, 220, 221, 231, 232, 233, 234, 238, 244, 247, 251, 256, 274, 275, 302, 303, 304, 306, 307, 308, 312, 313, 316, 317, 318, 319, 320, 324, 325, 338, 346, 347, 358, 359, 360, 361, 362, 364, 366, 367, 369, 370, 371, 372, 373, 432, 434

☐ Roger Williams - REP
☐ Marco Montoya - DEM
☐ John Betz - LIB

District 35, United States Representative
(Distrito Núm. 35, Representante de los Estados Unidos)

Precincts / Precintos: 101, 115, 116, 117, 119, 120, 121, 128, 134, 139, 164, 209, 223, 224, 401, 402, 403, 404, 405, 407, 410, 411, 413, 414, 415, 417, 423, 425, 426, 427, 429, 436, 438, 439, 440, 441, 442, 443, 444, 447, 448, 450, 451, 452, 463

☐ Susan Narvaiz - REP
☐ Lloyd Doggett - DEM
☐ Cory W. Bruner - LIB
☐ kat swift - GRN

Governor
(Gobernador)

All precincts / Precintos enteros:

☐ Greg Abbott - REP
☐ Wendy R. Davis - DEM
☐ Kathie Glass - LIB
☐ Brandon Parmer - GRN
☐ Write-in / Voto Escrito

Lieutenant Governor
(Gobernador Teniente)

All precincts / Precintos enteros:

☐ Dan Patrick - REP
☐ Leticia Van de Putte - DEM
☐ Robert D. Butler - LIB
☐ Chandrakantha Courtney - GRN

Attorney General
(Procurador General)

All precincts / Precintos enteros:

☐ Ken Paxton - REP
☐ Sam Houston - DEM
☐ Jamie Balagia - LIB
☐ Jamar Osborne - GRN

Comptroller of Public Accounts
(Contralor de Cuentas Públicas)

All precincts / Precintos enteros:

☐ Glenn Hegar - REP
☐ Mike Collier - DEM
☐ Ben Sanders - LIB
☐ Deb Shafto - GRN

Commissioner of the General Land Office
(Comisionado de la Oficina General de Tierras)

All precincts / Precintos enteros:

☐ George P. Bush - REP
☐ John Cook - DEM
☐ Justin Knight - LIB
☐ Valerie Alessi - GRN

Commissioner of Agriculture
(Comisionado de Agricultura)

All precincts / Precintos enteros:

☐ Sid Miller - REP
☐ Jim Hogan - DEM
☐ David (Rocky) Palmquist - LIB
☐ Kenneth Kendrick - GRN

Railroad Commissioner
(Comisionado de Ferrocarriles)

All precincts / Precintos enteros:

☐ Ryan Sitton - REP
☐ Steve Brown - DEM
☐ Mark A. Miller - LIB
☐ Martina Salinas - GRN

Chief Justice, Supreme Court
(Juez Presidente, Corte Suprema)

All precincts / Precintos enteros:

☐ Nathan Hecht - REP
☐ William Moody - DEM
☐ Tom Oxford - LIB

Place 6, Justice, Supreme Court, Unexpired Term
(Lugar Núm. 6, Juez, Corte Suprema, Duración Restante del Cargo)

All precincts / Precintos enteros:

☐ Jeff Brown - REP
☐ Lawrence Edward Meyers - DEM
☐ Mark Ash - LIB

Place 7, Justice, Supreme Court
(Lugar Núm. 7, Juez, Corte Suprema)

All precincts / Precintos enteros:

☐ Jeff Boyd - REP
☐ Gina Benavides - DEM
☐ Don Fulton - LIB
☐ Charles E. Waterbury - GRN

Place 8, Justice, Supreme Court
(Lugar Núm. 8, Juez, Corte Suprema)

All precincts / Precintos enteros:

☐ Phil Johnson - REP
☐ RS Roberto Koelsch - LIB
☐ Jim Chisolm - GRN

Place 3, Judge, Court of Criminal Appeals
(Lugar Núm. 3, Juez, Corte de Apelaciones Criminales)

All precincts / Precintos enteros:

☐ Bert Richardson - REP
☐ John Granberg - DEM
☐ Mark W. Bennett - LIB

Place 4, Judge, Court of Criminal Appeals
(Lugar Núm. 4, Juez, Corte de Apelaciones Criminales)

All precincts / Precintos enteros:

☐ Kevin Patrick Yeary - REP
☐ Quanah Parker - LIB
☐ Judith Sanders-Castro - GRN

Place 9, Judge, Court of Criminal Appeals
(Lugar Núm. 9, Juez, Corte de Apelaciones Criminales)

All precincts / Precintos enteros:

☐ David Newell - REP
☐ William Bryan Strange, III - LIB
☐ George Joseph Altgelt - GRN

District 14, State Senator
(Distrito Núm. 14, Senador Estatal)

Precincts / Precintos: 101, 102, 103, 104, 105, 106, 107, 108, 109, 110, 111, 112, 113, 114, 115, 116, 117, 118, 119, 120, 121, 122, 123, 124, 125, 126, 127, 128, 129, 130, 131, 132, 133, 134, 135, 136, 137, 139, 140, 141, 142, 145, 146, 148, 149, 150, 151, 152, 153, 154, 156, 160, 161, 163, 164, 200, 202, 203, 205, 206, 207, 208, 209, 210, 211, 212, 213, 214, 215, 216, 217, 218, 219, 220, 221, 222, 223, 224, 225, 226, 227, 228, 229, 231, 232, 233, 234, 235, 236, 237, 238, 239, 240, 241, 242, 243, 244, 245, 246, 247, 248, 249, 250, 251, 252, 253, 254, 256, 258, 259, 260, 262, 263, 266, 267, 268, 273, 274, 275, 277, 301, 305, 307, 309, 311, 313, 317, 318, 321, 323, 325, 328, 327, 328, 329, 330, 331, 332, 333, 334, 335, 336, 337, 338, 339, 340, 341, 342, 343, 344, 345, 347, 350, 351, 352, 354, 356, 357, 358, 360, 364, 369, 370, 371, 372, 373, 374, 375, 407, 409, 412, 415, 421, 422, 424, 426, 427, 428, 430, 432, 433, 434, 435, 436, 437, 438, 439, 442, 444, 454, 458, 460, 461

☐ Kirk Watson - DEM
☐ James Arthur Strohm - LIB

District 25, State Senator
(Distrito Núm. 25, Senador Estatal)

Precincts / Precintos: 302, 303, 304, 310, 315, 349, 362, 363, 366, 367, 406, 408, 411, 414, 416, 417

☐ Donna Campbell - REP
☐ Daniel Boone - DEM
☐ Brandin P. Lea - LIB

District 46, State Representative
(Distrito Núm. 46, Representante Estatal)

Precincts / Precintos: 105, 113, 116, 117, 118, 120, 121, 122, 124, 125, 126, 127, 129, 130, 131, 132, 133, 134, 135, 136, 139, 141, 142, 145, 146, 148, 151, 152, 156, 160, 203, 217, 223, 224, 436, 444

☐ Dawnna Dukes - DEM
☐ Kevin Ludlow - LIB

District 47, State Representative
(Distrito Núm. 47, Representante Estatal)

Precincts / Precintos: 232, 233, 234, 244, 245, 302, 303, 304, 306, 308, 310, 312, 314, 315, 316, 318, 319, 320, 324, 330, 333, 334, 336, 338, 346, 349, 359, 360, 361, 365, 367, 368, 369, 370, 371, 372, 373, 374, 375, 406, 417

☐ Paul D. Workman - REP
☐ Scott G. McKinlay - LIB

Many state and local races are less visible to voters, who may know little about the candidates in down-ticket races (those below president and Congress). For example, voters in this Texas county were called on to elect a commissioner of agriculture, a railroad commissioner, and numerous judges.

majority ethnic group. One implication, then, is that candidates in at-large systems do less to appeal to ethnic groups who are minorities within the city, who then find it harder to gain representation on the city council.

Despite these differences in candidate strategy among federal, state, and local campaigns, all candidates at any level of office make similar kinds of strategic decisions about their message and the kinds of voters they will target. State and local candidates seek to articulate a message that defines and promotes their candidacy. They analyze past election results, precinct by precinct, and pore over registered voter lists to identify likely supporters who can then be targeted with media and get-out-the-vote efforts. They work to contact those supporters and ensure their participation on Election Day. But in many state and local races, these efforts are difficult to see, aside from lawn signs and perhaps a volunteer with a clipboard knocking at your door.

The Push toward Professionalization

Even as state and local campaigns are, on average, less professionalized than federal campaigns, they have increasingly come to resemble federal campaigns—with more spending, television advertising, and use of consultants than in the past. For example, the average candidate for the California State Assembly spent $385,000 in 2014, while the average candidate for State Senate spent $504,000.[36] State parties are also driving professionalization. They conduct polls and hire consultants to help formulate strategy that can then be implemented by the party's candidates. Many political consultants focus their practice within a given state and advertise their detailed knowledge of the local terrain. To some extent, the push toward professionalization is simply an arms race: once one side raises enough money to hire consultants and air television advertising, the other side will try to do likewise. The push to professionalization is perhaps most evident in two types of elections: for ballot initiatives and referenda and for state judicial offices.

Ballot Initiatives

Ballot initiatives and **referenda** are proposals placed on the ballot that allow citizens to change law and public policy. This mode of decision making is sometimes called "direct democracy" because such measures are voted on directly by citizens rather than by elected representatives. Twenty-one

---

[36] These figures are the amounts spent by the average candidate in 2014 dollars. The data are from http://followthemoney.org/election-overview?s=CA&y=2014 (accessed 4/9/15).

states allow ballot initiatives while 25 states allow ballot referenda.[37] The number of initiatives or referenda varies by year. In 2014, there were 114 ballot measures across the country, down from a high of 226 in 2006.[38]

Although direct democracy does empower citizens in some respects, many ballot initiatives are hardly the results of grassroots organizing. Instead, interest groups and wealthy individuals work to place their proposals on the ballot and then spend money to promote them. A highly controversial ballot measure in a large state will ultimately cost supporters and opponents many millions of dollars. In 2008, the campaigns for and against California's Proposition 8, which sought to amend the state constitution to recognize marriages only between men and women, cost a total of $107 million. There is little that can be done to limit the amounts spent in ballot initiative campaigns. Supreme Court precedent forbids limits on donations to committees formed to support or oppose initiatives; it also forbids bans on corporate spending in ballot initiative campaigns. The logic is that initiatives, unlike candidates, cannot be corrupted by money, and thus there is no compelling interest that would allow restrictions on speech.[39]

With so much money involved, the tasks of getting measures on the ballot and promoting them now involve a wide array of campaign professionals. There are law firms who craft the wording of the initiative, consulting firms who specialize in gathering the signatures needed to get the initiative on the ballot, media firms who produce radio and television ads promoting or denouncing the initiative, pollsters who monitor the public opinion about the initiative, and direct mail firms who design and send letters to citizens about the initiative. Consultants often relish the opportunity to work on these campaigns, which offer them greater latitude to shape the campaign message than they might have working with an actual candidate. As one consultant said, "With ballot issues you build your own candidate."[40]

Judicial Elections

Thirty-eight states have judicial elections, of which there are three types.[41] Partisan elections pit opposing candidates identified with political parties

---

[37] http://ballotpedia.org/Forms_of_direct_democracy_in_the_American_states (accessed 4/9/15).

[38] http://ballotpedia.org/2014_ballot_measures (accessed 7/10/14).

[39] Richard Hasen. 2005. "Rethinking the Unconstitutionality of Contribution and Expenditure Limits in Ballot Measure Campaigns." *Southern California Law Review* 78: 885–925.

[40] Quoted in Johnson, *No Place for Amateurs*, p. 201.

[41] American Bar Association. "Fact Sheet on Judicial Selection Methods in the States." www.americanbar.org/content/dam/aba/migrated/leadership/fact_sheet.authcheckdam.pdf (accessed 7/14/14).

The Spillover Effects of Ballot Initiatives

In 2004, 11 states had ballot initiatives that would ban same-sex marriages by defining marriage as a union between a man and a woman. They all passed with overwhelming support. After George W. Bush's victory in the presidential election that year, the *New York Times* wrote that these initiatives, "acted like magnets for thousands of socially conservative voters in rural and suburban communities who might not have otherwise voted, even in this heated campaign."[1] Although Karl Rove, Bush's chief campaign strategist, denied he helped engineer the anti-gay marriage amendments to aid Bush's reelection, Ken Mehlman, who was Bush's campaign manager in 2004 and chairman of the Republican National Committee at the time, said he knew Rove "had been working with Republicans to make sure that anti-gay initiatives and referenda would appear on November ballots in 2004 and 2006 to help Republicans."[2]

Even if the anti-gay marriage amendments were part of the Republican strategy, the question is whether such initiatives — or any other initiative, like those advocating the legalization of marijuana — can affect candidate elections taking place at the same time. There are primarily two ways they can affect elections. First, initiatives can change the composition of the electorate by mobilizing people who did not plan to vote (or even by discouraging some people from voting). Initiatives can also change how people vote by priming voters' evaluations of candidates. As we discussed in Chapter 8, priming means that voters evaluate candidates in light of a particular issue — in this case, the ballot initiative issue — even though the candidate may not have taken a position on it or in any way be associated with it.[3] If ballot initiatives can prime candidate evaluations, then they may be an important way for interest groups to set the agenda in an election.

Political scientists have not agreed on whether the same-sex marriage initiatives tipped the balance toward Bush in 2004. After all, much of the debate in the 2004 election concerned Bush's handling of the War on Terror and the Iraq War. There is some evidence that the same-sex ballot initiatives primed voters in a way that was helpful for Bush[4] and increased turnout among evangelicals.[5] Even if political scientists do not agree on their effects, it is clear many political consultants do. Looking ahead to 2016, supporters of marijuana legalization plan to conduct signature drives to place measures on the ballot in at least six states, including some battleground states such as Nevada and Maine.[6] With polls showing that people between the ages of 18 and 29 — a group that typically votes Democratic and has lower turnout rates — overwhelmingly support legalization, these measures may have the potential to do for the Democrats in 2016 what many believe the anti-gay marriage amendments did for the Republicans in 2004.[7]

[1] James Dao. 2004. "Same-Sex Marriage Issue Key to Some GOP Races." *New York Times*, November 4.

[2] Marc Ambinder. 2010. "Bush Campaign Chief and Former RNC Chair Ken Mehlman: I'm Gay." *The Atlantic*, August 25.

[3] Stephen Nicholson. 2005. *Voting the Agenda: Candidates, Elections, and Ballot Propositions*. Princeton, NJ: Princeton University Press; Todd Donovan, Caroline Tolbert, and Daniel Smith. 2008. "Priming Presidential Votes by Direct Democracy." *Journal of Politics* 70, 4: 1217–31.

[4] Donovan, Tolbert, and Smith, "Priming Presidential Votes by Direct Democracy"; but see D. Sunshine Hillygus and Todd G. Shields. 2005. "Moral Issues and Voter Decision Making in the 2004 Presidential Election." *Political Science and Politics* 38, 2: 201–9.

[5] David Campbell and J. Quin Monson. 2008. "The Religion Card: Gay Marriage and the 2004 Presidential Election." *Public Opinion Quarterly* 72, 3: 399–419.

[6] Marijuana Policy Project. "MPP's 2014 Strategic Plan." www.mpp.org/about/mpps-2014-strategic-plan.html (accessed 7/11/14).

[7] Art Swift. 2013. "For the First Time, Americans Favor Legalizing Marijuana." Gallup Politics. www.gallup.com /poll/165539/first-time-americans-favor-legalizing -marijuana.aspx (accessed 7/11/14).

against each other. Nonpartisan elections also feature opposing candidates, but they run without party labels (although political parties may endorse them). **Retention elections** are referenda on sitting judges in which voters decide whether judges should remain on the bench. They do not select a replacement. In 2010, three justices from the Iowa Supreme Court lost their retention elections after the court ruled in favor of gay marriage, the first time in Iowa's history that a sitting judge had ever lost a retention election. Moreover, while campaigns for these offices were once staid affairs that featured little electioneering, they have come to resemble campaigns for executive and legislative offices as well as many ballot initiatives.

Judicial campaigns have become increasingly costly: the total amount of money raised by state supreme court candidates across the country jumped from $6.3 million in 1989–90 to almost $61.2 million in 2003–4.[42] Since then, state supreme court candidates have continued to raise similar amounts in cycles including a presidential election ($57.1 million in 2007–8 and $56.4 million in 2011–12) but less in those including a midterm election ($42.8 million in 2005–6 and $38.7 million in 2009–10). Judicial campaigns often attract the efforts of various party organizations as well as interest groups such as chambers of commerce, trial lawyer groups, and the Business Council of America, who donate to judicial candidates or spend independently on their behalf. In fact, in 2011–12, party and interest group funding accounted for a stunning 43 percent of the total spending in state supreme court campaigns—a new record.[43] Finally, these campaigns feature a larger number of television advertisements. State supreme court elections saw only about 23,000 ads in 2000, but more than 51,000 in 2012.[44] As in other sorts of campaigns, the ads are frequently hard-hitting, accusing judges of sleeping during trials, "putting criminals on the street," and the like.

One reason for the increased expense of state judicial elections is that, starting in the 1990s, business groups increasingly came into conflict with trial lawyers, consumer groups, and labor unions over tort reform. Tort reform

---

[42] James Sample, Adam Skaggs, Jonathan Blitzer, and Linda Casey. 2010. "The New Politics of Judicial Elections, 2000–2009." New York: Brennan Center for Justice and National Institute on Money in State Politics; Adam Skaggs, Maria da Silva, Linda Casey, and Charles Hall. 2011. "The New Politics of Judicial Elections 2009–2010." New York: Brennan Center for Justice and National Institute on Money in State Politics.

[43] Alicia Bannon, Eric Velasco, Linda Casey, and Lianna Reagan. 2013. "The New Politics of of Judicial Elections, 2011–2012." New York: Brennan Center for Justice and National Institute on Money in State Politics.

[44] Brennan Center for Justice. 2012. "New Data Shows Judicial Election Ad Spending Breaks Record at $29.7 Million." www.brennancenter.org/press-release/new-data-shows -judicial-election-ad-spending-breaks-record-297-million (accessed 4/17/14).

FIGURE 11.2 **Contributions to State Supreme Court Candidates, 1991–2012**

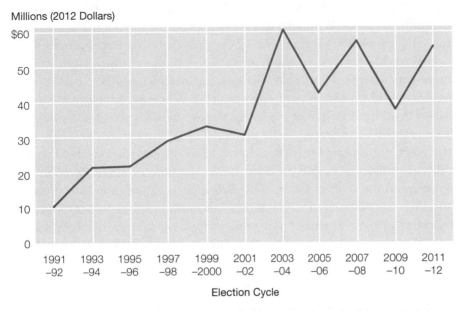

Millions (2012 Dollars)

Election Cycle

Note: 2012 dollar figures based on conversion rates from the even-numbered year of each two-year period.
Source: Data for 2000–2009 are from Sample, Skaggs, Blitzer, and Casey, "The New Politics of Judicial Elections, 2000–2009." Data for 2010–2012 are from Bannon, Velasco, Casey, and Reagan, "The New Politics of Judicial Elections 2011–12."

typically entails limits to the awards that plaintiffs can win from corporations and businesses for, say, an allegedly faulty product. Business groups favored these reforms, but trial lawyers and consumer groups did not. This conflict then began to spill over into the judicial arena, since appellate and state court justices would often hear tort cases on appeal and could adjust the amount of money awarded to plaintiffs. Thus, it made strategic sense for interest groups to insert themselves into state judicial campaigns. Judicial races had previously been so sleepy that these groups believed a sudden influx of spending could make a difference.

Whether the issue is tort reform, redistricting, or collective bargaining for state workers, in general it is cheaper to influence judicial elections than to help elect a favorable majority in the state legislature or a sympathetic governor. As one Ohio union official put it, "We figured out a long time ago that it's easier to elect seven judges than to elect 132 legislators."[45]

---

[45] Quoted in Sample, Skaggs, Blitzer, and Casey, "The New Politics of Judicial Elections, 2000–2009," p. 9.

Needless to say, such sentiments do nothing to allay the fear that expensive campaigns compromise the integrity of judges. A case in point involved a West Virginia supreme court justice, Brent Benjamin. In 2004, he defeated incumbent justice William McGraw with the help of Don Blankenship, the CEO of a West Virginia mining company, Massey Energy. Before the campaign, Massey Energy had been sued by Harman Mining Company for breach of contract. A jury ruled that Massey owed $50 million. Blankenship then spent $3 million in an attempt to defeat McGraw, establishing a group called "And for the Sake of the Kids," which aired ads accusing McGraw of "voting to let a child rapist out of prison." Three years after Benjamin won, the West Virginia supreme court heard Massey Energy's appeal of this $50 million verdict. Benjamin provided the swing vote in a 3–2 decision that overturned the verdict. Later, the U.S. Supreme Court threw out the West Virginia court's decision, arguing that Benjamin faced a conflict of interest so extreme that Harman Mining's due process rights may have been violated.[46] Such a scenario, however unusual, suggests that expensive judicial campaigns may bring with them unintended consequences.

Activists in State and Local Campaigns

The entry of interest groups into state judicial elections hints at a broader feature of many state and local campaigns: without much voter or media interest, dedicated activists, whether from state and local party organizations or interest groups, can powerfully affect these races. In state and local elections, activists can often work to influence the outcome without attracting much attention or even competition. For them, it takes fewer resources to get a larger benefit: greater influence over state and local races than might be possible in more visible federal races.

Rules that dictate off-cycle elections can have a particularly strong effect on the influence of interest groups, because they result in lower voter turnout. For example, in school districts with off-cycle elections, teachers are typically paid more than in districts with on-cycle elections—that is, teachers unions are more likely to get their desired outcome: larger paychecks. Elections with low turnout help to empower interest groups whose members are likely to vote and thus produce policy outcomes closer to their preferences.[47] Small wonder, then, that parties and activists have routinely sought

---

[46] *Caperton v. A.T. Massey Coal Co.*, 129 S.Ct. 2252 (2009).

[47] Sarah Anzia. 2011. "Election Timing and the Electoral Influence of Interest Groups." *Journal of Politics* 73, 2: 412–27.

to manipulate the timing of elections to maximize their electoral or policy goals.[48]

The history of political monopolies within American cities provides a second example. As discussed in Chapter 3, party machines have had sustained periods of influence in many cities, using a variety of rewards and punishments to choose candidates, mobilize voters, and ensure the continued loyalty of both. And although some of the most infamous machines no longer exist, urban politics still has its monopolies.[49] When Newark's mayor Sharpe James was challenged by Cory Booker in 2002, Booker's campaign saw its signs disappear, its supporters harassed, and its headquarters robbed. Some of these actions were perpetrated by Newark police officers aligned with the James administration. Over his five terms, James had assembled a strong organization of party officials, activists, and even municipal employees who were willing to work on his behalf and, in this case, intimidate a challenger.

State legislative elections provide another example.[50] In many state legislative districts, the outcome is largely a foregone conclusion because the districts are so politically homogeneous. The majority party can essentially monopolize the district. This makes the primary election the most important election, since the majority party's nominee will almost always win the general election. If term limits are also in effect, primary elections to choose a new nominee occur more frequently, and term-limited officials often compete in primaries for higher levels of office. Few, if any, state legislative primaries attract much attention from local news organizations or from voters, most of whom could not name their state representatives if asked.[51]

The result is that local party activists have considerable leeway to shape the outcome. As they do in city elections, local party organizations work to recruit candidates, influence the primary election, and ensure that the winner remains loyal to the activists' agenda while in the state legislature. They are not machines but rather networks of like-minded officials and activists, sometimes with a de facto leader and sometimes not, who coordinate to influence the election. The power of this network will almost always trump

---

[48] Sarah Anzia. 2012. "Partisan Power Play: The Origins of Local Election Timing as an American Political Institution." *Studies in American Political Development* 26, 1: 24–49.

[49] Jessica Trounstine. 2008. *Political Monopolies in American Cities: The Rise and Fall of Bosses and Reformers*. Chicago: University of Chicago Press.

[50] Seth E. Masket. 2009. *No Middle Ground: How Informal Party Organizations Control Nominations and Polarize Legislatures*. Ann Arbor: University of Michigan Press.

[51] Samuel C. Patterson, Randall B. Ripley, and Stephen V. Quinlan. 1992. "Citizens' Orientations toward Legislatures: Congress and the State Legislature." *Western Political Quarterly* 45, 2: 315–38.

that of potential candidates. Most candidates are not well known or personally wealthy, and thus they need the support of the local party to get on the ballot and to win. Because they must conform to the views of activists, these candidates will tend to be more ideologically extreme than the voters that elect them, and the parties in the state legislature will be more polarized along ideological lines.

An example of how such a network matters comes from the rural Central Valley of California, where Bill Thomas, a Republican member of the House of Representatives, held sway for nearly 20 years.[52] Thomas's support for a local candidate was considered crucial, and Republican office seekers curried his favor. His endorsement signaled others in the network, such as prominent donors, business leaders, and conservative groups, to support the chosen candidate. This network was directly responsible for punishing a Republican state legislator, Mike Briggs, who disappointed conservatives by voting for a Democratic budget plan in 2001; the plan included a tax increase that conservatives opposed. Briggs found himself with a primary challenger, Devin Nunes, who was 28 years old, reliably conservative, and, perhaps most important, a former campaign staffer for Thomas. Nunes beat Briggs in the primary and went on to win the general election.

The Paradox of State and Local Elections

The invisibility of many state and local campaigns gives rise to a paradox. State and local leaders are in some sense "closest" to citizens: they are intimately involved with the community they represent, and their decisions affect virtually every aspect of life there—from whether schools get new textbooks to whether potholes get filled. And yet state and local elections engage many fewer voters than federal and especially presidential elections. With little spending by the candidates and little attention from the media, voters are unfamiliar with the candidates and do not learn much during the campaign. The weakening of party machines, whatever its benefits, has been associated with a decline in turnout. As a consequence, state and local elections see some of the lowest turnout rates among all American elections. One study of California municipal elections found that the average turnout in mayoral races was 28 percent, and in city council races 32 percent.[53] These rates are much lower than in federal elections: turnout even in midterm

---

[52] See Masket, *No Middle Ground*, pp. 2, 31–32.

[53] Zoltan L. Hajnal and Paul G. Lewis. 2003. "Municipal Institutions and Voter Turnout in Local Elections." *Urban Affairs Review* 38, 5: 645–68; Neal Caren. 2007. "Big City, Big Turnout? Electoral Participation in American Cities." *Journal of Urban Affairs* 29, 1: 39–46.

elections has been higher than 32 percent in every election since 1792. Moreover, even when state and local elections coincide with a presidential election, bringing more voters to the polls, voters sometimes fail to mark a choice for state and local offices (a phenomenon called "roll-off").

Some of this lack of voter involvement is because many state and local races are not competitive. State and local races are no different from congressional races in this sense. Many localities are not politically diverse. Republicans simply do not have much hope in Berkeley, California, while Democrats stand little chance in College Station, Texas. Incumbents have a considerable advantage, especially those who hold full-time, professionalized offices. The inequalities among candidates so frequently noted in congressional races are similarly prevalent in many state and local races.

The lack of competitiveness also stems from direct actions taken by leaders, parties, and interest groups. Gerrymandering is part of this story: majority parties work, to the extent possible, to draw state legislative boundaries that will maximize the number of seats they hold. In addition, political monopolies within cities promote one party's reign in part via strategies that render elections less competitive and reduce voter turnout.[54] Activist networks seek to control the nominations process and primary elections, often limiting the choices available to voters by "clearing the field" of opposing candidates.

None of this is necessarily problematic in terms of the goals of democratic political systems. Low voter turnout could at times reflect a degree of satisfaction with state and local representatives and governments. The enhanced role of activists may be entirely appropriate, given that they feel much more strongly than the average voter about the issues that confront state and local governments. And representatives elected in uncompetitive races still may work to represent the interests of their constituents.

At the same time, a lack of competitiveness in state and local elections may create biases that have important effects on the process of governing. The power of activists, most of whom have strong ideological views, tends to produce leaders who are more ideologically extreme than voters. This bias toward ideologues creates polarization in government—whereby the two parties strongly disagree on policy and cannot reach effective compromises. The result of such polarization is that governments struggle to develop policy solutions to important problems. In California, which has one of the most polarized state legislatures, state budgets are routinely passed months after the ostensible deadline because Democrats and Republicans cannot agree on the appropriate levels of taxation and spending.

---

[54] Trounstine, *Political Monopolies in American Cities*, chapter 5.

Low levels of turnout in local elections also create biases in terms of who wins elections and which groups are represented in government. In particular, racial and ethnic minorities are often affected—a situation exacerbated when local elections are conducted at large instead of in single-member districts. In low-turnout elections, minority candidates are more likely to lose mayoral elections and elections for city council; consequently, the spending policies of local governments are often out of step with the views of minorities.[55] Thus, the lack of competitiveness and the invisibility of many local races create another sort of political inequality: conditions that seem distinctly unfavorable to minority ethnic groups.

Unsurprisingly, then, many reformers seek to make state and local elections more competitive. As noted in Chapter 4, this is one goal of clean elections laws. Competitiveness produces more vigorous campaigns, which, on average, make voters more interested and willing to participate. Proponents of campaign finance reform and term limits often intend just that, although, as we have discussed, these reforms may have little impact. But there are important trade-offs in making campaigns more intense, ones highlighted by the trends in ballot initiative campaigns and judicial elections. Contested campaigns tend to be more professionalized and more expensive: more money is raised and spent, more consultants hired, and more advertisements aired. Competitive races also attract the energies of parties and interest groups, who may spend even more money independent of the candidates. All of this can make for mean and rowdy campaigns, while the money flowing into them raises additional concerns about the possibility of corruption. This gets at the essence of the trade-off. Competitive elections provide more choices and more information for voters increasing the chances that they will participate. Yet, absent a transformation in campaign finance, these races are more expensive and often more negative. It is hard to have one without the other. This means that many people may find the solution to the paradox of state and local elections—that is, the idea that most people do not vote in elections for the offices that most directly affect their lives—unpalatable.

Conclusion

State and local elections may often seem like small potatoes. The candidates are typically anything but celebrities, and the campaigns are often unsophisticated. But they have considerable strategic importance. For ambitious

---

[55] Zoltan Hajnal. 2010. *America's Uneven Democracy: Race, Turnout, and Representation in City Politics*. New York: Cambridge University Press.

people, state and local offices can be important for incubating political careers. Barack Obama and Jimmy Carter began their careers as state legislators. Other presidents began their careers in elected office as governors, including Ronald Reagan, Bill Clinton, and George W. Bush.

State and local politics are especially important for candidates from groups that have traditionally been underrepresented in political office, such as women and ethnic minorities. Potential candidates from these groups face significant barriers if they want to start their political careers at higher levels of office, such as Congress. Success is more likely within state and local politics, where the barriers are lower and where they gain the experience, visibility, and viability needed to seek higher office.

State and local politics are also important to political parties and interest groups. Decision making at these levels affects a variety of policies that parties and groups care about, including taxation, schools, prisons, roads, and health care. Moreover, state and local elections offer parties and interest groups more opportunities for influence than do federal elections. They can work to choose and support candidates, knowing that the local candidates depend on this support. Parties and interest groups can work behind the scenes, because most state and local elections are rarely covered by the news media and thus largely invisible to voters.

KEY TERMS

professionalism (p. 311)

citizen legislature (p. 311)

coattails effect (p. 314)

ballot initiatives (p. 319)

referenda (p. 319)

retention elections (p. 322)

FOR DISCUSSION

1. What is legislative professionalism and how does it affect the advantages of incumbents in state legislatures and the impact of the national economy on state legislative elections?

2. How do the strategies employed in state and local campaigns typically differ from those in federal campaigns?

3. Why do many state and local races give political party organizations and interest groups a particular opportunity to influence elections?

4. What are the possible advantages and disadvantages of having state and local elections become more competitive?

CHAPTER 12

Voter Participation

In 2008, Barack Obama's campaign team created a website called MyBarackObama.com, neither the first candidate website nor the first attempt by campaigns to harness the power of the Internet. Eight years earlier, during the 2000 presidential primaries, John McCain demonstrated the fund-raising power of the Internet by raising more than $1 million in a single evening. In 2004, supporters of Howard Dean's primary campaign arranged meetings via Meetup .com. But in 2008, MyBarackObama.com took e-campaigning to a new level. It was not created to persuade people to vote for Obama; most people who signed on to the site had already decided to vote for him. Instead, it was created to get Obama supporters involved in the primary campaign against Hillary Clinton and John Edwards. One of the website's creators, Jascha Franklin-Hodge, explained that the Obama campaign "knew they didn't have the kind of political machine Clinton was going to come in with. They had to build their own machine, and the way to do this was with the online tools."[1]

People who logged on to MyBarackObama.com were immediately asked if they would be interested in canvassing neighborhoods, making calls on behalf of the candidate, or hosting a campaign event. They could even view the names of neighbors who were not registered to vote, print out their state's voter registration form, and read a script to help guide their conversations with those neighbors. On other parts of the site, supporters could make donations and commit to raising a certain amount of money for the campaign through friends and family. The website encouraged supporters to report what they were doing so that the Obama campaign could keep track of their activity. If people reported engaging in an exceptionally high number of activities, field directors from the campaign would contact them and ask them to manage other volunteers. Thus, the Obama campaign used MyBarackObama.com to find volunteer staff and to

---

[1] David Talbot. 2009. "The Geeks behind Obama's Web Strategy." Boston.com., January 8. www.boston.com/news/politics/2008/articles/2009/01/08/the_geeks_behind_obamas_web _strategy/ (accessed 6/6/11).

In 2008 and 2012, Barack Obama's supporters could log into MyBarackObama.com to volunteer for the campaign and follow him on social media outlets, such as Twitter.

recruit activists from communities across the country.

The Obama campaign in 2008 made use of other Internet tools as well, such as Facebook, Twitter, and YouTube, but it greatly expanded those efforts during Obama's reelection campaign. For example, in 2012, Obama's campaign regularly posted short animated clips, or GIFs, on Tumblr, uploaded pictures from the campaign trail to Instagram and Flickr, and created playlists on Spotify. In 2012, the Obama campaign also took the novel step of using Facebook to replicate door-to-door canvassing on a mass scale. It sent supporters, who had downloaded an app, pictures of Facebook friends living in swing states and asked them to click a button to urge their friends to take important steps during the

Core of the Analysis

- The rules that govern elections determine who is eligible to vote and how easy it is for an individual to participate.
- Because of its rules, the United States has lower voter turnout than other developed democracies.
- Citizens' participation depends on three factors: ability, motivation, and opportunity.
- These factors create participatory distortions when those who participate more have views that are unrepresentative of the rest of the country.
- Mobilization by political campaigns encourages people to participate and may be responsible for the recent increase in voter turnout.

campaign, such as registering to vote or going to the polls.[2] Mitt Romney employed many of the same Internet tools to reach his supporters, but his campaign used these platforms far less than the Obama campaign. For example, one study found that across all platforms, during a two-week period, the Obama campaign published three times the number of posts than the Romney campaign did. Although it is unclear exactly how Obama's and Romney's Internet activity affected the election outcome, it is clear that both campaigns believed the Internet could be used to encourage and facilitate electoral participation. One of the most important reasons people vote or volunteer to work for a campaign is because someone asks them to. Obama's campaigns in particular have demonstrated how the Internet can be used to find supporters and get them to participate merely by providing them with a little information and encouragement.

What Is Electoral Participation?

Political participation during the electoral season can take many forms. The most common form of participation is voting, but participation encompasses other activities as well, such as trying to persuade a friend or coworker to vote for a particular candidate or writing a check to the candidate's campaign committee. **Electoral participation** refers to the range of activities by which individuals attempt to affect the outcome of an election, including not only partisan activities, which favor a particular candidate, but also nonpartisan activities, such as participation in voter registration drives.

Forms of electoral participation vary along four dimensions: how often they can be performed, the personal resources required to engage in them, whether they are performed alone or with others, and how much information they convey about citizens' preferences, needs, and desires. For example, citizens have only one vote, but they can volunteer and donate as frequently as they like, especially if they have resources such as free time and money. This means that certain individuals can have an impact on the electoral process far beyond a single vote, which can create a **participatory distortion**. A participatory distortion occurs when a group of citizens with preferences and viewpoints that are unrepresentative of the general public has a greater impact on the political process than other citizens.[3] For

---

[2] Jenna Wortham. 2012. "Winning Social Media Votes." *New York Times*, October 7, B1.

[3] Sidney Verba, Kay Lehman Schlozman, and Henry E. Brady. 1995. *Voice and Equality: Civic Voluntarism in American Politics*. Cambridge, MA: Harvard University Press, p. 15.

example, senior citizens, who vote at higher rates than young people, are more concerned about issues such as social security and Medicare, while younger people care more about issues such as college tuition rates and environmental degradation. Because senior citizens vote more, however, elected officials pay more attention to their political agenda.

In addition, some types of electoral participation can be performed alone, such as voting or making a donation to a candidate, but others involve interacting with people. While some people may find the solidarity that comes from working with other people to promote a cause such as a candidate empowering, others might view such activity with trepidation because it requires speaking one's mind and carries the potential for conflict.

Finally, some forms of participation contain more information for elected representatives than other forms. Consider voting for a candidate versus writing to a newspaper to say why you support that candidate. Both actions are forms of electoral participation, but writing to a newspaper conveys more information than voting does. When citizens vote, their votes communicate their preference for one candidate over another, but not why they voted for that candidate. Winning candidates often claim a "mandate," suggesting that their victory means citizens support all of the policies they advocate. In fact, voters may disagree with many of the policy positions embraced by candidates but vote for them anyway because they seem more likeable or trustworthy than their opponent. When citizens engage in information-rich forms of electoral participation such as letter writing they provide candidates and elected officials with more specific guidance.

Trends in Participation in the United States

After the 2000 election, books with titles such as *The Vanishing Voter* and *Democracy at Risk* sought to explain declining levels of political participation in the United States.[4] A chief motivation for this was the trend in turnout in presidential elections between 1960 and 1996 (see Figure 12.1). With the exception of 1992, when the three-way race featuring George H. W. Bush, Bill Clinton, and Ross Perot piqued voters' interest, the turnout rate

---

[4] Thomas E. Patterson. 2002. *The Vanishing Voter: Public Involvement in an Age of Uncertainty.* New York: Knopf; Stephen Macedo, Yvette Alex-Assensoh, Jeffrey M. Berry, Michael Brintnall, David E. Campbell, Luis Ricardo Fraga, Archon Fung, William A. Galston, Christopher F. Karpowitz, Margaret Levi, Meira Levinson, Keena Lipsitz, Richard G. Niemi, Robert D. Putnam, Wendy M. Rahn, Rob Reich, Robert R. Rodgers, Todd Swanstrom, and Katherine Cramer Walsh. 2005. *Democracy at Risk: How Political Choices Undermine Citizen Participation.* Washington, DC: Brookings Institution Press.

FIGURE 12.1 Electoral Participation in Presidential Elections, 1952–2012

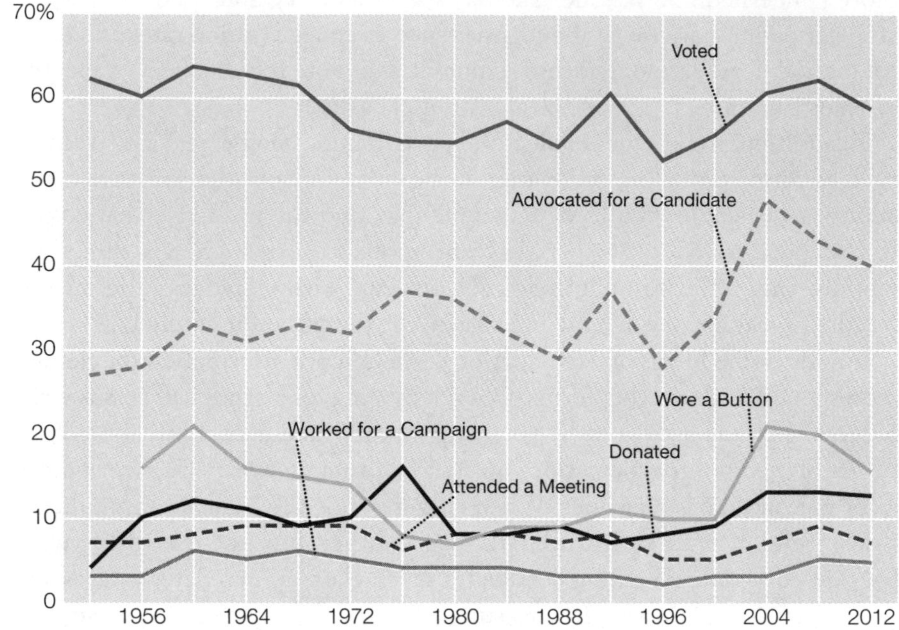

Source: Turnout rates based on voting eligible population. The pre-1980 data is from Samuel L. Popkin and Michael McDonald. 2001. "The Myth of the Vanishing Voter." *American Political Science Review* 95, 4: 966. The 1980–2012 turnout data is from Michael P. McDonald. 2014. "Voter Turnout." www.electproject.org/home /voter-turnout/voter-turnout-data (accessed 2/4/15). The nonvoting activities data is from the American National Election Study Cumulative File.

tended to decline during this period. Other forms of participation also declined, including displaying a candidate's button or bumper sticker, attending a meeting or rally for a candidate, or volunteering for a political campaign. The only form of electoral participation that defied the trend was advocating a candidate to family, friends, or coworkers.

Yet almost as soon as these books hit the shelves, the decline in electoral participation ended. From its low level of 53 percent in 1996, turnout in presidential elections increased to 62 percent in 2008, returning to the levels of the 1960s. Between 1996 and 2004, the percentage of people reporting that they had tried to persuade another person to vote for a particular candidate increased from 28 to 48 percent, declining slightly to 43 percent in 2008. The percentage reporting that they displayed a candidate's bumper sticker doubled from 10 percent in 1996 to 20 percent in 2008. The percentage saying they donated money to a candidate or party increased from 8 to 13 percent during the same time period. Electoral participation receded ever

FIGURE 12.2 Voter Participation in Midterm Elections, 1958–2014

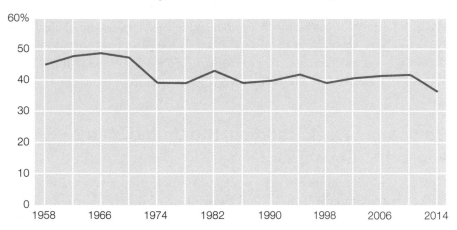

Source: Popkin and McDonald, "The Myth of the Vanishing Voter"; McDonald, "Voter Turnout."

so slightly in 2012, with voter turnout declining to 59 percent. Forty percent reported advocating a candidate and 15 percent reported displaying a sign or bumper sticker. The percentage donating remained stable at 13 percent.

Levels of electoral participation in the United States decrease sharply in midterm years, when turnout hovers around 40 percent, or 10 to 20 points lower than in presidential election years (see Figure 12.2). At 36 percent, the 2014 midterm election was the election with the lowest turnout since 1942. All other forms of participation are less prevalent in midterm election years as well. There is a particular drop-off in the participation of young people, making the midterm electorate significantly older than the presidential electorate.[5]

Voter turnout in midterm elections has held steady since the mid-1970s. The decrease in turnout in presidential election years between 1960 and 1996 did not occur in midterm elections. One reason is that people who vote in midterm elections are typically "habitual voters"—people who vote in most elections. People who vote in presidential elections include habitual voters as well as those who become motivated by the excitement and media coverage generated by the election and who are mobilized by the campaigns. In fact, the decline in voter turnout in presidential elections between 1960 and 1996 may

---

[5] Raymond E. Wolfinger, Steven J. Rosenstone, and Richard A. McIntosh. 1981. "Presidential and Congressional Voters Compared." *American Politics Research* 9, 2: 245–56; Robert A. Jackson. 2000. "Differential Influences on Participation in Midterm versus Presidential Elections." *Social Science Journal* 37, 3: 385–402.

derive from unexciting elections due mainly to how uncompetitive they were and declining investment by candidates and parties in **get-out-the-vote (GOTV) efforts**.[6] Both factors have changed in recent presidential elections. Not only have voters been more interested in the elections, but also candidates and parties have invested more in GOTV efforts. This investment appears to have produced results, as we will see later in this chapter.

Comparing Participation in the United States and Other Countries

Despite these recent increases in electoral participation, participation rates in the United States still lag behind those of many other countries, including many that are underdeveloped, such as Ghana, Nicaragua, and Sri Lanka. In terms of voter turnout rates, the United States ranks 31st out of the 76 countries that held presidential elections between 2004 and 2014 (see Figure 12.3).[7] Turnout rates in American midterm elections are even lower relative to those in other countries' parliamentary elections. If we compare the turnout in the most recent parliamentary elections of the 114 countries that held such elections between 2004 and 2014, the United States' 2014 turnout ranked 113th, just above Nigeria.[8]

This difference between the United States and many other democracies does not mean that Americans are less politically engaged. Americans actually report a stronger attachment to their party than do citizens of other countries. Americans are also more likely to believe that what they say has an effect on politicians and government.[9] Instead, many of the rules that govern elections in America depress citizen participation. For one, the United States does not make voting compulsory, as do 28 other countries, including Argentina, Australia, Brazil, Singapore, and Turkey.[10] In many of these countries, citizens can be fined if they do not cast a ballot. Compulsory voting is

---

[6] Donald P. Green and Jennifer K. Smith. 2003. "Professionalization of Campaigns and the Secret History of Collective Action Problems." *Journal of Theoretical Politics* 15, 3: 321–39.

[7] The analysis was based on data obtained from the Institute for Democracy and Electoral Assistance. Only the most recent presidential election since 2004 was used for each country. Countries with populations smaller than one million or who were considered to be "not free" in the year of the election by Freedom House were excluded from the analysis.

[8] Only the most recent parliamentary election since 2004, which was not held at the same time as a presidential election, was used for each country.

[9] G. Bingham Powell, Jr. 1986. "American Voter Turnout in Comparative Perspective." *American Political Science Review* 80, 1: 17–43.

[10] Institute for Democracy and Electoral Assistance. "Voter Turnout Database." www.idea.int/vt/compulsory_voting.cfm (accessed 6/6/11).

FIGURE 12.3 Comparing Turnout in Presidential Elections, 2004–14

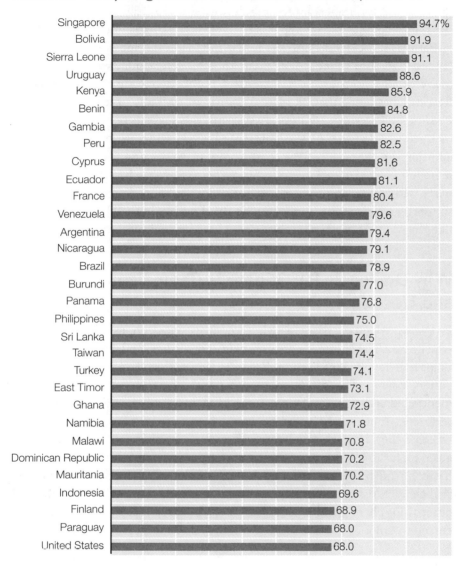

Country	Turnout
Singapore	94.7%
Bolivia	91.9
Sierra Leone	91.1
Uruguay	88.6
Kenya	85.9
Benin	84.8
Gambia	82.6
Peru	82.5
Cyprus	81.6
Ecuador	81.1
France	80.4
Venezuela	79.6
Argentina	79.4
Nicaragua	79.1
Brazil	78.9
Burundi	77.0
Panama	76.8
Philippines	75.0
Sri Lanka	74.5
Taiwan	74.4
Turkey	74.1
East Timor	73.1
Ghana	72.9
Namibia	71.8
Malawi	70.8
Dominican Republic	70.2
Mauritania	70.2
Indonesia	69.6
Finland	68.9
Paraguay	68.0
United States	68.0

Source: Institute for Democracy and Electoral Assistance, Voter Turnout Database.

estimated to increase turnout by 10 to 15 percentage points.[11] Second, Election Day in the United States occurs on a workday, while in many other countries it occurs on the weekend or a public holiday. Even though American employers are required by law to allow their employees to vote during

[11] André Blais. 2007. "Turnout in Elections," in *Oxford Handbook of Political Behavior*, eds. Russell J. Dalton and Hans-Dieter Klingemann. Oxford: Oxford University Press, pp. 621–35.

work hours without docking their pay, employees may be hesitant to ask for the time off. It is important to note, however, that holding elections on "rest days" instead of workdays appears to have only a small effect on turnout.[12]

Perhaps most significantly, as noted in Chapter 2, most elections in the United States use a winner-take-all method for determining winners, whereas many other countries use a system of proportional representation (PR). Research has found that PR increases turnout by 5 to 6 percentage points.[13] Because PR encourages multiparty systems, this suggests people may be more inclined to vote when they are presented with a wider variety of choices. In addition, PR makes elections more competitive because there are multiple members elected in each district. Since there is a good chance that any single party will win at least one seat, every party has an incentive to mobilize its supporters. In contrast, supporters of third parties in the United States feel like their vote is "wasted" if they cast a vote for their preferred party.

Why Do People Participate in Campaigns and Elections?

People who regularly participate in campaigns and elections differ from those who do not. They possess a greater *ability, motivation,* and *opportunity* to participate. The following section discusses factors that affect electoral participation, paying close attention to the forms of participation affected. As mentioned earlier, forms of electoral participation vary along a number of different dimensions, including how often they can be performed and whether they are performed with others. As a result, we cannot expect any given factor to affect every form of participation in the same way. Research has confirmed, however, that each of the following individual and contextual characteristics has an effect on participation *ceteris paribus*, meaning all other things being held equal. Within each subsection, the factors are discussed in order of the size of their impact on electoral participation.

Ability

The ability of an individual to participate in campaigns and elections depends a great deal on their education, income, and the amount of free time they have at their disposal. Although the reasons for these relationships might

---

[12] Blais, "Turnout in Elections," p. 627.

[13] André Blais and Agnieszka Dobrzynska. 1998. "Turnout in Electoral Democracies." *European Journal of Political Research* 33, 2: 239–61.

seem obvious, it is challenging to explain how and why education and income in particular matter for participation in elections.

Education Besides political interest, which is discussed later, a person's level of formal education is the strongest predictor of how much she will participate in politics overall. It seems to be especially important for forms of participation that are more time intensive and that require interacting with others.[14] The importance of education for participation has been well documented, but it is difficult to determine why it matters so much. The traditional view is that education provides citizens with the skills and resources necessary to participate in politics.[15] For example, primary and secondary education helps students understand how their democratic system functions, teaches them the importance of participating in that system by voting, and encourages students to discuss current events. These are, for example, the functions of high school civics classes. Primary and secondary education also increases students' aptitude as readers, writers, and speakers, which is also associated with electoral participation.[16] A spate of recent studies, however, show that attending college, by contrast, has more muted effects on participation because people who attend college are often already politically engaged.[17] Thus, even college coursework that focuses on political science or other social sciences has only a small impact on the likelihood of voting.[18]

Does this mean that a formal education is the only way to learn the skills necessary for electoral participation? Absolutely not. They can be learned in workplaces, churches, and other institutions that provide opportunities to organize events, put together presentations, or develop any other skill that is useful in politics. For example, churches have long fostered political activism in the black community by mobilizing and teaching civic skills. This is one reason black churches provided the organizational backbone of the civil rights movement. At the same time, however, educational attainment increases the chances that an individual will have access to the kind of job

---

[14] Verba, Schlozman, and Brady, *Voice and Equality*, p. 358.

[15] Verba, Schlozman, and Brady, *Voice and Equality*.

[16] D. Sunshine Hillygus. 2005. "The Missing Link: Exploring the Relationship between Higher Education and Political Engagement." *Political Behavior* 27: 25–47.

[17] Cindy D. Kam and Carl L. Palmer. 2008. "Reconsidering the Effects of Education on Political Participation." *Journal of Politics* 70, 3: 612–31; Steven Tenn. 2007. "The Effect of Education on Voter Turnout." *Political Analysis* 15, 4: 446–64; Adam J. Berinsky and Gabriel S. Lenz. 2011. "Education and Political Participation: Exploring the Causal Link." *Political Behavior* 33, 3: 357–73.

[18] Hillygus, "The Missing Link."

that teaches civic skills. For example, teachers and lawyers are more likely than blue-collar workers to acquire civic skills on the job.[19]

Income Income is another resource that enables individuals to participate in politics, although it matters much less than education for most forms of electoral participation. The one exception, unsurprisingly, is contributing to a political cause. For that form of participation, income is the strongest predictor of whether and how much individuals contribute. What is surprising, however, is that those with higher incomes are more likely to engage in every form of participation—even in protests, which are sometimes considered a "weapon of the weak." What is it about having a higher income that enables wealthier people to participate more than poor people? This answer is obvious for making a political contribution, but less so for other forms of participation. It is not that people with higher incomes have more free time. Careers that provide higher incomes, like those in medicine or law, typically provide very little free time. Another possibility is that people who have low incomes must spend more of their time and energy simply trying to get by. Indeed, once people achieve a comfortable standard of living, increases in income no longer increase their participation rates. When people feel they no longer must live from hand to mouth, they are more able to focus on other things, including politics.[20]

Free Time Although its effect on electoral participation is small compared to education, income, and the motivational factors we discuss later, having more free time on one's hands can lead to more electoral participation. This is especially true for forms of participation that require more of a time commitment such as working for a campaign.[21] As one might suspect, free time matters little for voting and donating since these forms of electoral participation can be performed relatively quickly.

Motivation

People who participate in an election not only possess the resources to do so but are also motivated to get involved. Motivations can be loosely grouped into two categories: those that are individual—such as a general interest

---

[19] Verba, Schlozman, and Brady, *Voice and Equality*, pp. 314–16.

[20] Raymond E. Wolfinger and Steven Rosenstone. 1980. *Who Votes?* New Haven, CT: Yale University Press, pp. 23–26.

[21] Verba, Schlozman, and Brady, *Voice and Equality*, p. 357, n. 40.

in politics—and those that are generated by the environment in which individuals live—such as a phone call from a campaign.

Political Interest The single most important individual-level factor affecting whether a person participates in campaigns and elections is **political interest**, which is simply a person's reported level of interest in government and public affairs. It matters the most for the willingness of a person to discuss the election with others, but it is also a strong predictor of whether one engages in forms of participation that require a time commitment such as attending a rally, as well as the decision to cast a ballot. It matters much less for donating to a candidate.

Although certain events can increase a person's political interest temporarily, it is a relatively stable characteristic that one either has or does not have.[22] Because it is stable over a person's lifetime, one must look to pre-adult factors to explain its origins. Parents can certainly pass their passion for politics on to their children, and formal education plays a role. Another source of political interest may be personality. Our basic personality traits can have an impact on how we think and act politically. For example, people who are open to new experiences—that is, those who are naturally curious and interested in learning—are significantly more likely to be interested in politics than people who are more conservative in their approach to life.[23] Recent research also suggests that genes may play a role in the creation of political interest.[24]

Political Knowledge Citizens vary substantially in how much they know about politics. This knowledge can take a variety of forms, including facts about how the political process works, familiarity with elected officials, and awareness of the current issues of the day. As a predictor of political participation, its effects are on par with formal education. It is a powerful predictor of voting and whether or not a person discusses politics, but it also matters for engaging in more time-intensive campaign activities. Interestingly, it has no effect on donating. Although political knowledge might appear to be a resource that increases one's ability to engage in politics, scholars usually treat

---

[22] Markus Prior. 2010. "You've Either Got It or You Don't? The Stability of Political Interest over the Life Cycle." *Journal of Politics* 72, 3: 747–66.

[23] Jeffery J. Mondak and Karen D. Halperin. 2008. "A Framework for the Study of Personality and Political Behaviour." *British Journal of Political Science* 38: 335–62.

[24] Robert Klemmensen, Peter K. Hatemi, Sara B. Hobolt, Axel Skytthe, and Asbjørn S. Nørgaard. 2012. "Heritability in Political Interest and Efficacy across Cultures: Denmark and the United States." *Twin Research and Human Genetics* 15, 1: 15–20.

it as an objective measure of how motivated a person is to participate in politics. It is an *objective* measure because a person must be able to answer a series of questions about politics correctly to demonstrate a high level of knowledge. In contrast, people need only claim to have a high level of political interest, which makes it a *subjective* measure of engagement. In general, people who are politically interested, better educated, wealthy, and white tend to have higher levels of political knowledge than those who are not. In addition, men are usually more politically knowledgeable than women.

Partisan Strength As discussed in Chapter 6, Americans typically identify with one of the two major parties or remain unaffiliated, referring to themselves as "independent." Partisan strength captures how strongly people identify with a party, with independents considered to be the weakest in partisan strength. It affects electoral participation because the more strongly a person identifies with a party, the more invested they are in its success. Overall, the size of partisan strength's effect on participation is less than education, political interest, and political knowledge, but roughly similar to income. It matters the most for voting, but also affects whether a person donates and discusses the campaign. Unlike political interest, partisan strength is unrelated to education, income, and gender, but age and personality seem to drive it. Partisan strength typically increases with age as people come to more strongly identify with a party. Personality affects partisan strength because some people have a stronger need to belong, as well as a stronger need for a structure to help them interpret their political world. Specifically, people who score high on extroversion (sociability), agreeableness (cooperative), and conscientiousness (high need for structure) are more likely to be partisans.[25]

Self-Interest People participate in politics because they derive some benefit from doing so. It can be a **material benefit**, meaning a person receives something tangible in exchange for participating. For instance, individuals may receive payment for collecting petition signatures to help get a candidate's name on the ballot. Individuals also participate in order to receive **solidarity benefits**, which are the intangible rewards that come from being part of a collective effort, such as friendship with fellow volunteers or status in the community. In addition, individuals may participate in order to receive **purposive benefits**, which consist of satisfaction for having advanced an issue

---

[25] Alan S. Gerber, Gregory A. Huber, David Doherty, and Conor M. Dowling. 2012. "Personality and the Strength and Direction of Partisan Identification." *Political Behavior* 34, 4: 653–88.

or ideological position, or for having fulfilled a duty. Ultimately, participating in a political campaign or election could bring all of these benefits, as participants benefit tangibly from getting paid for their work, enjoy the camaraderie among those working for the campaign, and feel good for having helped a worthy candidate.

Contextual Factors

Although our own particular qualities or characteristics affect our willingness to participate in politics, the broader environment in which we live also affects our participation. We consider two types of contextual effects: those related to campaign activities and those related to an individual's social context. In general, contextual factors have a weaker effect on electoral participation than most of the individual characteristics discussed earlier, but they are still important determinants of participation. Campaign mobilization activities can be especially effective at turning out voters who are on the verge of participating but just need an extra nudge. There is very little research on how environmental factors affect different forms of participation, so here we discuss their effect on participation in general.

Direct mobilization is often difficult and time-consuming work, but it is an effective way to encourage citizens to turn out at the polls. Here, a member of the Alaska Democratic Party goes door-to-door along an icy road in support of Senator Mark Begich's reelection campaign in 2014.

Mobilization The most important environmental factor promoting electoral participation is mobilization. **Mobilization** refers to the range of activities that candidates, parties, activists, and interest groups engage in to encourage people to participate. These activities usually occur during a campaign, but groups can mobilize citizens at other times and for reasons besides electing a candidate. They can encourage citizens to support certain legislation by writing letters to their members of Congress, or to show up at a town hall meeting to oppose an action of their city council. To be sure, the goal of those who mobilize is not simply to increase civic participation. It is to use that participation to achieve certain ends, such as the election of a candidate. Thus, groups target their mobilization efforts at those who share their goals.

Individuals and groups seeking to mobilize citizens do so directly and indirectly. They mobilize directly when they contact citizens and encourage them to act. They mobilize indirectly by using the social networks in which citizens are embedded to reach them, including workplaces, churches, schools, labor unions, neighborhood associations, and large national organizations such as the National Rifle Association (NRA) or the American Association of Retired Persons (AARP). During a campaign, for example, candidates seek the endorsement of community groups and national organizations in the hope that an endorsement will encourage group members to vote for the endorsed candidate. This saves the candidate some effort, not only because the groups assume some of the costs of communicating with their members but also because group members are more likely to trust recommendations from group leaders than direct appeals from candidates themselves.

Mobilization efforts work because people respond when someone asks them to get involved. This may be because people are flattered by the request, like the idea of being involved in a collective effort, or find it difficult to say no and then feel they must follow through once they have committed. Groups seeking to mobilize members of a community are likely to focus their attention on individuals who are already active in their community. Active people have two qualities that mobilizers appreciate. First, they are easy to reach because they belong to a variety of organizations. Second, they are more likely to be influential when they do participate because they have a large social network and greater status in their community. Similarly, mobilization efforts are likely to target those with more education and higher incomes.

As we noted earlier, much of the decline in turnout in presidential elections between 1960 and 1996 occurred because campaigns abandoned traditional mobilization activities, such as neighborhood canvassing. Instead, they turned to television advertising to communicate with voters.[26] Television advertisements, however, are not particularly effective at mobilizing voters. For example, eligible voters in media markets that witness a slew of presidential advertisements are no more likely to vote than those who live in markets that see no such advertisements. It does not make much difference whether the ads are predominantly positive (promoting a candidate) or negative (attacking a candidate). Although some commentators worry that negative advertising drives down turnout, as citizens' distaste for attacks makes them feel alienated from politics, the sum of the evidence suggests that negative advertising does not affect turnout in any consistent fashion.[27]

What are the most effective mobilization strategies? Research to date has found that the specific message used in mobilization activities does not matter a great deal. For example, reminding citizens that voting is their civic duty seems to be no more or less effective than reminding them that the election will be close and so "every vote counts." There is some evidence, however, that threatening to reveal a person's voting history to neighbors or to publish a list of voters in the local paper can be effective.[28] In general, how voters are contacted is much more important for mobilization than message content. One of the most effective strategies is in-person contact, as we noted in Chapter 5. Contacting eligible voters by having someone knock on their door and remind them to vote increases turnout by about 8 percentage points, according to one study. Telephone calls, which are somewhat less personal, have a smaller effect, and then only when the phone call seems "authentic"—a quality better provided by enthusiastic volunteers or trained professionals. A phone call that seems scripted or, worst of all, is merely a recorded message has little effect on turnout. Even more impersonal forms of communication, such as postal mail and e-mail, also seem to have little effect.[29]

The effects of campaign mobilization on citizens depend on the underlying capacity and motivation of citizens to participate. Citizens who are already

[26] Steven J. Rosenstone and John Mark Hansen. 1993. *Mobilization, Participation, and Democracy in America*. New York: Macmillan.

[27] Richard R. Lau, Lee Sigelman, and Ivy Brown Rovner. 2007. "The Effects of Negative Political Campaigns: A Meta-Analytic Reassessment." *Journal of Politics* 69, 4: 1176–1209.

[28] Alan S. Gerber, Donald P. Green, and Christopher W. Larimer. 2008. "Social Pressure and Voter Turnout: Evidence from a Large-scale Field Experiment." *American Political Science Review* 102(1): 33–48; Costas Panagopoulos. "Affect, Social Pressure and Prosocial Motivation: Field Experimental Evidence of the Mobilizing Effects of Pride, Shame and Publicizing Voting Behavior." *Political Behavior* 32, 3: 369–86.

[29] Donald P. Green and Alan S. Gerber. 2008. *Get Out the Vote!* 2nd ed. Washington, DC: Brookings Institution Press.

very interested in politics are typically unaffected by mobilization because they are already likely to vote. Citizens who have little interest in politics are also unaffected because no mobilization effort is likely to convince them to participate. Instead, it is citizens in the middle: those with some interest in politics who are often on the verge of voting but do not always end up making the effort. These citizens may need a reminder to vote, and campaigns can provide that.[30]

Starting in the 1998 midterm elections, the Democratic Party and its affiliated interest groups began to shift resources from advertising to voter outreach. The success enjoyed by the Democrats in the 1998 and 2000 elections led the Republican Party to focus more of their resources on voter outreach as well. As a result, 2004 saw unprecedented mobilization efforts by both parties—efforts that actually built on some of the mobilization research results we have described. This heightened focus on mobilization continued in 2008 and 2012. Thus, it is no accident that electoral participation has surged in recent presidential election years.

Social Contexts Family, friends, classmates, coworkers, and neighbors can all affect one's decision to participate by providing information, such as how to find the polling place where one is to vote. They also provide models from which individuals learn—either directly, as when a teacher educates students about American government, or indirectly, as when people become inspired by politically active role models and decide on their own to get involved in politics. Moreover, as we noted, people can decide to participate for the solidary benefits of participation: because they enjoy interactions with other people, such as their fellow volunteers on a campaign. We refer to the people with whom an individual communicates and interacts as that person's **social context**.

One of the most important social contexts for a child is the family. Parents can help to inculcate political interest and efficacy in their children. Some of this happens through mimicry. When children come of age politically, they may vote in part because they watched their parents vote. But besides providing modeling for their children, parents can deliberately try to instill political interest in their children. One important way they do this is simply by talking about politics. Conversations at the dinner table help to communicate parents' interest in politics to their children, who will then be more likely to become interested in politics themselves. Parents

---

[30] Kevin Arceneaux and David Nickerson. 2009. "Who Is Mobilized to Vote? A Re-Analysis of Eleven Randomized Field Experiments." *American Journal of Political Science* 53, 1: 1–16.

Conducting Voter Mobilization Experiments during Campaigns

One challenge for political scientists studying the mobilizing effects of campaigns has been in gaining access to real campaigns where they can run experiments. In the 1998 midterm elections, Alan Gerber and Donald Green decided to test the effectiveness of campaign tools, such as mailing postcards, phone calls, and in-person visits, in getting voters to the polls. Partnering with the League of Women Voters, Gerber and Green split the residents of New Haven, Connecticut, into three groups that each received one of the following treatments: a postcard encouraging them to vote, a phone call with the same message, or an in-person visit. For comparison purposes, a fourth group received no contact. After the election, Gerber and Green examined voting records to see who had actually voted. They found that turnout among people who had received an in-person visit was 9.8 percent higher than among those receiving no contact. Postcards yielded less than a 1 percent boost in turnout, while telephone calls had no effect whatsoever.

When Gerber and Green's study was published in 2000, it attracted the attention of campaign practitioners. Hal Malchow and Mike Podhorzer, campaign consultants for the American Federation of Labor and Congress of Industrial Organizations (AFL-CIO), recognized the importance of the Gerber and Green study for their work and conducted experiments during the 2004 presidential election to test how different types of campaign appeals affected AFL-CIO members. After 2004, Malchow and Podhorzer invited other Democratic political operatives to meet at regular lunches to share research on campaign effects. They called their unofficial group the Analyst Institute. In 2007, the Analyst Institute became an official consulting firm, describing itself as "a clearinghouse for evidence-based best practices in progressive voter contact."[1]

Under the leadership of a new executive director, Todd Rogers, the Analyst Institute began to conduct research challenging some of the conventional wisdom among political practitioners. For example, they found that simply asking people about their voting plans significantly boosts turnout, especially among people living alone: their turnout jumps by 10 percent. Rogers speculates that the reason is that adults living together talk through their plans to vote with each other, which helps them envision casting a ballot. A campaign worker can play the same role for people living alone, encouraging them to think through how they will get to the polls.

The Analyst Institute is not the only group running experiments in campaign mobilization these days. For instance, Rock the Vote has found that e-mail and text messages sent by well-known celebrities to young people encouraging them to vote are *less* effective than those with bland "senders," such as "Election Center."

In 2012, the Obama campaign fully embraced the experimental ethos and hired the Analyst Institute. As a result, the campaign soon found itself breaking conventional campaigning rules: they bought ads sporadically and six months out from the election, as well as ran a slew of ads with different campaign messages. Although some observers found this behavior puzzling, those who knew where to look could see the experimental method behind the madness.

[1] Analyst Institute. www.analystinstitute.org (accessed 6/6/11).

Source: Sasha Issenberg. 2010. "Nudge the Vote." *New York Times*, October 31, MM28; Sasha Issenberg. 2012. "How Obama's Embrace of Empiricism Could Swing the 2012 Race." *Slate*, May 22.

The family is an important influence on whether individuals participate in elections and politics in general. Children often follow the models provided by their parents' political participation.

who adhere to the convention of not discussing politics at the dinner table might be decreasing the chances that their children will be interested in politics.[31]

Another important social context is schools, as we have already noted when discussing the role of formal education. Taking part in certain types of high school activities, particularly those that emphasize student government and community service, make young people more interested in politics and likely to participate as adults. Although participating in sports teams does not have the same effect, high school activities that emphasize public performance, such as debate and drama, also appear to promote political

[31] Verba, Schlozman, and Brady, *Voice and Equality*; Molly W. Andolina, Krista Jenkins, Cliff Zukin, and Scott Keeter. 2003. "Habits from Home, Lessons from School: Influences on Youth Civic Development." *PS: Political Science and Politics* 36, 2: 275–80; Hugh McIntosh, Daniel Hart, and James Youniss. 2007. "The Influence of Family Political Discussion on Youth Civic Development: Which Parent Qualities Matter?" *PS: Political Science & Politics* 40, 3: 495–99.

participation.[32] We can see the effects of nonathletic high school activities irrespective of a student's family income or the education level of their parents.[33] This suggests that cutting them from high school curriculums, as many school districts across the nation are doing, may have troublesome consequences for the future political participation of younger generations. Families and schools are particularly important because they open up avenues for children to think about politics at a time when there is no formal way for them to participate. They cannot vote until they are 18, for example, and generally lack other opportunities to participate meaningfully in political life.[34] It is no wonder that a recent survey of ninth graders found that they did not believe politics would affect them until they were older.[35]

Later in life, social context continues to matter. Getting married can profoundly alter how often a person participates politically because the spouse becomes the central figure in that person's social context. In general, marital transitions (getting married or divorced, or becoming widowed) depress electoral participation in the short term as individuals adjust to their new personal circumstances. In the long term, the participation rates of married people converge, with spouses becoming more similar in, for example, whether and how often they vote.[36]

Social context also matters at the level of communities. In particular, people who feel as if they belong to a community are also likely to feel empowered and to participate. By contrast, those who feel alienated or marginalized may withdraw politically. For example, studies have found that poor individuals living in wealthy communities are less likely to vote than those living in poor communities.[37] A number of studies have also shown that Democrats and Republicans living in "enemy territory"—communities

---

[32] Daniel A. McFarland and Reuben J. Thomas. 2006. "Bowling Young: How Youth Voluntary Associations Influence Adult Political Participation." *American Sociological Review* 71, 3: 401–25; Jacquelynne S. Eccles and Bonnie L. Barber. 1999. "Student Council, Volunteering, Basketball, or Marching Band: What Kind of Extracurricular Involvement Matters?" *Journal of Adolescent Research* 14: 10–43; Paul A. Beck and M. Kent Jennings. 1982. "Pathways to Participation." *American Political Science Review* 76, 1: 94–108.

[33] McFarland and Thomas, "Bowling Young."

[34] Virginia Sapiro. 2004. "Not Your Parents' Political Socialization: Introduction for a New Generation." *Annual Review of Political Science* 7: 1–23.

[35] James G. Gimpel, J. Celeste Lay, and Jason Shuknecht. 2003. *Cultivating Democracy: Civic Environments and Political Socialization in America*. Washington, DC: Brookings Institution Press.

[36] Laura Stoker and M. Kent Jennings. 1995. "Life-Cycle Transitions and Political Participation: The Case of Marriage." *American Political Science Review* 89, 2: 421–33.

[37] R. Robert Huckfeldt. 1979. "Political Participation and Neighborhood Social Context." *American Journal of Political Science* 23, 3: 579–92.

dominated by the opposing party—are also less likely to participate and discuss politics than their counterparts living in friendlier areas.[38] Even young people living in areas that have a significantly older population are less likely to vote than young people living among a younger population.

Finally, a type of context that is even broader than community is an individual's generation. Different **generational cohorts**—people who came of age politically at about the same time—can have distinctive patterns of electoral participation. This is not necessarily because of direct interaction with others in their generation. Instead, distinctive patterns arise from the norms of behavior and the levels of civic and political engagement that were pervasive when that generation came of age. For example, people who came of age during the Great Depression and World War II were part of what has sometimes been called the Greatest Generation, the most civically and politically active generation of the twentieth century—one that stayed politically involved throughout their lives, even long after the Great Depression and World War II had ended. In contrast, Baby Boomers—those born between 1946 and 1964—have been less engaged in civic life and politics, even though many of them came of age in the 1960s and witnessed the civil rights movement and the Vietnam War protests up close. Subsequent generations—those sometimes referred to as "Generation X," "Generation Y," and "Millennials"—have continued the trend and are even less interested in politics than Baby Boomers.[39]

Why have later generations been less politically engaged than the "long civic generation" of the 1930s and '40s? One factor is technological change, beginning with the rapid arrival of television. In 1950, less than 10 percent of American households had a television set. By 1960, over 90 percent did. Between 1965 and 1995, the average number of hours Americans spent watching television per week increased from approximately 9 to 15 hours.[40] Television offers citizens alternative ways to spend their leisure time that often compete with other activities, such as volunteering for a local organization or participating in politics. One study estimates that every additional hour of television viewing per day is associated with a 10 percent reduction in

---

[38] James Gimpel, Joshua Dyck, and Daron Shaw. 2004. "Registrants, Voters and Turnout Variability across Neighborhoods." *Political Behavior* 26, 4: 343–75; Robert Huckfeldt and John Sprague. 1995. *Citizens, Politics, and Social Communication: Information and Influence in an Election Campaign*. New York: Cambridge University Press.

[39] Robert D. Putnam. 2000. *Bowling Alone: The Collapse and Revival of American Community*. New York: Simon & Schuster, pp. 250–51.

[40] Putnam, *Bowling Alone*, p. 222.

civic activism.[41] The arrival and penetration of the Internet, mobile phones, video games, and personal audio devices, such as iPods, may be having a similar effect. Today, young people spend as much time with these new forms of media as they do watching television: more than 30 hours per week.[42]

Changes in values may also explain why more recent generations are less likely to engage in politics than earlier ones. One value that has been embraced more broadly in recent generations is materialism.[43] Members of Generation X—those born between 1965 and 1979—are more likely than Baby Boomers or members of the World War II generation to say that having "a lot of money" is necessary for having a "good life."[44] They are also less likely to feel strong ties to their neighborhoods, churches, and local communities. Those with a preoccupation with earning money and a lack of connection to the community have little reason to become involved in civic activities or to vote.[45] The passing away of older, more participatory generations and their replacement by newer generations with different sets of priorities does not bode well for the future of civic and electoral participation in the future.

Opportunity

People may have the ability and motivation to participate, but still not do so because they lack the opportunity. They might not be eligible to participate, or the costs of participating—how difficult and time-consuming it is—may be too steep. As we discussed in Chapter 2, one must be an American citizen of at least 18 years of age to vote. These requirements for voting are far less stringent than in earlier periods of history, when women, African Americans, and other groups were barred from voting. The primary groups excluded today include the country's 75 million children and its 13 million permanent residents who work, live, and pay taxes here but are not citizens. Forty-eight states also bar felons from voting and 12 of these states bar ex-felons—those that have served their time in prison—from voting. These felon disenfranchisement laws prevent 6 million Americans from voting. Although these groups cannot vote, they can participate in elections in other

---

[41] Putnam, *Bowling Alone*, p. 228.

[42] Victoria Rideout, Ulla Foehr, and Donald Roberts. 2010. *Generation M2: Media in the Lives of 8- to 18-Year-Olds.* Menlo Park, CA: Kaiser Family Foundation, p. 2. www.kff.org /entmedia/upload/8010.pdf (accessed 4/12/11).

[43] Wendy M. Rahn and John E. Transue. 1998. "Social Trust and Value Change: The Decline of Social Capital in American Youth, 1976–1995." *Political Psychology* 19, 3: 545–65.

[44] Putnam, *Bowling Alone*, pp. 272–73.

[45] Putnam, *Bowling Alone*.

ways, such as by volunteering for a campaign. For eligible Americans, the costs of voting depend on the costs entailed in each step—registering to vote and casting a ballot.

Voter Registration In most states, if one is not registered one cannot vote. As discussed earlier in this chapter, it is unusual for a developed democracy to make citizens responsible for registering, which adds an additional cost to voting. This extra burden, however, is no accident. Voter registration was enacted by Progressive era reformers in the early twentieth century (see Chapter 3). They sought to challenge the political machines, whose power derived from their ability to mobilize immigrants and the urban working poor. The Progressives believed—often with good reason—that these machines were corrupt and that the methods by which they achieved high rates of turnout among immigrants and the poor were corrupt as well. They also believed that the vote choices of uneducated and illiterate people were manipulated by party bosses. Requirements for voter registration were intended to help prevent fraud by requiring citizens to appear periodically before local officials to verify their eligibility.

Both the timing of registration and the magnitude of registration requirements affect the cost of voting. The earlier a person must register before an election, the more difficult the process becomes because it is easier to remember to register when Election Day is near. Furthermore, if a person must travel to a distant location to register, that also imposes a cost. At present, no state has a registration closing date more than 31 days before an election. Similarly, the National Voting Rights Act of 1993, also known as the **Motor Voter Act**, requires states to allow voters to register when they are applying for a driver's license and public assistance programs, such as food stamps, or to allow Election Day registration. As a result, the costs of registering are now lower than they have been at any time since registration laws were first enacted. However, the Motor Voter Act did not significantly increase turnout in presidential or midterm elections. This raises the question of whether further weakening registration laws would actually increase turnout.[46] One registration reform that has been shown to lower the costs of voting is allowing voters to register at the same time that they vote. Same-day registration, as it is called, increases state-level turnout by approximately 5 percentage points.[47]

---

[46] Benjamin Highton. 2004. "Voter Registration and Turnout in the United States." *Perspectives on Politics* 2: 507–15.

[47] Highton, "Voter Registration and Turnout in the United States," p. 509.

Voting There are other costs associated with actually casting a ballot. About 85 percent of the people who are registered typically vote. What prevents the remaining 15 percent from getting to the polls? One possibility is that they do not know where their polling place is. Some states mail citizens polling place information or sample ballots, especially helpful in boosting the turnout rates for the less educated and the young.[48]

Many states have tried to boost turnout by experimenting with ways of making the act of voting itself easier. **Convenience voting** refers to methods by which registrants can vote without actually casting a ballot at a polling place on Election Day. One way to make voting easier is to allow citizens to mail in their ballots. Every state now offers some form of **absentee voting**, which enables citizens to vote by mail-in paper ballot prior to Election Day. Twenty states, however, require individuals to state a reason for why they cannot vote in person, while the remaining states and the District of Columbia allow voters to apply for an absentee ballot without justifying their request. Seven of these states, as well as the District of Columbia, make it even easier to cast an absentee ballot by allowing any citizen to request to receive one for every future election.[49] Oregon and Washington have gone a step further by requiring all citizens to **vote by mail**. In these states, county administrators automatically mail out ballots to registered voters approximately three weeks before an election. Voters can either return the ballot by mail or drop it off at a designated location. Aside from absentee ballots and voting by mail, some states allow citizens to vote a week or two early at county elections offices or designated voting centers. A handful of other states allow voters to vote over the phone or to submit their ballot by fax. Currently, no state allows people to vote over the Internet.

Convenience voting is designed to make voting less costly and to increase turnout. Although some earlier studies conducted in the 1990s suggested it had little effect on turnout, recent research using more sophisticated methods suggests that it does have an effect. Specifically, states adopting early voting with polls opening 45 days before an election saw a 3.1 percent increase in turnout, while those adopting no-excuse absentee voting saw an increase of 3.2 percent.[50] Voting by mail also appears to increase turnout.

---

[48] Raymond E. Wolfinger, Benjamin Highton, and Megan Mullin. 2005. "How Postregistration Laws Affect the Turnout of Citizens Registered to Vote." *State Politics & Policy Quarterly* 5, 1: 1–23.

[49] National Conference of State Legislatures. 2014. "Absentee and Early Voting." www.ncsl .org/default.aspx?tabid=16604 (accessed 6/11/14).

[50] Jan E. Leighley and Jonathan Nagler. 2014. *Who Votes Now?* Princeton, NJ: Princeton University Press, p. 116.

Still, it does so not among the most unengaged eligible voters but among the "low-hanging fruit"—those who need only a nudge to actually cast a ballot.[51]

Recently, many states have instituted voter identification laws that make voting somewhat less convenient. These laws require voters to show certain forms of identification at polling stations in order to vote. They are typically implemented in the interest of reducing voter fraud. As we have learned, people who vote are educated and politically engaged, so they are likely to learn about voter identification laws and to figure out how to comply with them. This is borne out by numerous studies that have found the implementation of voter identification laws to have a minimal impact on turnout.[52] Yet, even if such laws are relatively harmless, those who oppose them argue that they are unnecessary since there is very little evidence of voter fraud in the United States.[53]

Electoral Competitiveness Thus far, our discussion of opportunity has focused on voting, but there are many other ways to participate politically, especially in campaigns. One factor that affects the opportunity to engage in these other forms of participation is the competitiveness of the election. When elections are close, candidates, parties, and interest groups have an incentive not only to encourage voters to participate but also to create more opportunities for participation. For example, a person who lives in a battleground state during a presidential election has ample opportunity to attend candidate events, help canvass neighborhoods, and call friends, because presidential candidates set up campaign organizations in these states specifically to create such opportunities. Similarly, when a House or Senate race is competitive, candidates will provide the citizens of that district or state with more opportunities to participate.

Participating Online As mentioned at the start of this chapter, campaigns have been using the Internet to increase opportunities for participation. Candidates for major offices use their websites to provide supporters a means to donate money, pledge their time and effort, and sign up for alerts about

---

[51] Adam J. Berinsky, Nancy Burns, and Michael W. Traugott. 2001. "Who Votes by Mail? A Dynamic Model of the Individual-Level Consequences of Voting-by-Mail Systems." *Public Opinion Quarterly* 65, 2: 178–97.

[52] Jason D. Mycoff, Michael W. Wagner, and David C. Wilson. 2009. "The Empirical Effects of Voter-ID Laws: Present or Absent?" *PS: Political Science & Politics* 42, 1: 121–26; R. Michael Alvarez, Delia Bailey, and Jonathan Katz. 2007. "The Effect of Voter Identification Laws on Turnout." Social Science Working Paper. California Institute of Technology, pp. 1–27.

[53] Lorraine Minnite. 2010. *The Myth of Voter Fraud*. Ithaca, NY: Cornell.

further opportunities to get involved. Candidate websites usually ask supporters to provide their zip codes so they will receive news about opportunities within their communities.

The Internet also allows citizens to connect and create participatory events on their own. One example is Howard Dean's use of Meetup.com to keep supporters connected during his campaign for the presidency in 2004. Meetup made it possible for supporters to organize events at places, such as coffee shops and bars, where they could bring their friends and tell them about Dean. When Dean announced his candidacy in June 2003, he had just 3,000 supporters on Meetup, but by mid-November he had more than 140,000 supporters on the site and had raised over $15 million from them. Once the primaries began, supporters used Meetup to organize meetings where they would write letters to voters in key primary states, and to organize trips to those states to actively campaign. Dean's campaign may have faltered in the end, but his innovative use of social networking set a precedent and multiplied the opportunities for Americans to participate by making it easier for citizens to customize and localize events.

Group Differences in Electoral Participation

The factors that encourage electoral participation reinforce one another. For example, people with more education are likely to have higher incomes and jobs where they can develop the confidence and skills that facilitate electoral participation.[54] Their education and jobs also ensure that they are embedded in social networks through which they are likely to be mobilized. In addition, their education and income make it more likely that they will access the Internet and learn about opportunities to participate in a campaign. Understanding how these factors reinforce one another illuminates why certain groups in America are more likely to participate and why others are not. And when these groups have policy preferences that are unrepresentative of the general population, it creates participatory distortions because elected officials will pay more attention to their concerns.

Figure 12.4 illustrates group differences in electoral participation. It is important to note, however, that this figure is based on reported behavior in elections. Although researchers have long observed that reported political participation in surveys is higher than actual participation, recent research has demonstrated that certain kinds of people are more likely to misrepresent their behavior. Specifically, people who feel the most pressure to vote are

[54] Verba, Schlozman, and Brady, *Voice and Equality.*

FIGURE 12.4 Self-Reported Voting in the 2012 Presidential Election

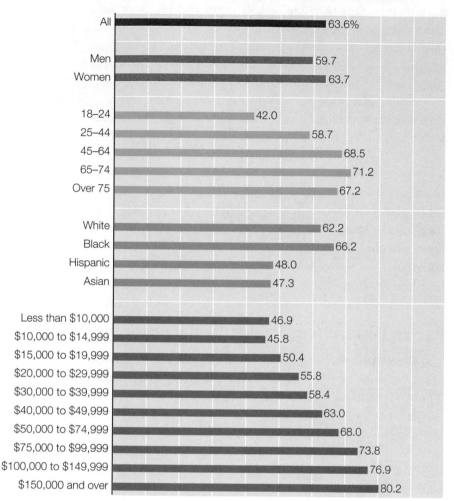

All	63.6%
Men	59.7
Women	63.7
18–24	42.0
25–44	58.7
45–64	68.5
65–74	71.2
Over 75	67.2
White	62.2
Black	66.2
Hispanic	48.0
Asian	47.3
Less than $10,000	46.9
$10,000 to $14,999	45.8
$15,000 to $19,999	50.4
$20,000 to $29,999	55.8
$30,000 to $39,999	58.4
$40,000 to $49,999	63.0
$50,000 to $74,999	68.0
$75,000 to $99,999	73.8
$100,000 to $149,999	76.9
$150,000 and over	80.2

Source: Current Population Survey Voting and Registration Supplement, 2012.

the most likely to lie about not voting. Who feels the most pressured to vote? They are the same types of people who do vote: those who are older, educated, wealthy, and politically engaged.[55] As a result, the differences in reported voting across education and income in particular, and to a lesser extent age, are very likely exaggerated. Interestingly, however, race and marriage are unrelated to over-reporting, but men are significantly more likely than women to lie about not voting. Unfortunately, it is extremely difficult

[55] Stephen Ansolabehere and Eitan Hersh. 2012. "What Big Data Reveal about Survey Misreporting and the Real Electorate." *Political Analysis* 20, 4: 437–59.

to validate a person's reported voting behavior, so political scientists working with surveys often must take a person's word at face value.

Here we describe some of the more important group differences in electoral participation, drawing on the discussion in the previous section to explain them. In the next section, we turn to a discussion of whether these differences matter for election outcomes and government policies.

The Wealthy and the Poor

An especially large disparity in voter turnout exists between those with high and low incomes. For example, in 2012 the reported turnout among citizens making more than $75,000 per year was almost 30 percentage points higher than those making less than $20,000 (77 versus 46 percent). From a certain perspective, this inequality makes little sense. The poor should be less satisfied with the political institutions and policies that make it so difficult for them to get ahead, and thus they should participate more. Meanwhile, the wealthy should be content with the status quo, since they have benefited from it. Yet this is clearly not the case for the reasons we have discussed: wealthier people typically have more education and a professional career that provides them with skills that are useful in politics. They are also embedded in large social networks that encourage their participation and can be easily reached by those seeking to mobilize them.[56]

The Old and the Young

As discussed earlier, young people are much less likely to participate than older people. In 2012, 41 percent of people ages 18 to 24 reported voting compared to 72 percent of those 65 and over. What explains this lower rate of participation among the young? First, young people move around a lot. With each move, they must re-register, which increases the cost of voting.[57] Their mobility also makes them more difficult to mobilize, because they are harder to track. Young people are also undergoing many other transitions—leaving school, getting married, starting new jobs, having children—that in the short term may depress participation because of the physical and psychological commitments they entail.[58] Of

[56] Verba, Schlozman, and Brady, *Voice and Equality.*

[57] Benjamin Highton. 2000. "Residential Mobility, Community Mobility, and Electoral Participation." *Political Behavior* 22, 2: 109–20; M. Margaret Conway. 2000. *Political Participation in the United States.* 3rd ed. Washington DC: CQ Press.

[58] John M. Strate, Charles J. Parrish, Charles D. Elder, and Coit Ford III. 1989. "Life Span Civic Development and Voting Participation." *American Political Science Review* 83: 443–64; Philip E. Converse and Richard Niemi. 1971. "Non-Voting among Young Adults in the United States," in *Political Parties and Political Behavior,* ed. William J. Crotty et al., 2nd ed. Boston: Allyn & Bacon.

Young people are much less likely than older Americans to vote. In recent years, groups like Rock the Vote have sought to mobilize young voters. Here, Talib Kweli performs at a Rock the Vote event.

these, the first two—leaving school[59] and getting married[60]—appear to depress turnout the most. As people settle into their jobs and marriages over time, and as their children become less dependent on them, the costs associated with political participation decrease. Independent of such life transition effects, however, aging has a strong positive effect on political participation. Although scholars are still debating why this is the case, many believe it can be explained by pure learning—that is, as one ages, one becomes more knowledgeable about the political system and how to engage with it. An accumulation of life experience also seems to spur engagement.[61]

---

[59] Benjamin Highton. 2001. "The First Seven Years of the Political Life Cycle." *American Journal of Political Science* 45, 1: 202–9.

[60] Laura Stoker and M. Kent Jennings. 1995. "Life-Cycle Transitions and Political Participation: The Case of Marriage." *American Political Science Review* 89, 2:421–433.

[61] M. Kent Jennings and Laura Stoker. 1999. "The Persistence of the Past: The Class of 1965 Turns Fifty." Presented at the annual meeting of the Midwest Political Science Association; Rosenstone and Hansen, *Mobilization, Participation, and Democracy in America*.

Whites and Non-Whites

Over time, certain groups in the United States have become more likely to participate, demonstrating that participatory inequalities are not immutable. Before the adoption of the 1965 Voting Rights Act, African American turnout was understandably poor due to discriminatory laws that effectively disenfranchised black Americans, especially in the South. The Voting Rights Act empowered the federal government to take over voter registration in southern states to ensure that African Americans could vote. This legislation quickly yielded results. Within 20 years, the gaps in registration rates between blacks and whites in the South—which had been 50 percentage points or higher in Mississippi, North Carolina, and Alabama—dropped to less than 10 points.

Today, African Americans vote at virtually the same rate as whites. Whites were 3 percent more likely to vote than blacks in 2000 and 5 percent more likely in 2004, but the voting rates of the two groups were identical in 2008 and the African American voting rate actually surpassed that of whites in 2012 (66 versus 62 percent). To put this in perspective, the difference in reported turnout between whites and Latinos was 18 percent in 2004, 16 percent in 2008, and 14 percent in 2012.[62] In 2012, blacks actually were significantly *more* likely than whites to report attending a meeting or rally for a candidate, displaying a lawn sign or bumper sticker, or working for a campaign. And for the first time, African Americans made campaign donations at the same rate as whites in 2012 (17 versus 16 percent, respectively), although they almost certainly contributed less money overall than whites due to their lower income. The electoral participation rates of blacks are especially remarkable because of their lower income and because they are typically less educated than whites. Part of the explanation for black electoral activism is mobilization that occurs in black churches. A more recent explanation has to do with the excitement surrounding the presidency of Barack Obama.

Latinos and Asian Americans participate at lower rates than blacks and whites. This is notable because these are the fastest growing minority groups in the country—in fact, Latinos are now the largest minority group (having surpassed African Americans), accounting for 17 percent of the population. However, ethnicity per se does not explain the lower participation rates of Latinos and Asian Americans. Lower levels of education and income are more important, as are the struggles with mastering the English language that immigrants often face.[63]

---

[62] Current Population Survey Voting and Registration Supplement, 2012.

[63] Wendy K. Tam Cho. 1999. "Naturalization, Socialization, Participation: Immigrants and (Non-)Voting." *Journal of Politics* 61: 1140–55.

Men and Women

Women were excluded from voting in most American states until passage of the Nineteenth Amendment in 1920. Today, women vote at a slightly higher rate than men, again demonstrating that participatory inequalities can be erased. In 2012, 64 percent of women reported voting, compared to 60 percent of men. The gap is especially large between unmarried men and women in particular: in 2012, only 46 percent of unmarried men reported voting, compared to 55 percent of unmarried women.[64] There are few disparities between men and women in whether they attend political meetings or work for campaigns. The traditional gender gap emerges in other areas: men are more likely than women to report donating and discussing politics, and to actually run for elected office. Men typically have higher salaries than women, which explains why they would donate more. The difference in engagement in political discussions may arise because men also report more interest in politics, demonstrate higher levels of political knowledge, and appear to be more comfortable engaging in the kinds of heated exchanges that political discussion often entails.[65] Another factor may be the perception that politics is a "man's world." When women do hold high-profile offices, girls become more interested in politics.[66] Thus, having few women in office may create a vicious cycle whereby young girls do not develop as great an interest in politics and then do not run for office themselves, perpetuating the underrepresentation of women in political office. See Chapter 5 for a more detailed discussion of some of the factors that lead women not to run for office.

Are Voters Representative of Nonvoters?

Would politics in America be dramatically different if everyone voted? The first question to answer is whether the same candidates would be elected. The second question is whether, once elected, those candidates would

---

[64] U.S. Census Bureau. 2012. "Table 9. Reported Voting and Registration, by Marital Status, Age, and Sex: November 2012." www.census.gov/hhes/www/socdemo/voting /publications/p20/2012/tables.html (accessed 6/12/14).

[65] Sidney Verba, Nancy Burns, and Kay Lehman Schlozman. 1997. "Knowing and Caring about Politics: Gender and Political Engagement." *Journal of Politics* 59: 1051–72; Stacy G. Ulbig and Carolyn L. Funk. 1999. "Conflict Avoidance and Political Participation." *Political Behavior* 21, 3: 265–82.

[66] David E. Campbell and Christina Wolbrecht. 2006. "See Jane Run: Women Politicians as Role Models for Adolescents." *Journal of Politics* 68: 233–47. See also Lonna Rae Atkeson. 2003. "Not All Cues Are Created Equal: The Conditional Impact of Female Candidates on Political Engagement." *Journal of Politics* 65, 4: 1040–61.

advance the same kinds of policies. If the answer to one or both of these questions is "yes," then it is evidence of a participatory distortion.

The conventional wisdom regarding the relationship between turnout and electoral outcomes is that higher turnout benefits Democratic candidates because nonvoters are more Democratic. Although the latter is true, research has demonstrated that increases in turnout do not consistently favor one party over the other.[67] The reason is, as we mentioned in Chapter 10, that few elections are close enough for high turnout to make a difference.

The relationship between turnout and policy (as opposed to candidate) outcomes, however, appears to be much stronger. Although an early seminal study on the topic concluded that in terms of issue preferences, "voters are virtually a carbon copy of the citizen population," evidence has been mounting that this is not always the case.[68] The relationship between turnout and policy preferences depends on the nature of the policy. Figure 12.5 shows that the differences between voters and nonvoters are relatively small on values issues such as gun control, the death penalty, legalizing marijuana, affirmative action, and abortion, but they are often quite large with respect to economic issues, especially spending priorities.[69] For example, while 82 percent of voters in 2012 favored reducing the budget deficit, just 62 percent of nonvoters did. In general, nonvoters are more in favor of government spending than voters, except in the case of spending on science and technology, which voters are more likely to favor (49 versus 39 percent). The one economic policy where we see little difference between voters and nonvoters involves the question of whether to increase taxes on millionaires. This small difference is very likely due to the fact that most people approve of such a tax.

These differences affect policy outcomes, however, only if elected officials ignore the preferences of nonvoters or discount them heavily. The evidence largely suggests that they do. Members of Congress are much more likely to vote in line with the preferences of voters than nonvoters in their district.[70] This is because voters tend to vote for people who share their values and views. Voters are also better at communicating their preferences to elected

---

[67] Jack Citrin, Eric Schickler, and John Sides. 2003. "What if Everyone Voted? Simulating the Impact of Increased Turnout in Senate Elections." *American Journal of Political Science* 47, 1: 75–90.

[68] Wolfinger and Rosenstone, *Who Votes?* p. 109.

[69] This analysis is modeled on Leighley and Nagler, *Who Votes Now?* chap. 6. They reach similar conclusions using earlier data from the American National Election Study and Annenberg National Election Study.

[70] John D. Griffin and Brian Newman. 2005. "Are Voters Better Represented?" *Journal of Politics* 67, 4: 1206–27.

FIGURE 12.5 Policy Preferences of Voters and Nonvoters in 2012

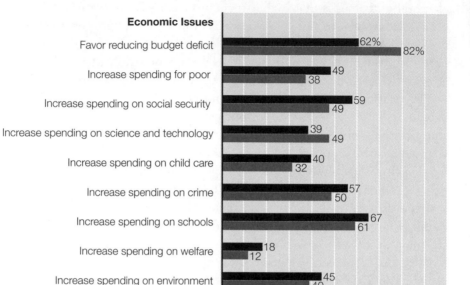

Difference   Voter   Nonvoter

Economic Issues

Favor reducing budget deficit — 62% / 82%

Increase spending for poor — 49 / 38

Increase spending on social security — 59 / 49

Increase spending on science and technology — 39 / 49

Increase spending on child care — 40 / 32

Increase spending on crime — 57 / 50

Increase spending on schools — 67 / 61

Increase spending on welfare — 18 / 12

Increase spending on environment — 45 / 40

Favor a millionaire's tax — 75 / 77

Average Difference — 8.7

Values Issues

Ban all abortions — 16 / 11

Favor more gun control — 49 / 45

Better if women stay in home — 43 / 47

Favor affirmative action in universities — 12 / 14

Government should help blacks — 16 / 17

Oppose death penalty — 73 / 73

Marijuana should be legal — 39 / 39

Average Difference — 2.3

Source: American National Election Study 2012 Time Series Study. Both face-to-face and Internet samples were used with appropriate weights to calculate these percentages.

officials than nonvoters. Finally and unsurprisingly, elected officials pay more attention to voters than nonvoters simply because they want to get reelected.

As we've discussed, nonvoters also tend to have lower incomes than voters, and research shows that proposed government policies are much more likely to become law when they are supported by the economically advantaged.[71] In fact, when low-income and middle-income Americans have different policy preferences than those with high incomes, research shows their preferences are largely ignored.[72] The influence of the wealthy may result from the greater frequency with which they contact their representatives, and the frequency and size of their donations to the representatives' campaigns. The fact that wealthy individuals are better organized than poor and middle class Americans is very likely a factor as well.

Conclusion

Political participation comes in a wide array of forms. Turnout in elections—as the most obvious and, in some ways, least demanding form of participation—captures the most attention. Turnout in the United States is low compared to other countries and actually declined from 1960 to 1996. In recent elections, however, turnout has increased, due in part to the mobilization efforts of presidential campaigns.

Of course, one might ask why anyone participates in politics at all. Some would argue that the costs of electoral participation outweigh its benefits.[73] After all, the likelihood that a citizen's vote will decide the outcome of an election is infinitesimal. Part of the story is that citizens may value participation in politics for other reasons. Citizens receive a variety of nontangible benefits from participation that make it enjoyable—such as a sense of satisfaction for fulfilling their civic duty or for helping a cause or candidate they believe in.

---

[71] Larry Bartels. 2008. *Unequal Democracy: The Political Economy of the New Gilded Age.* New York/Princeton, NJ: Russell Sage Foundation/Princeton University Press.

[72] Martin Gilens. 2005. "Inequality and Democratic Responsiveness." *Public Opinion Quarterly* 69, 5: 778–96.

[73] Andrew Gelman, Gary King, and W. J. Boscardin. 1998. "Estimating the Probability of Events That Have Never Occurred: When Is Your Vote Decisive?" *Journal of the American Statistical Association* 93: 1–9; Donald Green and Ian Shapiro. 1994. *Pathologies of Rational Choice Theory.* New Haven, CT: Yale University Press, chap. 4; John Ferejohn and Morris Fiorina. 1974. "The Paradox of Not Voting: A Decision Theoretic Analysis." *American Political Science Review* 68: 525–36; William H. Riker and Peter C. Ordeshook. 1974. "A Theory of the Calculus of Voting." *American Political Science Review* 62: 25–42; Anthony Downs. 1957. *An Economic Theory of Democracy.* New York: Harper & Row.

What affects the participation of those citizens who do involve themselves in campaigns and elections? We have suggested that ability, motivation, and opportunity are important factors. Ability is related to formal education, financial resources, free time, and the civic skills acquired at work and through involvement in community groups. The motivation to participate stems from an interest in politics and the encouragement that one receives from the prevailing social context and from candidates, parties, and groups who engage in mobilization. The role of social context suggests that participation is, in a sense, contagious. Parents who care about politics and vote are more likely to have children who are politically engaged than are parents who do not care or vote. Politically active spouses spur their partners to participate. People who are politically active also encourage other people in their social networks to participate. The role of mobilization demonstrates that campaigns themselves can affect the decision to vote and the decision to participate in the election in other ways. In fact, even mobilization efforts are contagious: when campaigners knock on a door and remind someone to vote, it makes other eligible voters in that household more likely to vote.[74] As we noted at the outset of this chapter, campaigns can matter not simply by persuading people how to vote, but by persuading them to vote.

Finally, having the ability and motivation to participate is not enough if one does not have the opportunity. In the case of voting, one has the opportunity to participate if one is eligible to vote and has registered. For other forms of participation, opportunities to participate are more likely to arise when elections are closer. Thus, citizens living in competitive jurisdictions will find themselves with ample opportunity to participate, while those living in noncompetitive jurisdictions will find they have fewer opportunities to flex their democratic muscles.

As we first noted in Chapter 2, political participation is intrinsic to many conceptions of what "good" elections look like. One such conception privileges the ideal of political equality. Egalitarians lament participatory distortions because they can produce electoral outcomes and policies that are not representative of what the general population wants. Yet, studies that have examined such questions argue that if all nonvoters participated, only some electoral outcomes and policies would change. The reason why only "some" would change is that an election must be close for the participation of nonvoters to make a difference, and close elections are becoming rarer in the United States. Beyond election outcomes, there is growing evidence that government is more responsive to those who participate than

---

[74] David Nickerson. 2008. "Is Voting Contagious? Evidence from Two Field Experiments." *American Political Science Review* 102, 1: 49–57.

to those who do not. Thus, the way that members of Congress vote appears to reflect the preferences of voters more than the preferences of nonvoters and the preferences of the wealthy more than the preferences of the poor.[75]

Such findings do raise important concerns about the quality of American democracy. At the same time, however, we must think critically about whether participatory equality is the most important ideal for elections and how it should be balanced with other ideals. Those who support imposing restrictions on voter registration claim that they prevent voter fraud and corruption and mitigate how much political parties can manipulate the electoral process. Moreover, some argue that it is more important for citizens to vote in an informed manner than for all citizens to vote. In this view, it is actually worse if more people participate but do not know a lot about the candidates or the issues facing the country. Needless to say, these debates cannot be resolved easily, but as we try to understand them, it is useful to recognize that increasing electoral participation entails trade-offs between competing values.

KEY TERMS

electoral participation (p. 332)

participatory distortion (p. 332)

get-out-the-vote (GOTV) efforts (p. 336)

political interest (p. 341)

material benefit (p. 342)

solidarity benefits (p. 342)

purposive benefits (p. 342)

mobilization (p. 344)

social context (p. 346)

generational cohort (p. 350)

Motor Voter Act (p. 352)

convenience voting (p. 353)

absentee voting (p. 353)

vote by mail (p. 353)

FOR DISCUSSION

1. How much does it matter for the quality of democracy if certain groups of citizens participate more in the political process than others?

2. How can voting be made more convenient for young people?

3. Are you interested in politics? If so, who or what encouraged your interest?

4. Do you benefit from participating in politics? How?

5. Looking ahead to 2016, what new techniques do you think candidates will use to mobilize citizens?

---

[75] Griffin and Newman, "Are Voters Better Represented?"; Bartels, *Unequal Democracy*, chap. 9.

CHAPTER 13

Voter Choice

On December 23, 2012, the *Boston Globe* ran an extensive story analyzing the 2012 presidential election. The bottom line? "[Mitt] Romney's problems went deeper than is widely understood. His campaign made a series of costly financial, strategic, and political mistakes that, in retrospect, all but assured the candidate's defeat, given the revolutionary turnout tactics and tactical smarts of President Obama's operation." "Democrats," the article reported, "followed the trail blazed in 2004 by the Bush campaign which used an array of databases to 'microtarget' voters and a sophisticated field organization to turn them out. Obama won in part by updating the GOP's innovation." This praise for the strategic prowess of the Obama campaign was commonplace. It was easy for commentators to think of all the smart decisions that Obama had made, and equally important, the bad decisions that his opponent, Mitt Romney, had made — most notably, allowing the Democrats to define him as an out-of-touch millionaire during the late spring and early summer of 2012.

But two months before the elections, a group of political scientists offered models that attempted to forecast the election's outcome. The models are based on an understanding of how voters incorporate factors such as the state of the economy and presidential approval into their choices. As we discussed in Chapter 9, these factors are largely outside either candidate's control but still powerfully affect presidential election outcomes. The August 2012 models estimated that Obama would receive 51.9 percent of the vote, on average. In fact, he received 50.6 percent, so the average forecast of the models, as well as the individual forecasts, were fairly close. More famously, former baseball statistics guru Nate Silver, blogging at fivethirtyeight.com for the *New York Times*, pegged Obama's vote at 50.8 percent in late August, calculating that the president's probability of reelection was about 70 percent. To be sure, election forecasting models are not always this accurate. In 2000, for example, the models predicted that Gore would receive about 56 percent of the vote, but in fact he received just over 50 percent. Still, more often than not, the political science models get it right — even though they do not take account of the general election campaign.

That presidential elections are so predictable flies in the face of many media accounts of presidential campaigns. These accounts often portray the election's outcome as uncertain, which helps create a dramatic narrative in which crucial voters are on the fence and every twist and turn of the campaign — even a single misstatement in a debate — could make the difference between winning and losing. More to the point, the predictability of presidential elections calls into question the importance of the campaign itself. If the campaign matters, how can presidential elections be forecast with such accuracy, even months before the election? Do Americans cast their votes based largely on broader economic and political realities, and not on campaign messages and events?

In this chapter, we focus on voters and their decisions about which candidates to support. We begin by exploring the reasons behind voting decisions. Our starting point is a fact we have highlighted through this book: many Americans do not follow politics very closely. As a consequence, their voting decisions are not based on a wealth of information about the candidates. Instead, American voters are more likely to rely on shortcuts and rules of thumb when making a decision. They tend to vote for parties that are aligned with the social groups to which they belong. They develop an attachment to the party itself, one that serves as a standing decision in elections for all levels of office. Most voters, but particularly those who don't pay attention to politics and do not have strong partisan attachments, take stock of the performance of the incumbent party, especially with respect to the economy, and reward or punish it accordingly. Thus, voting decisions often depend on long-standing social and political identities or evaluations of things that the candidates themselves cannot change.

Core of the Analysis

- Many Americans are not especially attentive to election campaigns and tend to rely on simple strategies for deciding among candidates.
- Individuals tend to develop a psychological attachment to a political party, and this attachment colors opinions about political issues and candidates.
- Appraisals of national conditions (especially state of the economy) are important factors for presidential vote choice.
- Campaigns can affect voters' decisions, but mainly when voters do not have preexisting views and when one candidate outspends another by a wide margin.
- Thus, campaigns are more likely to activate the partisan predispositions of voters than they are to persuade voters.

In 2000, models created by political scientists predicted that Al Gore would receive around 56 percent of the popular vote and win the election. However, he received just over 50 percent of the popular vote and lost in the Electoral College. What factors influence voters' decisions, and how can we understand them?

Does this mean, then, that political campaigns are irrelevant? Not at all. Campaigns remind people of their underlying attachments, thereby leading them to vote for the party or candidate they are naturally predisposed to support. But, as we discussed in Chapter 8, actual persuasion — changing someone's mind — is less common. Even so, under the right conditions, campaigns can move enough voters to shift the outcome of an election. We discuss several of those conditions in this chapter, such as how familiar the candidates are to citizens, and the balance of resources among the competing candidates. We conclude by considering whether the voting decisions of Americans are in line with democratic ideals.

What Influences Vote Choice

By and large, Americans do not spend a great deal of time following politics. This is true even in presidential elections, when politics seems extraordinarily salient. In surveys conducted in every presidential election from
1952 to 2012, fewer than half of Americans said that they were "very interested in the current campaign" (Figure 13.1). This has two implications.
First, as we have discussed, campaigns may have difficulty attracting the
attention of potential voters, some of whom might prefer watching football
or reality television, for example. This is one reason why many scholars are
skeptical about the ability of campaigns to persuade voters and shape election outcomes. Second, Americans may not have a detailed understanding
of the party platforms or the positions of the candidates running for office.
Their choices in elections may therefore depend on more limited information, and especially on factors that enable them to make choices relatively
quickly and easily. In the following sections, we consider five factors that
influence vote choice: social identities, party identification, the performance of incumbents, policy issues, and candidate traits.

FIGURE 13.1 How Interested Are Americans in Political Campaigns?

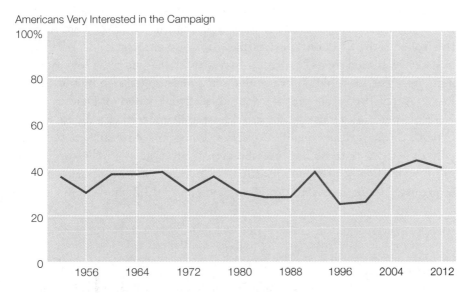

Americans Very Interested in the Campaign

Source: Data are from the American National Election Studies Cumulative Files, 1952–2012. Data are available at
www.electionstudies.org/nesguide/toptable/tab6d_6.htm (accessed 8/5/14).

Social Identities

In the aftermath of the wave of fascism that took hold in parts of Europe in the 1930s and 1940s, social scientists became fascinated with the potentially persuasive power of political communication. Some wondered, for example, whether people were easily swayed by propaganda, such as in a speech or radio broadcast, and whether propaganda might have allowed leaders like Adolf Hitler to gain and maintain power. In particular, scholars at Columbia University embarked on an innovative project, identifying a random sample of citizens in small communities—Elmira, New York, and Erie County, Ohio—and interviewing them multiple times during a presidential campaign.[1] These **panel studies** allowed researchers to understand how individuals changed their opinions in response to campaign activity.

In fact, the studies found that the campaign itself had little impact on citizens. Many citizens did not appear terribly knowledgeable about or interested in politics. They were not very responsive to the campaign or its mass media outreach. Instead, they maintained attitudes about the candidates that did not change much over time. Those whose attitudes did change—most often, from being undecided about the candidates to making a choice—tended to move in a predictable direction: toward the candidate that the individual was already predisposed to support.[2]

Why were voters predisposed to support a particular candidate in the first place? These studies revealed a crucial fact about voters' political attitudes: the attitudes depended on **social identities**. That is, voters were aligned with political parties because of class background, ethnicity, or religion. In part, this reflects the attention parties pay to group interests: the party that best serves the interests of a group may attract the enduring loyalty of its members. For example, in every election since the passage of the Voting Rights Act of 1965, about 90 percent of blacks have voted for Democrats. In 2012, 93 percent of black voters voted for the Democratic candidate Barack Obama. Similarly, the Republican Party's promotion of socially conservative policies—such as those limiting abortion—have garnered the support of most evangelical Christians. In 2012, 78 percent of white born-again or evangelical Christians voted for Romney. Figure 13.2 shows how various

---

[1] Bernard R. Berelson, Paul F. Lazarsfeld, and William N. McPhee. 1954. *Voting: A Study of Opinion Formation in a Presidential Campaign*. Chicago: University of Chicago Press; Paul Lazarsfeld, Bernard Berelson, and Helen Gaudet. 1948. *The People's Choice*. New York: Columbia University Press.

[2] The same finding emerged in a later study of the 1980 presidential campaign. See Steven Finkel. 1993. "Reexamining the 'Minimal Effects' Model in Recent Presidential Campaigns." *Journal of Politics* 55: 1–21.

FIGURE 13.2 2012 Presidential Vote by Social Groups

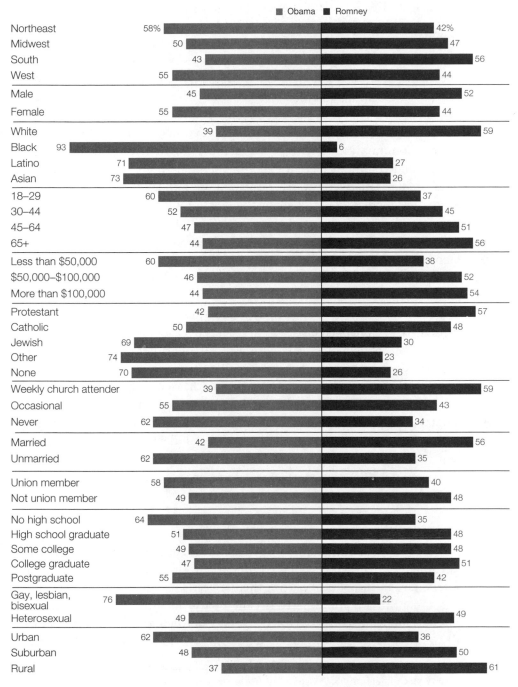

Source: 2012 National Election Pool exit poll, conducted by Edison Media Research (*N*=17,836 respondents).

social groups voted in 2012. These numbers shift from election to election, but many of the basic demographic contours of the vote have been in place since the 1960s.

Of course, voters who identify with a social group will not always automatically vote for the political party most aligned with that group. They may need some sort of "reminder"—one that essentially says: "People like you should vote for this candidate." The Columbia scholars argued that the degree to which those surveyed voted according to social identity often depended on their having contact and conversation with other members of their social group. Communication with other members of their church, workplace, school, and community often exposes potential voters to more politically interested and engaged voters—so-called **opinion leaders**. As the election nears, these individuals talk about the election in ways that rekindle long-standing allegiances. In the 1948 presidential election, for example, some wavering Democrats came to support the Democratic nominee, Harry Truman, when opinion leaders within Catholic churches and labor unions explained how Truman was for the "little guy," while Thomas Dewey was just another business-friendly fat cat.[3]

For voters who do not always pay much attention to politics, social identities serve as a relatively easy way to reach a decision. It does not take much information to align one's vote with a social identity. Moreover, any information necessary to do so may come without any effort on the part of the voter, perhaps just a brief conversation with a coworker or friend. And because we often trust coworkers and friends more than, say, political candidates, we will view their opinions as particularly credible. Explanations of voting that emphasize the importance of social identities implicitly suggest that campaigns have minimal effects on how voters vote, except insofar as they supply information that helps voters connect their social identities to their choices in a particular election.

Party Identification

Perhaps social identities are not the most important identities when it comes to voting. It might be that a more influential factor is the identification that voters have with political parties themselves. This idea of a psychological attachment to a political party is called **party identification**. The concept was developed by scholars at the University of Michigan drawing on nationally representative surveys conducted during the 1952 and 1956 elections.[4]

---

[3] David McCullough. 1993. *Truman*. New York: Simon & Schuster.

[4] Angus Campbell, Philip E. Converse, Warren E. Miller, and Donald E. Stokes. 1960. *The American Voter*. Chicago: University of Chicago Press.

TABLE 13.1 Parent-Child Party Identification Correspondence

	1958	1976	1992
Democrats	79%	62%	57%
Republicans	72%	56%	56%

Note: "Correspondence" refers to the percentage of partisan identifiers whose parents share their affiliation.
The parental party identification question was last asked by ANES for the 1992 study.
Source: Data are from the American National Election Studies Cumulative Files, 1952-2008.

Party identification does not mean identification with particular political ideologies or opinions. For example, to identify as a Democrat is not the same as identifying as a liberal. Nor can party identification be equated with how you are registered to vote or even how you vote at the ballot box, although it is highly correlated with each. Instead, party identification is like other social identities. We feel that we are a member of a group ("I am a Democrat" or "I am a Republican"), and we tend to feel positively about that group. So we cheer when our "team" wins and the other loses.

Where does party identification come from? It is learned relatively early in life, primarily from those who are closest to us for the most extended periods of time. Thus, our parents are the dominant influence on our party identification, although this tendency appears to be weakening (see Table 13.1). In 1992, a little less than 60 percent of citizens identified with the same party as their parents. Besides parents, other people and institutions—such as friends, schools, and churches—can also shape party identification.

The prevailing political context at the time that one comes of age also matters: people who enter young adulthood when a president is popular will be more likely to identify with the president's party than people who come of age when the president is unpopular. For example, young people who came of age when Ronald Reagan was president are still more likely to be Republicans than those who came of age under the unpopular and scandal-ridden Richard Nixon.[5] Regardless of its sources, party identification is typically formed by young adulthood. Because it is learned so early, it is a durable attitude. People tend not to change much, even as they grow

---

[5] Scott Keeter, Juliana Menasce Horowitz, and Alec Tyson. 2008. *Gen Dems: The Party's Advantage among Young Voters Widens*. Washington, DC: Pew Research Center for the People and the Press. http://pewresearch.org/pubs/813/gen-dems (accessed 7/22/10).

up, learn more, and see their circumstances evolve. In short, with party identification, where you end up depends in large part on where you start.

Of course, this discussion raises an important question: Does everyone develop a party identification? What about those people who identify as "independent"? To assess the true number of political independents, it is important to consider how party identification is typically measured. In a survey, respondents will be asked a question such as "Generally speaking, do you consider yourself a Republican, a Democrat, or an Independent?" If respondents identify as Republican or Democrat, they are then asked, "Would you call yourself a strong or a not very strong Republican/Democrat?" Respondents who say they are "independent" or express no preference are then asked, "Do you think of yourself as closer to the Republican or Democratic Party?" These questions measure the direction and intensity of party identification and are used to create a seven-point scale: 1. Strong Democrat; 2. Weak Democrat; 3. Leans Democrat; 4. Independent; 5. Leans Republican; 6. Weak Republican; 7. Strong Republican.

As measured by responses to the first in this series of questions, the number of independents (those who do not call themselves Republicans or Democrats) is rising: from 23 percent of Americans in 1952 to 40 percent in 2008.[6] But nearly all political independents think of themselves as closer to one party. Only 11 percent do not "lean" toward a party and could be considered "pure" independents—and, as Figure 13.3 shows, this percentage has actually declined since the mid-1970s. Moreover, independents who lean toward a party are almost as likely to support that party's candidates as those voters who call themselves Republicans or Democrats.

For those studying elections, party identification matters for three reasons. First, it functions as a filter or screen through which information must pass. In other words, we tend to accept information that comes from the party we identify with, or from sources closely identified with that party, and to discount information coming from sources on the other side.[7] This is why, as we noted in Chapter 9, partisans routinely think that their party's presidential nominee won every general election debate. Second, party identification also helps motivate people to vote; stronger partisans are more likely to vote than weak and leaning partisans, who in turn are more likely to vote than independents.

---

[6] See American National Election Studies. 2010. "Party Identification 7-Point Scale, 1952–2008. www.electionstudies.org/nesguide/toptable/tab2a_1.htm (accessed 4/13/11).

[7] Philip Converse. 1962. "Information Flow and the Stability of Partisan Attitudes." Public *Opinion Quarterly* 26: 578–99.

FIGURE 13.3 Trends in Party Identification, 1952–2012

A. **Democratic Party Identification**

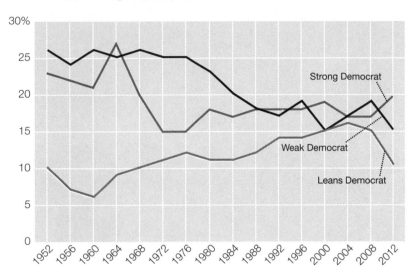

B. **Republican Party Identification**

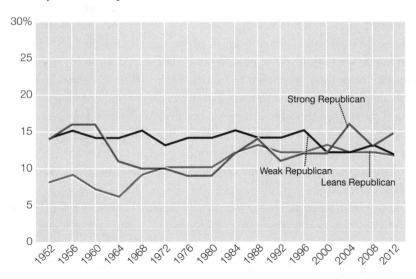

FIGURE 13.3 (continued)

C. **Independent Party Identification**

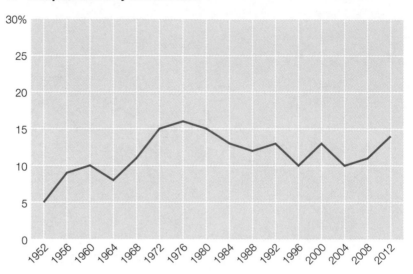

Source: Data are from the American National Election Studies Cumulative Files, 1952–2012.

Finally, and perhaps most important, party identification is a powerful predictor of how citizens vote. In presidential elections, approximately 90 percent of Democrats and Republicans vote for their respective party's nominee. Many races at other levels of office, such as for the U.S. House and Senate, also see high levels of party loyalty. In fact, partisan loyalty has been increasing over time, as shown in Figure 13.4.[8] To be sure, party loyalty is not an absolute. From time to time, partisans defect and vote for a candidate of the opposite party—for example, because that candidate is a talented incumbent who has no credible challenger. But defections are the exception rather than the rule. Because of this, campaigns typically try to reinforce partisan loyalties among their followers and to persuade independents to vote for their candidate.

Like social identities,[9] party identification functions as a useful shortcut for political decision making, especially when voters are not particularly

---

[8] Larry M. Bartels. 2000. "Partisanship and Voting Behavior." *American Journal of Political Science* 44, 1: 35–50.

[9] Some scholars see party identification as a social identity. For example, see Donald Green, Bradley Palmquist, and Eric Schickler. 2004. *Partisan Hearts and Minds*. New Haven, CT: Yale University Press.

FIGURE 13.4 Percentages of Self-Identified Partisans Voting for Their Party's Candidate in Presidential Elections, 1980–2012

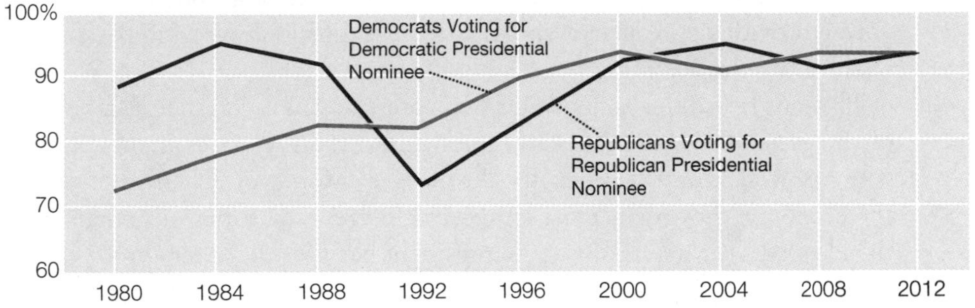

Source: Data are from the American National Election Studies Cumulative Files, 1952–2012.

well-informed about the candidates. Thus, party identification is particularly useful in races where voters know little about the candidates except for their party affiliation.

Incumbent Performance

A third factor in many voters' decisions is the performance of the incumbent party or officeholder. The most important criterion in evaluating performance is the state of the economy. When the economy is growing, voters tend to reward the incumbent party.[10] For example, an incumbent president is more likely to be reelected when the country is prosperous. But when the economy is growing slowly or not at all, voters tend to punish the incumbent president or, if that person is not running, the nominee of the incumbent party. As we discussed in Chapters 9 and 10, macroeconomic variables, such as changes in the average income of Americans, predict presidential and even congressional election outcomes. This lends credence to the idea that economic performance is a major factor when voters go to the polls.

How do voters use their perceptions about the economy to decide how to vote? For starters, voters rely more on their evaluations of how the economy has performed in the past rather than how it might perform in the future. Using past performance to decide between candidates is called **retrospective voting**, and is often encapsulated by a single question: "Are we better off now

---

[10] See, for example, Ray C. Fair. 1978. "The Effect of Economic Events on Votes for President." *Review of Economics and Statistics* 60: 159–72; Michael Lewis-Beck and Thomas W. Rice. 1992. *Forecasting Elections.* Washington, DC: CQ Press; Edward R. Tufte. 1978. *Political Control of the Economy.* Princeton, NJ: Princeton University Press.

than when the incumbent took office?" While basing one's voting decisions on the answer to this question may appear simpleminded, it is plausible that past performance predicts future performance.[11] In this way, retrospective voting provides an efficient shortcut for citizens looking to make choices about future leadership.

Previous research also indicates that voters rely more on their assessments of the national economy (**sociotropic voting**) than on assessments of their own financial situation (**pocketbook voting**).[12] Moreover, when voters assess the economy, they focus most on recent changes and, especially, changes in the election year itself.[13] Even if a president has presided over three years of a weak economy, if the economy shows strong growth in his fourth year, he is likely to be rewarded by the electorate. In this sense, voters are somewhat nearsighted: they see nearby, or more recent, economic events more clearly than events that occurred further in the past.

We should also note that voters' evaluations of the economy are affected by their party identification. In this sense, party identification creates bias in evaluations. When a Democrat is president, Democrats evaluate the economy more positively than do Republicans. Republicans exhibit this same tendency when a Republican is president. And even if partisans do pick up on more objective information about the economy, this does not mean that negative economic assessments will cause them to defect from their party's candidates. Nearly 90 percent of Republicans voted for John McCain in 2008, even though the vast majority of them believed that the economy was weak under the incumbent Republican administration. Ultimately, because partisans tend to judge more generously the performance of their officeholders, it is independent voters whose vote choice is most influenced by the incumbent party's handling of the economy.

Finally, incumbent performance often becomes more important as Election Day nears, as the campaigns tend to focus heavily on it.

Policy Issues

In a typical campaign, candidates spend a great deal of time talking about issues relating to government policy, such as the regulation of environmental pollution or the future solvency of Social Security and Medicare. When

---

[11] Morris P. Fiorina. 1981. *Retrospective Voting in American Elections.* New Haven, CT: Yale University Press.

[12] Donald Kinder and D. Roderick Kiewiet. 1981. "Sociotropic Politics: The American Case." *British Journal of Political Science* 11: 129–61.

[13] Larry Bartels. 2008. *Unequal Democracy.* Princeton, NJ: Princeton University Press.

voters make choices, do they factor these sorts of issue positions into their decision?

In Chapter 5, we introduced the median voter theorem, which posits that candidates take issue positions that are close to the hypothetical median voter, whose support is necessary to win the election. The median voter theorem assumes that voters make choices in a particular way: they evaluate the candidates' ideologies or their positions on issues and then choose the candidate who, on average, has positions most similar to their own. This strategy is called **proximity voting**—voters choose the candidates whose views are closest or most proximate to theirs.

Does proximity voting actually happen? Is voting really about "the issues"? In general, it is not. The strategy of proximity voting takes more time and effort than the other simple shortcuts that we have described. Voters do not often invest this kind of time and effort. To vote based on policy issues, voters first need to have opinions about those issues. But they often do not pay enough attention to politics to form opinions, especially about complex public policies. Even if they do have opinions, they may not pay enough attention to the campaign to discern where the candidates stand and which candidate is most proximate to them. Moreover, candidates do not always make their views clear. As we discussed in Chapter 5, candidates may have an incentive to be ambiguous.

One recent study estimated that less than half of the electorate has the requisite opinions on issues along with sufficient knowledge of candidates' views to engage in issue voting.[14] When issue voting does occur, it is usually limited to a particular group of voters within the broader electorate. These groups are called *issue publics*, and consist of voters who are more likely to have strong opinions about a particular issue, to learn where the candidates stand on this issue, and to vote for a candidate only if that candidate agrees with them. An example would be senior citizens, who are especially attentive to protecting their current Medicare benefits. However, this seems to be the exception and not the rule. Furthermore, there is some evidence that rather than voting based on policy, voters are more likely simply to adopt the policy positions of the candidates they already support based on party identification.[15]

---

[14] Michael Lewis-Beck, William Jacoby, Helmut Norpoth, and Herbert Weisberg. 2008. *The American Voter Revisited*. Ann Arbor: University of Michigan Press, chap. 8.

[15] Gabriel Lenz. 2009. "Learning and Opinion Change, Not Priming: Reconsidering the Evidence for the Priming Hypothesis." *American Journal of Political Science* 53, 4: 821–37.

Candidate Traits

Candidates spend a great deal of time promoting not only their views but also their biographies and personal qualities. Do voters draw on their perceptions of candidates' personal qualities, such as appearance or personality, when making decisions in an election? At one level, this seems a simple strategy that would not demand much time or effort on the part of voters. They could merely get an impression of the candidates as people, perhaps from television advertising or candidate debates, and then use this impression to select the candidate that seems the stronger leader, more honest, better looking, and so on. Indeed, conventional accounts of political campaigns often draw attention to personal qualities. In 1960, Democrat John F. Kennedy was considered youthful, energetic, but perhaps a bit inexperienced. His Republican opponent, Richard Nixon, was considered experienced and knowledgeable, but not especially trustworthy. In 1992, Republican president George H. W. Bush was considered honest and experienced, but out of touch with the problems of ordinary Americans. Many believe that Bush's image as a man detached from the people became fixed when he seemed perplexed by a price scanner in a grocery store during a campaign event. The Democratic challenger, Bill Clinton, on the other hand, was thought to be intelligent and compassionate (he told a crowd during the campaign: "I feel your pain") but not very honest. In 2008, Barack Obama was considered youthful, intelligent, and inexperienced (like his fellow Democrats Kennedy and Clinton), while John McCain's image as a maverick unafraid to buck the system was undermined by voter concerns about his age and temperament.

But do such qualities matter? There is some evidence that they do. For example, better-looking candidates appear to get more votes than less attractive opponents do. Similarly, the more positively people assess a candidate's personality—including traits such as honesty or capacity for leadership—the more likely they are to vote for the candidate.[16] Candidates also suffer when scandals, especially those involving allegations of official corruption, cast doubt on their character.[17] Other specific negative trait perceptions—Al Gore's untrustworthiness in 2008 and Sarah Palin's incompetence in 2012—have

---

[16] Chappell Lawson, Gabriel S. Lenz, Andy Baker, and Michael Myers. 2010. "Looking Like a Winner: Candidate Appearance and Electoral Success in New Democracies." *World Politics* 62, 4: 561–93; Donald R. Kinder, Mark D. Peters, Robert P. Abelson, and Susan T. Fiske. 1980. "Presidential Prototypes." *Political Behavior* 2, 4: 315–37.

[17] Tim Fackler and Tse-min Lin. 1995. "Political Corruption and Presidential Elections, 1929–1992." *Journal of Politics* 57, 4: 971–93; Daron R. Shaw. 1999. "A Study of Presidential Campaign Event Effects from 1952 to 1992." *Journal of Politics* 61: 387–422.

been damaging to particular candidates in presidential elections.[18] In addition to individual personalities, party images also seem to influence how voters see candidates' characteristics; certain traits are more likely to be "owned" by Democratic candidates (empathy) and others are more likely to be owned by Republican candidates (leadership).[19] Democrats who are able to establish themselves as strong leaders and Republicans who project caring appear to do relatively better at the ballot box.

At the same time, other evidence suggests that a candidate's appearance and personality may matter much less, and may be dependent on the nature of the race. For instance, one recent study demonstrates that attractive candidates tend to run in races where they have a better chance of winning.[20] Thus, if attractive candidates get more votes than less attractive candidates, it is unclear whether it was because of attractiveness or because the race was simply easier to win. The same logic may extend to other attributes of candidates, such as their personalities. A candidate's appearance or personality will typically matter most when there is little other information to draw on, such as in smaller races that feature unfamiliar candidates and attract little media coverage. In races where there is much more information—such as a presidential race—it is less clear that people's evaluations of the candidates' personalities actually decide their vote. In such races, people may have a preferred candidate for other reasons—especially because of party identification—and thus evaluate their party's candidate more favorably. Such biases are not absolute, however. In 2012, many Republicans rated Obama as more likely to care about "people like me." And many Democrats rated Romney as a stronger leader than Obama. Nevertheless, 90 percent of both Democrats and Republicans voted for their party's nominee, despite any misgivings.

How Do Campaign Consultants Think about Vote Choice?

Consultants and academics have similar views about how voters decide between candidates. As we explained in Chapter 5, consultants share the belief that voters are not particularly interested in or knowledgeable about politics. This is why they advise candidates to repeat a basic message over and over—often via a barrage of television ads. Similarly, consultants often

[18] Gabriel Lenz. 2012. *Follow the Leader: How Voters Respond to Politicians' Policies and Performance.* Chicago, IL: University of Chicago Press.

[19] Danny Hayes. 2006. "Candidate Qualities through a Partisan Lens: A Theory of Trait Ownership." *American Journal of Political Science* 49, 4: 908–23.

[20] Matthew D. Atkinson, Ryan D. Enos, and Seth J. Hill. 2009. "Candidate Faces and Election Outcomes: Is the Face–Vote Correlation Caused by Candidate Selection?" *Quarterly Journal of Political Science* 4, 3: 229–49.

Like political scientists, campaign consultants recognize party identification as a strong influence on vote choice. Campaign strategists look at the partisan composition of the district as a starting point in determining whose votes they can count on and whose they can hope to win through persuasion.

prefer emotional appeals over intellectual appeals, and negative appeals over positive appeals. Emotional appeals and negative appeals seem to be more likely to garner attention and more likely to be remembered.

Consultants, like academics, also believe that voters are strongly constrained by their partisanship and other predispositions. Recognizing these predispositions and acting accordingly is the hallmark of smart campaigns, which often have limited resources and thus need to focus their efforts on those voters most likely to help the campaign win. This is why consultants recommend not wasting time campaigning for the votes of opposing partisans, but instead focusing on delivering mobilizing messages to fellow partisans and persuasive messages to independents and weak partisans.

When Campaigns Matter

Although campaign consultants and political scientists share many beliefs about vote choice, they disagree over a key question: how much the campaign can affect voters' attitudes toward the candidates. Campaign consultants believe that their activities—television and radio advertisements, phone calls, direct mail, the Internet, social media, and person-to-person contact—help persuade voters and thus win elections. Political scientists are more skeptical but nevertheless acknowledge that campaigns can sometimes change voters' minds and even affect election outcomes. The crucial task is to identify *when* campaigns are likely to matter. Here we are particularly concerned with **persuasion**—a concept we introduced in Chapter 5 that means, in this context, convincing undecided voters to support a particular candidate or convincing the other party's supporters to defect. Later in this chapter, we will also consider alternative ways that campaigns may matter.

Campaigns have their largest persuasive effects when two conditions are met: the candidates are relatively unfamiliar to voters, and one side is able to dominate by virtue of better resources. When candidates are not well known, voters are less likely to have opinions about them. Although party identification is likely to affect their initial assessments, they will still be more susceptible to persuasive appeals by the candidates because they will not already have strongly held opinions about them.

Campaigns also matter more when one side can campaign more heavily than the other side. That is to say, campaigns matter more when one side dominates, typically when it has more money and thus a more extensive campaign organization, a larger presence on television and other media, and a better developed infrastructure for contacting and mobilizing voters. When opposing campaigns are more equally balanced in terms of resources, it is difficult for either campaign to get an edge. Television advertisements by one side can be matched with competing advertisements from the other side. The respective efforts of the two sides thus tend to cancel each other out. These two conditions suggest how much impact we should expect campaigns at different levels of office to have.

Presidential Elections

Despite the vast amounts of money that presidential candidates spend, presidential general election campaigns are less likely to decide election outcomes than campaigns at other levels of office. By the time the party conventions are over and the general election campaign has begun, the Democratic and Republican nominees are already relatively well known. They have been campaigning for months if not years, depending on when they began campaigning for the nomination. At the national party conventions, the parties spend several days promoting their nominees for a large television audience. Moreover, when incumbent presidents run for reelection, voters have had five or six years to get to know them, at least from the time their first campaign for president began.

Competing major-party presidential campaigns also tend to be roughly equal in terms of resources—including not only money but also motivation, information, and expertise. The assumption of equal resources has been valid since the passage of the Federal Election Campaign Act.[21] As discussed in

---

[21] Some dispute this notion of resource equality at the presidential level even during these years. See Bartels, *Unequal Democracy*.

Chapter 4, from 1976 to 2004, presidential general election campaigns were publicly financed. That is, both major-party candidates accepted equal amounts of funding from the U.S. Treasury the morning after they accepted their party's nomination for president. In exchange for this money, candidates agreed not to raise or spend additional money on their own behalf.

It is obvious that the campaigns of the two major parties have equal motivation. The presidential election is, in the words of the Republican media consultant Stuart Stevens, "the big enchilada." Both parties try hard to win. It is only slightly less obvious that they are working with equal information. Both the Democratic and Republican presidential campaigns have ready access to information about the preferences of voters via polling and focus groups. Opposition research arms both campaigns with data on the relevant issue positions and backgrounds of the candidates. And teams of experts work with the candidates and their teams on issue positions and policy papers.

The assumption of equal expertise is based on the observation that both sides bring very talented people to the presidential election contest. Consider the main consultants in recent presidential elections. In 2000, George W. Bush relied on the direct mail whiz Karl Rove, while Al Gore relied on the veteran media consultant and speechwriter Bob Shrum. In 2004, Rove and Shrum were again pitted against each other, this time with Rove working for Bush's reelection and Shrum working for John Kerry. In 2008, Obama turned to the Chicago-based media communications consultant David Axelrod, while John McCain ultimately settled on a longtime GOP message consultant, Steven Schmidt. In 2012, Obama continued to rely on Axelrod, along with organizational guru Jim Messina, whereas Mitt Romney turned to longtime GOP consultant and television ad expert Stuart Stevens. It is, in fact, difficult to find a presidential race in which one side seemed overwhelmed by the expertise of the other side—even though commentators are always willing to claim that the winners' team was that much smarter after the election.

Taken in combination, these equalities lead to the possibility that presidential general election campaigns will fight to a draw. The winner will be determined not by the campaign but by the broader conditions in the country, especially the economy. Of course, even if this is true as a general rule, there are moments when the campaign itself appears crucial. It is possible, even in presidential campaigns, for one side to get a financial advantage over the other. In the 2000 presidential race, George W. Bush outspent Al Gore in the battleground states late in the campaign, and the resulting advantage in advertising may have cost Gore four points of the vote—a large number in states such as Florida where the race was close.[22] In 2008, when Obama bypassed public funding and outspent John McCain by an enormous margin, Obama did better in most areas of the country than John Kerry did in 2004. More importantly, Obama did particularly well the more he outspent McCain. Obama's largest campaign spending advantages were in Florida (+$28 million), Virginia (+$16.3 million), Indiana (+$11.4 million), and North Carolina (+$7.2 million), each of which went for the Democratic challenger; these states had gone for Bush in 2004 by five, eight, twenty-one, and twelve points, respectively. In general, however, a presidential candidate needs a fairly substantial advantage over an opponent to shift voters in his direction, and, even then, this shift will likely be small.[23] This is why presidential election outcomes are rarely decided by the campaign. One study of presidential campaigns from 1948 to 2000 found that in only 5 of the 14 presidential elections did the campaign appear to have changed the outcome.[24]

Although presidential general election campaigns often have only a small impact, presidential primary campaigns are much more important. The primaries often see much larger swings in the candidates' fortunes than the fall campaign does. Moreover, events during the campaign itself are responsible for these swings. Unlike candidates in the general elections, candidates for the presidential nomination vary greatly in their resources. Some are heavyweights: politicians with national visibility and the campaign war chests, media attention, and party endorsements to show for it. In the 2012 Republican presidential primaries, Mitt Romney and Texas governor Rick Perry fit this description. Other candidates, however, struggle for visibility and can rarely raise as much money or attract the same level of attention as heavyweight candidates. In the 2012 Republican primaries, this describes candidates such as New Mexico governor Gary Johnson and Utah governor Jon Huntsman. These disparities in campaign resources help the heavyweights dominate the field, pulling voters to their side.

The candidates in presidential primaries are also much less well known than the eventual nominees will be. Although some may be national figures, as was Hillary Clinton in 2008, many others are familiar only to the voters of the state or district that they actually represent as members of Congress or as governor. Thus, voters do not have well-formed opinions about many

---

[22] Richard Johnston, Michael G. Hagen, and Kathleen Hall Jamieson. 2004. *The 2000 Presidential Election and the Foundations of Party Politics.* Cambridge: Cambridge University Press.

[23] Daron R. Shaw. 2006. *The Race to 270.* Chicago: University of Chicago Press.

[24] James E. Campbell. 2001. "When Have Presidential Campaigns Decided Election Outcomes?" *American Politics Research* 29, 5: 437–60.

primary candidates, leaving more potential for the campaign to influence these opinions. Furthermore, voters cannot rely on their party identification to make decisions: all of the candidates in a party primary obviously share the same party identification. As we discussed in Chapter 9, the primary campaign often matters in this fashion: a candidate's victories in the early caucuses and primaries signal to voters that the candidate is viable. This creates a bandwagon effect, as voters gravitate toward successful candidates, believing them to be able to compete effectively in the general election. In 2008, Obama's standing in the polls increased by about 20 points between the first caucus in Iowa on January 3 and the Super Tuesday primaries on February 5. This is a much larger swing than presidential general election campaigns create. Thus, primary candidates know that by campaigning effectively in these early primaries and caucuses, they build the momentum necessary to win the nomination.

Non-Presidential Elections

Campaigns for offices below the presidential level—for U.S. House and Senate, and for state and local offices—are more likely to influence voters relative to presidential general election campaigns. Again, familiarity with the candidates and resource disparities are reasons why. As we discussed in Chapters 10 and 11, citizens know much less about their representatives at lower levels of office. They often do not know the name of their congressional representative, to say nothing of their representatives in the state legislature, the state attorney general, and so on. Thus, their views about these people can be changed by a vigorous campaign. Oftentimes, this is what we see in the campaigns of challengers to incumbents in U.S. House elections. Campaign activity matters more for challengers because so few voters know them. Challengers with more money to spend become better known than poorer challengers over the course of the campaign.[25]

This makes campaign resource disparities all the more important. And, indeed, resource disparities are common in congressional, state, and local elections. One reason that incumbents often dominate these elections is because challengers cannot raise enough money to compete with them. This contrasts with presidential general elections, where, when the candidates both accept public funding, neither will be able to outspend the other overall. When challengers do raise money, it does move voters. In congressional

---

[25] Gary C. Jacobson. 2006. "Measuring Campaign Spending Effects in U.S. House Elections," and Laurel Elms and Paul M. Sniderman, "Informational Rhythms of Incumbent Dominated Congressional Elections," both in *Capturing Campaign Effects*, ed. Henry E. Brady and Richard Johnston. Ann Arbor: University of Michigan Press: 199–220, 221–41.

elections from 1972 to 2006, no challenger who raised less than $100,000 won. By contrast, almost a third of those who raised at least $1 million won.[26] Campaign spending is arguably even more vital for challengers in elections for state legislature, state supreme court, and city council.[27] In these elections, which attract relatively little media coverage, voters are not likely to see, hear, or read anything about challengers unless it comes from their campaigns. Thus, campaigns can be crucial to the outcomes of such elections, even if the dollar amounts spent on them are miniscule compared to what is spent in higher-profile races.

How Campaigns Matter

The preceding discussion focused on the conditions under which campaigns can persuade voters. But it has said much less about *how* campaigns persuade voters, as well as other possible effects of campaigns. In Chapter 12, we described how campaigns can mobilize citizens. Now we continue to examine how campaigns affect voters' attitudes toward the candidates. Three types of effects are important: persuasion, reinforcement, and priming.

Persuasion

As we have discussed, campaigns are more likely to persuade voters when voters are unfamiliar with the candidates and when one side can outspend the other. But this observation only scratches the surface when it comes to analyzing how campaigns persuade. Although resource disparities are important, much of campaigning is not simply about spending more than the opponent, it is about crafting specific messages that are intended to persuade voters. This is what campaign consultants focus on, using polling data, focus groups, and their own experiences to design advertisements, write speeches, and produce other kinds of media. It is also about choosing the appropriate time to air those messages so that they will have the maximum impact on voters. Unfortunately, we do not know very much about what kinds of persuasion strategies consistently work. Campaign consultants sometimes have

---

[26] Gary Jacobson. 2009. *The Politics of Congressional Elections.* 7th ed. New York: Pearson Longman, p. 46. Amounts are in 2006 dollars and thus adjusted for inflation.

[27] Anthony Gierzynski and David Breaux. 1996. "Legislative Elections and the Importance of Money." *Legislative Studies Quarterly* 21, 3: 337–57; Chris W. Bonneau. 2007. "The Effects of Campaign Spending in State Supreme Court Elections." *Political Research Quarterly* 60: 489–99; Timothy B. Krebs. 1998. "The Determinants of Candidates' Vote Share and the Advantages of Incumbency in City Council Elections." *American Journal of Political Science* 42, 3: 921–35.

polls or focus groups, but often they rely on guesswork and interpretations of past elections. Free from the daunting prospect of an election looming, social scientists tend to put little stock in such evidence, but more rigorous data are usually difficult to come by.

One aspect of persuasive messages that has been studied extensively is tone—that is, whether the messages promote a candidate (positive campaigning), attack that candidate's opponent (negative campaigning), or offer some combination of the two (contrast campaigning). Campaign consultants tend to place great faith in the power of negativity. One Democratic consultant put it this way: "The big question in most campaigns . . . is whose negative campaign is better. If it's negative, it works. If it's positive, save it for your tombstone."[28] But is negativity really that powerful?

There is some evidence that negative advertising is more memorable than positive advertising. This is because negative information typically stands out in our daily lives, which generally consist of positive interactions.[29] For example, we are much more likely to remember the couple next to us in a restaurant if they are arguing than if they are conversing pleasantly. But there is much less evidence that negative campaigning actually helps the candidate who goes on the attack. On the whole, negative campaigning makes voters feel less favorable toward the candidate being attacked, which is the goal. However, it also makes voters feel less favorable toward the attacker, and this backlash may be stronger than the effect on views of the attacked candidate.[30] Negative advertising is thus a risky strategy at best.

Besides tone, another aspect of messaging is issue content. In fact, a strategy that campaigns often employ to persuade voters is to focus on **wedge issues**. Strategies centered around these issues are designed to convince voters in the opposite party to defect from that party and vote for the other side. Here is one example of a wedge issue strategy. Latinos and African Americans tend to vote for Democratic candidates but at the same time maintain fairly conservative positions on social issues such as abortion and gay rights. In the 2004 elections, many believed that the Republican Party pursued a wedge issue strategy by sending anti–gay marriage direct mail pieces to Latinos and blacks in the eleven states where "defense of marriage" initiatives were on the ballot. Some of these mail pieces linked Democratic candidates

---

[28] Quoted in Richard R. Lau, Lee Sigelman, Caroline Heldman, and Paul Babitt. 1999. "The Effects of Negative Political Advertisements: A Meta-Analytic Assessment." *American Political Science Review* 93, 4: 852.

[29] Susan Fiske and Shelley Taylor. 1991. *Social Cognition*. 2nd ed. New York: McGraw-Hill.

[30] Richard R. Lau, Lee Sigelman, and Ivy Brown Rovner. 2007. "The Effects of Negative Political Campaigns: A Meta-Analytic Reassessment." *Journal of Politics* 69, 4: 1176–1209.

to support for a "gay agenda," thereby attempting to reduce the standing of these candidates among more socially conservative minority voters. Wedge issues are intended to take advantage of **cross pressures** within voters—that is, the fact that voters sometimes hold ideologically conflicting issue opinions (as in the case of a socially conservative Democrat). Voters who experience such cross pressures are more susceptible than other (non-cross-pressured) voters to persuasion during a presidential campaign.[31] At the same time, given that most partisans vote loyally for their party's candidates, wedge issue strategies may not be as effective as the strategies that parties pursue to solidify their ranks.

Another aspect of persuasion is timing: When can persuasive campaigning most effectively be deployed? Typically, campaigns increase their volume of advertising and other activities as the election draws closer, believing that this is when most voters begin to focus on the choice ahead of them. If so, the most important information is that which voters encounter immediately prior to casting their ballots. But there is a contrary point of view, which holds that candidates should start their campaigns early to define themselves and their opponents before all the noise of the general election begins.

Some evidence supports campaigning most heavily right before voters cast their ballots. A study of the 2006 Texas gubernatorial campaign of Rick Perry, which randomly assigned Perry's television advertisements to different media markets, found that the ads significantly improved Perry's vote share, but that the effect was temporary, fading within a week of the ads' airing.[32] A comparable analysis of other 2006 campaigns found a similarly rapid rate of "decay," suggesting again that campaign activities tend to have an immediate but short-lived impact.[33] Does this mean that early campaigning is always fruitless? Not necessarily. Moreover, given the substantial and increasing fraction of voters who cast their ballots before Election Day, campaigning "late" may actually mean campaigning at a consistently high level for weeks if not months.

---

[31] D. Sunshine Hillygus and Todd Shields. 2007. *The Persuadable Voter: Strategic Candidates and Wedge Issues in Political Campaigns*. Princeton, NJ: Princeton University Press.

[32] Alan S. Gerber, James G. Gimpel, Donald P. Green, and Daron R. Shaw. 2011. "The Size and Duration of Campaign Television Advertising Effects: Results from a Large-Scale Randomized Experiment." *American Political Science Review* 105, 1: 135–50.

[33] Seth J. Hill, James Lo, Lynn Vavreck, and John Zaller. 2007. "The Duration of Advertising Effects in Political Campaigns." Paper presented at the Annual Meeting of the American Political Science Association, Chicago.

Campaign Strategy and the Persuasion Model

Sasha Issenberg, writing online for *Slate* magazine,[1] describes in fascinating detail how the Obama campaign identified and targeted persuadable votes for his reelection:

"Republican operatives around the country have noted with a mixture of curiosity and anxiety that nearby mailboxes are less crowded with mailers making the case for Obama than they were four years ago. This may be the result of a strategic imperative: In many states, Obama has a clearer path to victory than Romney solely by mobilizing existing supporters than by finding new ones. But it could also reflect the fact that Obama's strategists do not think they have to rely, as have most campaigns over the last generation, solely on the mail for their targeted efforts to win over voters.

"Earlier this year, Obama put his volunteers' ability to do that to the test. The campaign administered an experiment in several states in which phone-bank volunteers were given a script with a few talking points and broad instructions to open up a conversation with a potential voter. Before and after these interactions, a professional call center surveyed the targeted voters to identify which candidate they supported, and campaign analysts set to work developing a statistical portrait of those who moved in Obama's direction after talking with a volunteer.

"The result of that analysis is the campaign's so-called persuasion model, which generates a score predicting, from zero to 10, the likelihood that a voter can be pushed in Obama's direction. (The score also integrates a voter's likelihood of casting a ballot altogether, so that field organizers focus the attention on those with the best chances of turning out.) A zero designates a voter likely to be repelled by the interaction, and actually pushed toward Romney or a third-party candidate; a one projects a minimal possibility of persuasion; a nine someone who can be easily pushed.

"Campaign strategists have traditionally been so fearful of triggering a backlash that they rarely entrust volunteers with persuasion efforts. When placed at a phone or given a clipboard to knock on doors, volunteers usually are given tasks that do not require them to discuss sensitive or complex topics—their role has typically just been asking voters who they support, and reminding those who declare their support to turn out.

"(While in 2008 Obama encouraged volunteers to make the case for the Democratic candidate in their communities, the campaign never saw it as a replacement for their paid persuasion strategy. One adviser from that campaign mockingly describes the 2008 sensibility as 'building this utopian society where people talk with their neighbors.' Obama's strategists certainly didn't let up in traditional channels, like television ads and direct mail, where they can deploy language and imagery delicately calibrated after polling and focus-group research.)

"'Persuasion calls are a more difficult thing for a volunteer to do because it's a lot easier to hang up on someone than slam a door in their face,' says Wisconsin Democratic Party

---

[1] Sasha Issenberg, "Obama Does It Better," from *Slate*, Oct. 29, 2012. © 2012 The Slate Group. All rights reserved. Used by permission and protected by the Copyright Laws of the United States. The printing, copying, redistribution, or retransmission of the Material without express written permission is prohibited.

chairman Mike Tate. 'You're not just asking someone who they're going to vote for or reminding them to vote—you're going to people who are undecided, who don't want to hear from you, and are often sick of politics.'

"Now, thanks to its experiments, the campaign feels confident enough in its ability to identify persuadable voters that it can direct well-trained volunteers to call them with pre-written scripts. (In an election year when so few voters are at all open-minded about the candidates, true persuasion targets are so dispersed that it is rarely efficient to send volunteers walking among their houses.) The messages are crafted for different kinds of persuadable voters. Obama's persuasion message for certain female targets threatens a 'return to an era when women didn't have control over own health choices.' Analytics are transforming the role, and value, of volunteers.

"Romney's campaign, meanwhile, appears to be selecting targets largely through the same method used in George W. Bush's 2004 campaign. After asking which candidate a respondent supports, the surveys that feed into Romney's microtargeting models also plumb for a voter's 'anger points.' *How angry does Obamacare make you? What about growing deficits?* With this data, Romney's targeters are able to model the likelihood that a voter will respond emotionally to one of its appeals—and if that person appears in the middle range between predicted support for Obama and Romney, the campaign will send a sequence of mail pieces on a related theme, like economics or social issues. While Republicans add modest pro-Romney 'advocacy' messages at the top of the scripts used at their Victory Center phone banks to identify potential supporters, they are relying on paid channels, not volunteers, to deliver persuasion messages."

Reinforcement

Because we have emphasized the challenges that campaigns face in persuading voters, it may seem as if campaigns matter only if they change people's attitudes. But campaigns can also be important by reinforcing attitudes. **Reinforcement** occurs when a campaign solidifies voters' preferences. Reinforcement is particularly likely to occur when most voters are already predisposed to support one party because of social group identities or identification with that party. For example, a voter may have a natural tendency to vote Republican but not know much about a particular Republican candidate and not feel strongly committed to this candidate. Campaign activity can increase this voter's level of commitment. Sometimes this is referred to as "rallying the base."

Although reinforcement is an important effect of campaigns, it is difficult to measure and thus somewhat underappreciated. Pre-election polls that simply ask voters whether they plan to vote Democratic or Republican will not capture how strongly voters feel or how certain they are. With further questioning, it might become clear that, early on in a campaign, many voters express a degree of uncertainty—one that disappears by late in the campaign, when voters have become devotees of their party's candidate and opponents of the other side's candidate. Of course, there is nothing automatic about reinforcement. A campaign might fail to rally its base. Such campaigns will naturally face long odds.

Priming

Not only can campaigns influence how people vote, they can also influence *why* they vote the way they do. That is, they affect the criteria that voters use in choosing a candidate, a process known as **priming** (Chapter 8). Why would campaigns be interested in priming? In any given election year, candidates know that they have some biographical details, personal experiences, and issue positions that give them an advantage, and some that do not. Campaigns will work to focus attention on issues that benefit them as well as issues that disadvantage their opponents. If the campaign ultimately focuses on issues beneficial to the candidate, this may help them win. Thus, campaigns are not simply about persuasion but about controlling the agenda and defining what the election is about.

Understanding priming helps answer an interesting question about elections, and presidential elections in particular: How can elections be so predictable and yet the polls fluctuate so much? We discussed in Chapter 9 (and alluded to at the outset of this chapter) how presidential elections can be forecast with considerable accuracy based on factors such as the state of the economy. And yet, during presidential campaigns, there can be notable swings in the polls—for example, in 2008, John McCain took the lead after the Republican National Convention, only to lose it two weeks later, never recovering it for the rest of the campaign. One explanation for why poll numbers eventually converge on the forecast is priming. As the election goes on, campaign activities tend to focus voters' attention on fundamental factors like the economy.[34] As these factors become more important criteria in voters' decisions, the polls move in the direction of the candidate favored by these fundamental factors—as, for example, an incumbent president would be favored if the economy were growing robustly. Of course, if the challenger to that incumbent president successfully changes the subject so that voters focus on some other issue, the incumbent may lose. A systematic study of presidential elections since 1952 shows the importance of priming: when candidates who benefit from the state of the economy and other

---

[34] Andrew Gelman and Gary King. 1993. "Why Are American Presidential Election Polls So Variable When Votes Are So Predictable?" *British Journal of Political Science* 23: 409–51; Thomas M. Holbrook. 1996. *Do Campaigns Matter?* Thousand Oaks, CA: Sage.

conditions emphasize these factors in their campaigns, they are more likely to win than similarly situated candidates who focus on some other issue.[35]

The 2000 election provides an illustration of the importance of priming. A pressing question after this election was why Al Gore did not win more of the popular vote, given how well the economy was doing in the year before the election and given his position as vice president under President Bill Clinton. One possible answer is that Gore's campaign agenda did not focus on the economy, and thus did not "prime" the economy in voters' minds. Gore was leery of associating himself even with positive aspects of the Clinton administration's record for fear that he would also be punished for Clinton's extramarital affair with Monica Lewinsky or other scandals. Thus, some voters may not have rewarded him for economic growth. Gore's strategy contrasts sharply with Obama's in 2008, which emphasized the weak economy and blamed the Republican administration.

Conclusion

The decisions Americans make about political candidates—and the campaign's role in influencing those decisions—are frequently the subject of concern. Commentators speculate about whether Americans make decisions that are well informed, which usually means that their decisions are based on specific knowledge of the candidates and especially voters' own views about issues. This concern speaks to the standard of *deliberation* that we introduced in the first chapter. Typically, that standard is applied to how candidates are campaigning or how the media covers campaigns. But the same standard could be applied to citizens. For one, healthy deliberation implies that citizens are themselves paying attention, willing to learn, and willing to contribute to the national conversation that happens in and around elections. Moreover, if the news media and candidates are expected to provide detailed information to voters but voters simply are not paying attention, then perhaps the voters bear as much or more responsibility as the quality of media coverage or campaign messages.

This perspective may give voters far less credit than they deserve. We have emphasized throughout this chapter that voters often rely on simple decision rules that do not require detailed information. For example, Americans often rely on long-standing psychological attachments to one of the two major political parties. They also draw on appraisals of the economy to evaluate

---

[35] Lynn Vavreck. 2009. *The Message Matters: The Economy and Presidential Campaigns.* Princeton, NJ: Princeton University Press.

incumbent performance. These strategies may be simple, even simplistic, but they may also be good shortcuts. What does it mean to say that something is a good shortcut? The question is whether voters who choose a Democratic or Republican candidate based on party identification would be likely to choose that same candidate if they had received and digested reams of information about the candidates. In other words, did the shortcut get voters to the same place that they would have reached had they devoted considerable time and energy to researching the alternatives? In many cases, the answer is probably yes. Some research has demonstrated that voting based on issue proximity calculations often gets citizens to the same vote choice they would have made had they relied solely on their partisanship. This is why social identities and party identification in particular may be reliable shortcuts. If so, then we might be slightly less concerned if voters do not follow the campaign closely.

A second concern raised about voters' behavior in elections concerns the impact of the campaign itself. Commentators sometimes worry that voters—particularly those who are not paying close attention to the campaign—could be unduly affected by clever television advertisements or other kinds of campaign appeals. This speaks to the standard of *free choice* that we have discussed previously. If campaigns can influence voters by airing ads that play on voters' fears with exaggerated attacks of the opponent, or ads that contained misleading information or even outright falsehoods, then perhaps voters' choices are not quite free but are instead being manipulated by the candidates.

By and large, such fears seem unfounded. Campaigns can be important for the voting process. They reinforce the views of partisans and occasionally persuade some voters who are on the fence. But their effects appear to stop well short of manipulation. Indeed, political reality—objective factors and conditions—significantly constrains how much campaigns can influence voters. Campaigns are hard-pressed to overcome political reality and voters' partisan habits, particularly when the efforts of one candidate are countered and offset by the efforts of the opponent. This is especially true for presidential election campaigns. The result is that presidents presiding over prosperous times typically win (for example, Reagan in 1984 and Clinton in 1996), and those presiding over recessions almost always lose (for example, Carter in 1980 and Bush in 1992). Only when voters know little about the candidates or when they cannot rely on shortcuts like party identification do campaigns appear more influential—and even then only when one candidate can outspend the other.

We are not suggesting that campaigns do not matter at all. For one, they might be important even if they do not persuade many voters. They provide information, mobilize voters, and force candidates to articulate policy positions that become the basis for subsequent accountability. Furthermore, in some cases, they do persuade enough voters to affect the outcome. Thus, the campaign can be the difference between winning and losing—certainly at lower levels of office and perhaps even in presidential elections from time to time.

This basic understanding of voters and vote choice is shared by political scientists and campaign professionals. Understandably, the people inside the campaigns, more so than academics viewing proceedings from afar, tend to think their actions are important to voters. But consultants and campaign workers comprehend, perhaps better than anyone else, how difficult it is to capture the attention of voters and score points. Ironically, it is precisely because it is so difficult to move voters that campaigns often develop a strong belief in how important it is to allocate resources effectively, message coherently, and win the daily battle with the news media.

KEY TERMS

panel study (p. 370)

social identities (p. 370)

opinion leaders (p. 372)

party identification (p. 372)

retrospective voting (p. 377)

sociotropic voting (p. 378)

pocketbook voting (p. 378)

proximity voting (p. 379)

persuasion (p. 382)

wedge issues (p. 388)

cross pressures (p. 389)

reinforcement (p. 391)

priming (p. 392)

FOR DISCUSSION

1. What is party identification and how does it influence the behavior of voters?

2. Why do scholars believe that most voters do not engage in issue voting?

3. Identify and briefly describe three ways in which campaigns might "matter" for voters.

4. Why is it that political scientists are particularly skeptical about the ability of presidential campaigns to determine election outcomes?

CHAPTER 14

Democracy in Action or a Broken System?

It is easy to imagine political campaigns as wars in which the candidates are generals and the people they direct — staff and volunteers — are the loyal troops that engage in combat. This conception of political campaigns is evident among practitioners and scholars. For example, Mary Matalin and James Carville called their book about the 1992 presidential election *All's Fair: Love, War and Running for President*, while the Republican consultant Ed Rollins called his autobiography *Bare Knuckles and Back Rooms*.[1] Lee Atwater, a consultant for presidents Ronald Reagan and George H. W. Bush, claimed that his favorite book was Sun Tzu's *Art of War* because "Everything in it you can relate to my profession, you can relate to the campaign."[2] It is not surprising, then, that Matalin's epigraph for *All's Fair* was the Vietnamese battle cry, "Follow me if I advance. Kill me if I retreat. Avenge me if I die."[3] Scholars are no less likely to use the war metaphor, as evidenced by book titles such as *The Battle for Congress, Campaign Warriors,* and *Air Wars*.[4]

To a certain extent, it is understandable why campaigns are depicted as wars. The word *campaign* itself derives from the Latin word *campus* ("field"), which originally referred to the period of time when an army was in the field. There are two problems with conceiving of political campaigns as battles, however. First, doing so makes it seem like there are no limits to the actions that political actors can

---

[1] Ed Rollins. 1997. *Bare Knuckles and Back Rooms: My Life in American Politics*. New York: Broadway.

[2] John R. Pitney. 2001. *The Art of Political Warfare*. Norman: University of Oklahoma Press, p. 13.

[3] Mary Matalin and James Carville. 1995. *All's Fair: Love, War, and Running for President*. New York: Simon & Schuster.

[4] James Thurber. 2001. *The Battle for Congress: Candidates, Consultants and Voters*. Washington, DC: Brookings Institution Press; James Thurber and Candice Nelson. 2000. *Campaign Warriors: Political Consultants in Elections*. Washington, DC: Brookings Institution Press; Darrell M. West. 2005. *Air Wars: Television Advertising in Election Campaigns 1952–2004*. Washington, DC: CQ Press.

take in pursuit of victory. What else could Matalin and Carville mean by the title *All's Fair*? Second, while the metaphor might be helpful for imagining the roles of political candidates and campaign workers, it is not very helpful for imagining the role of citizens. Are they soldiers? Civilians? Most citizens do not get involved in political campaigns beyond voting, so the soldier metaphor seems inapt. Civilians, on the other hand, can be viewed either as the people who stay behind to tend the home front and support the troops or as those who dodge sniper fire as they scrounge for food and water. Needless to say, these are poor ways to conceive of citizens in a democracy. Understanding campaigns means moving beyond martial metaphors and examining the role that campaigns play in a democracy.

Throughout this book, we have emphasized that campaigns in the United States reflect the country's laws and institutions, the strategic motivations of candidates, the choices that voters make, and the broader economic and historical context in which elections take place. In other words, campaigns make sense when one understands the incentives and constraints political actors face. The fact that there is an intelligible logic to how campaigns and elections function, however, does not mean that they are serving our democracy well. The challenge of evaluating campaigns animates this chapter. Our discussion starts with the assumption that the most important role political campaigns play in a democracy is to provide citizens with information to help them make a choice on Election Day. We then ask how campaigns might promote the democratic values of free choice, political equality, and deliberation that we discussed at the beginning of this book. The discussion concludes that, although campaigns in the United States are not perfect, they do facilitate important democratic processes. How they might be improved is a complicated matter, both in theory and in practice.

Core of the Analysis

- American campaigns and elections can be evaluated in terms of key democratic values, especially free choice, equality, and deliberation.
- The American tradition of free speech makes it difficult to reform political campaigns and further these three values.
- American campaigns generally uphold the free choices and equality of citizens.
- Some proposed campaign reforms have promise, but it is not always clear whether those reforms would work and whether citizens and politicians would agree to them.

Campaigns and Democratic Values

To help visualize the role that political campaigns play in democratic elections, imagine an election without them—that is, one with no television and radio advertisements, no phone calls from campaign volunteers, no glossy mailers, and no debates. Because the candidates would not be making appearances and speeches, news outlets would rarely cover the election. On Election Day, only the most politically engaged citizens would be aware that there was even an election going on, let alone know where they needed to go to cast their ballot. Only the most motivated of those citizens would actually vote. And those who did would know very little about the candidates.

As far-fetched as this scenario might sound, some candidates find it advantageous to employ a minimal information strategy. **Stealth candidates** refuse to campaign in the traditional sense—that is, by seeking party endorsements, making public appearances, and canvassing, precisely because they want to avoid questions from the press and keep their controversial views hidden from voters. Democrats in the early 1990s claimed many religious right candidates were running stealth campaigns in local races by avoiding public appearances and choosing to seek votes only in churches and on Christian radio. Although research has found little evidence of Christian Right candidates running stealth campaigns,[5] it is still a tactic that is occasionally used in local races, where it is easier for candidates to fly below the radar of the media. Yet, it is difficult to understand how such campaigns, which are designed to keep information from voters, serve democratic governance.

This discussion demonstrates that one of the most important democratic functions of political campaigns is to provide voters with information. Yet it is plainly clear to any observer that the quality of campaign information can range wildly. The goal of the following discussion is to use democratic theory to create a set of standards by which citizens can evaluate political campaigns. These standards are summarized in Table 14.1.

Free Choice

In a representative democracy, such as the United States, elections allow citizens to choose who will represent them in government. By definition, a choice involves selecting one of a number of alternatives. This means voters must be allowed to choose between at least two parties or candidates. If an election is uncontested, voters have no real choice. Yet, even when this

---

[5] Melissa Marie Deckman. 2004. *School Board Battles: The Christian Right in Local Politics.* Washington DC: Georgetown University Press.

TABLE 14.1 What Free Choice, Equality, and Deliberation Require
of Campaigns and Elections

Free Choice	• A choice of at least two candidates. • Citizens must play a role in determining the final set of candidate choices. • No intimidation, manipulation, or coercion of citizens.
Equality	• The votes of citizens should have an equal impact on election outcomes. • All candidates should be able to disseminate similar amounts of information. • The rules governing campaigns and elections must apply equally to all candidates.
Deliberation	• Candidates and citizens must have opportunities to deliberate before an election. • Citizens must have a high volume of campaign information from a diverse range of sources. • Candidates must offer reasons for the positions they take. • Candidates should not be required to refrain from criticizing one another.

minimal requirement has been met, free choice is not guaranteed. First, political scientists have long recognized the power of agenda-setting—that is, the ability to manipulate outcomes by constraining political choices.[6] As discussed in Chapter 3, party elites exercised this power prior to the fourth campaign era, when they chose which candidates would compete in the general election. The adoption of primaries by both parties following the dramatic protests of the 1968 Democratic National Convention signaled recognition that citizens must be involved in the nomination process. Free choice is also undermined when voters are coerced or manipulated into voting a particular way. Such coercion can take the form, as it does in some countries, of armed soldiers monitoring ballot boxes, or it can involve more subtle methods such as withholding information crucial for voters. When this happens, voters are no longer free or autonomous.

Political Equality

Political equality has always been a central value in the American political system. The principle of "one person, one vote" is a natural extension of the

---

[6] Robert A. Dahl. 1956. *A Preface to Democratic Theory.* Chicago, IL: University of Chicago Press.

belief that "all men are created equal." Equal access to the ballot box, however, is not sufficient to ensure equality. Inequalities can also arise during the campaign.

In *A Preface to Democratic Theory*, the political scientist Robert Dahl argues that preserving equal political influence requires that voters possess identical information about the choices confronting them on Election Day.[7] Here, *identical* means that candidates should be able to disseminate similar amounts of information to voters so that no one candidate or party can monopolize the avenues of communication in a campaign. The constitutional scholar Ronald Dworkin arrives at the same conclusion by arguing that citizens are equals not only as voters but as candidates for office as well.[8] In fact, Dworkin contends that we should be just as concerned about the equality of candidates for office as we are about the equality of voters. He argues that all citizens—including elected officials, candidates for office, and organized groups—should have a fair and equal opportunity to publish, broadcast, or otherwise command attention for their views. A candidate who controls the flow of political communication has disproportionate influence over citizen opinion.

Political equality also requires that election rules and regulations apply equally to all candidates. In his book *Just Elections*, Dennis Thompson argues that in a truly fair election, candidates would have "comparable opportunities to raise resources, unbiased rules for conducting primaries and elections, and impartial procedures for resolving disputes."[9] Some would argue that this is too demanding, because candidates may not be able to raise resources for good reasons—for example, because their views are unpalatable to potential donors.

Deliberation

Like political equality, deliberation has long been associated with democracy. In his eulogy of democratic Athens, Pericles called the period of discussion preceding a political decision "an indispensable preliminary to any wise action at all." But political decisions, and even elections, are not inherently deliberative. The side with the most votes wins, whether or not there has been discussion. The possibility that political decisions are made without such a discussion is particularly bothersome to those in the minority.

---

[7] Dahl, *A Preface to Democratic Theory*.

[8] Ronald Dworkin. 2002. *Sovereign Virtue: The Theory and Practice of Equality*. Cambridge. MA: Harvard University Press.

[9] Dennis Thompson. 2002. *Just Elections*. Chicago: University of Chicago Press.

In September 2011, CNN and the Tea Party Express hosted a presidential primary debate that was not endorsed by the Republican National Committee (RNC). In response, the RNC has passed new rules for 2016 that will penalize candidates who participate in debates that are not sanctioned by the RNC. This move helps Republicans assert more control over a debate process that many felt was unwieldy in 2012, but one can also argue it undermines democratic values, such as deliberation and political equality.

They would prefer a more deliberative campaign process so that they can try to persuade the majority. And even if they lose, such a process would leave them with the sense that they had a fair hearing.

How can we evaluate the deliberative quality of a campaign? First, there must be a large volume of information available to ensure that citizens receive at least a portion of it. Second, voters must be exposed to information from diverse sources, including candidates, parties, and interest groups, so that their views are not biased because they received information from only one side. Third, campaigns should provide reasons for supporting or opposing a particular candidate. If a candidate for office says "I oppose abortion," citizens may know where the candidate stands but not know the candidate's reasoning. When candidates offer reasons for their beliefs—for example, "I oppose abortion because I believe life begins at conception and that it is immoral to end a life"—it helps citizens understand their views and encourages more discussion. Finally, deliberation demands accountability. Earnest and honest discussion requires that candidates identify themselves and take responsibility for their words.

It is important to understand that deliberation does not require that candidates refrain from criticizing one another. Because deliberation requires candidates to be honest and substantive, attacks are a concern when they are misleading or irrelevant. However, such attacks must be distinguished from valid criticisms. For one, even if positive advertisements are more appealing than negative ads, politics inevitably involves disagreement, and it is important to clarify the disagreements among opposing candidates. Negative advertisements can actually be more informative in this regard than positive ads, which often mask differences and rely on innocuous images of flags, sunshine, and smiling children.

What role do citizens play in a deliberative campaign? Ideally, they would reflect on their own values and interests, spend time learning about the candidates and their issue positions, and vote for the candidate who best represents their views. A key part of a deliberative campaign for citizens is exposure to disagreeable viewpoints. This means they must inform themselves about *all* of the candidates and discuss the election with people who are supporting different candidates. Of course, as we learned in Chapters 12 and 13, citizens rarely behave this way in elections, but it is important to recognize that citizens play a crucial role in deliberative campaigns.

Freedom of Speech

The First Amendment of the Constitution of the United States says that "Congress shall make no law . . . abridging the freedom of speech." The First Amendment is normally interpreted as giving American citizens the legal right to speak freely and openly, without government regulation. Because free speech is a fundamental right in our country, it is difficult to regulate campaigns in ways that might promote some of the values just discussed, because such reforms would entail limits on speech and expression. For example, if political equality requires that candidates provide equivalent amounts of information to citizens, Congress could create a law that established spending limits in campaigns to prevent one candidate from spending more and thus providing more information than the other candidates. It could also create a law that prevented political candidates from supporting their campaigns with their own money to ensure that a wealthy candidate does not have an advantage over a less wealthy competitor. In fact, as we discussed in Chapter 4, Congress passed a law that did both things: the Federal Election Campaign Act of 1971. However, in *Buckley v. Valeo* (424 U.S. 1, 1976), the Supreme Court ruled that these provisions were unconstitutional because they violated the free speech protections of the First Amendment.

As a result of this commitment to free speech, the United States has one of the least regulated campaign systems in the world.[10] In fact, many of the

---

[10] Bruce I. Buchanan. 2001. "Mediated Electoral Democracy: Campaigns, Incentives, and Reform," in *Mediated Politics: Communication in the Future of Democracy*, ed. Lance Bennett and Robert M. Entman. New York: Cambridge University Press, p. 366.

laws and regulations that other countries have adopted to improve campaign discourse would very likely be overturned by the U.S. Supreme Court. For instance, political parties in Japan can use television advertising only to discuss policy positions and must refrain from mentioning the name or record of any individual candidate. Some other countries limit the duration of the campaign, or prohibit the publication of public opinion polls for a certain period of time before an election so that their results do not discourage people from voting. Even if Americans wanted to adopt such restrictions—which is by no means clear—they would likely violate the principle of free speech, at least as it is interpreted by contemporary U.S. courts.

In sum, the political values of free choice, equality, and deliberation require political campaigns and elections to have certain characteristics. First, free choice requires contestation, meaning that an election must feature at least two candidates, and that citizens control the nomination process. It also requires that a citizen's vote choice not be coerced or manipulated and that citizens have information about all of their vote choices. Political equality requires that citizens receive equivalent amounts of information about candidates and that the rules and regulations governing campaigns apply equally to all candidates. The value of deliberation concerns both the quantity and quality of information. Citizens must have access to a large amount of campaign information from a variety of sources. Deliberation also demands that candidates offer clear reasons for their positions and engage the arguments of their opponents. At the same time, deliberation requires citizen engagement. Even if Americans' commitment to free speech conflicts with some of these values, they are important values to keep in mind when evaluating campaigns.

The Reality of Political Campaigns

Is it realistic to expect campaigns to live up to all of the ideals discussed in the previous section? As we have emphasized, even if we agree that certain democratic values are important, there might be trade-offs among values, or limits on what we can reasonably expect from candidates and citizens. Thus, it is important to consider the "reality" of American campaigns.

What Do Citizens Want from Campaigns?

Do citizens want the kind of campaign that these values imply—one that focuses on substantive comparisons of the candidates and asks citizens to deliberate and participate in the electoral process? If not, then there arises a dilemma: Should campaigns be modeled on abstract values, even if citizens do not necessarily endorse these values, or should campaigns simply give citizens what they want?

What exactly do citizens say they want from political campaigns? It depends on how interested in politics they are.[11] Those who are interested in and informed about politics tend to favor more substantive and interactive campaigns—including candidate debates, town hall meetings where candidates interact with citizens, and, in general, more discussion of policy issues. Those who are less interested in politics, however, tend to favor campaigns that demand less of them, providing them with simple cues that enable them to make choices with minimal time and effort. For example, citizens who are not very interested in politics may be more interested in each candidate's résumé, including information about the candidate's political career, such as voting records, and personal life, such as credit scores and Department of Motor Vehicles records. Citizens who do not follow politics closely are thus most interested in getting a sense of who the candidates are as people. They do not necessarily want detailed analyses about where the candidates stand on the issues. Nor are they necessarily interested in investing time and energy in campaign events, such as town hall meetings, that provide venues for deeper discussion of the issues and the choices before voters in the election.

The fact that citizens do not necessarily agree about the "ideal" campaign makes it complicated to reform campaigns. That some citizens prefer less substantive campaigns does not necessarily mean that reforms aimed at making campaigns more substantive or deliberative should be abandoned. Instead, it may suggest that reformers should also look for ways to make campaigns more appealing to those who are not politically sophisticated—for instance, by finding ways to provide voters with simple, digestible information, such as a short description of the candidates' issue positions next to their names on a ballot. One must also consider the possibility that people who say they do not want to participate in more deliberative events might change their mind once they have experienced them. Research shows that jurors who are reluctant to report for jury duty—a highly deliberative exercise—leave the experience convinced of its value and enthusiastic about participating again.[12]

---

[11] Keena Lipsitz, Christine Trost, Matthew Grossman, and John Sides. 2005. "What Voters Want from Political Campaign Communication." *Political Communication* 22: 337–54.

[12] John Gastil, E. Pierre Deess, Philip J. Veiser, and Cindy Simmons. 2010. *The Jury and Democracy: How Jury Deliberation Promotes Civic Engagement and Political Participation*. New York: Oxford University Press.

How Do American Campaigns Measure Up?

Americans love to hate political campaigns. They complain about negative ads but rarely tune them out. They bemoan the tactics of candidates but rarely seem to punish candidates who push the envelope of campaigning. As a result, Americans may actually create incentives for candidates to do the things that Americans claim to dislike. James Madison referred to the "vicious arts"[13] by which candidates win elections; but a phrase like "vicious arts" is too strong. Evaluating campaigns by the standards of free choice, equality, and deliberation reveals a more mixed portrait.[14]

Free Choice Most campaigns and elections in the United States promote free choice. Since the early 1970s, citizens have been able to vote in primary elections for general election candidates. They usually have two or more candidates from which to choose, as well as access to information about their choices. Coercion or intimidation of voters in America is now quite rare. Although candidates do make misleading claims, it is difficult for them to lie outright without an opposing candidate or the news media challenging them. It is quite common for television news programs to include **ad watch** segments in which they dissect candidate advertising. In addition, organizations such as FactCheck.org monitor the accuracy of campaign advertisements, speeches, and interviews.

Certain aspects of American elections, however, do undermine individual free choice. Although citizens can now vote in primaries for all partisan offices, individuals who want to run in a primary must demonstrate their ability to raise money and earn endorsements from party elites, especially to participate in primaries for higher offices. For example, long before presidential primaries begin, individuals who want to contest them must perform well in the "invisible primary"—that is, the race for cash and endorsements that proves one is a viable candidate. Although public opinion polls do matter in this process, recent research shows that party elites have been largely successful in regaining control of this process.[15]

There is no question that citizens have access to an abundance of information about presidential candidates and candidates for statewide office, but they have much less information about candidates in local races. Motivated

---

[13] Alexander Hamilton, James Madison, and John Jay. 1961. *The Federalist Papers*. New York: Penguin, p. 82.

[14] This approach is advocated by and elaborated upon in Keena Lipsitz. 2011. *Competitive Elections and the American Voters*. Philadelphia: University of Pennsylvania Press, chap. 2.

[15] Marty Cohen, David Karol, Hans Noel, and John Zaller. 2008. *The Party Decides: Presidential Nominations Before and After Reform*. Chicago, IL: University of Chicago Press.

citizens can learn about the candidates if they make the effort, but most lack such motivation. At best, they "accidentally" pick up information through advertisements and local media coverage. A competitive election can help citizens learn because the candidates have more money to buy advertisements and the media have more of an incentive to cover the election. The problem is that many elections are not competitive.

Indeed, as we noted in Chapters 10 and 11, a surprising number of elections in the United States are not even contested—that is, there is only one candidate, or at least only one major-party candidate, running for office. Uncontested elections occur more often in local races and state legislative races, but some U.S. House and Senate elections are also uncontested. For example, 30 House races were uncontested in the 2014 midterm election.[16] Many other races are contested but feature only one major-party candidate. In recent years, there have often been 50 or more U.S. House races with only one major-party candidate. Most primaries for House, Senate, and statewide offices are uncontested. In fact, on average, just 30 percent of primaries featuring an incumbent are contested. Although one might argue that it is more important for the general election to be contested than a primary, keep in mind that many jurisdictions in the United States are dominated by one of the two major parties. In such jurisdictions, where the outcome of the general election is a foregone conclusion, one can argue that the choice voters make in the primary election is as important as in the general election, if not more so.

Even when races are contested by two major-party candidates, they are often not competitive. Although presidential elections remain consistently competitive, electoral competitiveness is declining in House and Senate races, in state legislative elections, and in most primary elections.[17] The level of electoral competition in local races is stable, but that is only because it is and has long been quite low. A recent study of mayoral races in 38 large cities from 1979 to 2003 found that the average margin of victory was 22 percentage points.[18] Most scholars consider a margin of less than 10 percent to be competitive. In short, a skeptic might argue that while citizens have a choice

---

[16] http://www.thegreenpapers.com/G14/uncontested.phtml (accessed 4/10/15).

[17] Gary C. Jacobson. 2009. *The Politics of Congressional Elections.* 7th ed. New York: Pearson/Longman; Richard G. Niemi, Lynda W. Powell, William D. Berry, Thomas M. Carsey, and James M. Snyder, Jr. 2006. "Competition in State Legislative Elections, 1992–2002," in *The Marketplace of Democracy,* ed. Michael P. McDonald and John Samples. Washington, DC: Brookings Institution Press, pp. 53–73; Stephen Ansolabehere, John M. Hansen, Shigeo Hirano, and James M. Snyder, Jr. 2006. "The Decline of Competition in U.S. Primary Elections, 1908–2004," in *The Marketplace of Democracy,* pp. 74–101.

[18] Neal Caren. 2007. "Big City, Big Turnout? Electoral Participation in American Cities." *Journal of Urban Affairs* 29, 1: 31–46.

of candidates even when an election is uncompetitive, they do not really have much of a choice if one of the candidates is certain to win.

Political Equality Competitive elections in the United States produce the highest levels of political equality. Competitive races attract Democratic and Republican donors, allowing both major party candidates to get their messages out. This is because political parties, political action committees (PACs), and individual contributors funnel their limited resources to races where they have the best chance of affecting the outcome. As discussed in Chapter 9, presidential elections exhibit the equalizing effects of true competition. These races are always well funded, so that major party presidential candidates invariably compete with one another on roughly equal terms. Yet, in virtually every other type of election in the United States, the lack of competitiveness means that opposing candidates compete on very unequal terms.

But is this a reason to condemn the American system? Not necessarily. First, it is important to consider whether strict equality of resources is required. The standard of strict equality makes sense when applied to voters. In a democracy, there is no legitimate basis for claiming that one person's vote should count more than another's. Political candidates, however, might not deserve equal resources: one of the candidates might actually be better for the job. The amount of money that candidates are able to raise reflects, in part, the confidence that citizens have in them. If citizens believe certain candidates to be untrustworthy or out of step with the district, they will not contribute to their campaigns. Likewise, PACs contribute to candidates who they believe will best represent their interests in Congress. As a result, some inequality in campaign resources may be natural.

But citizens and PACs give to candidates for other reasons that are less legitimate from the standpoint of political equality. For instance, PACs contribute to incumbents because they know they are likely to win, and the PACs want to ensure access and perhaps influence the way a politician will vote on a particular piece of legislation. Citizens may decide not to donate to candidates that they like simply because they do not think the candidates will win, thereby giving an advantage to the likely victor—who, in many cases, is also an incumbent. When campaign resource inequalities result from these kinds of calculations, they are more of a concern. It is impossible to say how much of the campaign resource inequality we see in campaigns today is due to legitimate and illegitimate reasons. Later we discuss some campaign finance reforms that might discourage giving to candidates for the illegitimate reasons described.

Another requirement of political equality is that the rules and regulations governing our electoral processes apply to all candidates equally. In one sense, our system reflects and promotes the goal of political equality: major-party candidates who run for any office in this country must abide by the same rules and regulations. But minor parties are uniquely burdened by a host of laws and regulations.[19] Consider the situation of minor-party presidential candidates. Whereas the names of the Democratic and Republican candidates automatically appear on the ballot in every state, minor-party candidates must petition state election officials to get their names on the ballot. As we noted in Chapter 2, this usually requires collecting a certain number of signatures from citizens, which can range from as few as 25 in states such as Tennessee to as many as 5 percent of a state's registered voters in states such as Montana and Oklahoma.[20] In addition, as detailed in Chapter 4, presidential candidates from the two major parties are automatically eligible for public funds to finance their general election campaigns. Minor parties, on the other hand, receive public funding *after* the general election, and then only if they receive at least 5 percent of the national popular vote and appear on the ballot in at least 10 states. Minor-party candidates are also not invited to participate in televised presidential debates unless polls show that at least 15 percent of the population supports their candidacy. Of course, an election system with no barriers to ballot access or public financing would be inordinately expensive and potentially confusing for voters. Still, the current system does not treat all candidates equally.

True political equality also requires that electoral disputes be settled by a neutral arbiter. In this country, elections are administered by individuals who are affiliated with political parties. In 33 states, the secretary of state or chief election official is chosen through a partisan election. In the remaining states, the position is usually filled by gubernatorial appointment. No state uses a nonpartisan election process. The most obvious consequence of having party loyalists occupying such positions is the potential for political bias. Most rules governing elections have consequences that benefit one party more than the other. For example, making it harder to vote by limiting voting hours or requiring voters to present a photo identification typically helps Republican candidates. Conversely, making it easier to vote usually helps

---

[19] Steven J. Rosenstone, Roy L. Behr, and Edward H. Lazarus. 1996. *Third Parties in America*. 2nd ed. Princeton, NJ: Princeton University Press; Samuel Issacharoff and Richard H. Pildes. 1998. "Politics as Markets: Partisan Lockups of the Democratic Process." *Stanford Law Review* 50: 643–717; Ian Shapiro. 2003. *The Moral Foundations of Politics*. New Haven, CT: Yale University Press.

[20] Rosenstone, Behr, and Lazarus, *Third Parties in America*, p. 21.

Democrats. Since most people do not want to wait in long lines, reducing the number of polling places in an area dominated by an opponent can lower turnout among her supporters.[21]

In addition, when there are election disputes, such as in Florida after the 2000 presidential election, partisan bias has the potential to affect the outcome of an election by swaying the decisions of election officials. This is often referred to as a problem of "foxes guarding henhouses"—even though election officials are supposed to protect the integrity of the electoral process, partisan self-interest may interfere with their ability to do so.

Deliberation American campaigns do offer opportunities for deliberation, but critics contend that they could offer more. Deliberation depends on both the quantity and quality of information provided to citizens as well as the level of citizen engagement. As we have discussed, the quantity of information depends on the competitiveness of the election. Because the majority of races in the United States are not competitive, citizens are arguably receiving less information than deliberation demands.

The quality of information depends on whether candidates address similar issues, offer specific positions on those issues, and provide the reasoning for their positions. Deliberative events such as debates offer an opportunity for candidates to communicate this kind of information. Debates require candidates to address the same topics—typically, those posed by a moderator—and give them time to explain and defend their thinking. But debates are not necessarily the best forums for deliberation. For one, their occurrence usually depends on the whims of candidates. Candidates who believe that their interests are not served by participating in a debate can avoid them. Moreover, the format of debates may reflect the strategic goals of the candidate more than what is "good" for the electorate. For example, candidates participating in presidential debates usually sign a binding contract that lays out the debate rules. In the past, these rules have stipulated that candidates have no more than 30 seconds to respond to a question and that the candidates cannot ask each other direct questions. These rules reduce uncertainty for the candidates and limit the possibility that they will make mistakes, both of which are desirable from the perspective of campaign consultants. Such restrictions could, however, undermine the "give and take" between the candidates and limit the deliberative value of the debate.

---

[21] Heather Gerken. 2009. *The Democracy Index*. Princeton, NJ: Princeton University Press, p. 16.

Outside of debates, candidates have much more flexibility and freedom in how they communicate with voters. Here again, competition is crucial in whether campaigns will live up to deliberative values. In competitive elections, candidates are much more likely to talk about the same issues—and thus engage in a true dialogue—during the campaign.[22] They are also more likely to offer specific statements of their issue positions.[23] For example, competition might make the difference between a candidate saying "I want to improve education" and "I want to improve education by giving students and their parents education vouchers so they can leave a failing public school." Obviously the latter statement provides voters with a better sense of the policies a candidate will pursue if elected. Increased competition leads to greater issue specificity because candidates in tight races must be clear about their issue positions to attract money and to aggressively confront their opponents. When races are not competitive, however, candidates are more likely to offer bland statements that convey little information to voters.

There have been efforts to increase the quality of information provided by American campaigns. The Bipartisan Campaign Reform Act of 2002 included a "stand by your ad" provision that requires candidates to state their approval of their advertisements—for example, "I am John Smith and I approve this message." In radio advertisements, this requires an audio statement by the candidate that offers identification and approval. In television advertisements, candidates must also personally approve of the ad through either a visual appearance or an audio voice-over. In addition, the candidate's name must appear at the end of the advertisement in "a clearly readable manner" for at least four seconds. Failure to comply with these provisions can result in a fine by the Federal Election Commission (FEC). More important, candidates who fail to comply with this requirement can lose their "lowest unit rate" status—political candidates are typically charged the lowest advertising rate possible for a time slot—for the duration of their campaign. This provision in the law is intended to reduce negativity, but it also forces candidates to take visible responsibility for their advertising, which contributes to deliberation.

Yet, even if campaigns provide a high-volume of balanced, diverse, and truthful information about all the candidates, an election cannot be truly

---

[22] Noah Kaplan, David K. Park, and Travis N. Ridout. 2006. "Dialogue in American Political Campaigns? An Examination of Issue Convergence in Candidate Television Advertising." *American Journal of Political Science* 50, 3: 724–36.

[23] Kim Fridkin Kahn and Patrick J. Kenney. 1999. *The Spectacle of U.S. Senate Campaigns.* Princeton, NJ: Princeton University Press.

deliberative unless citizens are engaged and making use of that information. But as we learned in Chapter 13, very few Americans are interested in elections, even when the presidency is at stake, and most rely on shortcuts, such as social identity and party identification, to make their vote choice rather than give serious thought to the candidates' positions on the issues. Thus, they share at least part of the responsibility for the fact that American campaigns are less deliberative than they could be.

Reforming Campaigns

The preceding discussion highlighted some strengths and weakness of American campaigns. For the most part, American campaigns protect the free choice and political equality of citizens, but they do not create equal opportunities for candidates. The resulting inequalities can undermine the deliberative quality of elections. Are there reforms that might make political campaigns better? As we have discussed throughout this book, identifying effective reforms is not easy. A reform may further one value while undermining another. For example, limiting candidate spending to help ensure that citizens have more balanced information from competing candidates would restrict freedom of speech. A reform may also simply not work. Consider televised ad watches, in which news programs evaluate the truthfulness of campaign advertisements. Ad watches have been shown to have the perverse effect of reinforcing the advertisement's content rather than countering it because viewers can only remember the ad, not the critique of it.[24] Or consider the idea that candidates and campaign consultants should pledge publicly not to campaign negatively. Such a pledge may fail because few candidates and consultants are willing to adopt or respect it and because citizens actually learn as much or more from negative campaigning as from positive campaigning.[25]

In this section, we examine seven reforms that advocates believe would improve the content and conduct of campaigns in the United States (see Table 14.2). We discuss their effectiveness, as measured by current research,

---

[24] Lori Melton McKinnon and Lynda Lee Kaid. 1999. "Exposing Negative Campaigning or Enhancing Advertising Effects: An Experimental Study of Ad Watch Effects on Voters' Evaluations of Candidates and Their Ads." *Journal of Applied Communication Research* 27, 3: 217–36.

[25] L. Sandy Maisel, Darrell M. West, and Brett M. Clifton. 2007. *Evaluating Campaign Quality: Can the Electoral Process Be Improved?* New York: Cambridge University Press; Richard R. Lau, Lee Sigelman, and Ivy Brown Rovner. 2007. "The Effects of Negative Political Campaigns: A Meta-Analytic Reassessment." *Journal of Politics* 69, 4: 1176–1209.

TABLE 14.2 Reforming American Campaigns and Elections				
Reform	Free Choice	Equality	Deliberation	Support among Public?
Publicly finance campaigns	✓	✓		Medium[a]
Make campaign donations anonymous		✓		None
Adopt the national popular vote		✓		Medium[b]
Reform the redistricting process		✓		Medium[c]
Create neutral election administration positions		✓		None
Use deliberative polls			✓	None
Create a national day of deliberation			✓	None
Use citizen juries to make recommendations			✓	Low[d]

[a] David Primo. 2002. "Public Opinion and Campaign Finance: Reformers versus Reality." *The Independent Review* 7(2): 207–19.
[b] Level of support based on number of newspapers endorsing the National Popular Vote, including the *New York Times*, *Chicago Sun-Times*, and *Los Angeles Times*, among others. Polls conducted for the National Popular Vote also indicate a high level of support, although it is unclear how much of a priority the reform is.
[c] Joshua Fourgere, Stephen Ansolabehere, and Nathaniel Persily. 2010. "Partisanship, Public Opinion, and Redistricting." *Election Law Journal* 9(4): 325–47.
[d] Based on the adoption of the CIR in Oregon.
Note: Support among the public is categorized as "low" support or "some" support, but could theoretically range higher. In the cases where we have indicated "None" we mean that most people have never heard of the reform, which is why there is no support for it.

as well as whether the public is likely to support the reforms. If citizens are not enthusiastic about a reform and do not understand its importance, then its chances of being adopted are slim.

Making All Elections Publicly Financed

Although presidential candidates have access to public financing, most other candidates for political office in the United States do not. Providing candidates with public financing would enhance political equality because it would help underfunded challengers compete with well-heeled incumbents. It would also improve electoral competitiveness, which encourages candidates to provide voters with the kinds of information that facilitate deliberation.[26] Public financing may also improve individual free choice by encouraging more people to run for office and ensuring that more elections are contested. But the effects depend on the amount of public funding provided. For example, Hawaii and Wisconsin provide only a small amount of public money to state legislative candidates, rendering their programs less effective. Other states, such as Minnesota and Arizona, provide more money and appear to have had greater success with respect to enhancing competitiveness.[27]

Citizens must therefore be prepared to fund public financing programs generously to make them work. There is little evidence, however, that Americans are willing to do so. For example, fewer than 12 percent of U.S. citizens filing federal tax returns typically check the box on their tax form indicating that they would like to donate $3 to the Presidential Election Campaign Fund (the source of public funding for presidential candidates).[28] Citizens are reluctant to check this box even though the tax form assures them that doing so does not increase the amount of tax they pay. As we noted in Chapter 4, even if a majority of citizens do support publicly financed campaigns in the abstract, they do not necessarily consider campaign finance reform an important priority.[29] Moreover, incumbent politicians have little incentive to pass a reform that would essentially give campaign funds to their opponents.

Making Campaign Donations Anonymous

Another way to reform campaigns would be to make all donations anonymous. This reform accepts the role of private donations; there may be nothing inherently wrong with citizens contributing to a candidate who they feel will represent them effectively. The potential problem is that some citizens may contribute to candidates because they want access or a favor in return. Making donations anonymous would eliminate this possibility, since candidates could never learn who had given them money. Candidates and political parties would no longer be able to accept checks

---

[26] Lipsitz, *Competitive Elections*.

[27] Kenneth R. Mayer, Timothy Werner, and Amanda Williams. 2006. "Do Public Financing Programs Enhance Competition?" in *The Marketplace of Democracy*, ed. Michael P. McDonald and John Samples. Washington, DC: Brookings Institution Press, pp. 245–67.

[28] Tax Foundation. 2008. "Presidential Election Campaign Fund Untapped by Obama Claims Little Support from Taxpayers." News Release. www.taxfoundation.org/press/show /23306.html (accessed 6/7/11).

[29] David M. Primo. 2002. "Reformers vs. Reality." *Independent Review* 7, 2: 202–19.

directly from individuals and PACs. Instead, an individual or PAC would give to a blind trust established in the candidate's or political party's name. It is possible that individuals could tell a candidate or party that they made a large contribution, but talk is cheap, and under this system anyone could make such a claim. Supporters call this idea the **donation booth**: just as ballots are cast in secret in the voting booth, donations would be made in secret as well.[30]

A relevant question is whether anonymous donations would reduce the amount of money—and, hence, the amount of communication—in campaigns. Many contributors might not give money if they do not think candidates will acknowledge their donations. Moreover, few Americans have heard of this reform, so its advocates will have the additional burden of explaining to citizens what it is.

Limiting Campaign Spending

Although U.S. citizens are ambivalent about public financing, they do support limits on campaign spending. Even so, there is considerable debate about how spending limits would affect elections. The debate hinges on the methodologically thorny question of whether incumbents or challengers get more bang (vote share) for the buck in campaigns. If challengers do, then spending limits would hurt them because they need to spend as much as possible to successfully compete against incumbents.[31] If incumbent spending is more effective, however, then spending limits would be helpful for challengers.[32] Irrespective of their effects, however, the Supreme Court has ruled that spending limits are a violation of free speech and, consequently, cannot be imposed on candidates. Candidates can, however, volunteer to limit their spending in exchange for public funding (see Chapters 4 and 9). Thus, public financing and spending limits are usually linked in our political system. This means that the fate of the latter depends on the fate of the former.

---

[30] Ian Ayres and Jeremy Bulow. "The Donation Booth." http://faculty-gsb.stanford.edu/bulow/articles/The%20donation%20booth.pdf (accessed 6/7/11).

[31] Gary Jacobson. 2009. *The Politics of Congressional Elections.* 7th ed. New York, NY: Pearson Education, p. 49.

[32] Alan S. Gerber. 1998. "Estimating the Effect of Campaign Spending on Senate Election Outcomes Using Instrumental Variables." *American Political Science Review* 92, 2: 401–11; Steven D. Levitt. 1994. "Using Repeat Challengers to Estimate the Effect of Challenger Spending on Election Outcomes in the U.S. House." *Journal of Political Economy* 102, 4: 777–98.

Reforming the Redistricting Process

As we discussed in Chapter 2, states typically redraw the boundaries of congressional and state legislative districts after the decennial national census. State legislatures are most often responsible for determining these boundaries, and their plans must be approved by the state's governor. This process means that any party that controls the legislature and governor's mansion can draw district lines in a manner that protects its members, as well as incumbents more generally. Thus, redistricting has been linked to two trends: the increase in the incumbency advantage and the decrease in electoral competitiveness. Both of these limit free choice and political equality. As discussed in Chapter 10, the proposals for reforming the redistricting process involve either bypassing the state legislatures and giving power to independent commissions or officially adopting redistricting guidelines that mandate enhanced competition.

There is some evidence that such redistricting reforms do, in fact, work against incumbents to enhance electoral competitiveness, but scholars continue to debate the magnitude of their effects.[33] The other question is who will pursue such reforms. As was the case with public financing, politicians often have little incentive to support redistricting reform, especially if they believe it would alter the boundaries of their own districts or cost their party seats in Congress or the state legislature. Surveys show that Americans who have an opinion about redistricting procedures tend to believe that district lines drawn by independent commissions are fairer than those drawn by state legislatures, but 40 percent of those surveyed had no opinion on the topic.[34] As a result, the biggest obstacle to adoption of redistricting reform is the low salience of the topic for voters. But as Californians demonstrated in 2008 when they voted to adopt such an independent redistricting commission, voter education and outreach can work.

Reforming or Abolishing the Electoral College in Presidential Elections

The Electoral College undermines citizen equality because the manner in which it functions makes the votes of citizens in battleground states worth more than those of citizens in non-battleground states. We have also

---

[33] See Michael P. McDonald. 2006. "Drawing the Line on District Competition." *PS: Political Science and Politics* 39, 1: 91–94; Michael P. McDonald. 2006. "Re-Drawing the Line on District Competition." *PS: Political Science and Politics* 39, 1: 99–102; Alan I. Abramowitz, Brad Alexander, and Matthew Gunning. 2006. "Drawing the Line on District Competition: A Rejoinder." *PS: Political Science and Politics* 39, 1: 95–98.

[34] Joshua Fourgere, Stephen Ansolabehere, and Nathan A. Persily. 2010. "Partisanship, Public Opinion, and Redistricting." *Election Law Journal* 9: 325–47.

discussed how the Electoral College creates incentives for campaigns to allocate more time, money, and attention to citizens in battleground states. Electoral College reformers tend to fall into one of two categories: those who would abolish or effectively bypass it; and those who would simply eliminate the "winner-take-all" rule—where the winner takes all of the state's electors—in exchange for a more representative allocation of electoral votes. As mentioned in Chapter 8, some reformers in the first category advocate requiring states to allocate their state's electoral votes to the winner of the national popular vote (this is the so-called National Popular Vote [NPV] movement). This reform is more likely to be adopted than the constitutional amendment that would be required to eliminate the Electoral College. A constitutional amendment requires the support of three quarters (38) of the states but the NPV could theoretically pass with support of just 11 states. This is because it will take effect as long as the states that adopt it have a combined total of 270 electoral votes between them—the number needed to decide a presidential election. The second class of reforms usually involves exchanging the winner-take-all rule for either a proportional allocation or an allocation of electoral votes based on electoral outcomes in individual congressional districts. Because basing electoral votes on candidate performance in congressional districts would politicize the redistricting process even more than it already is, most reformers prefer allocating electoral votes according to a system of proportional representation.

Although many Americans have a sense of what it means to live in a battleground state during a presidential election, only the most politically astute understand how the Electoral College works and why the NPV might be desirable.[35] Despite the lack of widespread popular support, NPV bills have been introduced in virtually every state. Ten states—California, Hawaii, Illinois, Maryland, Massachusetts, New Jersey, New York, Rhode Island, Vermont, and Washington—as well as the District of Columbia, have passed an NPV measure, which will take effect only when enough states have adopted the reform to provide the winner with an Electoral College majority (270). At this point, the law has been enacted by jurisdictions with a total of 165 electoral votes.

Adopting a national popular vote for president, however, would not necessarily enhance citizen equality. Candidates who currently campaign in battleground states because of the Electoral College would not allocate their

---

[35] Darshan Goux. 2006. "A New Battleground? Media Perceptions and Political Reality in Presidential Elections, 1960–2004." Paper presented at the American Political Science Association Annual Meeting, Philadelphia, PA.

resources evenly across the nation if there were a national vote. Instead, they would focus on areas of the country where large concentrations of swing voters reside. The bottom line is that candidates have finite resources and, as we have stressed throughout this book, will be strategic about how they use them.

Making Election Administration Neutral

Political equality requires that the rules and regulations governing elections be enforced in a neutral manner, but most election officials in the United States are party loyalists. One way to reform the system is to adopt a system of nonpartisan, professional election administration, as most of the world's democracies have.[36] For example, all Canadian federal elections are administered by an independent chief electoral officer (CEO), who is the only Canadian citizen who is not allowed to vote in federal elections. In addition to the CEO, no Canadian election official can engage in partisan activity, belong to a party, or make a contribution. Although it is unlikely the United States will nationalize election administration in the near future, rather than having elections administered by partisan secretaries of state, commissions could be formed to choose neutral election administrators. Such commissions might include representatives from major and minor parties to ensure that the enforcement of election laws do not discriminate against minor parties or the non-incumbent party. Once selected by the commission, these election administrators could serve for long terms to further insulate them from partisan politics.

In the wake of the 2000 presidential election, many hoped that Congress or the courts would address election administration reform. Their hopes have met with disappointment. As a result, election law scholars have offered alternative methods to enhance democracy. One scholar proposed a **Democracy Index** that would rank all states and localities based on election performance.[37] This has been implemented recently in the form of the new Pew Election Performance Index, which ranks states based on a variety of factors, including whether the state has a neutral election official, how easy it is to register, voter waiting times, and whether every vote is counted properly, among others. It is intended to influence through embarrassment; its proponents believe that states ranked at the bottom will want to improve their marks. Other scholars have recommended a more conventional approach

---

36 The Electoral Knowledge Network. http://aceproject.org/epic-en/CDMap?question=EM014&f= (accessed 6/4/14).

37 Gerken, *The Democracy Index.*

of pushing election reform packages through Congress and the state legislatures. History shows that election reforms can be passed when there is unified party control of the executive and legislative branches.[38]

Irrespective of the path to reform, the fair and neutral administration of American elections is likely to improve political equality. But reformers face an "invisibility" problem when pushing for election reform. Citizens become concerned about election administration problems only when the election is close. Once the election is over, they quickly forget about the problems. Furthermore, the practical consequences of administering elections in a partisan manner are not always obvious. If a Democratic administrator fails to provide a sufficient number of ballots to a Republican precinct, it may or may not influence who wins the election. Improving the administration of elections would be good for democracy, but this reform may seem less important unless citizens see that it affects election outcomes.

Increasing Opportunities for Deliberation

A final set of reforms is intended to improve opportunities for voter deliberation within campaigns. Many proposals focus on increasing the frequency of candidate debates and town hall meetings, the two most obvious forums in which candidates and voters interact. There are also some more innovative ideas for enhancing deliberation. One is the **deliberative poll**.[39] Deliberative polls, which were developed in the United States and have been used around the world, begin by identifying and interviewing a random sample of citizens about some set of issues or candidates. Then respondents to the poll are asked to travel (all expenses paid) to some location for two or three days, where they listen to a range of different speakers and arguments about the same issues or candidates. They are then reinterviewed, and changes in their opinions are taken as evidence of the impact of deliberation. Ideally, these deliberative polls are aired on television so that other citizens can watch what happens when fellow citizens are given the time and space to think deeply about issues or electoral choices. A companion proposal would have the federal government sponsor a national **Deliberation Day**, in which citizens are given paid time off from work to attend meetings to discuss the upcoming election.[40]

---

[38] Richard Hansen. 2010. "Election Administration Reform and the New Institutionalism." *California Law Review* 98, 3: 1075–1100.

[39] James S. Fishkin. 1995. *The Voice of the People: Public Opinion and Democracy*. New Haven, CT: Yale University Pres.

[40] Bruce Ackerman and James S. Fishkin. 2005. *Deliberation Day*. New Haven, CT: Yale University Press.

Another proposal is to convene **citizen juries**—randomly selected panels of people who deliberate for several days about the choices in an election—to develop recommendations on which ballot measures and candidates to support.[41] Voters learn about the recommendations and endorsements of these citizen panels through voting guides or sample ballots. In 2010, the Oregon state legislature implemented this concept with the creation of a Citizens' Initiative Review (CIR) panel to provide voters with recommendations on ballot initiatives. A study of the CIR's effects shows that voters who read its recommendations find them helpful and many report that the information provided by the CIR makes them take into account arguments and pieces of information they would not have considered otherwise.[42] These findings suggest citizen juries simultaneously increase deliberation and lessen the costs of voting for individual citizens.

Despite their potential benefits, it is unclear how eager citizens are to participate in a citizen jury or an event like Deliberation Day. Furthermore, individuals who are exposed to disagreement—a natural part of these deliberative exercises—can become ambivalent about politics and less likely to participate in elections.[43] Thus, achieving the goal of increased deliberation in campaigns and elections might come at the cost of lower participation.

There are some practical concerns as well. Deliberative forums are relatively expensive and place substantial demands upon the participants. These forums also require that the candidates or their representatives take an active part in the process, something they may be reluctant to do.

Conclusion

Campaigns in the United States are heavily influenced by rules and institutions, by the broader political reality, by strategic considerations, and by the voters themselves. The larger point is that campaigns function in a logical manner given the context of the American political system. This is not to say that campaigns are perfect or should not be improved. It is simply to say that they are neither inherently bad nor somehow irrational. They can be analyzed systematically and judged on their own terms.

---

[41] John Gastil. 2000. *By Popular Demand: Revitalizing Representative Democracy through Deliberative Elections*. Berkeley: University of California Press.

[42] John Gastil and Katie Knobluch. "Evaluation Report to the Oregon State Legislature on the 2010 Oregon Citizens' Initiative Review." www.la1.psu.edu/cas/jgastil/CIR/OregonLegislativeReportCIR.pdf (accessed 6/5/14).

[43] Diana Mutz. 2006. *Hearing the Other Side: Deliberative vs. Participatory Democracy*. Cambridge: Cambridge University Press.

But campaigns also play a vital role in democracy. So while they can be judged and analyzed on their own terms, they should also be measured against the standards of democratic theory. We have evaluated American campaigns in terms of three standards: free choice, political equality, and citizen deliberation. In some ways, American campaigns live up to these standards. When contested, campaigns force incumbent politicians to account for themselves, provide voters with information about their electoral choices, and encourage citizens to become politically involved. In other ways, American campaigns fall short, particularly because they are often uncompetitive, and competition directly facilitates each of these three values.

There are reforms that could improve the democratic performance of election campaigns in the United States, but it is not clear whether enough citizens or politicians support these reforms or whether reforms would withstand challenges on free-speech grounds. Perhaps the most practical and effective reforms would be establishing neutral election administration and adopting citizen juries as Oregon has. Neutral election administration would help guarantee that election rules apply to all candidates and parties equally. Creating institutions such as the CIR will provide voters with information from people like themselves who have had an opportunity to deliberate. And while parties and candidates will surely resist these reforms due to the increased uncertainty and risk that they would bring, they are likely less opposed to these reforms than many others, such as public financing and redistricting reform.

These changes will not make American campaigns perfect. In fact, even if all of the reforms considered here were to be adopted tomorrow, citizens would almost certainly still have reservations about their politicians and the election process. Some of this reflects partisan reactions to a competitive system: when your side loses, you tend to question the process. Some of this reflects the long and honorable American tradition of complaining about politics and politicians. But despite Americans' avowed distaste for election campaigns, surveys show that they still believe that their democratic system is the best in the world. Furthermore, campaigns in other parts of the world are beginning to look more like those in the United States. The question, then, is how to expand the engaging and informative aspects of the American experiment in mass democracy, as well as its overall fairness. The answer is critical to the long-term health of the American system of government.

KEY TERMS

stealth candidates (p. 398)

ad watch (p. 405)

donation booth (p. 414)

Democracy Index (p. 417)

deliberative poll (p. 418)

Deliberation Day (p. 418)

citizen juries (p. 419)

FOR DISCUSSION

1. Which of the values discussed in this chapter—free choice, equality, deliberation, or free speech—do you think is most important for campaigns in democratic elections? Why?

2. Given the challenges facing this country, how important do you think it is to reform our political campaigns?

3. Would you participate in a town hall meeting about local candidates? Why or why not?

4. The authors of this book argue that political campaigns receive a passing grade in terms of how they serve democracy. Have they convinced you?

GLOSSARY

501(c) organizations—Organizations that are exempt from federal taxation and may be able to engage in political activity, subject to certain restrictions

527 organization—Officially designated political organization under the tax code, and required to disclose its contributors to the Internal Revenue Service. These organizations came to the fore in 2004, the first election after BCRA's ban on soft money for parties.

absentee voting—The process by which citizens who cannot vote in person on Election Day request that ballots be mailed to their homes, and then vote by mailing those ballots to election officials

ad watch—A feature in media outlets in which journalists study campaign ads and comment on their content and truthfulness

agenda setting—The news media's ability to influence the issues that the public regards as important by selecting which stories to cover

at-large elections—Geographic units that elect multiple members as their representatives

analytics—In the context of American elections, the use of sophisticated statistical models to identify politically meaningful patterns within large sets of voter data

attack ads—Advertisements in which supporters of one candidate question the character, ethics, and/or integrity of their candidate's opponent

Australian ballot—A method of voting by secret ballot, widely adopted in the United States in the early part of the 1900s, that made it impossible for casual observers or party workers to determine for whom a citizen had cast a vote

ballot initiative campaigns—Campaigns surrounding specific propositions put directly to voters for their approval. Since there are no candidates, interest groups are the main actors in influencing voters.

ballot initiatives—Measures that affect laws or public policy and that are proposed by interested citizens and then voted on by citizens in elections

battleground/swing states—States that are competitive between the major party candidates and whose outcome may decide the presidential election

big data—In the context of American elections, large data sets containing extensive information on individual voters

Bipartisan Campaign Reform Act (BCRA)—2002 law that prohibited soft money spending by national, state, and local parties; limited soft money spending by outside groups; and increased individual contribution limits

blanket/jungle primary—Election in which all candidates for each office are listed on the ballot, and anyone registered to vote in that election may vote for any one candidate; typically, the top two vote-getters advance to a second, runoff election

blogs—Websites with regularly updated stories that often have a more personalized and conversational style; originally short for web logs

Buckley v. Valeo—1976 decision overturning the Federal Election Campaign Act's limits on spending by federal candidates as a violation of the First Amendment

Bush model—Campaign strategy focusing efforts on identifying partisans and getting them to the polls

campaign—An organized effort to persuade and mobilize voters to support or oppose a party or candidate

campaign agenda—The issue areas discussed during a campaign

campaign strategy—A campaign's understanding of how its candidate is going to win the election, who will vote for the candidate, and why

casework—The work performed by members of Congress or their staff to help constituents deal with government bureaucracies

caucuses—Relatively closed affairs in which registered partisans attend meetings at election precinct locations and vote to select delegates to the county or state party conventions

citizen juries—Randomly selected panels of people who deliberate about the choices in the election to develop recommendations for other citizens

citizen legislature—A legislature in which serving as a legislator is a part-time position that comes with relatively little salary or staff support

Citizens United v. Federal Election Commission—2010 decision holding that under the First Amendment corporate funding of independent political broadcasts in candidate elections cannot be limited

civil service—Government jobs or positions in which employment and promotions are based on professional qualifications and performance

clean elections systems—A system of campaign finance whereby candidates who raise a minimum amount of private donations qualify for public funding from the government. Once they accept public funding, they cannot spend any more money raised from private donors.

Clinton model—Campaign strategy focusing on identifying persuadable voters and reaching out to them with poll-tested, popular issue positions

closed primary—Election for the party's nominee in which only those registered as party members can vote

coattails effect—When a popular high-profile candidate is on the ballot, lesser known candidates in that candidate's party benefit from that candidate's appeal to voters— they "ride the coattails" of the high-profile candidate

communities of interest—Redistricting principle that districts should attempt to keep together citizens in areas that share a political history or set of interests

constituencies—Subsets of the American public for which interest groups or candidates claim to speak, such as ethnic or religious groups

contrast advertisements—Advertisements in which supporters of a candidate seek to favorably compare their candidate's record and positions to their opponents' record and positions

convenience voting—Absentee, early, or mail-in voting conducted before Election Day to facilitate turnout

convention bump/convention bounce— Increased support for a candidate resulting from the party's national convention

coordinated expenditures—Money that political parties spend to help cover a candidate's campaign costs in a federal election. Such expenditures are limited by law.

cross pressures—Two or more beliefs, identities, or issue positions that pull a voter in different partisan directions

delegates—People chosen to vote for the presidential nominee of the party at the national convention

Deliberation Day—A paid day for citizens to take time off from work to attend meetings to discuss an upcoming election

deliberative poll—A type of survey in which a random sample of citizens are asked about some set of issues or candidates, then attend a meeting in which they think about or discuss these issues more, and then answer a second set of questions to see if their opinions have changed

Democracy Index—A ranking of all states and localities based on how democratic their elections are

Democratic Party (1828–present)—Political party associated with Andrew Jackson, representing interests suspicious of entrenched commercial class; the first party to embrace mass democratic participation

Democratic-Republican Party (1796–1824)— Political party associated with Thomas Jefferson, representing a more limited view of federal governing power, preferring state and local governing authority; support was strongest in the southern and western states

donation booth—A blind trust established in a candidate's or political party's name into which individuals or PACs can make anonymous donations

Duverger's Law—Single-member, simple plurality election systems tend to produce two major political parties

earned media/free media—The publicity that candidates get by engaging in promotional activities

election—The selection of persons to hold public office by means of a vote

electoral participation—The range of activities by which individuals attempt to affect the outcome of an election

era of pre-democratic campaigns—Time between the ratification of the U.S. Constitution in 1788 and the widespread expansion of elected public offices in the 1820s

express advocacy—Specifically advocating the election or defeat of a candidate

Federal Election Campaign Act (FECA)—1971 law, substantially amended in 1974, that set limits on contributions to federal campaigns, provided for public funding of presidential election campaigns, mandated contribution disclosure and finance report filings, established the Federal Election Commission to oversee finance laws, and set limits on candidate spending. The last of these provisions was overturned by the Supreme Court.

Federal Election Commission (FEC)—The regulatory agency that enforces the laws governing federal elections

Federalist Party (1796–1828)—Political party associated with Alexander Hamilton, representing a more expansive view of federal governing power, especially with respect to regulating commercial interests; support was strongest in the northeastern states

field experiments—A form of research in which subjects (in the case of campaigns, voters) are randomly assigned into treatment and control groups, treatment groups

receive a particular stimulus, and outcomes are compared between the two groups; an important new way for campaigns to test outreach and persuasion

focus groups—A form of qualitative research in which a group of people is asked about their perceptions, opinions, beliefs, and attitudes toward a product, service, concept, advertisement, idea, or packaging. Questions are asked in an interactive group setting where participants are free to talk with other group members. In campaigns, small groups of persuadable voters are interviewed in depth to gather additional data and test specific issue positions.

framing—Choosing the language to define a debate and fitting individual issues into the contexts of broader story lines. The news media's ability to influence what the public thinks is at stake in a debate by categorizing issues into one of many possible interpretations.

franking privilege—The ability of members of Congress to send mail to constituents without postage

front-loading—Moving statewide nominating contests earlier in the calendar to increase their influence

front-porch campaign—Tactic whereby the candidate stays at home and allows his campaign team to arrange for select meetings with news media outlets

front-runner—Candidate perceived to have the money, experience, and popular support to win

generational cohort—A group of people who came of age politically at about the same time

gerrymandering—Drawing district lines to maximize some political interest

get-out-the-vote (GOTV) efforts—The efforts of candidates, parties, and interest groups to get citizens to vote

hard money—Money raised in accord with campaign finance laws

Hill committees—A term used to refer to the four major party campaign committees involved in congressional elections

horse race journalism—News reporting that focuses on which candidates are becoming more or less likely to win an election as well as what each candidate is doing to improve their standing in the polls

incumbency advantage—The vote share earned by an incumbent compared to what a nonincumbent would have earned if he or she had run

incumbent—The candidate in an election who already occupies the office

independent candidates—Persons running for office who are not affiliated with any particular political party

independent expenditure committees—Political action committees that can raise unlimited donations from various sources and then spend money to advocate for or against candidates

independent expenditures—A piece of campaign communication by an independent group that engages in express advocacy; party expenditures made without consulting or coordinating with a candidate

infotainment—Media content that provides a combination of information and entertainment, such as comedy news programs or coverage of celebrities

interest group—A collection of people with the shared goal of influencing public policy that does not run its own candidates for office

interpretive journalism—News reporting that includes analysis of the reasons why events happen and the likely effects that the events will have

issue advocacy—Advocating a position on a political issue without explicitly advocating for the election or defeat of a candidate

issue ownership—Concept that political parties have differential credibility on certain issues, and that their candidates try to win elections by convincing voters that issues they "own" are the most important for a given election

literacy tests—Knowledge questions asked by election officials at the polls; used to prevent blacks from voting in southern states, and were suspended in states where turnout was less than 50 percent of the age-eligible population by the Civil Rights Act (1965)

magic words—Words that make an advertisement subject to campaign finance laws and regulations

majority-minority districts—Districts in which racial or ethnic minorities form a majority of the population

malapportionment—Any significant differences in the number of citizens across districts

material benefit—A reward or payment received in exchange for political participation

median voter theorem—In a majority election, if voter policy preferences can be represented as a point along a single dimension, and if all voters vote for the candidate who commits to a policy position closest to their own preference, and if there are only two candidates, then a candidate maximizes her votes by committing to the policy position preferred by the median voter

microtargeting—Rating the voting behavior of every individual on the registered voter list based on a statistical model of the vote estimated from a large random sample

mobilization—The range of activities that candidates, parties, activists, and interest groups engage in to encourage people to participate

Motor Voter Act—A federal law requiring states to allow voters to register when they are applying for a driver's license and public assistance programs or to allow Election Day registration

narrow-casting—Targeting a message to a small audience using e-mail, direct mail, and telephone calls

negative campaigning—Campaign messages that consist of criticism leveled by one candidate against another during a campaign

news media—Regular communicators of information designed to reach large audiences

news values—The criteria reporters and editors use to determine what is newsworthy, such as how recently an event occurred and whether it was unexpected

one person, one vote—The principle that each person's vote should have equal weight in determining representation; first articulated in *Reynolds v. Sims* (1964)

open primary—Election for the parties' nominees in which registrants are allowed to vote in any primary they choose (but only in one)

open seat—An election in which no incumbent is running

opinion leaders—Individuals who follow politics and help inform other members of the group about issues and candidates

pack journalism—The tendency of reporters to read and discuss each other's stories and converge on a similar narrative about the campaign

panel study—Survey that interviews respondents at one point in time and then reinterviews at a later point in time in order to measure change in their opinions

participatory distortion—Occurs when certain groups of citizens have a greater impact on the political process than other groups

party-as-organization—The institutions, professionals, and activists that administer party affairs, including the official bodies that raise funds and create the rules for the party

party identification—A citizen's allegiance to one of the political parties, including both party preference and level of commitment

party-in-government—The members of a party who hold public office

party-in-the-electorate—The group of citizens who identify with a political party or regularly support candidates from one party

permanent campaign—The notion that candidates never stop campaigning because of the constant need to raise money for the next election cycle

personal vote—That portion of an elected official's vote share that can be attributed to their relationship with constituents

persuadable/swing votes—The number of voters in a given election who are not

committed to supporting a particular candidate. This is usually estimated by the percentage point difference between the maximum and minimum vote for a major party's candidates across recent elections.

persuasion—Convincing undecided voters to support a particular candidate or convincing the other party's supporters to defect

plurality rule—A way of determining who wins elections in which the candidate with the most votes wins (even if they do not get a majority of the votes)

pocketbook voting—Choosing between candidates based on how one's personal finances have faired during the incumbent party's rule

political action committee (PAC)—Private group organized to elect political candidates

political amateur—A candidate with no political experience

political interest—Having an ongoing interest in politics

political machines—Party organizations that mobilized lower status citizens to win office, and then used government to reward party workers and bestow services and benefits to their constituents

political parties—Group of people with the shared interest of electing public officials under a common label

poll taxes—Fee requirements for voting; typically used to keep blacks from voting in southern states, and outlawed by the Voting Rights Act of 1965

positive campaigning—Campaign messages in which candidates make an affirmative case for their election based on their background, experience, record, or issue positions

primary election—Election in which voters select the candidate that will run for the party in the general election

priming—The news media's ability to influence the criteria that citizens use to make judgments about people by selecting which stories to cover

probability sample—Some number of individuals from a certain population randomly selected and asked a set of questions; the key is that every individual in the population of interest has a known probability of being selected

professionalism—A quality of legislatures that captures how much work legislators perform and status they receive. In a more professionalized legislature, serving as a legislator is a full-time job with a substantial salary and staff support.

Progressive/"Bull Moose" Party (1912–14)—Political party associated with Theodore Roosevelt, representing disaffected Republicans who favored greater power and democratic prerogatives for the "little man" and regulation of major industries

proportional representation—System in which seats are allocated based on the percentage of the vote won by each party

proximity voting—Choosing a candidate based on how close the candidate's views are to one's own views across a range of relevant issues

public funding—Campaign funds provided by the government

purposive benefits—The satisfaction one derives from having advanced an issue or ideological position, or from having fulfilled a duty

quality challenger—A candidate with the experience and backing necessary to run a competitive campaign

reapportionment—Process of determining the number of representatives allotted to each state after the decennial census count

Reconstruction—Era immediately after the Civil War in which policies were enacted to protect the freedoms and rights of black citizens. Reconstruction policies were particularly important in the southern states, where Union troops were stationed to enforce these policies. The Reconstruction era ended at different times for different states, but many believe that the Compromise of 1877 effectively ended Reconstruction.

redistricting—Drawing new district lines after the decennial census count

referenda—Measures that affect laws or public policy that allow citizens to vote on a statute already passed by state legislatures

reinforcement—The notion that news consumers interpret information as giving added strength or support to their existing views. The process of solidifying voters' support for a candidate.

Republican L—The pattern formed by Republican-leaning states in the mountain west and southern states

Republican Party (1860–present)—Political party originally associated with Abraham Lincoln and representing interests opposed to slavery and favoring the continuation of the Union

retail politics—Face-to-face communication between candidates and voters of political positions and arguments

retention elections—Judicial elections in which voters decide whether a sitting judge should continue in that position; these elections do not feature a competition between the sitting judge and an opponent

retrospective voting—Choosing between candidates according to broad appraisals of whether things have improved or gotten worse under the incumbent

right to equal time—A Federal Communications Commission rule that requires most radio and television broadcasters to treat candidates equally when selling or giving away airtime

roll-call vote—At a party convention, the aggregation of state-by-state votes of delegates

same-day/election-day registration—System in which eligible citizens may register to vote as late as Election Day itself

semi-closed primary—Election for the party's nominee in which party registrants and those unaffiliated with any party are allowed to vote

single-member districts—Geographic units that elect only one person to represent the entire unit

social context—The people with whom one communicates and interacts, such as family, friends, classmates, coworkers, and neighbors

social identities—The portion of an individual's self-concept derived from perceived membership in a relevant social group, such as being Catholic, or African-American, or working-class

sociotropic voting—Choosing between candidates based on how one thinks the country has faired under the incumbent party's rule

soft money—Money raised outside the limits normally established by campaign finance laws

solidarity benefits—Intangible rewards for participation that come from being part of a collective effort

sorting—People's partisan preferences have become more closely aligned with their political views

sound bite—A short segment of sound or video used in a news report as an excerpt of an event or interview

stealth candidates—Candidates who refuse to campaign in the traditional sense because they want to avoid questions from the press and keep their controversial views hidden from voters

strategic voting—In an election with more than two candidates, voting for a candidate other than one's first choice in order to prevent an undesirable outcome

super PACs—PACs that can collect unlimited amounts of donations as a consequence of a recent Supreme Court decision, *Citizens United v. FEC*. Super PACs are required to disclose their donors.

survey research—A research method involving the use of questionnaires and/or statistical surveys to gather data about people and their thoughts and behaviors

term limits—Legal restrictions on the maximum time a person can hold a specific office

Tillman Act—1907 law banning corporate contributions to political campaigns

viability—Ability to win the nomination

vote by mail—When jurisdictions conduct elections by ballots that are automatically mailed to voters instead of using polling stations

vote targets—Estimates of how many votes a candidate will need to win the election. These are based on calculations of how many people will vote in a particular election, what percentage of the vote will be needed to win, how many votes can be counted on, and how many votes are persuadable.

voter identification/voter ID calls—Calls, usually via telephone, to every person on the voter list to ask about the candidates and issues in the upcoming election

Voting Rights Act of 1965—Congressional legislation designed to end discriminatory practices disenfranchising blacks, especially in the South

wedge issues—Political issues intended to persuade voters to abandon the party they traditionally support and support the opposite party

Whig Party (1832–52)—Political party that rose in response to the Democratic Party in the 1830s, representing voters concerned by Jackson's expansive view of the presidency and his attacks on commercial interests

wire services—A news agency that collects and distributes news stories to many outlets

CREDITS

INDEX